Informing with the Case Method:

a guide to case method
Research, Writing, & Facilitation

T. Grandon Gill

Informing Science Press

To Jean:
It's a pleasure
having you here

[signature]

Informing with the Case Method: A Guide to Case Method Research, Writing, and Facilitation

ISBN: 978-1-932886-44-3

Published by

Informing Science Press
publishing arm of the Informing Science Institute:

131 Brookhill Court
Santa Rosa
California
95409
USA
Phone: +1 707.324-317
Fax: +1 480 247 5724
ISPress.org
InformingScience.org

Printed in the US

This book is dedicated to my parents,
Elizabeth Gill (1927-2011) and Richard T. Gill (1927-2010),
who always loved my case studies.

Acknowledgements

This book has been made possible by the many faculty members who helped me learn how to write case studies—with particular thanks to Ray Goldberg at *Harvard Business School*, who got me started—and the many students who taught me much of what I know about facilitating a case discussion.

With respect to the book itself, I owe a particular debt to Betty Boyd and Eli Cohen, whose tireless efforts in the name of the *Informing Science Institute* has made the product of this book—and many other books—possible. Without their encouragement and tolerance for my awkward prose, this project surely would have been abandoned.

I would also like to thank those of my colleagues from the University of South Florida who voluntarily agreed to subject themselves to the first case method workshop ever constructed around this book and, of particular note, agreed to join me in a case development project that will—with any luck—lead to a transformation of our undergraduate capstone course. In this group are Kaushal Chari, Manish Agrawal, Al Hevner, Don Berndt, Joni Jones, Rick Will and Inge Wefes. I should also mention Bill Murphy, who enthusiastically agreed to represent the doctoral student community in this endeavor.

This material is based upon work supported by the National Science Foundation under Grant No. 1043919.

T. Grandon Gill
Informing with the Case Method
Santa Rosa, California: Informing Science Press.

Contents

T. Grandon Gill
Informing with the Case Method
Santa Rosa, California: Informing Science Press.

Preface

There are a number of marvelous books that address the topic of the case method. If you are interested in facilitating cases, you can look to the classic book *Teaching and the Case Method* by Louis Barnes, C. Roland Christensen and Abby Hansen (1994). The collection of essays on the subject, *Education for Judgment: The Artistry of Discussion Leadership* by C. Roland Christensen, David Garvin and Ann Sweet (1991) is a wonderful and inspiring read as well. If your interest is case-based research, it would be nearly impossible to find a more authoritative source than Robert Yin's (2009, 4th Edition) *Case Study Research: Design and Methods*, which (at last count) has been cited nearly 29,000 times, according to *Google Scholar*. There is even a new entry to the field, William Ellet's (2007) *The Case Study Handbook: How to Read, Discuss, and Write Persuasively about Cases* that is specifically aimed at the student. At first glance, then, the topic of case studies in education and research seems to be pretty well covered. Do we really need another book on the subject?

I write this book believing the answer is yes. While I have great affection for the classics, there are a number of issues facing *most* business faculty—not to mention faculty members from disciplines outside of business—that these books simply do not address. In writing this book, my intention is to offer some thoughts on some of these. Paradoxically, these omissions arise from the very fact that the authors of the classics are undisputed masters of their craft. Why this is a problem should become clear as I identify the three areas of focus for this book.

The first issue that I feel must be considered is using the case method with a novice audience. Consider the following. When I was enrolled in the MBA program at Harvard Business School (HBS) in the early 1980s, the curriculum consisted of nearly 900 case discussion (15 per week) and—perhaps—as many as 20 class periods given over to lecture-style presentations. When I teach a case-method graduate course at my own institution, on the other hand, I am constrained to 11 case discussions (a 12 week semester). As it happens, I am also the only course in the entire program that employs pedagogy reasonably faithful to the case method, as it is normally defined. The math is very simple.

By the last day of my semester, my students have as much experience discussing cases as I did on Thursday afternoon of the first week of my two year MBA program at HBS. With the exception of faculty teaching at those rare institutions that have chosen to widely adopt the case method, the situation I face is commonplace.

The second concern that existing books raise for me is their tendency to focus on isolated topics. Specifically, case facilitation, case writing and case research are treated as separable activities. I would argue that these three aspects of the case method—which I define quite broadly— are inseparable. For institutions that wish to achieve the full set of benefits provided by the case method, all three activities must be pursued in parallel. Perhaps this is why so few institutions have achieved success through the case method. In this book, I will argue that achieving such integration is precisely why those rare institutions have been *so successful.*

Once you start believing that the case method can be a key to institutional success, how you get there becomes a real challenge. At leading institutions featuring the case method, such as HBS, the philosophy is largely learned through a period of apprenticeship. For example, I did not encounter any of the references mentioned in the first paragraph— excepting Yin—at any time during my 5 year doctorate at HBS. Instead, I went out and wrote cases, facilitated discussions and did research under the guidance of faculty members who were masters of the craft. How can someone without the benefit of such an experience acquire such mastery? While I cannot offer any promises in this regard, I will at least provide some examples and easy-to-follow checklists that may be of service to individuals getting started.

My final concern parallels the second, but deals specifically with attitudes about the case method. Lip service paid to the case method is easy to come by. In fact, when I looked for articles questioning its value in the business literature, I could find only one. When it comes to the decisions that exert a major influence on a faculty member's career however, such as those relating to promotion and tenure (P&T), the pursuit of an integrated program of case teaching, writing and research does not carry much weight. In my own situation, the several dozen discussion cases that I have written were valued similarly to a typographical error when it came time for P&T; taken as implicit evidence that my commitment to "real" research was insufficient because I spent so much time on my "hobby".

Having passed that particular hurdle, I can now laugh at it. But it would have been nice to have some systematic arguments as to why case studies not only *can be rigorous*, they are likely to be *the most rigorous* form of research in many—if not most—settings where the fundamental test of our research vale is its applicability to practice. Drawing upon my recent book, *Informing Business* (2010), I argue that a compelling case for the case method can and should be made.

Finally, the vast majority of books that I have found on the case method in the classroom specifically focus on its application to business. My own experience, however, leads me to believe that the approach is readily transferable to other disciplines. Specifically, if a discipline involves the transfer of ideas to a community of practitioner experts operating outside of the academic environment, there is a very good chance that the case method may be relevant. The "real world" tends to produce complexity as the needs of stakeholders collide in a way that makes "fit", rather than "optimization" the most relevant goal. Where fit is the goal, judgment is nearly always required. And the case method is well suited to presenting situations where judgment is needed.

Professor T. Grandon Gill
Information Systems & Decision Sciences Department
College of Business
University of South Florida

November 2011

T. Grandon Gill
Informing with the Case Method
Santa Rosa, California: Informing Science Press.

Chapter 1

What is the Case Method Paradigm?

The case method may be defined narrowly or broadly. Narrowly defined, it is an approach to teaching whose roots are the "Socratic Method". In this method, real world examples are presented to students after which learning is facilitated through discussion and skillful questioning of participants. Defined more broadly, the case method is a philosophy applying to both education and research that is built upon the creation and analysis of complex real world examples.

In this book, I embrace the broader definition, which I refer to as the *case method paradigm*. My rationale for this choice should become clear as the book progresses. Certain types of situations lend themselves to a case-based approach that incorporates a set of common principles based upon discovery and synthesis. For those situations, it makes sense that both research and learning should follow similar patterns. Where a situation does not lend itself to the case method, it is doubtful that the use of cases in the manner I describe will serve the best interest of either research or education.

In this chapter, we briefly review the history of the case method then consider the practice of the case method, both in the classroom and in research. Finally, we examine some of the challenges the case method now faces. Although most examples are drawn from business schools—where the bulk of my experience resides—I would encourage readers from other fields to consider the broader implications for their own area. Later, in Chapter 2, I identify attributes of situations that make them particularly appropriate for case-based research and education. Many areas of study, such as education, share profiles similar to business across these attributes. In these disciplines, I would expect opportunities to apply the case method beneficially to be plentiful.

A Brief History of the Case Method

Throughout this book, I use the term *case method* to describe an approach to teaching and research that draws almost entirely upon real world examples for its knowledge acquisition and informing activities. In the classroom, this translates to employing pedagogy that revolves around the discussion of these examples. In research, it implies an emphasis on insights drawn from a small number of deeply understood situations in preference to inductions based upon a large number of less detailed observations.

The use of the term "case method" is a relatively recent development. Its underlying ideas, however, extend back thousands of years. Discussion-based instructional approaches, for example, are frequently associated with Socrates, the famed philosopher of ancient Greece and mentor of Plato. Indeed, instruction based upon questioning students, rather than lecturing to them, is often referred to as the "Socratic method" in his honor. The use of example stories, rather than abstract principles, to inform is common to nearly all religions, ancient and modern. In scientific research, many fields—including medicine and psychology—have long advanced through the careful study of individual case examples.

Origins of the Case Method

In a 2003 *Harvard Magazine* article, Harvard Business School (HBS) Professor David Garvin presented a history of the case method at Harvard, the institution that largely pioneered its use in the classroom. The first application was in 1870, at Harvard Law School:

> A newly appointed dean began to teach with cases in 1870, reversing a long history of lecture and drill. He viewed law as a science and appellate court decisions as the "specimens" from which general principles should be induced, and he assembled a representative set of court decisions to create the first legal casebook. To ensure that class time was used productively, he introduced the question-and-answer format now called the Socratic method. (Garvin, 2003, p. 56)

Law provided a natural home for the case method because, in many societies, such as the U.K. and other countries whose legal system is based on the British model of common law, the interpretation of the law is heavily influenced by legal decisions made in the past, referred to as precedents. Thus, to understand the law today, you must carefully review the outcomes of previous cases and apply inductive reasoning. This approach to the law can be distinguished from other legal systems, such as the civil law approach that dominates countries such as France, where an effort is made to incorporate a more comprehensive set of rules in the civil code, thereby reducing the role played by interpretation of past decisions.

Roughly 50 years after its original adoption, the case method had become the dominant pedagogy in U.S. law schools (Garvin, 2003). It was about that time that the case method moved to business schools. The pioneer in this area was, once again, Harvard.

HBS had been founded in 1908 as part of a growing movement to professionalize business education (Khurana, 2007), following the lead of two other Ivy League schools: Wharton (at the University of Pennsylvania in 1881) and Tuck (at Dartmouth, 1900). Although the school's first catalog emphasized cases and discussion based teaching[1], Garvin places the schools distinctive emphasis on the case method as beginning in 1920, when Wallace P. Donham, its new dean and a Harvard Law School graduate, forcefully advocated its use and provided resources for case development. By 1924, most of the instruction at HBS centered around the case method (Copeland, 1958, p. 28), by which time 20 MBA graduates were involved in case development (Barnes, et. al., 1994, p. 43).

The early HBS cases were very different from the cases of today, better described as simple problem statements rather than the complex descriptions of an administrative situation that would be typical of today's HBS case[2]. The approach to teaching differed as well. During this period, the pedagogy closely mirrored that of the law school, with the classroom protocol consisting mainly of the "facilitator" interrogating individual students. While the aim of the questioning differed between the two schools—the law school sought to have students distill the core legal concepts involved whereas the business school sought to ferret out weaknesses in the student's analysis or action plan (Barnes, et. al., 1994, p. 44-45)—the interaction was more like a series of dialogs than a discussion.

Case research in the early days of HBS also differed considerably from what we now view the case method. Much of the early research of that period consisted of detailed industry reports, particularly directed towards practice and was conducted hand-in-hand with the development of teaching cases. The ultimate hope was that these reports would lead to general principles of business that could be taught to students and communicated to executives. According to Rakesh Khurana (2007, p. 173), however, around 1930 this effort was largely abandoned "after several Harvard business professors argued that the effort to identify rules and principles applying to all situations was futile".

Following the Great Depression of the 1930s and World War II, business education began to grow rapidly, spurred by programs such as the GI Bill in the U.S. Towards the end of the 1950s, however, the effectiveness of then-existing research and education practices were called into question in studies funded by two major foundations[3]: Ford (Gordon & Howell, 1959) and Carnegie (Pierson, 1959). Interestingly, the net effect of these reports, particularly the one prepared by the Ford Foundation, was a bifurcation of research and teaching approaches. On the research side, the science-based professionalism that had been pioneered at Carnegie-Mellon was preferred[4] (Khurana, 2007). On the teaching side, however, there was considerable enthusiasm for the case method. In fact, the Ford Foundation funded a Visiting Professors Case Method Workshop at HBS between 1955 and 1965 in which over 200 faculty members from leading business schools (roughly 20 per year for 11 years) came to HBS for an entire summer to practice case teaching skills and to develop cases on their own (Garvin, 2003).

Viewed in retrospect, the changes to business education envisioned by the two foundations were highly successful in one regard, less successful in another. On the research side, their efforts to make business research more scientific in its approach and outlook were transformative. While some researchers—myself included (see Gill, 2010)—question whether today's business research serves a useful purpose, no one can doubt that as business researchers we have collectively made a strong commitment to appearing as scientific as possible. On the teaching side, however, the case method never established the same degree of traction in business education that it did in law schools. One reason for this may be that active foundational funding for developing case method teaching skills ended in the 1960s. Another may be that the impact of the two reports was far greater at the most prominent U.S. business schools than it was for the vast majority of business schools (Khurana, 2007, p. 292).

Current State of the Case Method

Today, the degree to which the case studies are employed in learning and research varies widely across and within disciplines. In education, cases are used widely but tend to be much shorter (e.g., 2-3 pages in length) than their counterparts in business. In selected social sciences, such as psychology and anthropology, case studies are widely used in research and range considerably in length, from short descriptions to entire books, such as Graham Allison's (1971) *Essence of Decision*, a case study describing the events of the Cuban Missile Crisis from various perspectives. In engineering and science, Clyde Freeman Herreid (2007) has spearheaded an effort to use case studies to teach problem solving, developing a large repository of short case study problems.

While many disciplines have adopted the case study as a tool, few actually develop and employ these case studies in the manner that I describe as "the case method" in this book. This statement is not intended to minimize the potential benefits of employing case studies in other ways, for both instruction and research. Rather, it is to emphasize the fact that this book is specifically intended to focus on a particular philosophy of teaching and research that is sporadically employed in business disciplines, but is even less common elsewhere. To clarify the distinction, we now turn to the use of the case method in the classroom and in research.

The Case Method in the Classroom

Even within the business disciplines, many views regarding what constitutes the case method in the classroom exist. In this book, I take a broad view of the case method by extending the term to research. In contrast, I take a particularly narrow of view of the case method in the classroom; a perspective that is based heavily on my experiences at HBS. I therefore begin this section with a completely fictional illustrative example of an HBS case discussion—written from the student's perspective—from which I distill a set of distinctive features. For the sake of completeness, I then identify other uses of cases in the classroom that I refer to as "quasi-case methods". I alert the reader to the fact that many instructors would argue that these are, in fact, equally valid case method approaches. In other words, when someone uses the term "case method", it is important to ask what he or she means.

Example: The Case Method at HBS

Imagine yourself sitting in a horse-shoe shaped amphitheater-style classroom with about 80 other students. It is about two minutes before the hour when class is scheduled to start. Friends and not-so-friends are scurrying to their seats, perhaps pressed for time as a consequence of the long lines that sometime form between classes for the Aldrich Hall restrooms.

The instructor, a distinguished looking woman in her mid-40s, is already at the front of the classroom poring over an array of papers laid out across the desk. There is no podium as you might see in a typical classroom. There is, however, a custom designed white board with many layers that can be moved up and down to allow a huge area to be exposed.

As you look down at your case, a 25 page single-spaced document that consists of about 10 pages of single-spaced text followed by 15 pages of charts, tables and clippings (from news sources, annual reports and the web), your palms begin to sweat. There were so many facts in the case that half of the text was highlighted by you as you prepared it in the previous evening. Unfortunately, this is too much of a good thing. There is so much highlighting that it no longer serves the useful purpose of helping you to identify relevant facts should you be called upon to do so. You then turn to the one and a half page outline developed by a member of your study group: Jing Lee, chosen because he had done his undergraduate degree at the University of New South Wales. You started wishing that it had been you—not he—that had created the outline. When you discussed the case last night, your group had collectively identified three options that the company, a bauxite mining and processing operation in Australia called AluminAux Ltd., could pursue in order to move forward. Jing had chosen the more conservative option, which was less risky since it did not require a major investment. Your own preference, on the other hand, involved establishing a new joint venture with a Nigerian company in order to gain a distribution foothold in Africa—despite the obvious risks of doing business on that continent. Unfortunately, Jing's notes offered little concrete support for your position; during the group meeting you'd scribbled some comments in the margin, but now you wonder how effectively you could open with them. You look forward to the afternoon's case, involving a financial services VP who finds himself questioning whether a particular investment vehicle is ethical. For that case, you were the one who had prepared the outline. You are confident that you have that one nailed!

The class goes silent and your pulse races. The professor scans the room. Her gaze fixes on you for a moment, but then her eyes move upwards, towards the top, most distant row of students (affectionately referred to as the skydeck).

Mary, what would you advise the CEO of AluminAux to do?

Immediately, you feel a sense of release. Although some professors prepared a set of study questions for each case, this instructor does not. Thus, you never knew what you will have to respond to when she cold calls you.

You feel considerable sympathy for Mary, who has been quiet most of the semester, as she opens. From the tremor in her voice, it is clear that she is very nervous. Nevertheless, her presentation is well organized—clearly indicating her preference for the same African option that you chose. Her country analysis, however, seems to drag on. The professor seems to think so too, first giving Mary a quizzical look and then, finally, asking:

I hate to interrupt, but is this taking us anywhere?

You turn back towards Mary and see the tension in her face. Hastily, she completes the analysis in a few seconds then states her conclusions in rushed fashion. As soon as it is clear she is about to end, ten hands go up throughout the classroom.

Yours is not one of them. This particular course, focusing on international business, has generated a lot of participation—perhaps because your section is over 25% international in its makeup. While all your classes treat participation as 50% of the student's grade, in some classes it is relatively easy to contribute. In this class, it is definitely not. Thus, you only raise your hand when you have something specific you *really* want to say.

As a result, you have mixed feelings about Mary's opening. With competition for air time being so intense, it would have been nice if the opener had taken a position you could disagree with—your contributions to the discussion have a lot more impact when you disagree with the consensus than when you agree. On the other hand, Mary has had a tough time motivating herself to participate throughout the semester, since she readily admits that public speaking and confrontation are not her forte. Thus, you are glad that you are not in the position of being forced to try to refute her points.

So you wait. A few of your classmates make inconsequential comments of agreement and your attention starts to wander. Then the instructor calls upon Jerry...

Jerry, with a Yale undergraduate degree and five years of experience working at a New York investment bank prior to enrolling at HBS, is one of the section's stars in participation. Aggressive to the point of arrogance, he seems to take particular delight in demolishing the arguments of others, even those who are weaker participants. Within the section he is greatly admired, though not particularly well liked.

And so the process of taking apart everything that Mary concluded in her opening begins. He questions her assumptions about the potential profitability of the Nigerian joint venture. He argues that she vastly underestimated the cash flows that could be derived from the more conservative strategy. Most importantly, he asserts that any Nigerian venture must be negotiated with public sector involvement—that involvement in the private sector is simply too risky.

Instantly, your hand shoots up. You look directly at the professor with a transparent, and somewhat theatrical, look of desperation on your face. She catches your eye and gives an almost imperceptible nod. You relax—you will be the next student calls because she knows exactly what you are going to say. You quickly flip your case to the proper page and a few seconds later she points to you. You begin:

> I am not sure that Jerry has taken into account Exhibit 4. If he had read the text closely, he would have noticed the following...

You begin to read a block of text that describes the potential Nigerian partner's role as their Deputy Minister of Finance for nearly a decade and his close relationships with the existing Prime Minister, who came from the same region of the country as he did. You sum your comment, which takes less than a minute in total, with the following:

> Although it does not explicitly state this in the case, I think this evidence strongly indicates that the proposed venture is being

> designed and sanctioned by the current government, and that its risk is therefore acceptable.

You hear some giggles from around the classroom. You shoot and you score, you think to yourself. Jerry immediately raises his hand to rebut you, but is thwarted by the professor who says:

> Given the support of the Nigerian government, what other risks do we need to worry about in analyzing the joint venture?

Nadia raises her hand and begins to discuss the question. Her presentation is not well organized, however, and seems to be an effort to point out all of the points she wanted to make, regardless of relevance. The professor recognizes this first, and begins to signal the fact by the manner in which she adds to the evolving outline on the classroom's boards. As the student makes each point, the professor scurries over to a different place in the board, using an exaggerated style of walking. Then she raises her hand to signal the student to pause, while she lowers one of the boards already filled and adds a comment to table that already has a similar one. At this point, Nadia recognizes the non-verbal message the instructor is communicating and quickly completes her contribution.

The discussion continues to flow around the potential risks of the joint venture. With about 20 minutes to go, the professor calls on Kassim—the section's only Nigerian student. His hand has been up and down for most of the discussion; thus, the choice to delay calling on him was probably a conscious choice on the professor's part, although you can never really know.

Kassim, in a deep voice accented by his Oxford education, begins to discuss the current situation political in Nigeria. Specifically, he points out that the recent discovery of a large oil field, sitting on the border of Nigeria and two of its neighbors, has produced severe regional tensions. Indeed, there is some fear that it may escalate into war. He concludes by saying:

> Thus, it would be a mistake in the current situation to believe that Nigeria would be a good choice as your gateway to Africa. While I believe that AluminAux can successfully enter the African markets, now would not be the time for to attempt that with a Nigerian partner.

He has, of course, completely demolished your point. Knowing that, were you making this decision you would have certainly opted for the safer option. Nevertheless, Kassim's statement does not disturb you. The fact was not in the case, nor was it known at the time of the case. Reality may undermine your conclusions, but the only reality that matters is that which appears in the case.

Having scarcely spent 3 minutes speaking for the first hour of the class, the professor now takes control. Interestingly, her summation centers around Kassim's point. Her particular perspective is that we, as managers, need to be particularly attuned to the possibility that events can radically change the competitive landscape. Thus, we need to consider the completely unexpected in assessing possible outcomes, and not become fixated on what our projections tell us.

As she wraps up, it becomes clear that she is not planning to tell us what decision the company actually made. Jerry raises his hand and asks. She replies:

> The company chose a variation of the less risky option presented in the case.

Jerry smiles knowingly at you, acting vindicated. The professor continues:

> Unfortunately, the rapid increase in the value of the Australian Dollar against the Euro, the Dollar and the Yuan that occurred last year meant that their margins were squeezed below break-even and, as a result, the company is now in the Australian equivalent of Chapter 11.

You smile back at Jerry.

Key Features of Cases in the Classroom

The fictitious example just presented was intended to illustrate a number of key features that distinguish the case method as practiced at HBS from other pedagogies, particularly lectures. Among the most important are the following:

1. *Discussion is integral to the case method.* Reading or even analyzing a case independently is not sufficient, although it is a necessary prerequisite to discussion.

2. *The facilitator can use many tools to direct the discussion.* Beyond posing questions and explicitly requiring a change of topic, the professor—whom I will henceforth refer to as the facilitator—can use many techniques, including expression and body language, to guide the discussion in a particular direction.

3. *Peer-to-peer contributions dominate the discussion.* Unlike the Socratic Method, which is dominated by question and answer discourse between the instructor and individual students, case method discussions are dominated by students responding to each other.

4. *In any group of learners, there is likely to be a large diversity in the characteristics of individual learners.* This applies not only to knowledge and experience, but also to attitudes towards the case method itself. Absent such diversity, we would expect the act of discussing the case to offer far less value.

5. *Individual relationships within the community of learners play an integral role in the dynamics of the discussion.* In most of the discussions I have witnessed, *who* made a point can impact a discussion as much as what was actually said. This is particularly true in cohort programs, where students come to know each other very—and sometimes too—well.

6. *Cases are recognized as being incomplete and it is generally assumed that there is no "right" decision.* With relatively few exceptions, good case studies do not have "right" answers. They do, however, have better and worse answers given the facts presented.

7. *Evidence supporting a particular decision may come from many sources, including the experiences of the discussion participants.* In business and many other research fields, lecture-based methods tend to specialize on a particular function or area of study. In case discussions, even when conducted in a curriculum organized by functions, there are few boundaries to what is considered relevant and contributions may even include material not in the case (such as Kassim's insights into the political situation in his native country in the illustration).

8. *We cannot necessarily assume that the actual decision made by protagonists in a case was the "correct" one.* Ever where students look up what management chose to do—increasingly possible today us-

ing the Internet—that decision was not necessarily the best one. A good case study tends to profile a difficult decision since the goal is to improve student decision-making skills not test to see if they can come up with the "best" answer.

I would also caution the reader about taking some aspects of the illustration too seriously—particularly the behavior of the instructor and that of the case's central figure (the "you" of the case). In the professor, I attempted incorporate all the characteristics of the ideal case instructor: extensive knowledge of the case, an intuitive feel for the case, the ability to guide the discussion without appearing to take control, a warm rapport with her students and a willingness to let others do the talking. I've never met any facilitator who mastered all these traits[5].

Perhaps even more importantly, the central figure profiled in the illustration would be typical of many, but far from all, students in an HBS MBA class. The individual portrayed has obviously bonded with the case method, enjoys jumping into the discussion, and spends at least as much time worrying about the discussion process as the discussion content. While that would certainly describe my own experience, it would certainly not reflect the experiences of the "Mary" in the illustration, or even the "Jerry". Point 4, relating to the diversity of learners, virtually guarantees that vast differences in attitude towards the pedagogy will exist. That is one reason why knowing something about the individual students in a case discussion class is given so much emphasis in the literature dealing with teaching using the case method.

Quasi-case Methods

In a teaching note for case method instructors, HBS professor Kasturi Rangan (1996) describes four distinct approaches to case teaching:

1. Lecturing a case
2. Theorizing a case
3. Illustrating a case
4. Choreographing a case

To his list, I would add a fifth approach based on my own experience:

5. Dialoguing a case

From this list, the illustration just presented would clearly be an example of choreographing. In this book, unless otherwise specified, this will be what I refer to as the "case method" when used in an instructional context. All five approaches are called the case method by some people, however, and all have value in some circumstances. Thus it is worth briefly considering the differences between them.

Lecturing a case

When in lecture mode, the instructor talks about the case, presents the students with the analysis that needs to be performed and outlines the conclusions that can be drawn from it. As would be appropriate in a traditional lecture, the instructor may be open to questions and may also ask questions of the class. But neither is central to the pedagogy, as the flow of information is not driven by these interrogations.

Lecturing a case is, in essence, a walkthrough. If there happens to be a "right" way to perform the analysis associated with a particular situation, lecturing may be the best approach to employing a particular case. The problem with relying too heavily on discussion in such situations is that students can learn the "wrong" way to approach a problem by listening to peers who have gone off track. I personally recall a few accounting cases from the first year of my MBA where allowing students to proceed in describing an approach to a problem (after it became clear that they had made an error) probably did more harm than good for the rest of the class.

Theorizing a case

When a case is used as a means of justifying a particular theory, Rangan (1996) calls it "theorizing a case". Under this approach, the theory or concept being presented takes center stage; the case becomes supporting material.

Like lecturing a case, theorizing a case requires that the instructor remain in control. Where it diverges from what I call the case method is in attempting to instill a *particular* mental model upon the participants. At the heart of the discussion-based approach to case teaching is a philosophy referred to as *constructivism*. Under this philosophy, participants create their own mental models over the course of the discussion process. Such learner-centered concept formation is unlikely to occur where the instructor has a particular theory in mind.

As was true for lecturing a case, theorizing a case may be completely appropriate in situations when the instructor wants the student to learn a particular set of concepts with little room for interpretation. It is also worth noting that in business, education and other social science disciplines, instructors often *are* interested in precisely that outcome: they have a particular theory that they want the students to learn. In Chapter 2, we return to that issue by considering when theory is most likely to be most valid, and when it is not.

Illustrating a case

In lecturing a case, the case serves as the raw material for a walkthrough. In theorizing a case, the case serves as evidence. In illustrating a case, the case is used to make the idea being conveyed more concrete. As a general rule, our brains are hard wired to acquire concrete knowledge more rapidly than abstract knowledge. By using a case as a concrete example, we may be able to improve the effectiveness of our informing.

Actually, cases can be wonderful tools for illustration. Chip and Dan Heath (2007), in their book *Made to Stick*, propose that we best recall communications with 6 characteristics:

1. Simple

2. Unexpected

3. Concrete

4. Credible

5. Emotional

6. Stories

Using the first letter of each characteristic, they refer to this as the SUCCESs framework. It is not at all unusual for a case study to have at least four of these characteristics. The characteristics "concrete" and "stories" come for free with the case format. Any half decent case writer will be able to incorporate some of the remaining characteristics.

The large disconnect between the case method and illustrating a case occurs when the first characteristic, "simple", is incorporated into the case. Nearly any textbook in the social sciences includes some case examples. These usually extend for a paragraph or so and their purpose is to illustrate a point. They are very sticky according to the SUCCESs criteria and they can make for interesting content in a classroom setting. They are simply not well suited for building the skills in judgment that are the focus of the case method.

Dialoguing a case

Dialoguing a case occurs where the flow of the class involves the instructor peppering individual students with questions about the case, rather than having students build upon each other's contribution without direct involvement of the instructor. Unlike the previously described lecturing, theorizing and illustrating approaches, it is necessarily very interactive. Unlike choreographing a case, however, the instructor controls the flow of the class through choice of students and selection of questions.

Inasmuch as dialoguing a case is very close to the Socratic Method and describes the approach to cases taken by many law schools, my inclusion of dialoguing a case among the quasi-case methods is certainly debatable. My own experiences with groups of students who are new to case discussions suggest that it can be very hard to avoid dialoguing. Unfortunately, being too directive undermines the constructivist learning that is the goal of the case method. For that reason, dialoguing will not be a central focus of this book.

The Case Method in Research

In business, the schools that are most effective in using the case method in the classroom also tend to engage in case method research. The synergy that exists between classroom and research use of cases is frequently not acknowledged. On the other hand, case method research can exist independently of case method pedagogy. As an illustration of such research, we turn to an example from the field of sociology.

Example: Extended Case Method Research

In the field of sociology, Michael Burawoy defines a process of using action research to examine theory as the "extended case method". He describes his own activities as follows (Burawoy, 1998, p. 5):

> The *extended case method* applies reflexive science to ethnography in order to extract the general from the unique, to move the "micro"

---

to the "macro," and to connect the present to the past in anticipation of the future, all by building on preexisting theory. In my own use of the extended case method I used my experiences as a personnel consultant in the Zambian copper industry to elaborate Fanon's theory of post-colonialism. I tried to expose the roots of consent to American capitalism by applying Gramsci's theory of hegemony to my experiences as a machine operator in a South Chicago factory. I have explored the nature of work organization and class formation under socialism by combining Szeleni's theory of class structure and Kornai's theory of shortage economy. This was based on laboring in Hungarian factories--champagne, auto manufacturing, and steel. Most recently I have worked my way outward from a small furniture factory in Northern Russia in order to develop theories of the transition from socialism to capitalism using Marxist notions of merchant and finance capital.

Burawoy (1998, p. 30) observes that the positivist research philosophy that dominates many fields that view themselves as "science" seeks to reduce the impact of context and can be undermined by manifestations of power (e.g., domination, silencing, objectification and normalization). Reflexive approaches, such as the extended case method "…takes context and situation as its points of departure. It thrives on context and seeks to reduce the effects of power…"

Key Features of Case Method Research

What I choose to describe as "case method research" closely parallels case method instruction. Drawing upon the illustrative example and the distinctive features of the pedagogy, features common to both include:

1. *Case method research tends to be exploratory in its goals.* Discovery, rather than explicit theory testing, tends to drive the case method research process.

2. *Case method research relies heavily on triangulation of data sources.* As was true in the classroom, evidence many sources and functional areas can and should contribute to the conclusions of a case method research project.

3. *Case method research often involves a researcher actively participating in the process being investigated.* Research where the researcher is also

a participant is sometimes called *action research*. It is common in case method research and its rationale can be viewed as one of objectivity vs. access. Whereas the standards of objectivity would suggest the investigator should stay as far removed from the process being investigated as possible, access to data may demand the opposite. This is not only true with respect to archived data (such as confidential company reports), it also holds for the quality of observations. A participant is likely to reveal a different set of views to an investigator who has also been acting as a co-worker than to a lab-coated researcher that he or she has never met.

4. *Case method research conclusions are constructed by the researchers involved.* Even when a researcher does not participate in the process being investigated, conclusions of the research are necessarily constructed by the researchers since they make the decision regarding what evidence is relevant and what is not.

5. *The intended outcome of case method research is more likely to be a better explanation of a process than a generalizable "truth".* As was true in the case method classroom, there are likely to be better and worse explanations for a particular observation. Even the most carefully made observation is unlikely to provide enough evidence to provide a compelling argument that some phenomenon is universally true; even if it were true in a particular situation, the lack of replicability inherent in the case method means that many other observations are needed before any degree of generalizability can be supposed.

In providing a list of general features of case method research, I am also implying something very important: *Just because an investigation involves in depth observations of a particular situation or set of situations does not necessarily make it case method research.* You may recall that I characterized lecturing a case and theorizing a case as quasi-case method approaches. Correspondingly, I would argue that going into a case research site with an inflexible agenda of supporting or refuting clearly defined theory is, in fact, quasi-case method research. My reasoning for this is more clearly established in Chapter 2. In that chapter, I develop the argument that certain types of environments that are more conducive to the case method in the classroom than others. Similarly, I argue that such environments are better served by the exploratory philosophy just described than by the rigid theory-testing approach that is frequently advocated in research methods classes and textbooks. This is not the same as arguing that rigorous theory testing is bad. Rather, it proposes that an appropriate research philosophy must take into account the complexity of the processes being investigated.

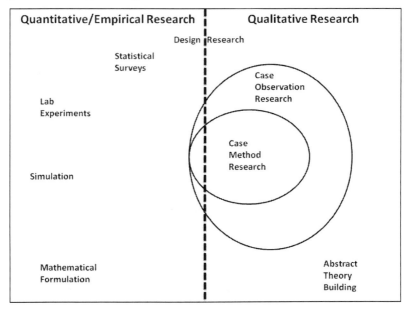

Figure 1.1: Positioning case method research with respect to other forms of research

Case Method Research vs. Qualitative Research in General

Having just argued that not all research involving case observations is case method research, I now consider the distinction between case method research and qualitative research in general. Qualitative research comes in many forms—some of which clearly fall outside of the case method paradigm. For example, activities such as abstract theory building, synthesis and design research are widely applied forms of qualitative research that have little to do with the case method. What is less obvious perhaps is that case method research may incorporate sampling protocols and analysis that will, from time to time, make it appear to be more like quantitative/empirical research than qualitative research. Where the unit of analysis is an organization, for example, the case study analysis may include statistical analysis of populations within the organization. It is the rare educational study that focuses on a particular course, for example, that does not include detailed analysis of student-generated outcome measures such as exam performance, grade distributions or evaluation results. Figure 1.1 serves to illustrate how case method research can be positioned with respect to other research forms.

Challenges Facing the Case Method

There is no shortage of challenges facing the case method today. In this section, I emphasize the obstacles to application in business research and education, the two areas where I have been involved in case method research as an active participant.

Limited Opportunities for Faculty to Learn the Craft

There would seem to be four principal ways to learn the craft of case discussion facilitation and research: through observation, through formal training, through apprenticeship and mentoring, or through trial-and-error. For a variety of reasons, all but the last of these opportunities are declining in availability. The last, on the other hand, is declining in attractiveness. I now explain why I hold this somewhat pessimistic view.

Opportunity to learn through observation

Learning to apply the case method through observation is much like learning through the case method itself. It requires that the individual have the opportunity to observe situations—e.g., facilitators leading case discussions, researchers going into the field with a flexible, exploratory agenda—in considerable detail, most beneficially as a participant. It demands that the individual construct his or her own perspective from these opportunities. It assumes a problem to which there are better and worse approaches, but that seeking the "right" approach will lead only to dead ends.

The obstacle here is that there are very limited opportunities for a faculty member, or future faculty member, to engage in such observation. At a few elite schools, such as Harvard and University of Virginia in the U.S., Ivey and IESE internationally, the case method predominates and instructional practices fairly faithful to the intent of the case method are followed. At other institutions, however, what passes for the case method differs substantially from what is described in this book, and is more akin to lecturing or theorizing with the case method, as described earlier[6].

The same problem applies with respect to observing case method research. Schools that produce case studies for teaching also tend to be comfortable with case method research. Largely as a result of the bifurcation of research and teaching that occurred in the 1960s, case method research tends to have a somewhat lower stature than theoretical or statistically grounded research at other institutions. Thus, it may be hard to find case method researchers to observe elsewhere.

Opportunity to learn through formal training

Foundation grant funding available from the mid-1950s to mid-1960s provided HBS with considerable incentive to train faculty members from other institutions in case method instruction. After that time, however, extensive summer teaching workshops in the craft were discontinued. While HBS continues to sponsor short seminars in case method facilitation, the school's limited efforts to promote the pedagogical technique are vastly less aggressive than their resources would allow. In part, this may be intentional. HBS deans repeatedly emphasize that they view the school's use of the case method as a competitive advantage with respect to other business schools. Would it make sense for them to erode that advantage by actively encouraging the use of the pedagogy at other institutions?[7]

More broadly, business schools seem reluctant to invest time and effort into developing the pedagogical skills of its doctoral students and faculty members. In his book *Managers, Not MBAs*, Henry Mintzberg (2004, p. 406) notes how faculty members protested when a course on pedagogy was included in their doctoral program. I have observed exactly the same phenomenon myself.

Formal training in case method research at business schools faces a different obstacle. Although the conventional wisdom is that case method research is hard to publish, I have never found that to be the case. Moreover, I have noticed that over the years many elite scholarly journals in MIS and management have accorded articles employing case research their top honors. The particular drawback of case research is that it tends to rely heavily on the investigator's own experiences. This being the case, doctoral students are often discouraged from pursuing it (outside of those schools heavily invested in the case method) and their formal training in the approach is limited to a session or two in a research methods class.

Opportunity to learn through apprenticeship and mentoring

For all the reasons just stated under the observation heading, the availability of individuals who can serve as mentors for faculty members seeking to learn more about the case method is limited. Similarly, for the reasons just stated under formal training, many individuals who *could* mentor doctoral students and junior faculty may be reluctant to do so, since it may not be a good fit with the junior faculty career path[8].

Risks of trial-and-error

In the absence of observation, instruction or mentoring, it remains possible to learn the case method entirely through a process of trial and error. Unfortunately, that might not be the wisest career choice in today's academic climate. A side-effect of institutional goals related to demonstrating a commitment to good teaching has been to raise the practical importance of student evaluations of teaching. While my own experience suggests that quality case method instruction usually performs very well according to these rudimentary and inaccurate metrics, my experience also finds that it can take a semester of two to nail down a new pedagogy. For junior faculty members and doctoral students in particular, a few bad classes could exert a significant negative impact on future career prospects. Precisely the same argument can be made with respect to experimenting with case method research.

Lack of Faculty with Experienced Observational Skills

To be a good case method researcher or facilitator, you need to be a good observer. To be a good observer requires practice. Although this last assertion sounds like the type of message that might appear in a fortune cookie, it has a strong basis in cognitive science. In order to absorb the details of a new situation, you need to incorporate them into working memory. The problem is that working memory has very limited capacity. As we practice with a concept or activity, the amount of that memory it requires is drastically reduced through cognitive processes known as chunking and automization (Gill, 2010). Thus, the more practice you have observing case situations, the better you become at being able to pick up relevant details. For novices, the onslaught of information that arrives upon visiting a new case site is like drinking from the proverbial fire hose.

When business schools started viewing business research as a science in the 1960s, they began to seek doctoral students and faculty members more like those of other sciences—in other words, individuals distinguished by their academic achievements rather than by their experience in practice. Such individuals will have had much less opportunity to develop the type of observational skills that facilitate effective case research and teaching.

Movement towards Non-classroom Pedagogies

The case method pedagogy has been tuned to the classroom. Today, however, we are seeing a strong trend towards pedagogies where the classroom is not the central focus. These include both distance learning and experiential learning approaches. While the benefits of these alternative paths to learning can be great, the case method of instruction—as presented in the previous illustration—requires considerable modification if it is to be effective in these situations (for more details, see Chapter 11). To compound the problem, those institutions that are most committed to the case method, particularly HBS, remain dominated by full time students in face-to-face classes. As a result, their apparent level of commitment to developing variations of the case method that take full advantage of the new instructional options has been limited.

Difficulty in Assessing Outcome Results

The resulting outcomes of employing case instruction and case research can be difficult to assess. In case method instruction, the problem tends to be one of measurement. In case method research, the problem involves concerns regarding the generalizability of case method research findings.

Growing "Assurance of Learning" movement

With higher education expenses growing far faster than the cost of living, faculty members and administrators are increasingly being required to provide concrete evidence that our students are actually learning. The challenge of providing such evidence when the case method pedagogy is employed is a frequent lament throughout this book. To compound the problem, public and accrediting agencies often disallow student perceptions as a source of evidence of learning. Thus, we find ourselves with a strong incentive to focus our curricula on conveying content—such as facts, formulas and theories—where learning can be demonstrated rigorously through testing.

As was the case with student evaluations, the well-intentioned act of measuring outcomes may take us in a direction that is exactly the opposite of what makes most sense from a learning standpoint.

N of 1

On the research side, the normal objection to case method research (as well as other forms of case observation research) can be succinctly framed as the problem of "N of 1". The concern is particularly prevalent in fields where statistically grounded empirical research methods are widely used. When applying the case method, you must resign yourself to the fact that in-depth observations take a long time to gather and, in consequence, you rarely get very many of them. Thus, questions of generalizability of the research will nearly always be raised by those who are more comfortable with the objectively rigorous facade that statistical testing presents[9].

Increasingly Litigious Society

Although most of the challenges with the case method have dealt with the research and instruction side of the process, there are also challenges with respect to enlisting appropriate case sites. At many organizations, particularly large organizations, the legal staff may raise objections to providing access to case writers. The problem may be compounded where the project is designated as "research" and is therefore subject to review by a panel intended to protect the rights and privacy of human subjects. The prickly issue this raises is that the organization's representatives now have to sign a form that explains their rights as research subjects. This almost a guarantees a trip to the legal department. It also means that we have just called our practitioner partners in the research "human subjects". While this terminology may seem appropriate to patients participating in a medical research study, it is bound to raise some eyebrows in a real world organizational setting such as business or education.

Conclusions

the case method paradigm has been explored. Covering ... use of case studies in the classroom and case method research, the paradigm is built upon a set of shared characteristics:

1. *It is exploratory.* Whether its venue is cases in the classroom or an organization in the field, participants enter the process without well-defined expectations regarding what will be discovered. No matter how unusual the case, the method strives to construct appropriate explanations and solutions.

2. *It is comprehensive, integrative and participative.* Understanding of a classroom case depends on the participation of the students; understanding of a situation in the field depends on the collective wisdom of the investigator and the individuals engaged in the observed activity—often including the investigator. This means that case method outcomes can be highly dependent upon participant skills.

3. *It is decision and problem focused.* Rather than being driven by theory, the nature of classroom cases and the exploratory philosophy of case method research tend to focus participants on understanding decisions rather than on conveying or validating theory.

4. *It assumes an environment in which distinguishing "better" and "worse" is important, while searching for "right" and "wrong" solutions is likely to be futile.* Even if objectively right and wrong approaches to a decision exist, case method participants—both researchers and students—can never expect to have sufficient information to firmly establish the validity of a particular decision. What is desirable, however, is to rank alternatives based on what is known, building a strong link between the case method and judgment skills.

5. *It is constructivist.* Conclusions and ideas developed through the case method are constructed by participants—whether they are students or researchers.

These characteristics make the case method well suited for certain types of environments, and poorly adapted to others. That fact is important because there are many obstacles to applying the method, the most important of which include the lack of skilled case method practitioners and the various risks associated with applying the method. Among the latter: the risk that research and classroom applications of the technique will be poorly received, that new approaches to delivering instruction may require us to rethink the conduct of case method instruction, that case method outcomes will not be convincing, and that legal concerns are likely to make suitable case method research sites harder to come by.

In light of these obstacles, the decision to employ the case method paradigm should not be taken lightly. In Chapter 2 we turn to identifying those domains where the case method paradigm offers sufficient benefits as to justify dealing with the many frustrations that its use can present.

Chapter 1 Notes

[1] The 1908 HBS catalog stated:

In the courses on Commercial Law the case system will be used. In the other courses an analogous method emphasizing classroom discussion in connection with lectures and frequent reports on assigned topics—what may be called the "problem method"—will be introduced as far as practicable." (Copeland, 1958, p. 27).

[2] As a representative example of an HBS case, circa 1920, Barnes, Christensen and Hansen (1994, p. 43) offer the following case:

BADGER MANUFACTURING COMPANY: BUYING HABITS OF CONSUMERS

The badger Manufacturing Company produces enamelware for kitchen use in a wide variety of articles and styles of several qualities. The company has recently decided to start an extensive advertising campaign in order to increase its sales.

What are the buying habits and motives of consumers purchasing such products, which the advertising manager of Badger Manufacturing Company should take into account in planning this campaign?

3 For example, the Ford Foundation report included the following statement:

> [There is] strong and widespread dissatisfaction with the quality of business education in American colleges and universities today. What passes as the going standard of acceptability is embarrassingly low, and many schools of business do not even meet these low standards. While the schools are bedeviled by uncertainty, there is growing recognition that the present situation is intolerable. The gap between what society needs and what the business schools are offering has grown wide enough for all to see (Gordon & Howell, 1959, p. 6).

4 Consider the following comments relating to the use of the case method as a research tool in the Ford Foundation report:

> Whether the aim is to improve our understanding of business behavior (i.e., to search for significant generalizations) or to develop better techniques and rules for decision-making, it is clear that business research needs to become more analytical, to develop more solid theoretical underpinning, and to utilize a more sophisticated methodology. This means not only more applied research of the sort that makes the best possible use of the methods of analysis that we now have, but also the development of new and more useful theories and concepts. This in turn requires that the business schools turn for help to the underlying disciplines such as the behavior sciences and mathematics and statistics, as well as to economics...

> None of the preceding discussion is intended to minimize the importance of field investigations, detailed case studies, and, in general, the systematic collection of more and better information about business behavior. This is the essential raw material for the study of business—but it is only the raw material. Similarly, case collection is an important activity for the business school, both because of its contribution to teaching and because of its value as training for the faculty member. But case collection by itself is not research in the usual sense of that term. It can, however, become the raw material for research since, through careful and discriminating analysis, signif-

icant generalizations can sometimes be drawn from the study of a large number of cases. (Gordon & Howell, 1959, p. 384-385).

[5] Personally, I fall short of the "perfect facilitator" ideal in far too many respects for my liking. Sometimes the weaknesses in my technique are not under my control (e.g., the classroom settings I teach in are wrong and the students are generally completely unfamiliar with the discussion dynamic coming into my classroom). Sometimes they are (e.g., I like the sound of my own voice way too much to be an ideal instructor). Fortunately, as I will point out many times in this book, while perfection is unattainable for most mortals, adequacy can readily be achieved with sufficient motivation.

[6] *Business Week*, as part of its annual ranking, asks schools to identify the percentage of case method instruction used in their MBA programs. The self-reported average is about 37% for the top 20 ranked U.S. schools and 42% for the 9 top international schools. Having done some spot checking of these rankings for a number of non-elite schools (that shall remain nameless), however, I have come to suspect that self-reports in the 20-30% range are more likely to represent closer to 0%, although case studies are doubtless used for descriptive purposes.

[7] I am quite sure that many HBS faculty members would strongly object to my speculation that HBS is not actively promoting the case method for reasons of maintaining a competitive advantage. My reasoning is as follows. First, case method instruction is what its graduates most remember and prize about the school (more on that in Chapter 2). Second, even a single case method instructor using HBS cases represents a phenomenal source of ongoing revenue for the school. Suppose a faculty member teaching graduate students uses 12 cases in a class that, over the course of year, is given to 100 students. At $4/case (standard HBS Publishing fee for a case download), HBS realizes $4800/year. Multiply that by a 35 year academic career and $168,000 in contribution to profit is generated over the instructor's lifetime. Based on this, the economic incentive to invest a few thousand in training doctoral students and new faculty from other institutions to use cases effectively should be obvious.

[8] In a rather perplexing illustration of this, I have found myself mentoring a number of doctoral students in both case method research and

instruction. None have been in business, however. Instead, they have arrived at my door from our School of Social Work and our College of Education.

[9] In my book *Informing Business* (Gill, 2010) I conclude that—in certain types of environments—statistical significance is likely to be wildly misleading. Thus I use the term "objective façade" in describing such research rather than simply saying objective. In Chapter 2, I explain briefly the rationale behind this usage, which—on the surface—seems to serve no purpose other than unnecessarily annoying nearly all of my research colleagues. The key point to understand here is that I advocate the case method paradigm precisely for those environments where other techniques are destined to fail.

Chapter 2

Why Use the Case Method?

Immediately before the conclusion of Chapter 1, I summarized a series of obstacles that face almost anyone employing the case method paradigm. Since many of these challenges are daunting indeed, our motivation to surmount them must be substantial before we even contemplate applying the paradigm. This chapter is intended to identify those contexts where the case method can be worth the effort. *It represents a significant departure from the remainder of the book, being highly theoretical in some of its elements. It is primarily directed at those believing in theory, but not the case method.*

Many of the objections raised against the case method, particularly as it is applied in the classroom, are a function of implicit beliefs about the nature of what students should be learning. I therefore begin the chapter by identifying some of the most common objections, then exploring the assumptions upon which they are based. The assumed complexity of the domain of study, or the lack thereof, proves to be the underlying factor common to these objections.

We then consider the nature of complexity. This analysis, summarized from my earlier book *Informing Business* (Gill, 2010), concludes that where the complexity of a particular domain of study is high, many of the teaching and research methods normally characterized as rigorous can fail, sometimes spectacularly.

Finally, we examine at how the characteristics of the case method paradigm are consonant with the characteristics of complex environments. Further adding to the potential value of the paradigm is the stickiness of case method approach, using the concept introduced in Chapter 1. Thus, I conclude that the case method is likely to be a justifiable choice when used in the appropriate setting. It may even be the "best" choice of those teaching and research alternatives currently available— although that is a very un-case method thing to say.

Arguments against the Case Method

In academia, often the most effective way to suppress a movement is to completely ignore it. Thus, relatively few direct assaults on the case method have been mounted, at least in the business and education domains with which I am most familiar. Instead, instructors lecture to their students and examine them on the concepts they have learned. Researchers eschew in-depth observational and analysis in favor of more purportedly rigorous statistical and theory-building approaches. Administrators seek the economies of classes so large that managing meaningful discussions becomes nearly impossible. Companies refer case development projects to their legal department for approval. All the stakeholders involved pay lip service to cases. But they are unconcerned should the case method fade away, like an unneeded vestigial organ.

A few brave souls, however, have come forward and actually presented arguments *against* the case method in the classroom. Since all these arguments have a grain of validity, the faculty member contemplating adopting a case method approach would do well to understand the concerns. I therefore begin by summarizing their arguments. I then consider the assumptions that seem to underlie these arguments, and show how they run counter to the precepts of the case method. I particularly focus on the pedagogical aspects of the case method in this section, since the *N of 1* objection discussed in the previous chapter pretty well dominates the opposition to case method research and is central to the chapter specifically devoted to case method resrarch.

Critiques of the Case Method Pedagogy[1]

The most systematic attempt to discredit the case method that I could find was written by Steven Shugan (2006), a widely cited scholar in the marketing field, in an editorial written for *Marketing Science*. He specifically identifies seven issues that he asserts warrant abandoning case discussions in the classroom. So as to avoid introducing my own interpretations, the introductory statement for each item is quoted verbatim as follows (Shugan, 2006, pp. 113-114):

> First, the Socratic case method is extraordinarily effective for teaching many skills (e.g., applying written law); however, it is ancient and inferior to the scientific method...

Second, the case method weakens the link between research and classroom, removing critical incentives for relevant research...

Third, surrendering teaching to those with little knowledge of the vast marketing literature cuts the quality of marketing education...

Fourth, the case method can teach false confidence...

Fifth, we could lose our best students. Better students, who have already acquired analytical thinking skills and confidence, might seek more scientific content and technical training...

Sixth, some great research might never reach the classroom because translating it into the case-method format is too challenging...

Seventh, the case method rarely exposes students to the latest tools for making better decisions...

If we look at these criticisms, we can detect a number of distinct assumptions. Let us consider them point-by-point:

1. *He equates the case method with the Socratic Method*—what I referred to as "dialoguing a case" in Chapter 1. In fact, the approach to case teaching that is applied in business (i.e., choreographing a case) is very different from the manner in which it is typically applied at law schools.

2. *He assumes that a case study developed for discussion is not a product of research.* This may be viewed as a matter of definition. What I will argue throughout this book is that developing a case is always research[2].

3. *He believes that the quality of a marketing education depends on the amount of knowledge of the vast marketing literature that has been acquired.* This assumption is made despite the fact that there is precious little evidence that systematic knowledge of that literature produces better marketers. It might, however, produce a better marketing professor by some standards.

4. *He believes that the case method causes students to develop excessive confidence, presumably as a result of their ability to come up with the "right" answer.* This assumption suggests, at least to me, that he be-

lieves that participants in a case discussion generally come in with an answer that will be validated by the discussion. Were that actually true, there would be no need for discussions.

5. *He speculates that our best students will be drawn towards the scientific and analytical approaches he prefers.* Here he assumes that knowledgeable individuals will be drawn towards the science of business, as opposed to the art[3].

6. *He asserts that great research can be too analytically demanding to be suitable for the case method.* The assumption here is that complicated procedures or formulations are not well suited to the case method. This is quite consistent with what was stated in Chapter 1 about avoiding the case method where there is a right answer. It also suggests that he believes that marketing research is either highly generalizable with respect to its findings or that research "greatness" can be assessed entirely independent of the size of its potential practitioner audience, since many of the examples he cited were very situation specific[4].

7. *He assumes that useful research mainly flows from academia to practice, as opposed to moving in the opposite direction.* In this assumption, he obviously diverges from that expressed by Jeffrey Pfeffer (2007, p. 1337) in management, who points out that the vast majority of tools used in practice were developed outside of academia.

Aside from a few points (i.e., 1 & 4) that lead me to question Shugan's familiarity with the case method as it is actually practiced, the core of his argument against the case method rests on the assumption that analytical techniques, mainly quantitative in nature, will ultimately lead us to a better understanding of business than the case method paradigm. This is an assumption that can reasonably be questioned. In some disciplines—such as the hard sciences—the matter has largely been settled and Shugan would be validated. In others, the arts in particular, the question is not even raised since it would seem silly to most of us. In business, education and other social science domains, however, the question of the suitability of quantitative vs. qualitative approaches remains far from settled.

In a recent debate hosted on the Harvard Business Review web site, Professor Barry Mitnik (2009) presents a similar set of arguments. Taken verbatim from the blog, they are as follows:

1. Cases are not "real" - they are accounts, not the real thing; can grow dated; and ignore actual "real world" experience.

2. A course full of cases lacks time to introduce the systematic content of a discipline and the results of modern research on management practice. Indeed, where can students acquire the knowledge tools necessary to properly assess a case? The case method developed in an era in which management research was in its infancy; that era is long past.

3. The standard caveat on the first page of every case warns that it was prepared "as the basis of class discussion rather than to illustrate either effective or ineffective handling of an administrative situation." Yet students need to know what practices are effective and ineffective -- just as they should be encouraged to examine those practices critically.

4. The case method makes the instructor a facilitator; students learn from their peers. But they also need to benefit from deep expertise. Professors must sometimes profess, not merely facilitate. Self-training, like self-medication, is best done under professional direction.

5. The case method says discussion should be many-voiced and critical. Yet the use of multiple methods of instruction, including the Harvard model, would go far more directly to achieve this aim, than to lock instruction into a pattern decades old.

Certainly his first point, that cases are not "real", is valid; it must be tempered by the fact that neither are mathematical models. This concern is echoed by management giant Henry Mintzberg (2004, p. 52), who makes the following comments:

> Reaching a logical conclusion and knowing how to convince others of it are certainly important aspects of managing. But overemphasized, as they are in the case study classroom, they can distort the whole managerial process. Managers have to sense things; they have to weave their way through complex phenomena, they have to dig out information, they have to probe deeply, on the ground, not from the top of some mythical pyramid [the organizational hierarchy]. The "big picture" is not there for the seeing; certainly not in any twenty-page doc-

ument; it has to be constructed slowly, carefully, through years of intimate experience...

Points 2 and 3 assume that existing business research will lead us towards effective solutions. Point 4 implies that facilitation does not benefit greatly from expertise in the domain being discussed. As was the case with Shugan's commentary, this suggests unfamiliarity with the actual practice of the case method[5]. Point 5 asserts that the case method should not be applied to all subject matter. Having made that point in Chapter 1, I would be hard-pressed to disagree with it here.

My Own Concerns

Drawing upon my own experience, both as student and facilitator, I will readily concede three weaknesses inherent in the case method, each of which is a function of the challenges presented in Chapter 1.

The first weakness is the dependence of discussions upon the skills of the facilitator. There are myriad ways that an instructor can mess up a case discussion—all of which I have been guilty of from time to time. He or she can over-control the discussion or under-control it. By doing the former, the case becomes transformed into a lecture or narrative; the latter tends to convey the sense that any solution proposed is workable—an entirely false notion. The instructor can choose a set of cases that leads the students to generalize ineffective rules; this is particularly true when what actually happened after the case is over-emphasized[6]. Perhaps worst of all, the instructor can ignore the inherently integrative nature of a case study and facilitate it solely from the perspective of his or her discipline. Experienced facilitators and course designers are aware of these pitfalls and can, to a certain extent, avoid them. Unfortunately, experienced instructors are increasingly difficult to come by—a fact upon which Mintzberg (2004, p. 65) and I agree.

The second weakness of the case method is that it depends heavily on the students. I can think of no pedagogical technique where participant "buy in" is more critical. No instructor can make a case discussion effective if the students arrive unprepared. A strong desire for consensus can also wreck a discussion. Cultural factors play an important role in participation that can easily be underestimated[7]. All this becomes particularly challenging when students entering the course have no prior case discussion experience. Unfortunately, at all but a few select schools, this student inexperience with the pedagogy is the rule.

Perhaps the greatest weakness of the case method is the frustrating inability to assess case method learning outcomes in any objective way. Where specific content or skills are being conveyed, they can be tested. Such objective testing is extremely difficult in case method courses.

I would describe the problem in the following terms. When you first pick up a new case study, you are placed in the ultimate low-structure decision-making situation. For a business case, chances are the industry is one you've never thought about, the company is one you know little about or have never heard of, the product (if applicable) is one you do not care about, and the protagonist may well be entirely different from you in personality, nationality, and gender. You are then asked to place yourself in that protagonist's shoes and make a decision. There are enough variables in this equation, however, that you will find yourself "bonding" with some cases considerably more than others[8]. The variability of such bonding is considerable, yet plays a big role in your ability to analyze it. For example, imagine how hard it is to put yourself in the decision-making mindset of a manager who you detest, who is working in an industry you abhor, for a company that you would gladly see go out of business. If you use case exams to assess what a student has learned, the error introduced by the variability in bonding is likely to be considerable. Moreover, instructors themselves tend to "bond" with different approaches to analyzing a case, so the grading variability for a given exam will also tend to be great.

The Big Question

Excluding Mintzberg's (2004) criticisms and my own pragmatic concerns, the central theme of the arguments offered against the case method is as follows:

> *Other forms of business research generally offer a better path to solving business problems than the case method. It therefore follows that the case method—which can be time consuming both in research and in the class-room—is generally not the best choice for business research and education.*

The big question—the one that will be central to this chapter and this book—therefore becomes: *Do other forms of business research, particularly those heavily invested in theory and quantitative methods actually offer a better path to solving business problems? More broadly, is the case method suitable for any domain?*

My analysis of this question hinges on the assumed complexity of the environment being studied. To that topic we now turn.

Complexity and Fitness Landscapes

This presentation draws heavily on my recent book *Informing Business: Research and Education on a Rugged Landscape* (Gill, 2010) and the works that preceded it. Thus, I will try to keep my presentation as brief as possible.

The Nature of Complexity

The way that I view complexity is guided by a simple model developed by well-known evolutionary biologist and complexity theorist Stuart Kauffman (1993). Imagine that you are presented with a decision, the typical starting point of a case, and that there are a set of factors—for the time being limited to Yes/No choices that you can control—that are described by n different variables: $x_1, x_2, \ldots x_n$. Let us also assume that there is some value Y that tells us the fitness of any particular combination of Yes/No values for the factors that you choose. In its most general form, we could model the situation as follows:

$$Y = f(x_1, x_2, \ldots x_n)$$

where Y is fitness (dependent variable) and $x_1, \ldots, x_n$ are the Yes/No factors we have identified as impacting fitness (independent variables). In the simplest case, each variable x_i exerts an independent impact on fitness y_i, leading to the relationship that follows:

$$Y = c + y_1 + y_2 + \ldots + y_n$$

where c is a constant term, reflecting base-case fitness.

Relationships such as the one just described can be characterized as *decomposable*. A particularly common form of decomposable relationship is assumed by the linear regression and structural equation modeling tools that are widely used in business research, i.e.:

$$Y = c + a_1x_1 + a_2x_2 + \ldots + a_nx_n$$

What such a decomposable relationship necessarily implies is that there is only one set of values for $x_1, \ldots, x_n$ where further changes to any single variable will reduce fitness. Stated another way, decomposable landscapes have one, and only one, fitness peak. In a practical sense, *decisions made on decomposable landscapes have a single right answer*.

Many decisions, however, involve relationships that are not decomposable. For example, the desirability of water skis vs. snow skis as a present to your spouse will likely depend on whether the January plane tickets that accompany the skis are to Colorado or to Florida. Kauffman captures such interactions by describing landscapes in terms of their N,K property. N is the number of 0,1 factor determining fitness (x_1, ..., x_n in our example), K is the number of interactions present, which may range from 0 (decomposable) to N-1 (every variable interacts with all N-1 other variables). What is important about N,K landscapes is that as soon as K gets bigger than 0, you will start to see the emergence of many local fitness peaks. In fact, when K gets to it maximum value (N-1), the number of local peaks can be estimated at:

$$2^N/(N+1)$$

The typical decision in business or education is likely to have many controllable factors. What that means, on a highly complex landscape, is a huge number of peaks. For example, if there are 8 elements to the decision, there will be about 28 (256/9) different peaks on maximally complex landscape. While there will always be a "best" peak—as a matter of definition—several of these local peaks are likely to be nearly as good. Thus, a search for an appropriate combination (a "good" answer) makes more sense than an exhaustive search for the optimal answer (the "best:" answer).

Aside from having multiple peaks, decomposable landscapes differ from their complex counterparts in a number of other important ways. In a decomposable fitness relationship involving a large number of factors, each factor will, on average, exert a very small impact on fitness. This is simple arithmetic—if ten variables impact fitness independently, then each variable will on average account for 10% of the fitness range. Where interactions occur, the situation is entirely different, since changes to one variable in the interaction work on fitness with the combined effect of all the variables involved. This is illustrated in Figure 2.1. A good way to understand this is by considering hypothetical fitness function for cooking. Even though baking powder is added in tiny amounts and plays no particular role in determining the taste or caloric content of a dish, watch what happens to the overall fitness of a cake recipe if you happen to forget to put it in.

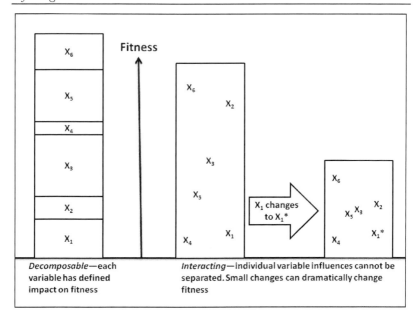

Figure 2.1: Decomposable vs. interacting contributions to fitness, and how little changes to variables in interacting systems can lead to big effects

The fact that interactions can have a large effect also exerts a profound impact on the appropriateness of studying phenomenon outside of their natural environment. Where the contributions to fitness are decomposable, incremental changes to fitness observed in one setting will be completely generalizable to another setting. Even if you can only explain a small portion of overall fitness—say you have only studied the effects of x_1 and x_2 in Figure 2.1—your conclusions should not be invalidated by subsequent research. In other words, the replicability of findings should be strong.

Where interactions are present, there can be no such confidence about generalizing results. Suppose variables $x_1, \ldots, x_n$ are under your control, while another set of variables $b_1, \ldots, b_m$ are beyond your control—either because you do not know they impact fitness or because they are aspects of the situation (e.g., the location of a production facility or classroom) that are not under the control of the decision maker. Further suppose the fitness function is actually of the form:

$$Y = f(x_1, x_2, \ldots x_n, b_1, b_2, \ldots b_m)$$

In this case, any relationships observed between fitness and your choices $x_1, \ldots, x_n$ are predicated on the values of $b_1, \ldots, b_m$, some of which you may not even be measuring or aware of. As long as there are no interactions between your x's and your b's, the problem may not be too severe. Should such interactions exist, however, any relationships you observe in the context of one set of b's may not hold in the context of alternative b values. Indeed, the relationships between the x values and fitness may prove to be radically different where high interaction levels are present and the b values are different. One way to protect against this is to determine the values of all b variables and assert that you do not necessarily expect results to apply for a different set of b's. The problem then becomes the b's whose impact on fitness is unknown. To prevent this type of error, heroic efforts are justified in order to systematically identify all factors impacting fitness in the situation being investigated. Anything less is not rigorous.

Substantial N,K complexity comes with a number of other properties that can be vexing to researchers. Consider the existence of theory fragments—theories that are intended to explain some, but not necessarily all, of the fitness associated with a particular situation. As K gets reasonably large, we can expect to find, *in some region of the landscape*, evidence for virtually any plausible relationship. Thus, observing such a relationship—even at a high level of statistical significance—is unremarkable. What is critically important, and much harder to determine, is the precise boundaries over which the relationship is expected to hold.

A particularly troubling aspect of N,K landscapes surfaces when they are populated by adapting entities—such as decision-makers. Designed as a framework for modeling evolutionary processes, the assumption is generally made that entities will migrate towards fitness peaks from generation to generation, as high fitness entities will survive more readily than low fitness entities. If the entities are adaptable decision-makers, on the other hand, and fitness represents the consequence of a decision, we would expect relatively rapid migration towards high fitness combinations. The clustering around peaks that this produces raises havoc with multivariate statistical tools, such as linear regression, a phenomenon the statistician Terry Sincich and I first observed (Gill & Sincich, 2008).

To summarize, *if we assume decision-makers locally maximize the fitness of their decisions—one of the fundamental assumptions that underlies most mathematical economics—then attempts to study these decisions using the empirical techniques widely used in business and education research will be prone to statistical illusions.*

Bringing together the key points relating to what I have just said:

1. A complex landscape will have many local fitness peaks, meaning a diversity of locally optimal behaviors is almost sure to exist on such landscapes.

2. Treating unknown variables as random error on a complex landscape can lead to very misleading findings; the generalizability of partial theories (theory fragments) is likely to be very low, the benefits of systematic study of any situation is likely to be high.

3. Discovering the boundaries of a particular behavior on a complex landscape is vastly more interesting than discovering that the behavior exists, since the diversity of fitness peaks means that almost any moderately sensible behavior will prove locally optimal somewhere.

4. The use of empirical statistical techniques that assume decomposability as their base case (such as multiple linear regression) is likely to yield as many illusions as insights.

All of these observations are directly related to the mathematical properties of complex N,K landscapes. Given a complex N,K landscape exist, we would expect them to occur. They also imply a general set of principles that are consistent with researching behaviors in a complex system:

Principle I: *Pay particular attention to distinguishing peaks from non-peaks.* **Rationale:** Entities will tend to migrate towards peaks; when entities exhibiting unusual behavior are identified, it is important to determine whether they are in the process of migrating or have arrived at a new peak.

Principle II: *Use every source of evidence possible in determining what does and does not impact fitness.* **Rationale:** Determining the boundaries of an observed behavior is at least as important as understanding the behavior itself, since lack of generalizability is a constant threat in complex behavior. Since any undiscovered or ignored interaction can dramatically impact behavior, a small number of in-depth observations are likely to be more valuable than a large number of casual observations. On the other hand, discovering that one set of factors impact fitness are completely decomposable in their impact on fitness from another set of factors is incredibly valuable information, since it justifies studying the two groups of factors independently (e.g., in a lab setting).

Principle III: *Study the mechanisms by which fitness is increased in preference to the contributors to fitness in a particular situation.* **Rationale:** The specific contributors to fitness are expected to vary widely by observation in a complex system. This is not necessarily true of the techniques for exploring fitness. In genetics, for example, a few simple processes, such as mutation and crossover, are proposed to be the underlying source of genetic diversity. In the theory of evolution, the process of survival of the fittest describes how species evolve; evolutionary biologists spend much more time exploring its mechanisms than is trying to predict what specific characteristics would contribute to organism fitness in general[9].

Principle IV: *Be suspicious of attractive theories, whether mathematically, conceptually or empirically derived.* **Rationale:** Theory fragments will rarely generalize beyond the assumptions and observations upon which they are based in a complex environment. Only a systematic and exhaustive study of the factors involved in the theory that demonstrates their independence (decomposability) from the remaining factors influencing fitness would justify the theory. This further underscores the value of studying the boundaries of observed behaviors as opposed to focusing exclusively on behaviors themselves.

Principle V: *Assume that outliers are valid observations and avoid statistical approaches that average effects.* **Rationale:** In systems assumed to be decomposable, unusual observations are normally attributed to randomness or to observational error. For this reason, they are frequently discarded. In complex systems, it makes more sense to assume that unusual observations are evidence of unexplained interaction and are therefore worthy of extra study for the insights they can provide.

We return to these later in the chapter.

The General Argument for Complexity

What makes the list just presented particularly relevant to domains such as business and education is that there is an underlying justification for expecting that living systems will tend to evolve into complex systems. The reasoning is as follows:

- Most living systems do not exist by themselves on a static landscape. Instead, they are impacted by other, co-evolving systems that change the fitness landscape over time, sometimes very rapidly—since the presence of discontinuous change is a characteristic widely observed in complex systems (Bak, 1996).

- Where changes to the fitness landscape are frequent or rapid, decomposable landscapes—which necessarily have a single fitness peak that all entities will eventually attain—are very brittle. Consider the devastation that occurred in the 19th Century, for example, when blight virtually wiped out the potato crop that had become nearly the universal staple of the Irish diet.

- More complex landscapes, on the other hand, are resilient because entities on such landscapes tend to spread themselves out. As a result, whatever new fitness function evolves, there will likely be some entities that are at or near high levels of fitness. Diversity does not come without cost however; with many local peaks, we may reasonably assume that some entities will routinely be trapped on peaks of relatively low fitness.

- Thus, as Kauffman (1993) theorizes, living systems should tend to migrate towards a relatively narrow region of complexity that exists between the chaos of the N,N-1 landscape and the order of the N,0 landscape.

- We might also reasonably suppose that the greater the rate of fitness change being experienced, the greater the benefit of complexity (i.e., the higher the K value in N,K terminology).

The practical difficulty presented in applying the N,K model is that fitness functions do not advertise their N and K values. As a result, some researchers will assume that N is manageable and K is close to 0. For these researchers, the greatest promise to advance the science will be theory building, mathematical analysis and statistical studies. These techniques have produced great advances in other fields of science, why should we not expect the same in fields such as management or education? Other researchers, however, will perceive N to be very large and K to be high. To such researchers, attempts to build attractive theory, mathematical models of behavior or draw conclusions from statistically derived evidence are likely to seem futile, if not naïve. To them, fields such as management and education may seem closer to art[10] than science.

In other words, what types of research and educational techniques are most appropriate depend very heavily on the assumed the complexity of the system being studied. As illustrated in Figure 2.2, the domains of study with which I am most familiar, business and education, could be located is a variety of places. How do we place them?

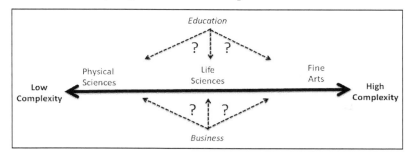

Figure 2.2: Where to place the domains of business and education on a continuum of complexity

While there is no definitive way of being sure, it is also fair to say that the presence of complexity leaves a trail of breadcrumbs. Taken directly from *Informing Business* (Gill, 2010), I propose that the following characteristics will tend to be observed frequently in nearly every complex systems populated with adapting entities:

1. *Different approaches to fitness succeed.* Where highly dissimilar examples of high fitness can be identified, the presence of multiple local fitness peaks distributed across the landscape is suggested. Dissimilarity is particularly important in this context,

since similar examples of high fitness could simply be entities close to the same peak.

2. *Inconsistent changes to fitness result when variables are changed in different contexts.* Inconsistent changes to fitness—resulting from manipulating the same variable in the same manner—mean that a variable's effect cannot be established independent of the values of other variables that determine fitness. Using a previous example, omitting the baking powder from a cake recipe may drastically reduce the fitness of the resulting cake, even though the quantity of the ingredient is small and its impact upon taste negligible. This differs from decomposable landscapes, where the impact of a particular variable is always the same, and if many variables participate in determining fitness, the average incremental impact of each will be relatively small.

3. *Inconsistent research findings.* Fitness behavior in a particular setting that varies significantly from findings well supported by previous research; like the second, this suggests a situation-dependence that implies interactions between variables. It could also indicate the presence of a dynamic component to fitness. On theoretical grounds, entities existing on a dynamic landscape will be more likely to survive if a diverse set of high fitness peaks are always occupied. Replication research will tend to be unsupportive of conclusions on such a landscape.

4. *Little changes sometimes make a big difference to fitness.* When a landscape is decomposable, changes in most variables exert a predictable (and usually small) impact on fitness. Where the underlying landscape is complex, variable changes can act through interaction and a small change can dramatically change fitness. For example, what would have happened to the fitness of the Mona Lisa if daVinci had employed a few extra milligrams of paint to make the smile just a bit more obvious?

5. *Stickiness of entities.* Ruggedness implies local peaks and entities on established peaks naturally resist incremental change; when change does occur, it tends to be discontinuous in nature. When you are on a fitness peak, incremental change always leads to a decline in fitness; this assertion is purely a consequence of how we define "peak". When attempting to migrate to another peak, changing many attributes tends to entail either

high risk or extended periods transitioning through valleys of low fitness. Thus, entities that have already reached fitness peaks are likely to try to remain on those peaks for as long as possible. Only entities who know that they are not on a peak (e.g., new entrants to an industry) or whose particular peak has been disrupted (e.g., manufacturers of photographic film in an age rapidly transitioning to digital photography) will be sufficiently motivated to engage in radical change. When such change does occur, it will be rapid.

6. *Turbulent dynamics.* Punctuated equilibrium behavior has been observed as a characteristic common to many complex landscapes.

I develop the case for the complexity of an educational setting in Appendix E, a copy of a paper that I wrote with my colleague Joni Jones (Gill & Jones, 2010). Later, I use it as an example of the case method of research. For now, we apply the list of complexity indicators to assess the complexity of business.

The Complexity of Business Environments

At the outset, let me assert that it would be nothing short of a fool's errand to attempt to characterize the complexity of all business environments. Indeed, the very assumption of complexity presupposes that some regions studied will be very complex, while others less so. Nevertheless, it is an interesting exercise to consider the degree to which business appears to conform to the list of six complexity indicators just presented. Since this was the principal subject of several chapters in *Informing Business* (Gill, 2010), I summarize the evidence in Table 2.1.

In the broader sense, I would argue that the near-total failure of business research to impact practice—well described in Jeffrey Pfeffer's (2007) *Academy of Management Journal* article titled "A Modest Proposal"—is a strong indirect indicator that the assumptions upon which we are basing our research are flawed. Since these assumptions largely hinge upon the notion that the phenomena we are studying exist on relatively decomposable environments, the validity of that assumption *needs* to be questioned.

Table 2.1: Evidence of complexity in business environments

Complexity Indicator	Examples of evidence
Diversity of fitness approaches	The large diversity of firms that emerge within most industries and in most countries; existence of distinct "schools" in many fields, such as economics, alternative generic strategies such as those proposed by Porter (1980)
Inconsistent incremental changes to fitness	Inconsistent preferences widely demonstrated in behavioral economics literature; failure of policy changes to produce intended results.
Inconsistent research findings	The extraordinarily low level at which research successfully replicates in marketing (Hubbard & Armstrong, 1994), finance (Hubbard & Vetter, 1991), accounting, economics and management (Hubbard & Vetter, 1996)
Sensitivity to small changes	Behavioral economics studies demonstrating framing, priming and other examples of how minor variations in problem presentation can exert major decision impacts; numerous anecdotal examples where small factors led to major changes in impact
Stickiness of entities	Large literature on resistance to change; theoretical frameworks such as Christensen's (1997) disruptive technologies model
Turbulent dynamics	Extensive literature reporting turbulent dynamics; the widespread impact of bubbles and panics

Another broad indicator of underlying complexity is the failure of experts in predicting system behavior. This phenomenon occurs both because the dynamics of punctuated equilibrium makes complex systems inherently unpredictable and because practical expertise tends to develop around individual fitness peaks, leading to loss of generalizability when new situations are encountered. Examples of this phenomenon are repeatedly encountered in the context of business and economics, as I discuss in *Informing Business*. More broadly, it is well supported by the research literature (e.g., Shanteau, 1992) and in books such as Nassim Taleb's (2007) *The Black Swan*, a compelling account of why business and economies cannot expect to anticipate the events that will ultimately exert the greatest impact upon them.

Complexity and the Case Method

In considering the role that can be played by the case method in a particular field, it is useful to think back to the five principles of research in a complex system presented earlier in the chapter and compare these with the characteristics of the case method presented at the end of Chapter 1. As illustrated in Table 2.2, the close relationship between the two lists should be readily apparent.

Table 2.2: Research Principles and Case Method Characteristics

Research Principle (from Chapter 2)	Case Method Principle (from Chapter 1)
I. Pay particular attention to distinguishing peaks from non-peaks.	4. It assumes an environment in which distinguishing "better" and "worse" is important, while searching for "right" and "wrong" answers is largely fruitless.
II. Use every source of evidence possible in determining what does and does not impact fitness.	2. It is comprehensive, integrative and participative.
III. Study the mechanisms by which fitness in increased in preference to the contributors to fitness in a particular situation.	3. It is decision and problem focused.
IV. Be suspicious of attractive theories, whether mathematically, conceptually or empirically derived.	5. It is constructivist.
V. Assume that outliers are valid observations and avoid statistical approaches that average effects.	1. It is exploratory.

Beyond the evident fit between the characteristics of research that makes sense in a complex system and the case method, the use of cases—independent of the formally defined case method—provides a number of benefits for informing. As noted in Chapter 1, for example, the "story" has long been known to be a particularly resonant form of communication (Heath & Heath, 2007; Gill, 2010). The development of cases for research and their use in the classroom therefore increases the likelihood that the knowledge contained within them will diffuse.

The story format provides particular benefits when used to inform experts in a complex environment. As a general rule, experts tend to be very reluctant to abandon or reject knowledge that they have already acquired. The resistance is so pronounced that I refer to it as the *Law of Abandoned Expertise* (Gill, 2010). This law presents a particular problem when conveying abstract knowledge in a complex environment because the ideas will tend to fall into two categories: consistent and inconsistent with the expert's observations. Where the knowledge is consistent, no informing occurs (since the expert learns nothing from the knowledge). Where the knowledge is inconsistent, it will probably be rejected or ignored by the expert. I hasten to add that in a complex environment, the expert is not necessarily wrong in doing so.

When knowledge is framed as a story, on the other hand, any embedded ideas do not directly conflict with the expert's existing experience (unless the story *directly* relates to the expert's situation). Thus, it can bypass much of the expert's resistance. Moreover, the expert can extract those elements of the story that he or she does perceive to be relevant and credible and act upon those, even though other elements of the story are rejected as being inapplicable. In other words, the expert plays an active role in constructing the meaning of the story personalized to his or her situation. Will this be the meaning that the researcher or facilitator anticipated? Not necessarily. But knowledge *has succeeded in diffusing* and the fact that the expert has become actively involved in its interpretation makes it all the more likely to stick.

Conclusions

Why use the case method? The answer depends mainly on what you believe about the world that you are studying. If you believe that is it governed by a manageably small set of straightforward principles that are awaiting discovery, then I would be hard-pressed to recommend the exertion required to employ the paradigm. To be sure, you might want to lecture a case or two, maybe theorize some others just because stories are so sticky. On the whole, however, you would be well justified in treating your colleagues—who bought into the whole constructivist, participative approach to knowledge creation—as having fallen prey to a largely unscientific philosophy that is little more than a cult.

Alternatively, if you believe that the world you are studying is truly complex, you are likely to see the case method as one of the few rigorous approaches to better understanding that is available to you. Cases are far from objective and far from complete in how they model the world. But at least, if done properly, they make a systematic attempt to gather and synthesize all the information that is available to the investigator and offer the student a chance to explore the type of novel situation they are likely to encounter in practice. To be sure, you might use statistical analysis from time to time to detect patterns in your observations that you may have overlooked. On the whole, however, you would be well justified to look at those colleagues who attempt to offer simple mathematical and conceptual theories that do not replicate and who apply statistical techniques without even wondering if their assumptions make least bit of sense as self-indulgent tools of a system that has failed to offer the world any measurable value. They have sadly confused the appearance of science with actually being scientific.

The debate between these two perspectives has, quite obviously, yet to be resolved in fields such as business and education. Furthermore, there is some hope that a compromise may be reached: even in a complex world, there may be decomposable elements that can be carved out and studied mathematically or statistically. Observant believers in a world that is largely decomposable will nevertheless concede that, from time to time, interactions have a confounding effect.

The key message of this chapter is that *where substantial complexity is present in the system being studied, the case method is a valid approach—and possibly the most valid approach available—for exploring and learning about it.*

Chapter 2 Notes

[1] The majority of this section was lifted, with only minor revision, from *Informing Business* (Gill, 2010), where the impact of complexity on research and teaching were treated in far greater detail. I justify this act of self-plagiarism by the fact that it was while writing the material on the case method for that book, I decided a book specifically devoted to the paradigm was warranted.

[2] There is another amusing aspect to the fact that Shugan does not see cases as a form of research. In *Informing Business*, I present the argument that one of the reasons my own discipline (MIS) is failing is that what we research (mainly behavioral) has become entirely decoupled from what we teach (mainly technical, at least in terms of student numbers). Under my definition, case research provides the perfect opportunity to correct that, by bringing our research into the classroom.

[3] The speculation that the top students will invariably be drawn to the more analytical/quantitative schools is somewhat undermined by the fact that HBS—the least quantitative/scientific of the elite business schools—also has the highest yield (percentage of applicants choosing HBS when also accepted by other schools) of these schools by far, coming in at roughly 90% (Datar, Garvin & Knoop, 2008).

[4] For the sake of illustration, the first example of "great" marketing research Shugan (2006, p. 113) cites findings "that demand leads distribution for most motion pictures, so studios should focus more attention on movie design and advertising over exhibitor incentives and owning theaters". It is hard to imagine that this particular decision would be made routinely by more than a few dozen people in the world. Thus, its greatness must derive either from its generalizability to other situations or from the elegance of the analysis presented. Paradoxically, the topic sounds like a great opportunity for a case study.

[5] I would infinitely prefer to give a lecture in an area where I was completely unfamiliar (provided I had a textbook to draw from) than facilitate a case study in an area where I had no practical exposure. It would be much easier for me to hide my ignorance while lecturing, since I could exert control over the process.

[6] I feel that Mintzberg (2004) is quite correct in asserting that most cases do not have enough information to make anything remotely resembling an informed decision. Thus, students need to make assumptions well beyond what is presented in the case in formulating their decisions or action plan. Over-emphasis on the outcome of a case implies that the facts of the case led to the result whereas, in reality, the cause-and-effect relationship likely involved many factors that the students were unaware of.

[7] In one of my graduate courses, for example, I had three sisters from China who sat together for the entire semester and never said a word in class—despite the fact that they generally came in well prepared. I spent the whole semester wracking my brain with respect to what to do. I mentioned the situation to a colleague who had been teaching in the Far East at a conference after the course was completed. Without even an instant of hesitation, she asserted that I should have separated them after the very first class. As soon as I heard the suggestion, I judged it to be a good one. Quite honestly, however, the thought never occurred to me until my colleague offered it.

[8] Very near the beginning of my marketing course at HBS, for example, I experienced a bonding to the "Butcher Wax" case that we discussed in the very first week of the course. My study group was astonished by my passion for the case. It derived from two sources. First, on several occasions I had spent more than a day applying Butcher Wax (principally used in bowling alleys) to the living room floor of my family's summer cottage in New Hampshire. Second, when I was in elementary school, our class took a tour of the Butcher Wax factory, compliments of one of my classmates, the late Susan Butcher (later the four-time winner of the Iditarod dog sled race).

[9] There is a very interesting exception to the general rule that biologists do not assign fitness values to individual traits but are more interested in the general processes by which fitness increases. The field of eugenics was preoccupied with developing exactly this type of theory: determining what specific traits led to the "ideal" human. What is particular interesting about this field—whose practical application was most evident in Nazi Germany—was that its theoretical leaders were the same individuals who were most influential in the development of those multivariate statistical techniques that, as I have already noted, start with the assumption that observations are drawn from a decomposable landscape. For example, Karl Pearson, one of the leading contributors to the field of statistics (e.g., Pearson correlation coefficient, p-value, Pearson chi-square) occupied a joint chair in Statistics and Eugenics at University College and was a founder of both the leading statistical journal of the day, *Biometrika*, and the *Annals of Eugenics*. When he retired, his chair was divided into eugenics and statistics chairs. Succeeding him as Chair of the Department of Eugenics was Ronald Fisher, the

vocal advocate of 5% statistical significance testing whose many contributions to statistics are too numerous to mention here (Ziliak & McCloskey, 2007, p. 219).

[10] I point out in *Informing Business* (Gill, 2010) that one can describe a work of art using the N,K model as well. The problem is, the complexity of art is huge (e.g., N represents the pixels in a picture, K the interrelatedness of them, and fitness changes frequently with taste)—far beyond the levels of complexity we routinely assume in the social sciences.

Chapter 3

Introduction to Case Design

Not too long ago, in May 2009, I attended a doctoral program reunion at Harvard Business School. As a special activity for the attendees, we discussed a case titled *Harvard Business School* (Datar, Garvin & Knoop, 2008). One of the things that struck me during that discussion was the intensity with which some of the participants savaged the recent case offerings of HBS—particularly the case under discussion. In many ways, I agreed with the group, having noticed the same problem in the recent cases that I have used in my own classes.

The source of the problem with that particular case, however, had little to do with whatever general problems may or may not afflict recent HBS cases. Rather, it had to do with the fact that the case was actually designed to be part of a multi-case research project documenting MBA programs at HBS, Stanford, University of Chicago, INSEAD, Yale and the Center for Creative Leadership (see Thompson, 2008).

> **Critical take away:** *when you use a case study for a purpose other than that for which it was designed, chances are that it will bomb.*

From this observation, it follows that spending some time thinking about your design before you write a case is likely to pay big dividends by the time the case is completed.

This chapter takes a broad overview of case design, with particular emphasis on identifying designs that match the *purpose* and *audience* for which the case is intended. We begin, however, with an invitation to examine three sample cases that will be used as illustrations throughout the chapter. At the end of the chapter, we also consider how cases may be repurposed to achieve multiple design objectives.

Three Little Pigs

When I teach the case writing workshop at the University of South Florida (USF), I always begin by having students read the series of three sample cases included in Appendix A, presenting the same story (*very loosely* modeled after the "Three Little Pigs" tale[1]) in different ways. We then discuss how the cases differ in design, attempting to map each to different purposes. I invite you, the reader, to look over these cases before proceeding to the next section, although it is not entirely necessary. If you choose to do so, you may also want to check off which case would best meet the different needs listed in Table 3.1.

Table 3.1: Select the case that best meets the described objective from Three Little Pigs A, B & C (Appendix A)

A	B	C	Comments
			Objective is to examine cause and effect, typically in a situation where phenomenon being observed are too complex for a controlled experiment. May be single case or part of a collection of cases.
			Objective is to create a case study that can be used as the basis for class discussion. Typically, such cases present a situation which requires discussants develop and/or evaluate solutions.
			Objective is to provide a concrete example of some phenomenon of interest, with the objective of creating a more lasting impression than could be achieved with a more abstract form of presentation.
			Objective is to provide an example of the analytical process (quantitative or qualitative) that is appropriate for a particular situation, often used within the context of a lecture.
			Objective is to present a contextually rich situation that can be analyzed using one or more approaches. It is similar to the traditional word problem in intent.

Categories of Cases

There is a rich variety of cases that can be developed. While a relatively small percentage of cases are suited to or representative of the case method, virtually any type of case can be highly effective if its design meets its objectives. In this section, I summarize some of the most common designs and uses of cases that I have observed. These include both case method and non-case method designs.

Research Cases

A research case nearly always explores cause and effect. Th
common purposes for these cases are proposing theory, expanding
theory, testing theory or clarifying theory.

There are many variations of design possible for research cases: single
case designs, multi-case designs, longitudinal designs and combinations.
These are described more fully in Chapter 5, devoted entirely to the
subject of research case design. What is common to all case research
designs, however, is the willingness to sacrifice some of the objectivity
that statistical, logical and mathematical approaches offer in exchange
for the ability to consider and integrate observations and information
triangulated from as many sources as possible. As pointed out in Chapter 2, the more complex the domain, the more sensible this sacrifice
becomes. When presenting the empirical results of Galileo's experiment
conducted on the Leaning Tower of Pisa, his emotional state at the
time he released the balls and the cultural norms of the day can be ignored without particular loss of rigor. The same cannot be said, however, when we try to develop a theory to explain the phenomenon of
persecution he later faced as a consequence of his experiments and
insights into the laws of nature.

The role of theory in research—not limited to case research—can be
divided into building and testing. The two approaches are not necessarily distinct, however, as theory building and testing may be combined
in a single research process. This is illustrated by researchers Colquitt
and Zapata-Phelan (2007), who published a study of the distribution of
Academy of Management Journal[2] (AMJ) articles by category for selected
years (3 year intervals). The conceptual chart, presented as Figure 3.1,
identifies five roles: reporters, builders, qualifiers, testers and expanders.
It is possible to design case-based research for any of these roles. Because of its inductive character (as described in Chapter 1), case method research designs are more likely to gravitate towards the left side of
Figure 3.1—reporting, theory building and qualification—since designing a case method research project specifically to test a theory implies
both a heavy weight being given to the theory being tested and a non-
exploratory frame of mind. These would seem to be inconsistent with a
belief in the complexity of the environment. It is also somewhat counter to the enthusiasm most case researchers feel towards studying outliers that other researchers might tend to discount as suitable test sites.

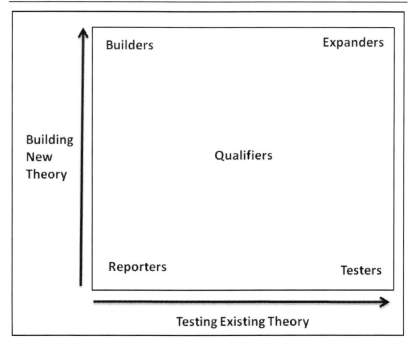

Figure 3.1: Theoretical contributions of empirical research, from Colquitt and Zapata-Phelan (2007, p. 1283)

The very existence of the reporter category in Figure 3.1 demonstrates that it is possible to develop a theory-free research case that is presented purely as an observation. It is, however, likely to be very difficult to get such a case published—at least in business, where our bias towards theory-related research is very strong (Hambrick, 2007). That was not always true, however. According to Colquitt and Zapata-Phelan (2007), in the years 1963, 1966 and 1969, roughly 75% of all AMJ articles were classified as reporter articles. On the other hand, in 2002, 2005, and 2007 *not a single reporter article* was published (recall that AMJ is the journal that *allows* non-theory articles, at least in principle). Instead, roughly 75% of the articles were about evenly divided between the *qualifier* and *expander* roles.

Discussion Cases

Discussion cases are, quite obviously, intended to serve as the basis for discussions, most commonly in a classroom setting. The case designer must take care *never* to forget that fact. Unfortunately, that fact is easy to forget (which is why discussion cases need to be contrasted with other case designs). Nearly all case method discussion cases involve some type of decision. In my own teaching, however, I have encountered three relatively common variations: the choice case, the design case and the sense-making case. To understand how these differ, it is useful to first think about what a case method analysis and discussion is intended to achieve. To accomplish this, we take a brief digression into problem solving.

Problem Solving and Educational Objectives

In their landmark book, *Human Problem Solving* (Newell & Simon, 1972), cognitive scientist Alan Newell and Nobel Laureate Herbert Simon synthesized decades of research into how we solve problems. At the considerable risk—nay certainty—of oversimplifying, they described the problem solving process as consisting of three components:

1. *Intelligence.* The process of acquiring information and procedures relevant to the task being performed.

2. *Design.* The process of developing appropriate (and sometimes inappropriate) alternatives and plans that relate to the decision.

3. *Choice.* The process of evaluating and selecting one of the alternatives.

It should be self-evident that this process is iterative. If choice suggests that designs are inadequate, then further design may be required. If insufficient information or procedural knowledge is available, then further intelligence is needed. As we learn more about the brain, it is easy to quibble about whether or not the intelligence-design-choice (IDC) model really describes the highly connectionist, non-symbolic nature of what seems to take place as we think. But, as a conceptual scheme, it has the virtues of being both simple and sufficiently flexible so that it can be applied to most problem solving situations without requiring bizarre interpretations.

For those in the education field, one of the most widely used conceptual schemes is Benjamin Bloom's (1956) *Taxonomy of Educational Objectives*, which identifies key skills that students need to learn in order to become effective problem solvers. These consist of knowledge, comprehension, application, analysis, synthesis and evaluation.

Table 3.2: Bloom vs. Newell & Simon

Bloom[3]	Newell & Simon
Knowledge of terminology; specific facts; ways and means of dealing with specifics (conventions, trends and sequences, classifications and categories, criteria, methodology); universals and abstractions in a field (principles and generalizations, theories and structures): Knowledge is (here) defined as the remembering (recalling) of appropriate, previously learned information.	**Intelligence** Acquisition and internalization of information and problem constraints. *Lower level intelligence skills:*
Comprehension: Grasping (understanding) the meaning of informational materials.	Knowledge Comprehension
Application: The use of previously learned information in new and concrete situations to solve problems that have single or best answers.	*Higher level intelligence skills:* Application Analysis
Analysis: The breaking down of informational materials into their component parts, examining (and trying to understand the organizational structure of) such information to develop divergent conclusions by identifying motives or causes, making inferences, and/or finding evidence to support generalizations.	**Design** Creation of plausible strategies for action that meet problem constraints.
Synthesis: Creatively or divergently applying prior knowledge and skills to produce a new or original whole.	
Evaluation: Judging the value of material based on personal values/opinions, resulting in an end product, with a given purpose, without real right or wrong answers.	**Choice** Selection of appropriate strategy from the available options.

As illustrated in Table 3.2, the Bloom (1956) and Newell & Simon (1972) conceptual schemes are highly compatible. Both suggest: 1) problem solving involves a number of different activities, and 2) real world problems normally require that the problem solver engage in *all* these activities, although the relative measure of each may vary.

Because it is the simpler of the two conceptual schemes, I generally use the IDC conceptual scheme for classifying discussion cases.

Discussion/Choice cases

In a discussion/choice case, the alternatives that the decision-maker is considering are clearly presented to the reader. This may be done in the case itself, or may be directed by the facilitator through pre-case questions or other means.

The discussion/choice case places a particular emphasis on judgment. Although evaluation and choice are sometimes presented as the highest level skills[4], choice cases tend to be the easiest to discuss since they revolve around concrete alternatives. When developing cases for a group of participants who are not experienced in case discussions, the choice case is an excellent choice. It also tends to be the easiest to facilitate, since the likelihood of the participants wandering into uncharted (and sometimes erroneous) territory is reduced by the concreteness of the options. I would characterize *Three Little Pigs (B)* as a discussion/choice case.

The fact that a choice design centers the discussion on choosing between alternatives does not mean that intelligence and design can be ignored. The details of the case (intelligence) provide the basis upon which the judgment must be made; very often, it incorporates the task of sorting out what is and what is not relevant is central to the process. Furthermore, it is the rare choice case that does not leave open the possibility of an alternative that has yet to be considered by the decision-maker protagonist of the case, opening the opportunity for further design.

Discussion/Design cases

The discussion/design case differs from the discussion/choice case in that the participants need to develop their own alternatives from the information in the case. This tends to come about in two ways. Either the alternatives are not provided in the case or all the alternatives are presented are bad.

If you are dealing with a highly experienced group of case participants, the discussion/design case tends to be very effective. It tends to be much less effective with novice participants. My experience is that cases that do not supply any options tend to produce blank looks from the uninitiated; those that supply only bad alternatives tend to focus the attention of participants overly much on the task of choosing the lesser of two evils. Facilitators may be able to remedy this situation by providing in-depth pre-case questions.

The *Three Little Pigs (C)* case *might* be used as discussion/design case. It presents a complicated decision situation and does not fully elaborate on the alternatives available. I would probably be reluctant to use it that way. When I designed the case I intended that it should leave the impression that there might be a "right" answer. Generally, where there is a right answer, I am uncomfortable with framing the decision as a matter of judgment, which is where the value of discussion is most pronounced. Doing so conveys a flexibility that is not consistent with the outcome of the process that I intend (i.e., in such situations I want everyone to end up knowing *how to find the right answer* AND to be convinced that *the single approach presented is the appropriate one*). Furthermore, even if Three Little Pigs (C) did not have a right answer, the wealth of numbers, charts and combinations would make any resulting discussion very hard to manage.

A real world example of a discussion/design case is the EMBA 2002 (A) case, provided as Appendix G, which describes my actual experiences with a new class. After one session of the class, several students had protested violently about the workload of the course, among other things, in emails to the director of the program. At the end of the (A) case, the first of a sequence of 3 cases, I offer two extremes as alternatives: completely caving in to student demands and being completely uncompromising. I also make it clear that I did not think much of either course of action. Thus, participants discussing this case need to come up with other alternatives.

Of all the case designs, the discussion/design format probably offers the participants the greatest opportunity to practice all three IDC skills. That may be why a great many HBS cases—written by experienced case writers for experienced discussion participants—tend to fall into this category. Facilitating these cases with a much less experienced group, I often feel that I am being overly directive in my involvement. Generally, students do not mind this; by comparison with the lectures that

make up most of our programs, the experience is still quite er
Nevertheless, I am not sure that I am realizing the full benefit
case method by so doing.

Discussion/Sense-making cases

From time to time, I use case studies that focus on the intelligence
aspect of the IDC model, instead of on a decision. I refer to these as
discussion/sense making cases because they usually involve an organization or individual that appears to be making inappropriate or ill-
considered decisions. The object of the discussion, then, is to figure out
why the decisions being made are more sensible than they first appear
to be. The easiest way to illustrate this is through an example of a case
that I used up until recently: Tektronix, Inc. (Austin, Nolan, Westerman
& Cotteleer, 1999). It is sufficiently old that I do not feel that I am
committing an ethical breach by letting the cat out of the bag[5].

Example: Tektronix: Global ERP

The Tektronix case is about a large scale implementation of an enterprise requirements planning (ERP) system at a company that made
three distinct types of products: high end color printers, analog test
equipment and voice/networking equipment. The company described
had an absolutely appalling set of existing information systems across
its various divisions and the case describes the process by which it installed its ERP. For those unfamiliar with ERP systems, they are
among the most complex types of information systems available, tying
together the accounting, production and marketing functions of the
company into the same system. As a result, putting them in place is
quite risky. Indeed, some say the criterion for a successful ERP is one
where the implementation that does not put the company out of business. Thus, the decision to build such a system should not be made
lightly.

Given this background, the story presented in the Tektronix case—
which does not leave the reader with a clear decision to make—offers a
number of very odd lessons. Among the questions a sensible participant might ask are:

1. Why is the company intent on putting in a high risk technology whose greatest ultimate benefit would be tying together the operations of divisions that have entirely unrelated products?

2. Why is the Chief Financial Officer supervising the installation?

3. Why does the CFO appear not to care about measuring the return on investment (ROI) of the system?

4. Why did they choose the most generic ERP vendor without even bothering to look at competing products? Indeed, the company decided to change its business processes to meet the needs of the technology—something you almost never want to do.

5. Why did they seem so willing to experience cost overruns in order to keep the project on schedule?

When I first selected the case for use in one of my courses, I was looking for a case that covered ERP installations—an important topic in an MIS capstone course—so I skimmed it without paying attention to the seemingly bizarre approach to implementation. The week before I facilitated it for the first time, I prepared it in depth. Was I surprised...

The first time I facilitated the case, I centered on using the case to identify "things you would normally not want to do in a sensible ERP installation" and, I fully admit, I lectured more than I facilitated. While I was facilitating the case a second time, however, as a student was discussing the company's various product lines, the real meaning of the case jumped out at me. At least one of the company's divisions—its color printing unit—was destined to die a horrible death at the hands of its competition because the industry was changing. The only possible way the division could survive was if it were sold to a large printer company; one that could provide the volume and economies of scale that Tektronix could not. Every day such a sale was delayed reduced the value of the division to a potential acquirer. The problem was, Tektronix's existing information systems were so weak that it would be nearly impossible to value the division. Thus:

1. The real impetus for the system was in clarifying the value of individual divisions, not in tying them together.

2. CFOs typically take a very active role in mergers and divestitures.

3. The ROI would be derived from the higher sale price of the division; such a fact would not be made public in the company, however, since it is not good for morale to learn your division is being tidied up for sale.

4. Plain vanilla technology and easy to understand processes are best when you do not know what technology your new owner is likely to use.

5. Speed was absolutely imperative if the color printing division was to be worth anything by the time you got rid of it.

Since that time, I have framed the case as a detective story: How could it be that these strange decisions make sense? The case has proven to be very engaging for the participants framed in this way. It also offers what I consider to be a very important lesson: when odd decisions appear to be made, it is better to seek an explanation than to assume that the decision-makers are clueless.

Illustration Cases

Arguably, cases intended to serve as illustrations do not fall within the case method, as I have described it. They are, however, the most common type of case—particularly prevalent in textbooks and in practitioner-oriented outlets, such as the *Harvard Business Review*.

The power of illustration cases is that they tend to be about the most resonant form of communication available. Recall the SUCCESs framework of Chip and Dan Heath (2007), originally presented in Chapter 1:

1. Simple

2. Unexpected

3. Concrete

4. Credible

5. Emotional

6. Stories

I cannot think of any message that is more likely to conform to this framework that a well written illustrative case. Thus, as a tool for communications, they tend to be unparalleled in their stickiness. The drawback of these cases is that they tend to be far less suitable for discussion.

Example cases

Example cases are a type of illustration case used principally to clarify and support concepts. When an instructor lectures a case or theorizes a case, it is almost always an example case that is used. What distinguishes an example case from a case method research case is the fact that example cases normally include the desired interpretation along with the case description. In addition, the triangulation and systematic approach employed in case research is neither necessary nor desirable in an example, since too much detail and complexity tends to interfere with the clarity of the message and the flow of the narrative.

To illustrate an example case, I present a story that I have used several times, most recently in *Informing Business*[6] (Gill, 2010), to illustrate the barriers to effective informing that frequently arise. The example is not the result of extensive research or confirmation of facts on my part. To the contrary, I rely on a single source and choose it simply because it made such an impression on me when I first heard in as a doctoral student. The very fact that I remembered it for so long, and keep repeating it, illustrates the unusual power of a resonant example.

Example: Morison's Naval Gunnery Case

Within the innovation literature, a widely cited example that highlights the challenges of achieving acceptance of an idea is presented in Elting Morison's *Man, Machines and Modern Times* (1966). The case study, summarized below, describes the obstacles experienced in attempting to convince naval authorities of the validity of a new way to fire the guns installed on U.S. naval vessels.

By way of context, achieving accuracy when firing shipboard guns has always been more problematic than achieving comparable accuracy with land-based artillery. The main source of the difficulty is the rolling of the ship, causing the angle of the gun's barrel to be continuously changing. As late as at the turn of the 20th century, individual gunners had to develop personalized approaches to compensating for the movement. Morison (1966, p. 21) describes the process as follows:

First of all, the rapidity of fire was controlled by the rolling period of the ship. Pointers [gunners] had to wait for the one moment in the roll when the sites were brought on the target. Notice also this: There is in every pointer what is called a "firing interval"—that is a time lag between his impulse to fire the gun and the translation of this impulse into the act of pressing the firing button. A pointer, because of this reaction time, could not wait to fire the gun until the exact moment when the roll of the ship brought the sights into the target; he had to will to fire a little before, while the sites were off the target. Since the firing interval was an individual matter, varying obviously from man to man, each pointer had to estimate from long practice his own interval, and compensate for it accordingly.

Another factor impacting accuracy involved the gun sights. Although telescopic sights were sometimes provided to enlarge the target, they were attached to the gun barrel and "recoiling with the barrel, jammed back against the unwary pointer's eye" (Morrison, 1966, p. 21). Thus, while useful in estimating target range, they were virtually never used during the actual firing process.

In 1898, an English officer—Admiral Percy Scott—developed an alternative approach to firing guns that involved continuous aiming. This approach involved three relatively minor changes to the physical equipment—changing the gear ratio on the guns, mounting a simulated target on the mouth of the gun, and changing the telescopic mountings so they did not recoil into the pointer's eye upon firing. More significantly, a major change to firing procedures was required: having the pointer continuously adjust the gun elevation so that it was always on the target. The results of this innovation were astounding:

In 1899 five ships of the North Atlantic Squadron fired five minutes each at a lightship hulk at the conventional 1600 yards. After twenty-five minutes of banging away, two hits had been made on the sails of the elderly vessel. Six years later one naval gunner made fifteen hits in one minute at a target 77 by 25 feet at the same range—1600 yards; half of them hit in a bull's-eye 50 inches square (Morison, 1966, p. 22).

In 1900, while serving in China, Scott met a junior U.S. naval officer, William S. Sims, who eagerly embraced the new approach and made the modifications necessary to institute the technique on his own ship.

After a few months of practice, he demonstrated astounding improvements in accuracy, after which he began to communicate his findings with his U.S. Navy superiors in a series of 13 reports. Described by Morison (p. 22):

> Over a period of two years, he reiterated three principal points: first, he continually cited records established by Scott's ships, the *Scylla* and the *Terrible*, and supported these with accumulating data from his own tests on an American ship; second, he described the mechanisms used and the training procedures instituted by Scott and himself to obtain these records; third, he explained that our own mechanisms were not generally adequate without modification to meet the demands of continuous-aim firing.

From an informing perspective, these messages demonstrated two things. First, the quality of the information was rigorously supported by multiple sources of the evidence. Second, the usefulness of the approach to the client (i.e., the U.S. Navy) was shown through outcome-based measures. Thus, the conditions of both rigor and relevance were clearly met. What transpired thereafter, however, illustrates how quality and usefulness may not be sufficient to ensure that effective informing takes place.

Morison (1966) described the Navy's reaction as taking place in three stages. During the first stage, Sims's reports were simply ignored. Indeed, after being filed away they were largely consumed by cockroaches—the 19th century analog to media failure. From an informing standpoint, this represents failure to attend to the channel. This failure of informing appears to have an underlying source that is mainly motivational in character: the individuals who received the correspondence had no particular interest in their contents.

After his initial efforts failed, Sims adopted a more strident tone in his reports and also began circulating them to other naval officers in the fleet. Described by Morison (p. 28-29):

> Aware as a result that Sims's gunnery claims were being circulated and talked about, the men in Washington were then stirred to action. They responded, notably through the Chief of the Bureau of Naval Ordnance, who had general charge of the equipment used in gunnery practice, as follows: (1) our equipment was in general as good as the British; (2) since our

equipment was as good, the trouble must be with the men, but gun pointers and the training of gun pointers were the responsibility of the officers on the ships; and most significant (3) continuous-aim firing was impossible.

The third of these was based on experiments, conducted in Washington Navy Yard, where it was found that five men could not operate the gears fast enough to achieve the rate of changes in the gun barrel angle that were required to support continuous aiming. In his rebuttal to the last point, Sims pointed out that the fixed platform test was invalid; instead, the rolling of the ship provided momentum to the gun barrel that actually made continuous aiming much easier.

From an informing standpoint, the three elements of the response from Washington clearly illustrate a practical challenge to achieving resonance: the existence of prior mental models. The client belief that U.S. equipment could not be inferior to that used by the British made accepting Sims's premise much more difficult. The belief that the accurate gunnery could only be achieved through training and that the task was a ship's responsibility—rather than that of the bureau—caused the client to question the relevance of the information. Finally, knowledge of the existing test caused the client to question the veracity of the information. Conceptually, then, prior mental models distorted the information during the communications process. As a consequence, the client's interpretation of the message did not match the sender's intent.

Returning to the narrative, Sims's increasingly agitated tone ultimately led to the third stage: "name-calling". Described by Morison (p. 31):

> He was told in official endorsements on his reports that there were others quite as sincere and loyal as he and far less difficult; he was dismissed as a crackbrained egotist; he was called a deliberate falsifier of evidence.

In this stage, the principal obstacle to informing was less a matter of distortion resulting from prior mental models than of outright refusal to change existing models. There was no longer any desire to believe Sims; indeed the clients had an active interest in disbelieving him. Morison (1966, p. 36) further argues that a secondary but critical further source of resistance came from the implications that would necessarily result from the acceptance of the idea. Gunnery had always been perceived as an art rather than a science. As such, it has occupied a relatively low status position in the increasingly technological Navy. Sims's innovation would transform the nature of the task—increasing the status of gunnery with respect to other shipboard activities (such as ship handling) and prospects for promotion. In the context of an organization that had only recently made the transition from sail to steam and was still adjusting to its aftereffects, the motivation to accept the information that Sims was communicating was low indeed. This demonstrates that, in the informing context, failure to consider or accommodate the client's intrinsic motivation can lead to a complete breakdown of the informing process. When such motivational conflicts are present, message distortion is no longer the issue. The complete unwillingness of the client to modify existing mental models is the source of the problem. The described nature of the communication also indicates the important role that emotions can play in the informing context.

Ultimately, Sims broke the informing deadlock by writing directly to Theodore Roosevelt, then President of the United States. Roosevelt brought Sims back to the U.S. and assigned him to the post "Inspector of Target Practice," where he continued for six years. During that period, his innovation diffused throughout the Navy and he was ultimately acclaimed as "the man who taught us how to shoot." He eventually was promoted to Admiral and had a warship named after him (USS William S Sims, DE/FF-1059). This would be an example of a case where intrinsic motivation failed using a particular channel. As a result, an alternative channel was needed and considerable extrinsic motivational force had to be applied.

In summarizing this case from an informing standpoint, we can see three key elements of what we'll refer to as resonance. Even after rigor and relevance have been established, the content needs to be *internalized and made available for later recall*, something that did not happen for the early letters owing to lack of motivation on the part of the client. The amount of *distortion* between the sender's intent and the client's interpretation needs to be minimized, a failure evident in the first response received by Sims: a consequence of initial differences between sender and client mental models. Finally, the client must be *willing to restructure his or her mental models* to incorporate the content, another motivational issue that is also subject to significant emotional forces. If any of these prerequisites of resonance are not met, the informing can fail.

In considering the above example case, notice how I did not invite interpretation by the reader. This is fairly typical of example cases and entirely atypical of discussion cases or case method research case. *The purpose of the example is to convey a particular point of view.*

Showcases

The showcase is an case designed specifically to highlight the benefits of an entity or approach. They can be found all over the web, often in the form of customer success stories and testimonials.

The showcase is really just a version of the broader illustration case. It is worth identifying specifically, however, for one particular reason: the showcase is usually case that an organization *wants you to write* when you are developing a case. As I discuss later, in Chapter 7, when writing a discussion case it is important to keep reinforcing the fact that the purpose of the case being developed is to stimulate a useful discussion. Often, that will be sufficient to prevent a showcase scenario from developing.

In my own experience, I have participated in two case writing projects that fell through by virtue of showcase issues. The first involved a well-known Silicon Valley entrepreneur who wanted to raise money and felt the draft that I had written would not sufficiently motivate investors—which, of course, was not its purpose. The second experience was more unusual. After the president of a large sub-prime credit card processing company had already approved a case that I had written on the company's information systems architecture, the chairman and founder decided that I should not release the case, even in a disguised version. His objection was that it made the industry—which absolutely pummels its low-credit-score customers with fees and penalties—look too attractive. He did not want to encourage competition and did not like the fact that I had showcased the business. Interestingly, these represent the only two instances that I have experienced where a completed case draft that I prepared was not released. Hence my concern with showcases…

Fables

A fable is a story, generally not based on observation, intended to communicate a particular lesson. Obviously, my *Three Little Pigs* collection of Appendix A would be an example of a fable—the lesson being the suitability of different designs to different purposes.

In a number of books on case writing that I have encountered, some of the cases they provide strike me as closing in on fables. The author who wrote the case clearly had a particular lesson that he or she wanted to convey and the case was not based on a real situation. This observation is not necessarily a criticism; Aesop's fables and many of parables that make up important religious texts have survived for millennia longer than any case study I am ever likely to write. Fables are a very sticky form of communication.

Fables tend to be less prevalent in business settings. The overriding problem with fables is that where complexity is present, it is very hard to be completely realistic without a model upon which to base the case. Some business researchers argue that there is no role for fictionalized cases in any form. As will become clear in when I discuss design cases next, I feel that position may be a bit extreme. Fables and fiction have their potential uses. They are, however, the antithesis of the case method.

Design cases

Design cases are hypothetical scenarios that attempt to define of clarify the consequences of a design activity. In information systems, we often develop *use cases* as part of the process of designing an information system. These cases attempt to describe how a typical user will interact with an information system that has yet to be built. They can be very useful in achieving that outcome. By attempting to make the abstract system concrete in the minds of the reader, issues often surface that might otherwise have been ignored.

Example: Court Information System

Not too long ago, I was involved in a consulting project that involved developing a training program for a new court technology system that had yet to be built. The problem facing the curriculum developers was that no one was actually sure what the final system would look like, since it was being built using an agile approach that meant its scope kept changing. Making the problem more serious: the court wanted training to commence even before the finalized system was completed.

Because I did not have a handle on what the system was supposed to do or how it was supposed to work, my first step was to spend several days interviewing the project manager. Collaboratively, we developed a detailed (11 single spaced pages) case detailing a day in the life of an operator of the proposed system. As a result of this case, several design changes were made. We then developed a series of special case scenarios—along with a case that detailed an operator positioned at a different station—intended to illustrate the full scope of the project. Our intention was to use these materials as part of facilitated discussions in training the incoming operators.

The ultimate result of the case development was significant, but not in the direction originally intended. When the cases and scenarios were presented to other high level managers in the court outside of the information technology group, they became concerned over the scope of the proposed job—something that they had not fully comprehended prior to the case development. The cases clarified what was being done, raising red flags in the process. As a result, the entire project was scaled back. Instead of creating an entirely new type of system operator, the decision was made to maintain the existing organization and incrementally add to the activities of existing jobs.

From time to time, I encounter design cases developed for discussion purposes. In my classes, I used to assign the *KPMG Peat Marwick: The Shadow Partner* (Eccles & Gladstone, 1991) case occasionally. The problem with such cases tends to come when participants question their credibility. An example of a book that takes the same approach is Jay Barney and Trish Clifford's (2010) *What I Didn't Learn in Business School: How Strategy Works in the Real World*. It is a book-length case study that imagines a consulting assignment from the perspective of a new business school graduate and attempt to illustrate how the frameworks and theory taught in school need to be tempered by real world circumstances[7].

Exercise Case

Exercise cases are constructions intended to develop analytical skills with detailed problems are presented in a realistic setting. Conceptually, they represent an extension to the dreaded "word problem" that vexes many young math students who have learned to manipulate symbols algebraically, yet have no inkling as to how these symbols relate to the real world. I group these into two categories, those intended to be facilitated and those offered as an assignment for independent study.

Walkthrough Case

A walkthrough case is designed to serve as a complex example that typically requires the facilitator to lead participants through a series of steps. I would probably use *Three Little Pigs (C)* as a walkthrough case— in the unlikely event I were ever to use it—precisely because it includes so much messy information that it seems unlikely that any type of meaningful discussion could be conducted if I did not take full control of the process. It should be noted that many "facilitators" that I have observed tend to treat every case as if it were a walkthrough case. While there is certainly pedagogical value to this approach in many situations, it is not the case method.

Where I most commonly use walkthrough cases in is preparation for similar assignment cases. For a database class that I teach every once in a while, I have prepared a couple of pairs of cases, one pair focused on extracting information from a database and one pair focused on designing a database to handle a specific business situation (presented in the case). For both pairs, I walk the students through one in class, then give them the other to prepare as an assignment.

Both the members of the design pair were closely modeled on business situations where I had personally developed a database. Thus, they might be viewed as disguised real-world cases. They were not discussion cases, however. While there is latitude in database design, the examples were constructed such that most of the design decisions were heavily constrained by the situation. The difference between "right:" and "wrong" did not rely heavily on judgment. The correct choice was more a matter of whether or not the system being designed would work.

Assignment Case

An exercise case is similar a walkthrough case except it is designed for the student to analyze, independently or in groups. As a matter of definition, any case used as an examination becomes an exercise case— whether or not it is designed that way[8].

Repurposing a Case Study

It is not that unusual to find that a case study intended for one purpose can be repurposed to meet another need. In this section, we consider two possible scenarios: repurposing the discussion case for research, and repurposing the research case for discussion. It quickly becomes evident that the former is generally much more feasible than the latter.

Repurposing the Discussion Case for Research

In my experience, it is not unusual for discussion cases to prove more useful for research purposes than cases designed as research cases. With the near disappearance of "reporter" research, described earlier in this chapter, the typical research case will include a great deal of theory and literature review. While I have no particular objection to such content (so long as they are not taken too seriously), journals typically have explicit or implicit space constraints. The practical result is reduced space for the case descriptions[9]. The rich tapestry of details that a case can provide may therefore prove to be a bit threadbare in the actual write up. None of these theory or literature review elements take up space in a typical discussion case.

So how does a discussion case become a research case? The first step is to consider at the timing of the case. A discussion case normally focuses on a decision to be made. A research case focuses on exploring cause and effect. It stands to reason that if a discussion case is extended to look at the decision made and its consequences, you have a promising basis for a research case. In the *Three Little Pigs* series, for example, the (A) case—describing the aftermath of the wolf's rampage and the events leading up to the outcome—could be viewed as a research case. The (B) case, describing the pigs trying to decide what to do in advance of the wolf's attack, is our discussion case. The *EMBA 2002* case series is another example. That series—unlike the *Three Little Pigs* example— was written as a sequence. The (A) case describes a decision to be made. The (B) case describes the actual decision. The (C) case describes its consequences.

Discussion cases can prove to be particularly useful sources for multi-case research designs. This topic is discussed in greater detail in Chapter 5, where research designs are considered. In brief, if you can find two or more cases in very different contexts that illustrate the same phenomenon, you have the basis for proposing that phenomenon may be generalizable. If, at the other extreme, you find two cases in very similar settings with highly different outcomes, you have the basis for arguing that an observed phenomenon is very situation specific. Joni Jones and I make this argument in the research case included as Appendix E, which draws heavily on earlier teaching cases that described the one of the courses that was the focus of the research case. The research design of that case is more fully discussed in Chapter 5.

Of all the case research that I have published, the most significant in terms of its impact—both on the research of others and on my own research—was inspired and largely based on two teaching cases (Gill, 1995a). I describe that research in the example that follows.

Example: High Tech Hidebound

In the early 1990s, I taught a number of introductory MIS classes to students in the MBA and Executive MBA programs at Florida Atlantic University. The course was taught as a traditional case method course, using cases from HBS as its source.

Being my first case facilitation experience, I was surprised by how much I learned in this process. One lesson, in particular, was how cases could interrelate. Two cases that I used were particularly surprising in this respect. One dealt with the cookie chain, *Mrs. Fields' Cookies*. The other dealt with one of the earliest adopters of automated trading driven by sophisticated financial computer models, *Batterymarch Financial Management*.

What was amazing about the discussions of these two cases was that they tended to proceed down the same path, in spite of their superficial differences. In common, both cases involved companies that:

1. Were founded by CEOs who were more than a bit inclined to make statements that skirted the border of confidence and arrogance.

2. Replaced tasks formerly performed by humans with computers (at *Mrs. Fields'* computers took control of nearly every aspect of cookie production; at *Batterymarch*, they controlled the portfolio and trading functions)

3. Relied heavily on quantitative computer models

4. Had evolved organizational structures that were vastly more streamlined than those of their competitors

5. Had experienced growth and performance that were extraordinary by industry standards

6. Had been described by the press and in research publications as being the future of the 21st century organization.

What these cases also had in common was that the class discussions of them left me with a very uneasy feeling. Having developed computer models as a consultant for almost three years, I was very aware of the fragility of these tools. The thought of having my day-to-day activities controlled by one was disheartening—in spite of the fact that both companies were paragons of success as described by the respective cases.

In 1993, my department chair passed me a call for papers on IT and organizational learning. Based upon my experiences in facilitating these two cases, it occurred to me that replacing humans with computer models might be framed as an organizational learning issue; this was mainly based on what the term sounded like, since I had no idea what the organizational learning literature discussed[10]. I therefore began researching what happened to each company after the point in time of the discussion case, and to gather more information to flesh out the cases themselves. The results of this research led me to seventh common factor:

7. Both companies had experienced a disastrous reversal of fortune beginning just about the time each case had been written.

As it happens, at the same time I was doing this I was also researching the emerging field of complex adaptive systems. It struck me that the notion of punctuated equilibrium could explain the rapid decline. Both companies had become highly tuned to their particular environment, gaining great efficiencies. At the same time, many of these cost savings were realized through eliminating or deskilling personnel who traditionally performed an important environmental sensing function (traders at a financial firm, store managers and franchisees at a food service chain). As a result, both firms were extremely vulnerable to rapid environmental change. When it occurred, they did not have individuals in place that could make sense of the change and react to it.

The paper breezed through the review process—to my considerable surprise—and had major impact on my future thinking. At least one other researcher reported to me that it exerted a profound impact on his early thinking on the subject of knowledge management[11]. The important lesson to be learned here is that significant research outcomes can be the result of a carefully constructed discussion case.

Developing teaching cases can also provide the entry mechanisms into an organization that can lay the ground work for ongoing research cases. That will be further discussed when we specifically turn to the case writing process in the next chapter.

Repurposing the Research Case for Discussion

Turning a research case into a discussion case involves a different set of challenges than moving from discussion to research. My own view is that the research to discussion repurposing is much more difficult for two reasons:

1. The research case, dealing with cause and effect, usually occurs after the optimal timing for the discussion version. Even if the case is rewritten so that the period of decision becomes the focus, if the research has been published there are bound to be students who will find the article and let their analysis be overly influenced by it[12].

2. The research article's attempt to mold the case to the particular theory or set of theories being studied will tend to make the research much more appropriate to lecturing a case or theorizing a case than to a case method discussion.

The type of research case study that would be an exception to these generalizations would be the reporter research case. As noted previously in the chapter, however, that type of research case has virtually disappeared, at least in business research.

Conclusions

Every case design presents its own unique set of challenges. In this chapter, I have summarized a wide variety of styles that a potential case writer might consider. While a relatively small percentage of these fit with the case method, as I have narrowly defined it within this book, nearly all can be highly effective given the right circumstances and informing objectives. Thus, the case developer's most important decision becomes identifying how the case is to be used.

In the broadest sense, the case designs in this chapter fall into four categories:

1. *Research*: to study and explain cause and effect.

2. *Discussion*: to offer an engaging framework for discussion in the classroom or elsewhere.

3. *Illustration*: to provide a concrete example that improves understanding and retention.

4. *Exercise*: to provide the basis for a problem solving exercise.

The first two of these designs are most closely associated with the case method. For the remainder of the book, we will therefore focus our attention on these two forms. Somewhat paradoxically, however, I will frequently present illustrative and exercise cases within the text. Hopefully, my doing so will convince the reader that I am not opposed to using cases for these purposes. Informing is tough enough without rejecting useful approaches on ideological grounds.

Once the case study's purpose has been decided, the case writing process can begin. In the next chapter, we introduce the elements of that process that tend to be common to all types of case studies. In subsequent chapters, we turn to issues specific to research and teaching case development.

Chapter 3 Notes

[1] According to *Wikipedia*, the first well known version of the Three Little Pigs was included in *Nursery Rhymes and Nursery Tales* (London, c.1843), by James Orchard Halliwell-Phillipps.

[2] By almost any measure, AMJ would certainly be in the top five of all business research journals in terms of academic prestige.

[3] These descriptions of Bloom's categories are extracted from Gunter Krumme's (1995) web site that was originally posted at the University of Washington. Since then, the site has been relocated to a private site

(as noted in the references). It remains, however, a very convenient reference and is widely cited all over the Internet.

[4] There is a tendency to rank skills as higher order and lower order, particularly when Bloom's taxonomy is presented, which suggests that evaluation is the "best" skill—although later versions of taxonomy actually place synthesis-type skills on top (Kratwohl, 2002). Personally, I feel that such a ranking tends to underestimate the importance of knowledge and practice in doing anything practical. This is another reason I prefer Newell & Simon's (1972) intelligence-design-choice model when classifying cases.

[5] Perhaps I am actually doing the individuals using the Tektronix case—if there are any besides me—a favor. As best I can determine, the teaching note for the case (Austin, 2001) ignores the point entirely, not discussing how their approach was consistent with preparing to sell off parts of the firm at all. My strong suspicion is that the company preferred the note be written that way, so the case writers acquiesced.

[6] The example case presented is taken directly from *Informing Business* (Gill, 2010).

[7] I assigned Barney & Clifford (2010) to a class before reading it, since we were doing a case session on redesigning the MBA and it seemed like a good fit, as well as having decent reviews. What I found some virtues (many of the lessons presented in the second half of the book) along with confirmation that writing an imaginary case that is realistic is very challenging. For example, the central premise—that a chemical company had developed a new fabric that was virtually indestructible but that could not be dyed (i.e., it could only be used to make white clothes)—was right out of a 1951 Alec Guinness movie, *The Man in the White Suit*. That the authors failed to credit the film left a bad taste in my mouth. Their protagonist claimed to be ignorant of clothing and fashion yet mentally estimated the price of the outfit that everyone he encountered was wearing. The notion that a chemical company would even consider entering the fashion industry with a product line consisting solely of white dress shirts struck me as ludicrous, the team leader of a consulting project was intentionally withholding valuable information from the rest of the team for the sake of achieving "objectivity", and so on. As the book proceeded, the premises and analysis became more realistic; the characters grew less absurd. But, reading the

book reinforced my opinion that if you are trying to portray a complex world realistically, it is a lot easier to start with reality.

[8] The fact that using case analyses for examination purposes makes the case an assignment case is worth underscoring. While almost universally used in case method discussion courses, it is not altogether clear to me what these examinations are measuring. I fully agree with Mintzberg (2004) when he criticizes discussion cases as being vast oversimplifications of real situations. What redeems them, in my opinion, is the discussion process and how it encourages individuals to try out new perspectives, to recognize the value of getting the perspectives of others and to value careful observation over mindless application of theory or analysis. Not one of these benefits seems to be realized in the course of taking a three hour exam. Add to the fact that such exams can only measure proficiency, not learning (which would necessitate a pre-test) and the huge variance in how much an individual bonds with a particular case and it is not evident how one should interpret and weigh exam performance. More will be said on the topic of assessing case method learning in Chapter 10.

[9] My contention that theory and literature reviews will crowd out case details would only seem to apply if you are in a field that prizes refereed journal publications, such as business, education and most of the social sciences. In fields that favor other forms of research communications, such as scholarly monographs, I see no reason why theory and case details cannot more peacefully co-exist.

[10] As an amusing side note, I had to look up what organizational learning meant. Unfortunately, the references were so jargon intensive that I still was not sure after reading them. So I simply made up a definition that made sense to me. A decade later, when I started tracking down references to the research, I discovered that a number of quite distinguished researchers referred to my definition in introducing the topic. It is incidents like this that leave me a bit suspicious with respect to the efficacy of out theories and constructs.

[11] I discuss how I assessed the impact of High Tech Hidebound and contrast it with other research I have conducted in *Informing Business* (Gill, 2010). Let me quickly add that while I judge that impact to be relatively high *compared to my other research*, we are talking about a bar that

is placed at a very low setting when assessing the impact of *any* of my research.

[12] It is true that students will often attempt to look up the outcome of the decisions made in any case where the names are not disguised. The problem with the research case is that it also supplies a reason why. Without ready-made explanation, knowing that something happened will not be particularly beneficial to the student. A good case facilitator will always explore a student's reasoning and, if no reasoning underlies the student's assertion, will gently (or, sometimes, not so gently) make sure that fact is apparent to all present.

From a practical standpoint, the fact that research cases explain the "why" of an outcome may be less of a concern than it first sounds. Given the way many research cases are written, many students will not have a clue as what the investigator is talking about even after a careful reading of the research article. That we, as researchers, imagine that the findings we report in such articles will diffuse to practice once they are published demonstrates, once again, the marvelous optimism that we bring to work with us every day.

Chapter 4

The Case Writing Process

Whether a case study is written mainly for discussion or research purposes, there will be common themes to the writing process. For each
type of case, you need to identify an appropriate case site or collection
of sites. You need to motivate professionals, managers and administrators to participate in the project and to provide you with access to organizational data and personnel. You need to identify the specific problem you want to study. You need to collect data using a variety of techniques that include interviews, observation and access to existing records. You need to write the case while, at the same time, soliciting organizational input on what has been written. Finally, you need to ensure
the organizations and individuals involved agree to your use and/or
publication of the case.

In later chapters (Chapters 6 and 7), we address those aspects of the
case writing process that are specific to research and discussion cases,
respectively. The purpose of this chapter is to examine the common
themes. My treatment is a bit more mechanical than the reality is likely
to be. Like all processes of creation, every experience is unique and
each presents its own challenges and opportunities. For inexperienced
case writers, the chapter should identify a number of issues that they
may have not considered. For the experienced case writer, perhaps it
will serve as a reminder of things that it is sometimes easy to forget. At
least, that is how I use the tools provided in my own case writing.

Identifying Case Sites

I have found that it is generally much easier to identify possible case
sites than you might, at first, think. You just need to know where to
look. Obviously, the best sources of ideas will vary widely by disciplinary area. What works for business cases will not necessarily work for
educational cases, public policy cases, or medical cases. I mainly focus

on business sources in this section, since that is the principal area of my experience. My hope is that the general philosophy I propose will prove adaptable to other areas.

Public Sources

There are a number of public sources that can be useful in identifying a case site. I have found four to be particularly useful in my own case writing:

1. *Local Newspaper:* Local newspapers frequently publish features that deal with locally-based businesses and other types of organization. Not only can these identify possible sites, such sites derive from the subset of organizations that are not publicity-shy. Once, when I was teaching a doctoral course in the case method at *Florida Atlantic University* (FAU), I contacted the company profiled in the *Boca Raton News'* weekly "Small Business Extra" section for three weeks in a row. All three agreed to become case sites.

2. *Products:* Sometimes you will purchase or otherwise use a product that you are enthusiastic about. When that product is made by a small local business, your involvement with it can often serve as an entree into a case writing scenario. In the early 1990s, I wrote a case study on Galacticomm, Inc., the company responsible for one of the most technically advanced electronic bulletin board systems (BBS) on the market, and—as a result of the case—had the opportunity to become acquainted with its remarkable 20 year old CEO.

3. *Research Publications:* While I have expressed reservations about repurposing research cases for other purposes, if an organization has participated in a research activity and allowed its role to be published, there is a good chance it will be receptive to further research or teaching case development.

4. *The Internet:* Often, the depth of an organization's web presence will signal its receptiveness to publicity. In addition, a comprehensive web site can help you learn a great deal about an organization that can be useful in getting the site to agree to participate.

Networking Sources

Although public sources can be used to identify potential case sites, I have always had my best luck through networking. Among the sources that I have found effective at locating case sites are included:

1. *Students:* Students have been the source of a substantial fraction of the cases that I have written; almost a third, to be precise. Part of this has been because the graduate case classes I teach have always tended to include a large number of working students. Often, they will have an interest in getting a case written on their own organization. One particularly way to way to surface case ideas is to assign a project or case writing exercise. Although my experience in this area has been in business, I have seen a similar approach used in education, where student-supplied cases became central to a course on counseling gifted students (Gill & Shaunessy, 2006).

2. *Colleagues:* Once faculty members become aware that you are developing cases, either for teaching or research, they may, from time to time offer suggestions through their own network of contracts. Most of my education cases were the result of contacts that I made in faculty workshops. Several business cases also came through this source.

3. *Professional organizations:* Industry and professional organizations, including university alumni groups, can be an excellent source of potential case sites. At least two cases that I wrote came from this source.

4. *Advisory boards:* Many colleges and departments in professional schools have advisory boards set up to help ensure the relevance of the educational content being offered. Three cases that I wrote came from this source. The last of these, in addition to being incorporated in several of my graduate courses, has been used as the basis of an undergraduate case competition whose finalists presented at spring 2010 board meeting.

5. *Former case sites:* Where an organization has a positive experience during the case writing process, they can often be enlisted to help identify other sites, or to participate themselves in subsequent cases. A couple of the organizations I developed cases

for participated in subsequent cases and several other sites have been identified with the help of former case protagonists.

6. *Conferences:* Conferences—particular those where cases are presented—can prove to be effective venues for identifying case sites and, equally important, colleagues who wish to collaborate on case development projects. One of my educational cases was a direct result of a contact I made during a technology in education symposium hosted by my university.

Beyond these sources, I speculate that social networking sites, such as *Facebook* and *Linked In* on the Internet, may be utilized to good effect in identifying possible sites. I also strongly suspect that special interest sites that host discussions on particular subjects could prove to be excellent venues for this purpose. Since I have yet to try these approaches, however, I cannot directly vouch for their efficacy.

The list of sources I have provided is doubtless far from comprehensive. Nevertheless, it should suggest the general picture I am trying to paint: if you are actively seeking case sites to work with, there are many ways of looking that stand a good chance of success.

Case Writing Checklist

Back in the late 1990s, I taught my first doctoral course on the case method. As I designed the course, I couldn't imagine how I was going to fill up two or three class sessions with specific thoughts about how to write cases. All I really wanted to say was:

1. Write as if you actually care about informing your reader, instead of writing to impress a reviewer.

2. Try to use sentences that are half as long as those you use in any other type of writing.

Even given my prodigious ability to generate unnecessary length, I was not convinced that I could devote six hours to making these two points. Thus, I set myself to the task of outlining the entire case writing process. The result, the case writing checklist (Appendix B), is particularly aimed at the development of teaching cases but is adaptable to research cases as well.

I would characterize the checklist as a "worst case" scenario—describing the unusual situation where you need to do everything "right". I cannot think of any case development project where I had to devote time and energy to every item on the list. On the other hand, I have had to address every item on the list carefully on at least one occasion.

Much of the remainder of this chapter will be devoted to explaining some of the more generic elements of the checklist. Elements that tend to be more specifically related to whether a case is being written for research or for discussion are covered in later chapters. These include design (Stage 1 of the checklist), organizing the write up (Stage 6) and gaining approval (Stage 7).

Acquiring the Case Site

The most pivotal point in the case writing process is the first meeting with a representative from the case site. Prior to that meeting, neither the potential organization nor you, the case writer, have invested very much time into the project. Once the meeting has occurred, approval to proceed has been granted, and work begins, both parties have skin in the game. From that point on, it is likely the project will continue to completion so long as both parties are faithful to what they promised initially.

Preparing for the First Meeting

The case writer's greatest sales tool is his or her own knowledge and skills. Whether justified or not, being a faculty member at an institution of higher learning gives you considerable credibility in the eyes of most practitioners. My experience has been that most organizations that participate in a case study do so for access to the knowledge that my position implies. That means the very worst thing a case writer can do is come into an organization unprepared.

Knowing the landscape

There are two forms of preparation for a case. One is building a rich knowledge of the domain in which the organization being studied functions. Unfortunately, this type of knowledge cannot be acquired quickly and is unlikely to be justified by the opportunity to write a single case. Over time, however, a researcher can build up a portfolio of experience within a particular domain. In business, this might refer to a particular industry or type of job. In education, it might refer to a particular subject or pedagogy. For other fields, appropriate types of specialization can be determined.

Knowledge of the landscape represents expertise acquired over the long term that can be enhanced by repeatedly directing your attention towards cases of a particular type. I would caution potential case writers against assuming it corresponds directly to academic discipline or functional specialization. Regrettably, our research—in business, education and most other social sciences—tends to encourage the development of disciplinary silos. Such silos keep the knowledge that we need to acquire down to a manageable level, usually at the cost of oversimplifying. The whole point of the case method, however, is to recognize the intrinsic complexity of real world problems by studying them in the setting in which they occur. A disciplinary or functionally narrow mindset will not impress professionals who recognize that decisions cannot be made by treating them as if they are taking place in the carefully controlled context of a lab. Thus, a landscape specialization would normally involve sites within a common domain—such as an industry, region or organizational type—while, at the same time, integrating functional perspectives.

The benefits of becoming expert in a particular landscape are great, however. The more you know, the more attractive a partner you become to potential case sites. The more you know, the greater the number of case opportunities that will become available to you.

Knowing the organization

The second type of preparation a case writer needs involves the organization being studied. Whereas it may be impractical to become expert in an entire landscape, it has become increasingly easy to find details on the organizations you are interested in writing about. The obvious tools include:

- *Search:* Google the protagonist and other relevant keywords. Social networking sites have also become increasingly valuable sources of information.

- *Research:* Examine research databases for relevant literature on the organization and industry. *Google Scholar,* as well as field-specific online databases such as ABI/Inform (for business) can be used for this purpose.

- *Web:* Browse organization-department-project web sites. Study strategic plans and mission statements for organizations. These usually can be found for businesses, educational institutions and public sector organizations.

- *Repositories:* Look for similar cases in sites like HBS (business) or MERLOT (many fields).

- *Public records:* Many times, useful information about organizations and participants can be found in the press and other records (e.g., LexisNexis search).

Coming into an organization and quickly demonstrating that you have acquired specific knowledge that relates to their situation is the most powerful inducement to participating in case development that I know of. I illustrate what I mean in the example that follows, which is extracted from a more comprehensive description presented Chapter 11 of *Informing Business* (Gill, 2010).

Example: Expert Systems: Where are they now?

In terms of citations and other standard metrics of research productivity, my most successful research project was a multi-case study that I undertook to determine what had happened to the systems profiled on a list of successful expert systems published in the late 1980s.

The systems I surveyed were drawn from a published list of 111 commercial expert systems in the trade book *Expert Systems: Tools and Applications* (Harmon, Maus & Morrissey, 1988), of which 97 were U.S. based. Based on my own knowledge, acquired mainly during my dissertation research, I knew that some had been abandoned and, presumably, some remained in use. Thus, I decided that system status would be a reasonable measure of fitness. Rather than sampling selectively, I decided that the entire list of U.S. systems would be examined.

The approach to data gathering occurred in two stages. It began with library research on each of the individual systems. I acquired the able assistance of three undergraduates—Chuck Taffinder, Martha Griffith and, especially, Allyn Rodriguez—who joined the project for course credit, and to whom I remain indebted to this day. Together, we combed the library for references on each of the systems, creating a folder for each one.

The conduct of the actual interviews is one aspect of the research with which I remain comfortable to this day. Expending nearly 300 hours of phone time[1], I was able to obtain usable responses—from a user, developer, or manager of the system—for 81 of the 97 systems on my list. The average time I spent on each phone interview was roughly 45 minutes, but ranged from 10 minutes (for systems that were never completed) to over 2 hours. The interview protocol included both Likert-scale variables and free form answers (see Gill, 1995b for the actual instrument employed). Most of the phone time was actually spent attempting to locate suitable participants; while the Harmon, Maus and Morrissey (1988) book included contact information for many of the systems, nearly five years after the fact relatively few entries were still accurate. For several systems this process took days, particularly in light of the fact that email and web pages were virtually non-existent in the commercial world at that time. I kept a large status chart on the wall upon which I marked my progress.

In preparation for each interview, I wrote up a preliminary description of what each system did—based upon the public descriptions we were able to find in the first phase of the project—and tentatively scored where I thought the system would end up on the task change portion of the questionnaire. During the course of the actual interview, if a respondent provided a value substantially different from what I had anticipated, I would ask about the response. In most cases, the explanation led me to better understand the precise nature of the task change brought about by the system; in some cases it turned out the respondent had either misinterpreted the question or did not understand it, in which case he or she was given the opportunity to revise the response.

The study's response rate exceeded 80% (81 out of 97 systems) and many of the missing 17 systems may not have ever actually existed. I am convinced that the reason for this very high rate was the preparation. As soon as a suitable respondent was on the line, I would detail what we already knew about the system. This distinguished me from the typical survey call. Another factor that may have contributed was the fact that my sample consisted entirely of systems whose participants had been positively disposed towards publicity in the past. This high response rate almost certainly contributed to the favorable peer reviews that led to two publications (Gill, 1995b; Gill, 1996) in my field's top journal, *MIS Quarterly*.

The First Meeting

The first meeting with a representative of the potential case site, whom I will henceforth call the client[2], can be instrumental in setting the tone for the case development process, as well as in determining whether or not the process goes forward. Generally, there are four objectives that I seek to accomplish in a first case meeting:

1. Convince the client of the potential value of participating in a case, as well as alerting the client to the type of commitment involved.

2. Convince the client that I am the right person to develop the case.

3. Identify potential areas of interest that can serve as case topics, without necessarily settling on one.

4. Arranging a second meeting and listing the action items (for both case writer and client) that should be completed by that meeting.

Whereas many of the items on the case checklist can be omitted, it is very rare that I will leave a first meeting without having made some progress in each of these four areas.

Value of a case: To disclose or not to disclose

If the individual you are meeting with has not participated in writing a case study before, there are likely to be many elements of the process that are unfamiliar. Unfortunately, not all of these will be attractive. Done properly, case writing tends to take up more time than expected. It does not generally lead to the type of PR piece that an organization can post on its web site. It can have unforeseen future consequences (since we can never truly foresee the future). It can even bruise the feelings of some individuals in the organization. The obvious question then becomes: do you mention all these things *before* the organization has committed to write a case? Or do you let them discover them on their own?

For my part, I like to err on the side of disclosing too much—even when some problems I envision may not materialize. I usually begin by providing the interested manager with a set of frequently asked questions (included as Appendix C) that details the set of central issues in the business case development process. Since these issues are presented in the appendix, I will not repeat them here. I would encourage case developers from other disciplines to customize lists based on their own experiences. For example, when I have written cases on issues facing instructors in higher education[3], I would note a number of differences:

- The time commitment associated with those cases tends to be lower, since there are fewer people to talk to and relevant materials are often already collected together as part of a course package.

- Privacy issues, such as access to student data or students themselves must be addressed more fully.

- In some departments, even discussion case studies may be treated as human subject research, and may therefore require approval or exemption from an institutional review board (this is discussed more fully in chapters specifically devoted to research and teaching cases).

- In an academic setting, I always encourage—practically beg— the client to participate as a co-author. The benefits of doing so are usually evident to the client and it reflects the collaborative reality of the case writing process.

- I worry much less about the case release process. At public institutions in particular, there are often legal strictures[4] that would make refusing to release a case virtually impossible.

My justification for over-disclosing, as opposed to minimizing, the costs of participating in case development tie directly to my view of the case as a tool for informing. Complex informing occurs best through networks of enduring relationships[5] rather than through documents or short encounters. Thus, I treat every case development project as the potential start of a long term relationship through which ideas will continue to diffuse in both directions for many years to come. I believe that such a relationship will be quickly soured if the case development process plays out in a manner that is vastly less attractive than it was originally portrayed. Should that happen, even if the client continues to participate—either out of a sense of honor or as a result of the "sunk cost"—I lose in the long run by winning in the short run.

The right person and the right attitude

As I mentioned earlier in the chapter, merely being a faculty member at a college or university will be viewed as impressive by many potential clients. As members of that particular guild, we are well aware (or should be) that any awe inspired by the title is largely misplaced[6]. Nevertheless, it works in our favor in trying to get a case development project going. What can help the process along is creating a short summary resume identifying your accomplishments and experience; one that forgoes the common tendency to list every meeting attended by more than two people as a presentation. Particularly in professional fields, resumes of a dozen pages are viewed unfavorably. A few major accomplishments always mean more than hundreds of minor accomplishments. An overly long resume suggests that you do not know how to tell the difference. Having said this, it always makes sense to expand upon your experience with the particular landscape upon which the case takes place.

Attitude can play an important role in the convincing a client that you are the right person for the case. Here, I particularly refer to attitude towards the client's knowledge. One of the major sources of the failure of business research to diffuse is that we have completely forgotten that our practitioner clients are experts. As a case writer, you would do well never to forget that. I attribute most of my success in acquiring case sites to the fact that I am always emphasizing what I am learning from the client (for a discussion case, to this I add what my students *will be learning*). What is equally important, I fully believe what I am saying. Case development is an informing process, with most of the information moving from client to case writer.

Oddly enough, I suspect the fact that I continually acknowledge the client's expertise causes them to develop the impression that I am far more insightful than I actually am. Sometimes, it takes years to disabuse them of this mistaken conclusion. I feel it best not to rush the process.

Before concluding my comments on presentation, I would forcefully add that what works is likely to be function of fit between the case writer and client. The approach and attitude I describe will not work with all clients. It would also be inconsistent with the personalities of many case writers. I would never encourage a case writer to attempt an approach that feels wrong; if for no other reason, because I am very skeptical about it working. As with all complex activities, achieving fitness is a matter of putting together the right mix of behaviors for the particular situation. Any time you are given hard and fast rules, they tell you far more about the rule giver than about what will actually work.

Potential topics

Choosing a potential topic is one of those areas where research and discussion case writing can be quite different. As a result, it is discussed further in the chapters specifically devoted to each type of case (Chapters 6 and 7). In brief, the search for suitable discussion case topics nearly always benefits from interviewing the client about decisions he or she is currently trying to make. Research case topics, on the other hand, come in two forms: topics the investigator wants to study and problems the client wants investigated further. While these may occasionally overlap, often they do not. When such is the case, I would propose that *the underlying philosophy of the case method should draw us towards researching client problems.* I have already asserted this previously in this book and will continue to assert the same in future chapters.

Much of the time, the first case meeting will have been inspired by a brief encounter or phone call with the client where possible topics have already been presented. These can certainly serve as a starting point for the conversation. I would discourage the case writer from locking in a topic too early, however. Some of my best cases have been the result of discarding what I initially thought the case was about and addressing a decision or outcome that emerged only after I knew more about the client's situation.

What you need to leave with

The one thing you can *never* afford to do during a first case meeting is forget your objectives. What I have found is that if progress is not made on all four objectives, you are destined to repeat the first meeting over and over again with the same client. Unfortunately, as academics we have acquired a particularly high tolerance for meetings where nothing is accomplished—so long as each of us gets the opportunity to share our wisdom with the collective gathering[7]. In the professional world, the series of endless meetings is similarly common, but is not embraced as an art form as we have chosen to do in academia.

Establishing a set of concrete action items and deliverables intended to move the process forward can be particularly useful in preventing paralysis from happening. Few clients will remain steadfast to their commitment once they conclude that their time is being wasted.

The Second Meeting

Since it is practically impossible to achieve what I have said you *must achieve* in the first meeting, a second meeting will nearly always be required to finalize the deal. By this point, however, a topic has usually been identified and the question of the process being used for case development will normally be addressed. For that, we turn to the subject of information gathering.

Information Gathering

Information gathering tends to occur in two stages. The first is a discovery stage, where the information gathered helps to determine the structure of the case. The second is a tuning stage, where the case has been fully outlined and, perhaps, even drafted; information is then needed to fill in the gaps and remove inconsistencies. Before beginning either stage, however, it is important to establish ground rules for data gathering, something I generally like to get done during the second substantive meeting.

Setting Ground Rules

When a case study centers on a single individual, as it often does in instructional settings or in small businesses, the case development process can be quite streamlined, since the same individual provides most or all information. Most case studies in organizations, however, require data from multiple sources and also interviews of key participants. As a case writer, you can save yourself headaches and misunderstandings if you establish procedures from acquiring information from these sources prior to beginning data gathering.

Interviews

There are three practical issues that I have typically faced with respect to interviews: scheduling, reviewing quotes and interview protocols. We'll briefly consider each in turn.

Scheduling: With respect to scheduling, many clients would prefer not to have a case writer coming and going to conduct interviews at will; others may not care. I have found three basic approaches tend to dominate:

1. *The client arranges all interviews.* This allows the client to have maximum control over the interview process, determining who is interviewed as well as when and where interviews are conducted. In smaller organizations, this approach dominates.

2. *The client designates an assistant to help arrange scheduling.* In larger organizations, this seems to be the most common approach, since it frees the client from handling the detailed logistics.

3. *The case writer is provided free access to individuals in the organization.* This approach is sometimes used, particularly when the case writer has other roles—such as engaging in action research or consulting—that lead to the perception that he or she is (informally at least) a member of the organization.

I have not found that it particularly matters which approach is taken. Organizations willing to participate in case development are usually not of a type desperate to control information flows. The key thing is to ensure a common understanding is reached before interviews begin to occur.

Reviewing quotes: An issue that is potentially more contentious than scheduling is the review of quotes and interview results. Nearly all organizations have a political dimension. It is unlikely that the case writer, however experienced, will understand every nuance of what is said during the early stages of data gathering. As a result, it is quite possible that in reporting the results of an interview, either in what is quoted or in general descriptions of what was said, potentially sensitive or embarrassing statements may be reported.

There are really two issues here. One is that of accuracy. Sometimes, *with the permission of the client and the individual being interviewed,* it makes sense to record interviews. The other issue, and the more difficult one, is that of sensitivity. Where a conflict may occur is when the contact individual—the one I have referred to as the client—wants the case writer to report what he or she is learning as the process proceeds. That can lead to the perception that the case writer is acting as a spy; a perception that may not be altogether inaccurate.

My own preference for handling this is to make a blanket declaration to the client, before interviews commence, that I will always provide individual interviewees with copies of any statements or quotes I make regarding their interviews *before* I include them in any draft. I also make this clear to the interviewees before the interview begins. To the extent the parties believe me—as they normally will—this procedure relaxes the process somewhat.

Another interview issue relates to the question of acquiring direct quotes from participants. Returning to the subject of recording interviews, one alternative is to transcribe them verbatim. In a research case, this is likely to be the best choice. For a discussion case, on the other hand, what I will often do is to paraphrase a quote based upon my notes, then ask the interviewee if that is an reasonable approximation of what he or she said and, if so, if I can use it as a quote. Sometimes, when I get a particularly interesting statement, I will also work with the person being interviewed to create the block quote on the spot. The purpose of this exercise is to produce quotes that are clear, accurate and as faithful to the interviewee's intended meaning as possible; it is most definitely not to introduce my own spin into the mix.

Protocols. I return to the subject of interview protocols when I discuss research cases specifically. Because my position is that being faithful to the case method involves maintaining considerable openness to discovery, I tend to avoid strict protocols. It is just too hard to predict how an interview will proceed before it begins when the objectives are exploratory. On those occasions when I have developed them, I always clear them with the client before using them in an interview.

Access to other sources of data

In most organizational settings, you will need access to data from a variety of sources in order to properly triangulate your findings. Examples of such data could include company reports, consulting reports, emails, memoranda, slide shows, financial data, projections and budgets, performance evaluations, strategic plans, and so forth. Such sources can be invaluable. Organizations may be nervous about providing such access to an outsider, however. If they are not, then they are naïve.

There are two principle issues I encounter in dealing with such information. The first involves confidentiality, the second involves copyrights.

Confidentiality. With respect to confidentiality, there are three practical steps I would recommend:

1. Offer to sign a non-disclosure agreement even before being asked to do so. You should read the agreement before signing it, of course. In a business case writing scenario, you may also find you need prepare a short, easy to understand, addendum identifying any parts of the standard agreement that are inapplicable to the case development process.

2. Be very careful about using university technology, such as an institutionally provided laptop, to store any confidential case-related information. Depending upon your local public records law (see an earlier chapter note regarding the regulations in Florida, where I work), such information could be demanded by reporters or even competitors.

3. Do not demand access to lots of information at the outset of the case. As the client becomes more comfortable with you, he or she will likely be willing to dump reports and other documents on you (often confidential and even more often unread by the client), counting on you to alert them to anything sensitive.

Copyright. With respect to copyright, it is critical that the case writer determine who holds the rights to any information incorporated in a case. Particularly where 3rd party reports or images are involved, the fact that they are used by the organization does not necessarily mean that they can be incorporated in the case. I recently developed a case with a company, for example, that had an injunction brought against them because one of their clients posted images (of herself) on her web site and the photographer claimed the copyright.

Because most faculty members are aware of this type of issue, either through their research, course materials or both, I simply point out that considerable problems can arise if a case is found to violate copyrights of others. Should this happen to me (it has not, as of yet), my first stop would be my university's general counsel. Academics are often granted special exemptions—in the U.S. at least—as a result of "fair use" statutes. These statutes are so amazingly vague, however, that a lawyer will definitely be required to assess the situation.

Once the ground rules for interviews and data gathering have been established, the case development activity can commence in earnest. My experience is that this process generally divides into two stages, discovery and tuning.

Discovery Stage

During the discovery stage, every new fact you learn could—potentially—alter the nature of the case. At least, that is the way it should be. Generally, I have found that most of my time during this period is spent in relatively low structure interviews. My objectives in these interviews tend to be threefold:

1. Finding out what the interviewee knows with respect to the case topic

2. Identifying any other sources of data that I should acquire, either for my own information or as possible case exhibits or appendices.

3. Identifying anyone else I should be talking to.

During the discover process, it is quite possible that the case topic will either be refined or changed. This is more likely for discussion cases than for research cases[8]. In my own experience, change of topic may occur for several good reasons:

- *The decision being examined has been made, despite the client's claims that it has not been.* This is not unusual, particularly in business, since most situations requiring decisive action do not improve with age. Sometimes, this can be addressed by rolling back the time period profiled in the case. The problem with that is that interviews and other information gathering may have taken place in the post-decision environment, at which time perspectives have been altered by the choice that was actually made.

- *The decision proves to be uninteresting.* Upon careful analysis, it seems as if only one option makes the slightest bit of sense. Building a case that pretends the situation is more conflicted than it actually is violates the integrity of the case. It is generally better to focus on a different decision.

- *You develop a vastly different perspective on the situation than the client.* As was the case for the uninteresting decision, constructing a case that presents a perception contrary to your own is problematic. This has happened to me a couple of times. In both of these situations, I was able to switch to a related situation where the client's perceptions and my own were more closely aligned.

Implicit in the notion that "change of topic" offers a practical solution to these difficulties are two beliefs. The first belief is that another more suitable topic can be found at the client's organization. The second belief is that you remain comfortable working with the client. My own experience has *always* been that a client's supply of potentially interesting decisions in inexhaustible. Perhaps that is because I find business and education to be very engaging. I have, on a couple of occasions, parted ways with a client without a case owing to a difference in perspectives. The decision was always mutual and was not accompanied by any particular ill-will.

Tuning Stage

During the tuning stage, your goal is to gather the information needed to make your case complete and credible. At this point, discovery is no longer the object. Rather, the focus is on getting specific questions answered and on acquiring supporting materials for exhibits (teaching cases) or appendices (research cases).

My experience has been that when very specific information is required, the client will often undertake the task of acquiring it. By the time these materials are needed, you will usually have a very specific outline that you have prepared for the client. For that reason, he or she is likely to clearly understand both what you need and, more importantly, why you need it.

Putting the Case to Words

Since "case writing" best describes the entire process detailed in this chapter, the actual composing of a case needs an alternate name: putting the case to words. Nowhere does the research case diverge more significantly from the discussion case than in this part of the process. Discussion cases are written to inform students and to set the stage for further informing through participative learning. Research cases are written to inform other researchers. Their respective goals in reading the case, pre-existing mental models and vocabularies tend to be very different. More is the pity…

There are, however, a few areas where the same issues need to be considered. Two areas I have found to be of particular importance are reviewing individual segments and considering the pros and cons of co-authorship.

Reviewing individual segments

In most case studies that involve an organization—whether they be for purposes of discussion or research—a number of individuals will be interviewed and, subsequently, drafts of the case will be circulated. Earlier in the chapter, I recommended interviewees be allowed to re-view and modify their segments before they were seen by anyone else. I am less comfortable with a blanket recommendation regarding how to circulate segments of the case. Such reviews of work in progress are important. They accomplish two important purposes: they help to elim-inate factual errors that may have crept into the case and they help to determine if your overall perception of the situation is aligned with that of the organization.

For compact cases that focus on a decision being made by a single individual, the process is usually self-evident. That individual, and that individual alone, is usually given access to pre-draft segments of the case. Where the process becomes more complicated is in situations where several units of an organization are involved, such as different departments. In principle, it would probably be desirable to have each department comment on their own piece before passing it on to the client (who is likely to be more highly placed than either department head). The counter argument would be that in situations where organi-zational politics are in play, such a process could lead to tensions be-tween the units, each of whom wonders what was written about the other.

Generally, I build a relatively close relationship with the client contact over the course of a case development project. For that reason, my natural inclination is to have that individual do whatever initial review-ing I believe the case requires. Prior to such reviews, I always empha-size that I tend to "make up" material in order to "fill in the blanks" when I am missing facts or interpretations of those facts, and that the major purpose of the review is to ensure that the final product is entire-ly factual. I find this technique for eliciting knowledge to be highly effective in developing discussion cases[9]; when my attempt to fill in a gap correctly fails, the client is quick to let me know about it. More often, however, my surmises have proven to be correct[10]. The big ad-vantage of this approach is one of speed. It takes much less time to write a case when surmises are substituted for missing facts and it takes the client much less time than would an interview to verify all the facts before incorporating them in the text. The price you pay as case writer is the occasional chastisement you get from the client for getting something completely wrong. As long as you have told the client in advance what you have done (and why you do it that way) the resulting rebuke is not terribly serious and the nature of the correction to be made is crystal clear.

Lest what I have written makes it sound as if every case development project is going to be a political hornet's nest, let me assure you that my experience has generally been the opposite. Most of my case development projects, both for discussion cases and research cases, have involved few entanglements in organizational politics. They can occur, however. Like many of the items on the checklist, it is best to anticipate that they will occur then be pleasantly surprised when they (usually) do not prove to be a serious obstacle.

Co-authorship

When writing a case study, the case writer should always at least consider offering the participant or participants the opportunity to be listed as a co-author. There are both pros and cons to doing so, although my strong opinion is that the pros generally outweigh the cons in case method research.

Pros of participant co-authors

There are many advantages to having participants serve as co-authors. Among these are the following:

1. With their name on the case, client co-authors have greater incentive to go over what is written very carefully.

2. Having a client included on a research case blurs the distinction between participant and subject. Should an institution require human subject approval for a case research project, this should reduce any stumbling blocks.

3. In most case development projects—at least ones that I have participated in—client co-authorship is best describes how the case was actually written.

4. It reinforces that notion that case research and writing is effectively a collaborative activity between research and practice.

The last of these points has special weight for me. The central theme of this book is that the case method can serve as an effective informing tool. There is no better way to ensure that such informing takes place than through collaborative research (and I most definitely include developing cases for discussion under the category of research).

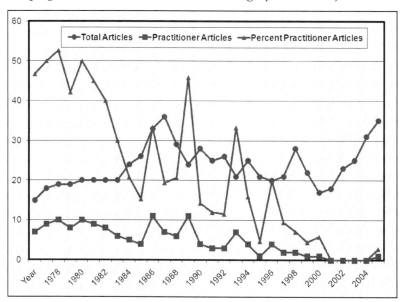

Figure 4.1 Articles published in MIS Quarterly each year versus articles where at least one co-author was a practitioner.

Unfortunately, in my field at least, the degree to which we are actively collaborating with practice seems to be declining. My colleague Anol Bhattacherjee and I documented this in a recent article published in *MIS Quarterly* (Gill & Bhattacherjee, 2009) where we examined the how the number of practitioner coauthors in our field has changed over time. The chart we prepared, presented below as Figure 4.1, shows a disturbing trend as such collaborations have virtually disappeared in the MIS field's premier journal. I believe we should be doing everything possible to reverse this trend. Successful collaborations with practitioners beget future collaborations and the formation of enduring relationships. I earnestly believe that that this is what we should be striving for if we want to survive.

Cons of participant co-authors

There are some disadvantages of participant co-authors as well. Some are valid; some are largely a consequence of nonsensical way in which we sometimes assess research productivity.

The nonsensical reason for not including practitioner co-authors is that a lot of universities judge research productivity by weight, not content, and therefore assign values based on percentage of co-authorship. Some go even one step beyond that. When I went up for promotion to professor the last two times (once failing, subsequently succeeding), I was required to assess my individual percent contribution for each article where I had co-authors[11]. I have never seen a more compelling demonstration of a failure to understand complexity in my life. I could just as reliably have answered the question: "What percentage of a cake's quality is the result of the baking powder?" To be honest, I even had a hard time with the notion that I should allocate myself 100% contribution for my sole authored papers. I like to flatter myself by thinking that I am open minded enough to be influenced by other researchers (properly referenced, of course), and that to attribute 100% of the resulting article to me alone is nothing short of hubris.

Nevertheless, if your university is obsessed by rankings and depends on crude research productivity metrics as the source of those rankings, you may feel pretty stupid if your institution drops several places because your role was only 50% and not 100% (or 33% instead of 50%, or 25% instead of 33%, etc.) as a result of voluntarily adding a practitioner co-author. Fortunately, since discussion cases do not tend to contribute to rankings under any circumstances, the temptation to yield to self-serving impulses is greatly reduced for these projects.

The valid reason for not including participant co-authors is that they may choose to be excluded. This would most likely be the situation when the choice has been made to disguise a case. That is our final topic of this chapter.

Disguising a Case

Once a case study has been written there will usually be a question with respect to whether or not it should be disguised. There are really two questions here:

1. Should specific details, such as individual names and sensitive numbers (e.g., financial data, teaching evaluation scores) be disguised?

2. Should the entire case be disguised?

In general, it often makes sense to disguise the former. With respect to names, we need to recognize that most decent case studies—whether they are developed for research or for discussion—will end up indexed on the web. That means a search for the participant's name will produce the case, often on the first search page. I recall one incident from my own experience where I wrote a case on a company in a real-estate related industry and spent several paragraphs extolling the expertise of the company's founder. About five year later, I found myself subpoenaed for my testimony. The party bringing suit was upset with the case protagonist as a result of a business deal that went sour; his argument was that if the protagonist was so expert, then the deal should not have broken down. I was therefore brought in to testify to the expertise of my former case client. The suit was later dismissed as being entirely groundless. But the episode illustrates how case studies can be used outside of their intended purpose. Since that time, I have always discussed the pros and cons of disguising a case with potential case clients.

Names and numbers can usually be altered without greatly impacting a case's integrity. The fact that some disguising has been done should, however, be noted in the case—perhaps as a footnote or parenthetical comment.

I am much less comfortable with fully disguising a case. In a business case, such disguising might involve changing the company's name, location or even industry. In an educational setting, it might involve changing the institution, the course content or even student characteristics. The problem such disguising introduces is the following. In a complex environment, the further you move away from the original setting, the more likely you will fail to account for some interaction that you are not aware of. Nevertheless, sometimes a highly disguised case is very successful[12]. Normally, this will be because it addresses issues that are far afield from its actual setting. Writing such a case, however, is a hard act to pull off.

Conclusions

As I asserted at the outset of this chapter, every case writing experience will exhibit its own set of peculiarities. If you are to be professional in your case writing activities, however, you should be able to anticipate a large fraction of them. This chapter has provided an initial set of these to think about. Additional items are suggested in the later chapters specifically devoted to writing each type of case.

One particular message of this chapter deserves to be highlighted, since it is less a matter of common sense than most of what has been presented. Perhaps the most important goal of a case-writing activity of any sort should be to form enduring relationships with the professionals or organizations profiled in the case. Such relationships can become important informing channels through which knowledge can diffuse in both directions. There are few things more valuable, to the academic researcher in particular, than the opportunity to be an observer as an organization or professional develops. We turn to that subject next, as we consider case development strictly from the research perspective and identify the particular benefits of longitudinal designs.

Chapter 4 Notes

[1] 300 hours of phone time is a rough estimate based upon the fact that just one of the monthly phone bills was over $2000. I know this because Carol Saunders, my department chair, relayed this fact to me, also mentioning that I had—in that single month—exceeded the entire department's phone allowance for a semester. That she passed on this news with an amused look served to further confirm my belief that I had been uncharacteristically wise in my choice of department.

[2] In informing science, the term *client* usually refers to the party being informed. In consulting, it is the person who pays you. Neither of these meanings is intended by the use of the term to refer to the case site. It is just a convenient term that conveys a certain degree of professionalism and also suggests that the case site itself should accrue benefits from participating in the case development process.

[3] Most of the discussion cases on higher education courses that I developed ended up in the short-lived journal, now repository, known as

Informing Faculty. These can be accessed through the *Informing Science Institute's* web site.

[4] In Florida, for example, we have a "Sunshine Act" that means a reporter could ask to see virtually anything on my computer except for student grades. In other words, as soon as I start to write a case it could become public *provided* an individual knew what to ask for. The law does not allow them to simply fish around on my computer, however—they need to ask I provide something specific. Thus, as long as I do not go announcing to the press that a case is under development, it is unlikely that information would be revealed. Were I to be in a situation where I felt there was any danger of private information being compromised, I would use one of the computers that I purchased with my own funds, just to be on the safe side.

[5] The importance of relationships in complex informing processes is discussed extensively in *Informing Business*. Its research roots derive from in the early agricultural technology diffusion studies, well described in the late Everett Rogers' (2003) seminal book *Diffusion of Innovations*.

[6] Okay, I over-generalized. Not *all* academics are as unimpressed with their personal brilliance as their accomplishments seem to warrant. Fortunately, most researchers who are convinced that they deserve their own special category between God and man would not deign to engage in the mundane activity of writing discussion cases. For my part, I will try to contain the occasional impulse to present myself as the *God of All Things Case Method.* Being human, I will doubtless fail from time to time, for which I hope I will be forgiven.

[7] Perhaps if teaching loads were set higher at research universities, we academics could satiate our desire to lecture and otherwise listen to our own voices through teaching, thereby reducing our desire to do so at meetings. Sadly, I believe that particular appetite may be insatiable.

[8] A research project that keeps changing its topic is too much like a random fishing expedition to suit even my wanton disregard of formal research protocols.

[9] I suspect that the technique of "making stuff up" is frowned upon in the development of research cases, although you would never know it from reading some of them.

[10] I recall one CEO turning absolutely white upon reading a draft I had presented him and stating:

"I can't believe we told you all that…"

I quickly explained that they had not, in fact, told me much of what I had written about their strategy. Rather, my narrative reflected my attempt to make sense of the bits and pieces they had told me. This is an example of how skills honed in analyzing cases can be put to good use in creating them.

[11] By the way, if you are ever on the game show *Jeopardy* and the answer given is "What numbers are guaranteed never to add up to 100" I would suggest you respond: "What are individual researcher estimates of their own relative contributions to a given article?".

[12] A good example of this is the *Concordia Casting* case, used for decades at HBS. Virtually everything about that technology-related case has been disguised. In fact, it has gone through several revisions and, in each one, the technologies involved have been changed. But, as it turns out, the case is not about technology.

T. Grandon Gill
Informing with the Case Method
Santa Rosa, California: Informing Science Press.

Chapter 5

Designing Case Method Research

The most important thing to do when designing case research is clarifying what you want to accomplish. When developing cases for discussion, I strongly recommend letting the protagonists involved play a major role in establishing the direction of the case. Where a research case is the goal, on the other hand, the investigator is likely to drive the design. The only type of case where this principle is unlikely to hold is for cases purely exploratory in nature.

In this chapter we specifically consider the question of case research design. Although the options for such design are nearly limitless, there are some general principles that can be helpful both in design and in justifying a particular research project to reviewers. These include mapping the case to common research objectives, the choice of single vs. multi-case designs and building a justification of validity into the research.

We begin the chapter where every case researcher is likely to begin, by considering the recommendations of Robert K. Yin. We then examine how the objectives of case research can be formulated in terms of a fitness landscape. Alternative design patterns are considered next, with single vs. multi-case and snapshot vs. longitudinal approaches being contrasted. That leads to a discussion of how design decisions can reinforce the perceived validity of a case research project. Finally, we consider case method research as it relates to human subject protections.

Many other design-related issues exist that the case writer should consider. Among these are included the degree to which the investigator participates in the activity being researched, case length, anonymity and publication outlets. These topics and others are postponed to Chapter 6, where the focus will be the actual conduct and writing of research cases.

The Objectives of Case Method Research

In Chapter 1, the notion that case method research is a subset of case research in general was illustrated in Figure 1.1. Before we consider research designs, it makes sense to explore this distinction in greater detail. Understanding these distinctions becomes particularly important in light of the fact that an extraordinarily influential book on the subject of case research design already exists (Yin, 2009). What we will find is that the distinctions between how Yin and I treat the subject of case research design—which turn out to be quite substantial in many areas—stem largely from my narrower area of focus, the assumptions about the environment that I make and—based on those assumptions—the objectives I see as being appropriate for such research. It is to the objectives of case research that I now turn.

Complexity and Research Categories

At the very beginning of Yin's book, he lays out a table of relevant situations for different research. In Table 5.1, I start with his table (shown with a slightly grey background), then add a column and a few rows. Yin's focus was on identifying situations for different empirical research methods. His columns represented:

1. The types of questions the method is likely to answer.

2. Whether the researcher needs to take control of behavioral events.

3. Whether the focus is on the present or the past.

To this, table I add two rows, representing conceptual theory building and logical/mathematical theory building. The purpose of doing so is to cover more broadly the types of research normally done in the social sciences.

In addition, I add the column "Suitable for Complex Landscapes". Using the ideas introduced in Chapter 2, I argue that any research method that limits the number of variables being considered (e.g., experiment, survey, conceptual theory, logical/mathematical theory) or relies heavily on analytical tools that make the default assumption of landscape decomposability (e.g., survey analysis tools, logical/mathematical theory) is likely to lead to misleading results for phenomena taking place on complex landscapes.

Table 5.1: Mapping of research methods to situations and complexity. Grey cells are from Yin (2009, p. 8), remaining cells added by me.

Method	Questions	Control of Events Required	Contemporary Focus	Suitable for Complex Landscapes
Experiment	how, why?	Yes	Yes	No
Survey	who, what, where, how many, how much?	No	Yes	No
Archival analysis	who, what, where, how many, how much?	No	Yes/No	Yes
History	how, why?	No	No	Yes
Case study	how, why?	No	Yes	Yes
Conceptual theory building	how, why?	No	Yes/No	No
Logical, mathematical theory building	how, why?	No	Yes/No	No

The point of adding the rightmost column is to highlight the fact that if you believe the underlying landscape being studied is complex, the number of suitable techniques for research diminishes significantly. Moreover, it is not clear to me why archival analysis, history and case study methods are presented separately. A systematic case study, whether for research or discussion, will nearly always analyze archival data and examine the history leading up to the point profiled. Repeating the conclusion of Chapter 2, it is the complexity of the landscape that drives the technique.

Objectives for Case Method Research

Assume, then, that we limit the use of the term "case method research" to situations where the landscape being studied is assumed to be complex. What types of findings can we reasonably expect to obtain?

The unlikelihood of attractive theory

Let us start with an easier question: what can we *not* expect to find? The answer here is *attractive theory* (Gill, 2010). The properties of such theory are:

1. Compactness

2. Generalizability

3. Stability over time

A complex system, by its very nature, consists of many elements that interact at a high level in an environment where fitness is dynamic; as we noted previously, this is how complexity is defined in a wide array of fields, such as evolutionary biology (Kauffman, 1993) and management (Wood, 1986). Attractive theory would seem to be the very antithesis of what we could reasonably expect from such systems.

There is probably not a more heretical position that one could take in the social sciences than to doubt the existence of an undiscovered attractive theory that will one day allow us to fully understand the systems we are today investigating. Even seemingly sensible researchers—such as Clayton Christensen, whose disruptive technology theory maps almost perfectly to the biological notion of complex fitness landscapes—has the following to say about the future of educational research:

> … the contention that … phenomena are unfathomably complex, with unpredictable outcomes, is not unique to education. For example, prior to 1700, people said similar things about understanding the natural world. Some things seemed so inexplicable that the only plausible explanation was the wrath of the gods. But the development of the scientific method changed all that, and now we understand and can predict with reasonable certainty many things in the world around us. For example, understanding gravity allowed humans to predict that if someone walks off a cliff, he or she will fall—and therefore we do not need to collect experimental data on that particular question. We can predict the level of stress at which a given material will fracture, the conditions under which certain elements will bond chemically with others, and so on. (Christensen, Horn & Johnson, 2008, p. 161-162).

Physical systems, such as the ones just described, avoid the problems of interaction through principles such as superposition and the formation of repeated structures. The laws that govern them remain static over time. They are not fitness landscapes, with participants continually adapting over time. By what property of reasoning by analogy would we expect the theories that govern human behavior to similarly simplify?

Theory vs. conceptual schemes

If complex systems are unlikely to yield attractive theory, why should we even bother investigating them? My response is that such research may yield *conceptual schemes* that are useful for controlling or predicting their behavior. Conceptual schemes is a term I picked up from reading *The Elusive Phenomenon* by Fritz Roethlisberger[1] (1977) and expanded on in a recent paper (Gill, 2011). On the surface, a conceptual scheme looks a lot like theory. It has some very important differences, however:

1. Theory seeks to describe the underlying *truth* of things; a conceptual scheme contents itself with being a *useful* way of looking at things.

2. Theory can be supported or refuted; since a conceptual scheme is not intended to be viewed as truth, research tends to focus on determining the *boundaries* over which it is useful.

3. The meaning of theory should be independent of how it is presented; in order to be useful, conceptual schemes must integrate with the existing mental models of the client.

The last of these points implies that the most appropriate conceptual scheme for one client may be different for another, even applied to the same situation. For example, the ego-id-superego model of the mind proposed by Freud may still serve as a useful conceptual scheme for a particular therapist despite the fact that a scientific basis for the three elements is unlikely ever to be established.

The goals of case method research

This analysis, supplemented by my assumption that the most appropriate domain for case method research is complex environments, leads to the following conclusion:

The objective of case method research is the development of conceptual schemes and determination of their relevant boundaries so as to allow a client improved control over activities or prediction of behaviors within a complex environment.

To the social scientist who believes that the apparent complexity of the systems we study is merely an illusion that results from our ignorance, the case method as I describe it would obviously be of little interest. Indeed, what I have suggested might well seem little short of contemptible since it implies that I have given up on the noble quest for truth. My response to that criticism would be that we must all play the hand we are dealt. If the environments we choose to study are truly complex, we need to conduct our research accordingly. Albert Einstein reportedly said that insanity is doing the same thing over and over again and expecting different results. Until the results of research-developed theory in areas such as business and education produce improvements that are replicable and unambiguous, those of us who think there has to be a better way should be pardoned for wondering if prevailing research methods are tinged with such madness.

What may be less obvious about the conclusion, on the other hand, are two important corollaries:

1. Since the most suitable conceptual scheme can vary in accordance with a client's existing mental models, case method research will not necessarily propose its own conceptual scheme. It may instead offer a narrative that an expert client can use as scaffolding upon which to build his or her own personal conceptual scheme.

2. If we do not find ways of communicating our conceptual schemes to practice, the case method is a pointless activity. Having conceded that we are unlikely to arrive at truth and that our results are likely to be messy (i.e., not attractive theory), what is the merit of any research we generate that is not put to work?

These two corollaries explain both this book's pre-occupation with informing and its position that case method instruction and research should not be viewed as independent activities, since they are far more similar than they are different.

Case Study Research and Yin

It is extremely unusual to find case study research in the social sciences that does mention the book *Case Study Research: Design and Methods* by Robert K Yin (2009). Now in its fourth edition, the book is informative, concise and clear. It is also one of the most widely cited research methodology works in the social sciences. If you are doing case study research, you can and should cite it.

Research vs. Teaching Cases

Having offered this ringing endorsement for Yin, I must now sound a cautionary note. Much of his book is written from the perspective of the search for theory that, as indicated in the previous section, may be overly ambitious when a complex environment is being investigated. He also takes a somewhat unflattering view of discussion cases, making the following statements:

> [This book] is not intended to help those who might use case studies as a teaching tool... For teaching purposes, a case study need not contain a complete or accurate rendition of events... Teaching case studies need not be concerned with rigorous and fair presentation of empirical data; research case studies need to do exactly that. (Yin, 2009, p. 4-5)

While his statement might be true of some types of cases used in teaching (e.g., fables, showcases), I would argue that discussion cases generally should strive to be as rigorous as research cases and that, as far as the case method is concerned, the distinction between the two case forms is best made with respect to the point in time that is profiled vis-à-vis a particular decision. On the dimensions of quality and accuracy, I would assert that they should be held to equivalent standards.

Quotable Yin

Aside from serving as an excellent overview of case design, Yin is an invaluable resource when it comes to defending case method research. Some of the key points that I have found most useful now follow.

Point 1: Lack of rigor

Case study research—whether it is what I call case method research or as it is more broadly defined by Yin—has always been subject to concerns about its rigor. On that score, there can be little doubt that the researcher's mental models (including prejudices and ideologies) will impact the conclusion of all case research. The impact of this can be reduced by focusing on reporting, rather than interpreting, the details of the case in the write up. But, as I discuss at length in *Informing Business* (Gill, 2010), the human cognitive system requires information pass through a series of filters before it is incorporated into our mental models. These filters exhibit allow information confirming what we believe to pass far more readily than information contrary to our beliefs. Thus, despite our best efforts, true objectivity is likely beyond us.

What Yin points out is requiring that case research be perfectly rigorous is not the fundamental issue. The relevant criterion for rigor needs to be *a comparison with other available techniques*. As a result, what we really need to be considering is the relative merits of research method efficacy for a particular domain—such as Table 5.1 and the discussions of Chapter 2. Here, the inherent weaknesses of case research may appear trifling in comparison with other methods when complex landscapes are the object of study.

Point 2: Generalizability and the N of 1 problem

Yin (2010, p. 15) frames the often asked question as follows:

"How can you generalize from a single case?"

His response, which I consider an elegant defense, is not to view a case as an *observation* but as an *experiment*. With observations, we tend to want many so we can test their statistical properties. With experiments, on the other hand, a single instance—supplemented, perhaps, with a few replications—can be entirely convincing.

While I agree completely with his reasoning here, I must also acknowledge its limitations for research on a complex landscape. For such landscapes, the assumption must be that nothing can be generalized without further evidence. The same, however, applies to experiments, surveys and other approaches—returning us to Point 1. Thus, like Yin, I encourage multi-case designs and longitudinal studies that permit the boundaries of a phenomenon to be explored. When conducting case method research, a single case research project *is* probably better viewed as an observation than as an experiment. The collective result of a case research program, however, is more like a survey of the landscape than a statistical sample. In such a survey, each observation is taken with considerable care and multiple observations are not taken at the same point so we can average them and determine their standard error. Nor would we consider averaging the results of all or observations across the landscape, as illustrated by Figure 5.1.

Figure 5.1: In understanding this landscape, are the most interesting properties really likely to be its average elevation and standard deviation? (Photo of Bryce Canyon National Park, Utah, taken by the author).

Point 3: Case studies are long

Yin combines two meanings of length in his discussion of this point: long to conduct and long write-ups. He argues that neither is necessarily inherent in the case method. With respect to the write up, he asserts:

> alternative ways of writing the case study [include those] in which the traditional, lengthy narrative can be avoided altogether (Yin, 2010, p. 15)

He further argues that the type of field research and ethnographic data collection (e.g., through interviews or action research) that are hugely time consuming may be avoided in some designs utilizing the phone or the Internet.

I am somewhat less than convinced by the first of these arguments when it comes to the case method. As I have defined it, the case method has a strong exploratory component to its nature. If a case write up is overly streamlined, I see considerable danger of it transforming into a case example, rather than an example of case method research. My view therefore is that a case research report should be as long as it needs to be in order to present a full picture of the situation being studied and, ideally, not a word longer. The fact that this length will, in many circumstances, exceed the desired length of a journal article can be inconvenient, to be sure[2]. That inconvenience should not influence the ultimate form of the write up, however.

With respect to the length of the research itself, I fully agree with Yin's assertion that the process does not have to be never-ending. I would suggest, however, that his assertion might be a bit disingenuous. If an investigator were to follow all of Yin's (generally excellent) suggestions regarding the design and conduct of case research, I find it hard to imagine that the process could be conducted expeditiously. Much as I view the case writing checklist discussed earlier, I tend to think of the worst case scenario as that research situation where rigor demands following *all* the best practices.

To justify my apparent advocacy of cutting corners, I return to Point 1. Rigor must be judged with respect to the rigor of the available alternatives. Recall that one aspect of complexity is the time dimension; relationships in a complex system are continuously changing. Excepting longitudinal research (which takes a lot of time by design) and historical case research (in which time is frozen), the more lengthy the research process, the greater the likelihood that the situation being observed will have changed between the start of the research and its ultimate publication. Unlike theory, which is assumed to be timeless, the conceptual schemes developed through case method research often come with an expiration date. Given that case method research tends to be justified by its usefulness, are the demands of rigor really satisfied by lengthy development times? This is not an excuse for sloppiness. It is a concession to the realities of complex environments. And, as another practical matter, the easiest way to disillusion a client is to act as if his or her time has little value.

Point 4: Cases are less valid than randomized field trials

Yin (2009, p. 16) points out that case studies are generally viewed as inferior in their ability to demonstrate causality than randomized field trials. This is the common refrain of those who advocate experiments. In defense of case research, however, he points out that information derived from a case study may serve to complement what is learned from such trials.

As we enter the domain of highly complex environments, on the other hand, I tend to be very suspicious of the information we are likely to gain from randomized trials. The problem is that the outcomes of such trials are likely to be impacted by so many interacting factors that we have not considered; the "control" provided by the trial is far more likely to present the illusion of rigor than actual rigor itself. Consider, for example, the two student comments on made on the first version of the programming course, Ism3232, that I taught (from Appendix E):

> *Comment 1:* I thought the course was wonderful. [Instructor A] made information for the class accessible in many, many ways. The CD for the class is the greatest thing. I wish I had other classes like this one. My overall evaluation of [Instructor A] is perfect. I have not had a better teacher at USF.

> *Comment 2:* Up to this point I am still wondering why this monster became a professor. He is a self-righteous person. He needs to go back where he came from.

These two students were taking the same course and attended the same section. Had I gathered extensive survey information on each student, I still very much doubt that I would have been able to gain much useful insight into the nature of the problem from summary measures. Even if I asked the right survey questions, there is no guarantee they would have given honest answers. Had I been able to spend 5 minutes in open and frank conversation with each student, on the other hand, I feel relatively confident that I could have made headway on the problem (and identified what the first liked so much about the course, and what the second hated).

As I discussed at length in *Informing Business* (Gill, 2010), it makes considerable sense to explain error as randomness where the environment being studied is presumed to be decomposable in nature. Where interactions dominate the landscape, on the other hand, it is a misleading approach. I am here reminded of a marvelous quote included in Ziliak and McCloskey's (2008, p. 245) equally marvelous book, *The Cult of Statistical Significance*. It was part of a letter from William Sealy Gosset[3] to Egon Pearson:

> [O]bviously, the important thing... is to have low real error, not to have a "significant" result... The latter seems to me to be nearly valueless in itself... You want to be able to say not only "We have significant evidence that if farmers in general do this they will make money by it," but also "we have found it so in nineteen cases out of twenty and we are finding out why it doesn't work in the twentieth." To do that you have to be as sure as possible which is the 20th—your real error must be small.

Here, once again, we see the difference between theory—which seeks to describe the truth—and conceptual schemes, which roll up their sleeves up and go to work.

Yin's Case Study Skills

For the most part, Yin's treatment of case study research strikes me as admirable in both content and presentation. When adapted to case method research, it makes sense to pay particular attention to areas where he talks about exploratory research.

One remaining area where he and I differ is with respect to case study skills. His list (Yin, 2009, p. 69) consists of the following:

1. Able to ask good questions

2. Be a good listener

3. Be adaptive and flexible

4. Have a firm grasp on the issues being studied

5. Unbiased by preconceived notions

Aside from my belief that the last of these is impossible, my main objection to the list itself relates to the fourth item when applied to case method research. To me, the phrase "issues being studied" suggests a disciplinary interpretation. For example, a business faculty member whose discipline is finance and whose specialty is capital markets might assume he or she possesses the requisite expertise to do case research on a small family-owned company considering going public. What I would argue, however, is that case method situations are normally sufficiently complex so that practical familiarity with the landscape (e.g., industry, small business, family-owned companies), rather than the specific issues of the case, may be more valuable. The amount of information that a case writer must process in the initial stages of conducting an investigation is huge; practice observing similar settings vastly increases the rate at which that information can be digested.

The other characteristic missing is broad communications skills. Being able to ask good questions and listen well are, of course, part of the equation. But the ability to inform the client, detect areas that are sensitive and areas that are not, and to write the case in an engaging manner are critical if case method research findings are to be put to work.

The same skill set applies, of course, to the development of discussion cases. Once again, this reinforces my belief that the two forms of case development are far more similar than different.

Case Method Research Questions

In Chapter 2, the rugged fitness landscape model was introduced. In this section, we consider how case method research can serve to help us better understand such a landscape. This treatment starts from the assumption that the phenomenon being investigated exists on a fitness landscape—meaning that there is some underlying desired metric that we are seeking to improve or maximize—and that the landscape is complex.

A. How do we estimate fitness?

Common to all the research questions is the need to assess the fitness of a given situation or strategy. Generally, this will be an important part of most case method research. True fitness is generally impossible to measure (Gill, 2010). Even if you think you have a handle on it, factors that are entirely unpredicted can impact an entity's survival or value. A company may determine the ideal location for a plant, yet a meteorite could hit the facility the next day. A lawsuit brought against a school system as a result of an accident could cause it to close down a program that seemed to be doing wonderfully at enhancing learning. In the aftermath of the unexpected, we may come to realize that a particular approach was far less fit than it seemed to be. This is a central point made in Nassim Taleb's (2007) book *The Black Swan*[4]. Thus, in a complex setting, we must always estimate fitness, we can never be certain of it.

Estimating fitness will depend heavily on the context of the situation. Thus, the question of how it is estimated will nearly always be an important element of case method research. In an educational setting, we might use measures such as test performance, attrition, student evaluation ratings, peer assessment and so forth to build our estimate. In a business setting, we might use share price, profit margins, sales, customer satisfaction surveys, product quality ratings, repeat purchases, efficiency, performance assessments, and so forth. The particular metric being used may not generalize well, even over time, as illustrated by the following example.

Example: Change in Fitness for Ism3232

In the case presented in Appendix E, high attrition was not viewed as a negative in the early years of the programming course. At that time part of the purpose of the course was to serve as a gatekeeper to a major where enrollments were growing so fast that they taxed the department's resources to the breaking point. Thus, attrition rates were not deemed particularly important aspects of the overall fitness of the course. Indeed, on at least one occasion, a colleague intimated to the instructor—which happened to be was me—that I might be letting too many students get through.

Within just a year or two, as part of a nationwide trend brought on by the end of Y2K and the bursting of the Internet bubble, MIS enrollments had plummeted. By the time the number of undergraduate majors had bottomed out, they had dropped over 80% from their peak values in the department. Suddenly, the fitness *of the department* depended on attracting potential majors and ensuring that every opportunity to succeed was given to them.

One may argue, of course, that the true fitness of a course should be determined not by practical considerations but by how much students learn. We can be reasonably certain, however, that such learning is unlikely to occur if the major is discontinued.

B. What Factors or Combinations Contribute to Fitness?

In its most exploratory form, a case study can serve to identify the key factors contributing to fitness in a given situation. Assuming a situation-appropriate estimate of fitness has been acquired, an interesting question involves determining what factors contribute to changes in the estimate and what factors do not.

There are two variations on how we might answer a question like this. One would be a longitudinal strategy, where we watch what happens when we change a single factor or combination. The bad news here is that if the factor acts as part of an interaction, there is a good chance that the effect of such a change will not replicate in other situations. The good news is that because of the interactions involved, a change to a seemingly minor factor may exert a large impact on fitness. What this means is that in situations where similar interactions are present, the opportunity to produce *material* fitness increases may be present and *not obvious*. This is precisely the type of finding researchers seeking to inform practice should be striving for.

Example: Grading Curve in EMBA 2002 (B) Case

The EMBA 2002 (A) case, presented as Appendix G, describes a case method course that, after a single class session, appears to be careening out of control. The instructor has received emails from a number of students and from the program director complaining about the workload, the selection of work assigned, his approach to scheduling work and his attitude. The situation was a very uncomfortable one.

As the case progresses, through the (B) case, the instructor begins to suspect that the *real* problem is that the course grading curve—as specified on the first day—was lower than what the students were used to. Through an email included in the (B) case, the instructor is able to verify this experimentally. He then offers to use a curve comparable to that used by most of the instructors in the program (a minor modification to the grading curve of no particular significance to the instructor). The outcome: the attitudes of the students miraculously transform. The remainder of the course proceeded without incident; the students were delightful, the evaluations positive, and the instructor was subsequently asked to teach the course again.

The other type of finding that may be uncovered by this research question is combinations of factors that represent entirely different paths to fitness. For this question, multi-case cross sectional designs may be appropriate. The idea is to find high fitness examples where fitness is achieved in very different ways.

Example: Cross Class Comparisons

The central theme of Appendix E is demonstrating how different strategies can nevertheless lead to equivalent states of fitness. Three different classes are profiled (Ism3232.A, Ism3232.B and Ism6155.A). Two of these are the same course taught by different instructors employing radically different designs (Ism3232.A and Ism3232.B). Virtually every design attribute that we would normally consider important is different—yet both exhibiting high fitness. A second pair consists of two different courses taught by the same instructor employing entirely different designs (Ism3232.A and Ism6155.A). Despite the differences in design, both of these courses exhibit high fitness as well. The conclusion drawn from this is that the fitness of a particular class results from finding suitable design combinations, rather than trying to find the "best" value for each design element (as would be perfectly appropriate on a decomposable landscape).

C. What Search Strategies Are Used to Increase Fitness?

Another interesting research issue for the case method is identifying possible techniques for attaining increased fitness. This is one area where theory, as well as conceptual schemes, could be the objective of the research. The reason for the difference is the fact that complex landscapes can, and often are, the product of a relatively small number of invariant processes. The obvious example here is genetics, where a small number of mechanisms, such as mutation, combination and cross-over, are used to explain the ever evolving gene pool. On the other hand, in complex systems involving humans, it may also be the case that heuristic techniques, wide in variety and rapidly evolving over time, may account for most of the adaptation towards fitness.

Because search strategies for increasing fitness *may* prove more generalizable than the actual factors that contribute to fitness itself, it makes sense to report these in sufficient detail in any report destined for practice. (Note that when case studies deal with education, practitioners may well mean other researchers while they are wearing their teaching hats). Techniques for estimating fitness and searching for increased fitness are among the types of knowledge that diffuse most rapidly (Gill, 2010).

D. Have We Reached a Fitness Peak?

Related to the previous objective, a case method research project can present an argument that a particular set of factors results in a position at or near a local fitness peak. There are a variety of ways that a researcher can argue that a peak has been attained or nearly attained:

1. *Benchmarks:* Demonstrating that fitness estimates for the observation are high relative to similar situations.

2. *Active experimentation:* Particularly in a longitudinal study, demonstrating that a process of searching for fitness has taken place and that further changes seemed to have minimal or negative effect.

3. *Expert assessment:* Opinions of experts in the domain that high levels of fitness have been achieved.

4. *Pegging the estimator:* Some estimators of fitness cannot extend beyond a certain point (e.g., attrition in a class cannot go below 0%, profit margins cannot go above 100% of revenue). Once an estimate of fitness reaches these levels, attempts to gauge the peak more accurately are likely to be ineffective.

Careful readers will doubtless note that with the possible exception of the last of these, none actually guarantee a true "peak" has been reached. In most cases, this is likely to be immaterial. Very high fitness is of sufficient interest in most practical circumstances.

Example: Demonstrating Peaks for Three Classes

In Appendix E, it was important to demonstrate that all three classes studied had reached a level of performance at or near a fitness peak. Evidence provided came from all four sources previously listed, including:

---

1. *Benchmarks:* For both sections of Ism3232, student evaluations were at historical highs and attrition was at historical lows. In addition, by tracing the evolution of Ism3232.A longitudinally, it was possible to demonstrate that these estimators had not been influenced by a watering down of course content.

2. *Active experimentation:* The longitudinal study of Ism3232.A showed a pattern of active experimentation, some of which appeared to increase fitness and some failing to do so. Extensive data was gathered as part of this process through an end-of-semester survey that students in that section filled out.

3. *Expert assessment:* Both Ism3232.A (2007) and Ism6155.A (2005) had been named the winner in an international innovative instruction competition sponsored by the *Decision Sciences Institute.*

4. *Pegging the estimator:* Student course evaluations and attrition rate measures had become so positive in all three courses that further improvement would have been nearly meaningless.

Collectively, these provided strong support for the high, near peak fitness of the classes described.

E. What are the Limits to a Conceptual Scheme?

A case can serve as a counter-example to an existing conceptual scheme. Assuming that the landscape being studied is recognized as being complex, this does not "disprove" the conceptual scheme in any way. It simply demonstrates that its domain does not extend to the region of the landscape.

Boundary limitation can be accomplished by finding two different outcomes resulting from superficially similar situations or from showing that small changes in a longitudinal study can lead to very different outcomes.

Example: MSDN and High Tech Hidebound

The reviews of my original High Tech Hidebound manuscript required that I make only one significant change. The reviewers asked that I develop a counter-example to the two cases I presented (i.e., *Mrs. Fields' Cookies* and *Batterymarch Financial Management*). Recalling the example presented in Chapter 3, the two original cases had the following characteristics in common:

1. Were founded by CEOs who were more than a bit inclined to make statements that skirted the border of confidence and arrogance.

2. Replaced tasks formerly performed by humans with computers (at *Mrs. Fields'* computers took control of nearly every aspect of cookie production; at *Batterymarch*, they controlled the portfolio and trading functions)

3. Relied heavily on quantitative computer models

4. Had evolved organizational structures that were vastly more streamlined than those of their competitors

5. Had experienced growth and performance that were extraordinary by industry standards

6. Had been described by the press and in research publications as being the future of the 21st century organization.

What I needed then was a case example that was superficially similar but which had a significantly different outcome. The example I came up with was Microsoft, with specific reference to its *Microsoft Developer Network* MSDN program.

With the two earlier cases, Microsoft shared attributes 1, 5 & 6. It also, quite obviously, had the capability to employ computers in any way it chose to. What impressed me about its MSDN program in particular was the way it spared no expense in reaching out to its developer community, providing multiple forums for sharing information. Because developer communities tend to be at the leading edge of technology in organizations, I argued that Microsoft would have a powerful advantage in anticipating and reacting to trends as a consequence of these relationships. This, I contended was a fundamental difference between that company and its otherwise similar counterparts in the paper.

While it remains fashionable to bash Microsoft for a variety of reasons, the fact remains that the company has successfully navigated the waters of two gigantic shifts in its industry: 1) from standalone text-based computers to networked graphic operating systems, and 2) from desktop-centric to Internet-centric software. For a large company occupying fitness peaks in pre-transition environments, this is a remarkable accomplishment for an organization. I remain convinced that its tight relationship with its developers was a major contributor to this success.

F. Can We Extend a Conceptual Scheme?

On a rugged landscape, the safest assumption is always that any phenomenon observed is local to the particular region. Where two dissimilar case studies observe the same phenomenon, we have evidence that our conceptual scheme is robust. This is best illustrated by taking examples from very different regions of a landscape and showing that they exhibit similar patterns of behavior. This was illustrated in Chapter 3 with the High Tech Hidebound example.

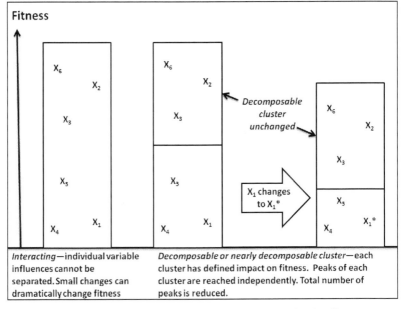

Figure 5.2: The existence of decomposable clusters in the fitness space simplifies study of fitness

One particularly important type of extension of boundaries that case method research may be able to identify is the existence of *decomposable or nearly decomposable clusters* of factors within the fitness landscape. Rather than assuming that individual variables act on fitness independently (as is true for a decomposable landscape), it assumes that clusters of variables do so, as illustrated in Figure 5.2. For example, researchers might discover that factors relating to motivation and factors relating to skills already acquired act decomposably on learning rate (a highly unlikely finding, to be sure, but bear with me for the purposes of the example). That would provide a justification for experiments or surveys dealing only with motivation, controlling for other factors through techniques such as random block assignment. It also would provide a rationale for theory fragments relating only to motivation that only explain a portion of fitness. None of these widely used approaches are truly rigorous if interactions between motivation and other non-motivational variables exist.

The existence of decomposable clusters (or nearly decomposable clusters, since true decomposability is unlikely to be provable on a complex landscape) also impacts the number of peaks and search strategies. With respect to peaks, each cluster will have its own set of peaks and the total number of peaks will be the product of the two (once you reach the peak of one cluster, you have a choice of peaks for the others). This division can lead to a significant drop in the peak count. Using Kauffman's formula for estimated peaks in a complex landscape ($2^N/(N+1)$), suppose we decompose 8 variables into 2 clusters of 4. Peaks change from:

$$\sim 28 = 2^8/9$$

to

$$\sim 10 = (2^4/5)(2^4/5)$$

Search strategies may also change, since variables in each cluster can be changed and their impact observed independently.

This type of landscape survey research will necessarily require a lot of case studies, so it is likely to involve some type of meta-analysis. Such a design would not, itself, represent case method research. The goal of demonstrating cluster decomposability, on the other hand, might drive the selection of case sites.

Alternative Case Research Designs

The choice of a case research design will necessarily be a function of research question and opportunism. In case method research, it is not uncommon for opportunism to be the driving force. This sounds unscientific, without a doubt. But recall, once again, that there is little justification for the case method if our findings are not put to work.

Single Case Designs

Single case designs may involve a single snapshot or a longitudinal set of observations. The benefits of single case designs are their simplicity and the depth of investigation they permit. The principle drawback is that they offer few insights, if any, as to how widespread the phenomena being reported are likely to be.

Single snapshots

Perhaps the least versatile of the designs, the single case snapshot is a detailed look at an entity at a single point in time. While this design is typical of discussion cases, it often leads to objections when employed in a research setting. It is truly the despised N of 1 design.

Despite these concerns, there are a variety of valid reasons for developing single case snapshots. Among these:

1. *The situation being observed is very interesting.* If we accept the fact that diffusion is an integral part of the research process, then an interesting story brings with it high informing potential. What makes a case interesting is a departure from the conventional wisdom (i.e., widely held conceptual schemes) that is not so large as to strain credibility (Davis, 1971).

2. *The situation illustrates techniques for searching for improving fitness.* As noted earlier in the chapter, techniques for adapting to higher fitness can be expected to generalize better than research reporting factors that impact fitness.

3. *The potential audience includes practicing experts.* On a complex landscape, the reader of the case plays an integral part in assessing its quality. The reason is that the expert reader may be in the best position to assess whether the activities described in a case would apply to his or her particular situation in the landscape.

4. *The case is part of a program to collect observations on a particular landscape.* Just because a research project consists one case does not mean that it cannot also be part of a more systematic effort to survey an entire landscape.

5. *The case is viewed from the perspective of alternative conceptual schemes.* Where multiple conceptual schemes exist that could be applied to a given situation, even one example may be used to explore the potential applicability of each to the specific case.

The last of these can be illustrated by a well-known example.

Example: Allison's Essence of Decision

One of the best known examples of case study research is Graham T. Allison's (1971) *Essence of Decision: Explaining the Cuban Missile Crisis*. This book takes a look at a single incident in U.S. history, the 1962 Cuban Missile Crisis and analyzes it from three different perspectives:

1. *The rational actor model.* In this model, the entities involved— normally treated at the "country" or "group of senior decision makers" level—are treated as rational decision makers. Events are described as if the situation evolved like a giant chess game.

2. *The organizational process model.* In this model, participants are viewed as organizations imbued with allocations of authority by organizational unit, a set of standard operating procedures and established decision-making processes that ultimately produce a plan of action as their collective output.

3. *The governmental politics model.* In this model, the organizations involved are decisions are viewed as consisting of self-interested agents whose motivation is to maximize their own position within each organization, particularly as it pertains to power. Unlike the second model, each group within the organization seeks to locally optimize its own situation, leading to decisions that often include elements that are not necessarily consistent with the whole. This s largely because they are arrived at independently.

Allison leans towards the last of these perspectives, arguing that it best explains the case. I would argue, however, that this conclusion will largely depend on the mental models of the client reading the case.

None of the perspectives described is likely to represent "truth" in any real way. I make this assertion because political scientists are among the expert categories least able to predict the future based on present circumstances[5].

Longitudinal cases

The longitudinal case can be used to bring an experimental flavor to a single case research activity. Typically, the focus of the longitudinal case is on what happens in response to each change that occurs. Because other factors (e.g., industry, students, employees) often remain constant over the course of the process during which other variable values change, potential conclusions, or at least speculations, about cause-and-effect can be proposed.

The potential weakness of the longitudinal case in complex environments is that, over time, we can expect the fitness landscape on which the environment exists to change. Thus, it is not always clear whether a change observed subsequent to an action taken by the entity under study is entirely due to the action taken or to other factors not measured.

Multiple Case Designs

Case research can benefit greatly from incorporating more than one case. In general, these designs are intended to investigate the applicability of a conceptual scheme across a particular landscape of interest. From a publication standpoint, multiple case designs tend to be viewed favorably by comparison to their single case counterparts. In some situations, this preference may be justified.

Multiple case treatments

Multiple cases are often presented as a form of quasi-experimental treatment. As simplifying rules, I would propose the following:

1. Where the goal is to show a conceptual scheme is widely applicable, investigate cases that are a dissimilar as possible and show the scheme holds across them.

2. Where the goal is to establish the boundaries of a conceptual scheme, choose very similar cases that have very different outcomes (this can also be done with longitudinal case designs).

It is also possible to employ hybrid designs, as the following example illustrates.

Example: A Tale of Three Classes

Included as Appendix E of this book, this multi case action research project was intended to highlight the complexity of the IS education space. This particular research represented an amalgam of research questions, but was particularly focused on Question E (What are the limits of a conceptual scheme?) in that its goal was to show that no conceptual scheme could be applied that would explain the entire landscape.

In order to demonstrate complexity, the research employed a hybrid multi-case/longitudinal design. In order to demonstrate that that content could not be treated as decomposable from the other key elements of the instructional setting (e.g., instructor, delivery approach), two courses with similar content but different instructors were examined (Ism3232.A and Ism3232.B). In order to demonstrate that content was not decomposable, two courses with very different content but the same instructor were included (Ism3232.A and Ism6155.A). In order to demonstrate that delivery method alone was not a determining factor, a single course that evolved from classroom delivery to delivery that was largely online and self-paced was examined longitudinally (Ism3232.A). This longitudinal analysis also was used to illustrate how seemingly small changes to a course could lead to large changes in apparent fitness. The design is illustrated in Figure 5.3, taken from the actual article.

As mentioned in a previous example, all three courses were—at the time the cross-sectional profile was taken (Fall 2007)—at a very high fitness level based upon multiple sources of evidence. What was particularly significant about this was the fact that Instructor A and Instructor B in the case (myself and Joni Jones, respectively) ran our programming courses in a manner that was as different as could be imagined (the differences are highlighted in Table 2 of Appendix E). The history of the course, presented in the longitudinal version of Appendix

---

E, illustrated that such high fitness outcomes were far from typical for the course. The longitudinal analysis further showed how both high fitness and low fitness outcomes could be achieved by the same instructor and could be impacted by seemingly minor changes to the course (illustrated in Table 3 of Appendix E).

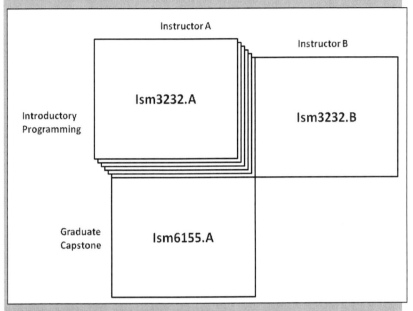

Figure 5.3: General Research Design.

As a consequence of demonstrating that dissimilar treatments had similar outcomes (cross course comparisons) while similar offerings sometimes had very different outcomes (longitudinal comparisons) a strong case for landscape complexity was made.

Statistical multiple case designs

With enough case studies in a multiple case design, it may even be possible to establish statistical significance using the cases being researched. Where many variables are involved, the number of cases required rises substantially; I've seen reviewers express concerns when the number drops below 50-60. That implies either a very long data gathering process or, perhaps, an analysis using existing case observations (e.g., undisguised discussion case write ups).

Covering the statistical analysis of large samples of rich data is beyond the scope of this book[6]. In *Informing Business* (Gill, 2010) I spend an entire chapter describing my own foray into statistical analysis of a large number of cases. The purpose of that chapter, however, is not to praise the approach but to critique it. The statistical techniques that we use to analyze large samples with many attributes almost uniformly assume decomposability of effects as a starting point. Results of these methods cannot be trusted if some measure of fitness is the dependent variable (Gill & Sincich, 2008). Thus, as a case method researcher, I have grown increasingly suspicious of my own quantitative findings.

Having made this disclaimer, I would certainly not turn down a large sample of cases with a summary of case attributes. I might even be willing to apply techniques such as analysis of variance to determine what attributes, on average, most contribute to fitness. My motivation in doing so, however, would not be to report these averages per se. What would interest me most is identifying high fitness examples in the sample that appear inconsistent with these averages and low fitness examples that conform to the averaged "best practices". These cases would be the particular subject of further study. Whereas most statistical methods appear to work best when plausible reasons for excluding outliers can be manufactured, the case method works best when outliers are used to help map out the boundaries of the rugged landscape.

Fortunately, case method researchers do not have to rely solely on statistical evidence to build their arguments or support their findings. Instead, they can employ the flexibility in the types of data acquired and in the types of methods employed to buttress support for their conclusions. This use of multiple sources of evidence is generally referred to as triangulation.

Triangulation

One of the greatest benefits of case research is the ability to triangulate during data acquisition. Before I would willingly participate in a case method research project, I would want to be sure that that I was likely to have access to a variety of data sources as part of the design. Triangulation can, however, extend considerably beyond using multiple data sources.

There are four generally accepts forms of triangulation (Yin, 2009; Patton, 2002): data triangulation, investigator triangulation, theory triangulation and methodology triangulation. Each can be employed within a case method research design.

Data Triangulation

Data triangulation involves acquiring data from multiple sources. As discussed in Chapter 4, this form of triangulation tends to be situation specific and also applies equally well to the development of both research and discussion cases.

Investigator Triangulation

Investigator triangulation is achieved by having more than one investigator. This would be particularly applicable to research cases, and can be very useful in addressing concerns of the subjectivity of observations. For example, if it can be shown that two investigators subjectively characterize the same set of observations similarly, inter-rater reliability can be established. An example of this technique is now described.

Example: Strategic Systems Research Project

The strategic systems research project was developed as both a course activity for the graduate MS-MIS capstone (see Appendix F) that I taught and to serve as the basis of a long term research project. The project revolved around fostering a deeper understanding of the nature of "strategic information systems"—not just for the students in the class, but within the MIS community at large.

The role played by each individual student in the project was to choose two systems (drawn from a list of over a hundred systems compiled by the instructor and a doctoral student) then to:

a) Conduct a detailed archival review of all available information on each system

b) Classify the systems according to schemes developed in references provided by the instructor, and

c) Trace their impact to the present day.

Once a student had completed a draft report, it was then reviewed by either the instructor or a doctoral candidate who would comment on its completeness, its reasoning (all classifications had to be justified with an explanation based on information related to the specific system) and

---

its overall quality. The comments were then returned to the student, who incorporated them into the final system description.

Each system description constituted a case study derived from whatever data sources were available (which varied widely by system). In the first phase of the project, two completely independent cases on the same system were prepared; the independence of the studies was enhanced by preventing the same system from being studied more than once in the same or adjacent semesters. In the second phase of the project, consolidated reports were prepared by a third group of students who determined what material differences, if any, existed between the two independent reports. The final stage involved creating an online database of the case studies containing the consolidated reports and source data. By the time this stage was completed, in 2007, nearly 400 separate documents had been prepared[7].

The principal impact of the research project to date[8] has been to confirm a suspicion that began to emerge in my earlier expert system research: large databases of examples cannot be assumed accurate. As was the case with expert systems, quite a number of the systems listed as "strategic" to their firms in the literature may have never existed as more than a press release. For many other systems, the strategic character of their impact was hard to justify. Here we see concrete evidence that in questioning the rigor of case method research, it is wise to do so not against an objective standard of truth, but rather against the standard set by other research method alternatives.

Theory Triangulation

Theory triangulation[9] involves considering a case from more than one theoretical perspective. We earlier saw an example of this in Allison's (1971) *Essence of Decision*. In Chapter 6, this approach is considered further. It serves to demonstrate that the investigator is open to multiple points of view, which can be viewed as a defense against subjectivity.

Theory triangulation can also represent a defense against what I have referred to elsewhere as *powder puff tests*. In hypothesis testing, there is little challenge to demonstrating that a plausible theory is more likely than no theory whatsoever. As a consequence, it is easy to reject ridiculous null hypotheses (e.g., system usefulness *does not* contribute to system use). Rigor, however, demands that we consider challenging hypotheses. A good way of achieving this it to compare two plausible theories (conceptual schemes) against each other and then assess which more comfortably accommodates the facts of the case. We saw an example of this in the earlier Allison (1971) example.

Methodological Triangulation

Methodological triangulation involves employing different research methodologies in a case research project. Obviously, one aspect of this can be found in data triangulation, since some data collection activities (such as surveys) may require active investigator involvement whereas others, such as searching through an archive of emails, may involve a more passive approach.

One particularly common form of triangulation involves mixing qualitative and quantitative methods. Within a case study situation, for example, the principle unit of analysis (e.g., the company, the course) may consist of many sub units (e.g., the employees, the students) that can be surveyed or otherwise studied using the tools of statistical analysis. From a publication perspective, such a combination of methodologies is advantageous, since the open minded reviewer will nearly always be able to find some methodological aspects of the research that meets his or her approval.

Example: Ism3232 Course Survey

As discussed in Appendix E, in 2004 I decided to implement a survey in Ism3232.A (the undergraduate programming course) that would provide detailed information about the course as it evolved. The purpose of the survey was not research-oriented (or, more accurately, was not publication-oriented). Instead, it was intended to provide detailed information that could be used for tracking purposes. Sections included:

1. Items on student demographics

2. Items on student past experience with computers (coursework, professional experience and recreational experience, as in computer games)

3. Items reflecting time commitment and workload relative to other courses

---

4. Detailed feedback on each assignment

5. Items regarding student reactions to how content was delivered

6. Items relating to student satisfaction

7. Items relating to student perceptions of learning gains

Some examples of questions asked are included in Exhibit G of Appendix I.

The survey typically consisted of 250-300 items presented on a spreadsheet. Students received extra credit (in the form of a + added to whatever letter grade they received) for completing the survey, leading to response rates that were typically 60-70% enrolled students. Anonymity was preserved by having students send the completed survey to a departmental assistant who provided the instructor with a list of students submitting forms (for extra credit purposes) but not the forms themselves until roughly a month after grades had been submitted.

Although the survey was not intended as a research instrument, the historical data record it provided proved instrumental in identifying areas of the class that were successful and that needed changing. As case study manuscripts involving the course were prepared, the quantitative results from the survey provided an excellent supplement to the qualitative description and to more general measures of fitness (such as teaching evaluations, grades and attrition.) In total, analysis of survey results was incorporated into about 10 refereed case study publications[10].

Human Subjects Issues

Case research, almost as a matter of course, involves observing human activities. As such, particularly in the U.S., it may require oversight by an institutional review board (IRB). Such boards were established principally to address valid concerns in three areas:

1. *Privacy*: ensuring that the privacy of human subjects is appropriately protected

2. *Informed consent*: verifying that subjects are informed of, and consent to, all experimental risks

3. *Appropriate design:* validating that research designs maximize privacy and eliminate unnecessary risks.

The intent of these boards and the associated institutional policies is admirable. Unfortunately, they are not necessarily attuned to the multiple methodologies, flexible goals and adaptive nature of case method research. When dealing with medical or psychological experiments, they reasonably demand documentation of an unambiguous set of research questions, a clearly defined experimental method and, where applicable, specific interview protocols that detail every question to be asked. It is not unusual for an exploratory case method research project to begin without any of the aforementioned documentation. It would therefore not be unreasonable for such an IRB to conclude that the research is too nebulous to be permitted.

Yin (2009) points out that the attitudes towards case research of IRBs are likely to vary widely from institution to institution. He recommends informally sounding out individual IRB members prior to submitting a proposal—sound advice, to be sure. It may also be possible to acquire an exemption from IRB requirements for a number of reasons. Some reasonable arguments might include the fact that there are no "human subjects" in case method research. Particularly in action research methodologies where practitioners are enlisted as co-authors, everyone involved is an expert and everyone involved is an investigator. Under such circumstances, even figuring out who should be signing informed consent documents can be confusing. It is also not unusual for case research to evolve from other relationships, such as consulting engagements[11], that do not normally require IRB approval. At what point should an IRB become involved in such a fluid process? Finally, there are specific exemptions in the U.S. guidelines for protecting human subjects that apply to standard educational practices. We return to these in Chapter 7, where we look at specific issues related to discussion case development. In Appendix I, I also include an evaluation plan that succeeded in making it through the USF IRB for an NSF grant that involved the development and evaluation of discussion cases.

However one chooses to handle the protection of human subjects during case research, it is critical that the issue be addressed in the research design. Generally, the earlier in the process it is considered, the less likely it will become a problem as the project unfolds.

Conclusions

Employing a research design that is a good fit with your research objectives and that demonstrates that attention was paid to validity can greatly increase the likelihood that the research will be credible (and published!) As a result of its exploratory outlook, case method research needs to incorporate considerable flexibility into whatever designs it employs. That does not absolve the researcher from the responsibility of planning what can be planned. At a minimum, such a plan should include:

- A rationale for why case method research is likely to be more appropriate than other forms of research

- A general category of question or questions that the intended research is intended to answer

- A design framework (e.g., single case or multi-case, cross-sectional or longitudinal) and justification as to how that framework is suitable for investigating the questions being asked

- A plan to address the validity issues that are frequently the basis of criticisms leveled against case research

- A means of gaining approval or exemption from institutional review standards for human subjects research, where applicable.

With these items accomplished, it the researcher is in a good position to commence the case research and write up, the subject of the next chapter.

Chapter 5 Notes

---

[1] Fritz Roethlisberger (1977) was a collaborator with Mayo on a number of important research projects, such as the famous Hawthorne experiments.

[2] With respect to the length of case studies and journal page counts, I speak from experience. A few years ago, I was designated to be the editor of a special issue of the *Decision Sciences Journal of Innovative Educa-*

tion (DSJIE), where I was an Associate Editor (AE). The call for papers specifically requested case research and I submitted one study of my own. The editorial for that manuscript were then assigned to another AE for obvious reasons. The reviewer comments came back fairly critical but, to my mind, most were right on the mark. There were two, however, that I simply could not abide: I was told to cut the submission's length by over 33% (from over 30 pages to 20 pages) and I was told to make in more anonymous. I explained to the Editor-in-Chief that I would eagerly incorporate all the remaining comments, but felt that the required length and anonymity changes would threaten the integrity of the piece. When he indicated that he was uncomfortable overruling the AE, I withdrew the piece, resigned from the journal as AE, offered my resignation as editor of the special topic issue (which was accepted) and let my membership to the *Decision Sciences Institute* expire. Such a fit of pique is not characteristic of me. But I am sufficiently passionate about case method research that I did not feel right about being party to silly rules that could undermine its rigor or perceived rigor.

As a matter of closure, my co-author Joni Jones and I incorporated all the changes suggested by the DSJIE reviewers—which, I repeat, were quite excellent overall, excepting the two regarding length and anonymity—and submitted it to the *Journal of IT Education* (JITE). There the review process went much more smoothly.

As it happens, because the *Informing Science Institute* allows free use of its publications within its other publications, the JITE article became the research case that is presented as Appendix E. For that reason, I am very grateful to DSJIE for enforcing its policy, however much I happen to disagree with it.

³ Gosset was, in fact, a brewer employed by Guinness whose initial research in statistics was published under the pseudonym Student. He was responsible for the Student's T test—the precise test used to assess the significance of coefficients in multiple regression models. Ironically, he did not see much practical use for significance testing. He was much more interested in the economic value of applying statistical techniques. As Ziliak and McCloskey (2008) describe it, that attitude often put him in conflict with Ronald Fisher, whose advocacy of significance testing was unwavering.

[4] The title of the book *The Black Swan* comes from the fact that since all swans in Europe happened to be white, the probability of a black swan was estimated to be zero. That estimate remained in force until, lo and behold, black swans were observed in Australia. His point is that there some things you simply cannot estimate based on past experience. This reasoning applies to fitness—there is simply no way we can be entirely sure if our measures accurately determine the underlying fitness of an entity.

[5] Consider the case of Soviet experts who, when asked in 1988, split almost 50-50 on whether or not the communists would still be in control by 1993 (Tetlock, 2000).

[6] There are many treatments of multivariate techniques and survey analysis that the reader can refer to that are equally applicable to large samples of case studies.

[7] The entire strategic systems project represented a total of between 5,000 and 10,000 self-reported student-hours of labor, conducted over a period of 5 years (10 semesters).

[8] As of this writing, I am still trying to figure out what the archive can best be used for in a research context. Because it is historical in nature, I do not feel the time pressure I would have otherwise experienced with such data in hand.

[9] In deference to its originators, I will not refer to theory triangulation as conceptual scheme triangulation, although that is obviously what I mean.

[10] The precise number of studies incorporating results from the Ism3232 survey depends on how you classify discussion cases (3) and non-specific teaching briefs (2).

[11] That case studies result from consulting arrangements is frequently the pattern in business.

Chapter 6

Conducting Case Method Research

Writing a research case, or any field case, can entail a considerable investment in time. In the previous chapter, the importance of design was emphasized. There are, however, many other practical considerations that must be addressed when writing a research case. In this chapter we address a number of these.

The first point to be made is that design does not necessarily precede the identification of a suitable research case site. Because of the heavy investment of time required by field research, the researcher would do well to permit a bit of opportunism to creep into his or her selection of projects. Very often, observation will suggest an incongruity that warrants further research. The case researcher should be open to such inspiration.

Another important issue is researcher involvement in the case being studied. At one extreme, we have the dispassionate observer who takes care never to interfere with the situation under study, even when possessing knowledge that could be beneficial to those being observed. At the other extreme we have the participant-researcher, actively involved in the process under study. I will argue that neither of these perspectives is inherently better than the other—and that a balance between the two is often the most sensible approach.

In composing the research case itself, two issues that invariably surface are length and anonymity. For reasons I will detail, length will likely be a constant battle in case research write-ups. Anonymity proves to be a double edged sword—the demands of rigor argue both for maintaining it and abandoning it entirely. Thus, we find that the policies of the outlets we choose can exert a significant, and not altogether healthy, influence on the expression of our research.

Despite these challenges, I have found that—contrary to popular myth—well constructed case research is generally well received by even the most elite of research journals. The trick is to ensure that you have followed the rules of research cases, and have not confused a research case with its discussion case counterpart.

Agile Research Methods

Perhaps as a result of my own background in management information systems (MIS), I see strong parallels between how we conduct research and how we build information systems. Traditional research protocols exhibit many parallels to the systems development lifecycle (SDLC) that, for several decades, was the gold standard for building information systems. In the past couple of decades, however, alternative approaches that are considerably more flexible—collectively referred to as agile development methods—have come to play an increasingly important role in building systems. I propose that case method research is more effective when it uses these latter approaches as a model. In this section, I explain and develop this proposition more fully.

Traditional Research Lifecycle

The traditional research lifecycle begins with a researcher, motivated by some identified hole or inconsistency in the research literature or grant opportunity. That researcher then sets out to find sites perfectly suited to addressing the research question, creates an appropriate design, then (and only then) begins data gathering. Once systematic data gathering is complete, analysis is conducted. Based on the results of the analysis, books, papers and other reports, such as conference presentations and seminars, are prepared. I would illustrate this overall research approach as follows:

Design → Investigate → Analyze → Disseminate

A certain amount of research that explores complex landscapes actually proceeds according to this plan. My experience suggests this to be particularly true when research is conducted under strong external constraints, such as requirements established in a research proposal (e.g., a doctoral thesis, grant-funded research). In case method research, however, you may pay a heavy price for strictly adhering to such a protocol. I illustrate this with an example from my own experience.

Example: Expert System Tools and Tasks

To illustrate the challenges that traditional design presents in the context of case method research, I use my doctoral dissertation as an example. Prior to describing the dissertation process itself, it is useful to present some background that will clarify how it emerged. I entered the HBS doctoral program after spending three years as an agribusiness consultant at a now defunct firm called *Agribusiness Associates*. While working there, I had taken my rudimentary knowledge of computer modeling (acquired during a summer job between my two MBA years in 1981) and built it into a full-fledged modeling and simulation practice. Without the benefit of any formal training (and relying heavily on my intuition) I had developed a diverse set of models that included studies of high fructose corn syrup production plants, citrus prices, soft drink syrup distribution, duck processing, pesticide application, and restaurant home delivery effectiveness. These models had been quite profitable for the firm (generating about $250,000/year in average billings) and had led to three promotions within my first 18 months, by which time my title had become Senior Vice President, Technical Services. These models were also becoming an increasing source of unease to me, however. After all, I had no formal training in the area and was therefore basing them heavily on my intuition and self-taught programming skills. I had this nagging suspicion that there was more about computer modeling that I needed to know.

In early 1985, I made the decision that I would return to school for my doctorate. My choice of the MIS discipline was based almost entirely on the opportunity it offered to further develop my computer skills. At that point in time, I had never read an academic MIS article in my life[1]. My choice of classes was entirely consistent with this motivation[2], with less than 1/3 of my course work being directly related to business research—compared with over 50% taken in the computer and cognitive sciences field at Harvard's GSAS and MIT's Graduate School of Engineering. This balance did not go unnoticed by my HBS advisors, nor was it discouraged. To the contrary, it was applauded. Thus, I had no concern about selecting a highly technical dissertation topic.

Expert systems, the topic area I settled upon, are a type of computer application where the knowledge of human experts is encoded into rule-like forms in order to perform tasks that would otherwise be very hard to program. My interest in expert systems developed as a result of both my course work and some teaching case studies of operational systems that I wrote with Dr. John Sviokla—a newly appointed assistant professor at the time. With my interest in building things, I quickly became enthused by the broad array of tools available for constructing such systems. I also noticed that while the rapidly expanding research and practitioner literature continually emphasized the importance of achieving task-tool fit, it provided absolutely no practical guidance on how such fit should be achieved. I therefore decided that determining how the underlying characteristics of a task determine the most appropriate tools for constructing a corresponding expert system would be an interesting topic to study. Having given them no particular reason to disagree, my dissertation committee approved.

Starting in the fall of 1988, I began visiting companies while, at the same time, doing a longitudinal study of the development of a large system by a local startup firm that had been founded by MIT faculty members. With a $10,000 research travel and expense budget, I could go practically anywhere. During the early stages of my investigation, I travelled to California to visit AI tool makers, to Houston to watch an expert gate scheduling system being implemented, and to numerous sites along the U.S. East Coast to meet with system managers and developers. I learned a great deal from these conversations and observations. Perhaps the most important thing I learned was that I had chosen a dissertation topic that was of no concern to practice.

As it happens, there were many interesting issues and problems that I did observe. For example:

1. Did developers choose tasks based on the tool they had available or did they choose the best tool for the task?

2. Did knowledge of a particular tool influence how developers perceived the task they were trying to implement?

3. The systems I examined included both successes and systems that never made it past prototype stage. One thing I noticed was that systems that took away the user's discretion without offering something in return almost never made it into actual use.

The problem was that my design was not built around looking for or at these issues. As a result, I gave them a page or two in my "directions for future research" section and filed it away for later reference[3]. In the meantime, I continued to push forward on my original topic[4]. The result was a dissertation that was breathtaking in its uselessness to any conceivable audience.

In many ways, the traditional approach to research that I have described parallels the SDLC in information systems. The SDLC was born out of the chaos that computer systems experienced in the mid-1960s, when programs started to become too big for a small team of developers and too expensive to be written off if they failed to deliver. It represented an attempt by management to exert a greater degree of control over systems development and delivery. Although there are many variations, most correspond roughly[5] to a pattern of:

Design → Construct → Test → Implement

Similar to traditional research, the expectation is that each stage will be completed in sequence and activities in one stage will not begin until all activities of the previous stage are completed.

The SDLC still has many adherents, and remains widely used for certain types of applications—particularly those where the objectives or reliability, control and accountability trump other all concerns. Its uncompromising use does, however, present a number of practical issues. As a general rule:

1. *It takes a very long time to build a system.* As a result, in a dynamic environment it is not unusual for designs to become obsolete even before system construction is completed.

2. *It is extremely rigid in its policies.* For example, to ensure that users accept a system once it is created, they may be required to sign off on mock-ups of the interface. Modifications to these are often frozen to prevent scope creep and frequent changes that slow development.

3. *It encourages users to bypass formal development processes.* Rather than involve an MIS department that would require the SDLC, user departments will find ways to construct systems on their own, even though they may introduce serious problems (such as security holes) by doing so.

The traditional research lifecycle suffers from precisely the same weaknesses. It takes a long time to plan. The demands of rigor require that a research protocol—once established—be followed faithfully. Where potential clients of the research need results in a hurry, they tend to bypass formal research channels and strike out on their own. Consider, for example, the popularity of "self-help" books of questionable pedigree in comparison with scholarly works in fields such as psychology.

Agile Methods

In systems development, one response to the weaknesses of the SDLC has been the development of agile methods. The methods, which include techniques such as successive prototyping and rely heavily on the use of tools that blend design and construction, can—in their most extreme form—lead to a lifecycle that is the polar opposite of the SDLC. For example, their principles include[6]:

1. *Rapid development.* The emphasis of these tools is to get a working system—often providing limited functionality—out to users as soon as possible. Functionality is then enhanced through successive versioning.

2. *Flexibility in design.* Rather than mapping out a complete design in advance, design decisions are strongly influenced by an iterative process guided by user feedback and performance results of earlier versions.

3. *Heavy user involvement.* Rather than providing users with a completed system at the time of delivery, users are integrated into the development process and often make key design decisions along the way.

Naturally, in addressing the problems of the SDLC, agile methods introduce a number of potential problems of their own. For applications that have security, reliability, accountability or long term architectural implications, excessive reliance on agile methods can create serious risks for the future. Users tend to be focused on their own problems. System security, backup and architectural issues may not be perceived as being of concern—until such time as they actually occur and massively disrupt user activities. Also, agile development tends to be locally focused on the problems at hand. As such, it tends to discount long term system integration issues[7]. Thus, for some applications, strict controls such as those provided by the SDLC might prove a better choice.

For others, agile methods provide a pathway to getting useful systems up and running quickly.

Agile Research Methods

The core principles of agile software development can be translated directly to research[8]. To adhere to these principles, the research lifecycle must be:

1. Completed rapidly, from design to dissemination.

2. Flexible in its conduct with respect to any initial research design

3. Conducted in close collaboration with the potential users of the findings—this would refer to practitioners in most professional research contexts.

Just as was true for software development, we would not expect agile research methods to be equally appropriate in all research settings. If your research requires the construction of a $10 billion super-collider, you'd better have some very well defined research questions and methods in place to justify the expenditure. If your research is studying a treatment involving human subjects in a life and death setting, safeguards against casual changes to the research protocol need to be enforced. If your research is intended to address a very well defined question that needs to be asked in a particular way, agility might simply be a code word for sloppiness.

On the other hand, for research conducted in a dynamic and complex environment where practice has traditionally been skeptical of academic research findings, agile research methods might be just the approach to transform the situation. We now consider its three elements in turn.

Rapid completion and dissemination

One of the key forces driving a complex landscape is changes to the fitness function. These changes may be the result of the landscapes internal dynamics or of the behavior (e.g., co-evolution, discontinuities) of related systems. The more complex the system, the more dynamic the fitness landscape tends to be.

For research to be useful in such a landscape, it often must be conducted and disseminated quickly. There are many researchers who believe that domains evolving so rapidly are not an appropriate area for academic study; that we should instead be focused on studying those principles that endure. This is certainly a noble sentiment. Unfortunately, in a complex landscape there are likely to be very few of these principles. Certainly, in my research domain of MIS there is relatively little we could assert about building systems today that would have been equally true two decades ago. And even less if you choose to exclude the immediately obvious.

Case method research, as I have defined it[9], can be conducted very rapidly. Indeed, it often *has to be conducted quickly* because the problem-focused approach of case method research proceeds at rate dictated by the landscape. Events will not wait for the researcher before unfolding. Only delays in writing up the research and lengthy publication cycles will tend to elongate the complete cycle. Thus, consistency with agile research methods would advocate publishing working papers—for example, registered with the SSRN[10]—as quickly as possible, then revising as necessary.

Flexibility in design

As described in the earlier example, the traditional research lifecycle often puts the investigator in a bind. Some design documents—such as a dissertation proposal or an approved grant proposal—require that a particular set of questions be addressed and prevents the design from being modified in the event the original questions prove uninteresting or the researcher encounters other questions that are more interesting. Examples of what might make for an interesting question could be virtually any item from the list of questions presented in the previous chapter and might be inspired by:

- *Unexpected observations*: Results inconsistent with our predictions, which would include most outliers.

- *Oddly similar pairs of observations*: Results we expect to be different prove to be similar.

- *Oddly dissimilar pairs of observations*: Results we expected to be similar are very different.

- *Patterns in sets of observations*: The emergence of patterns that suggest relationships that were not previously hypothesized.

- *Evidence that our original research questions are not interesting to practitioners:* This could be true because practitioners already feel they know the answer or because they see little benefit to answering the question accurately[11].

- *Evidence that questions other than the ones you asked are of greater interest to practitioners:* As the context of the case unfolds during the course of an investigation, it may become clear that a related question, requiring a modification to the research design, would be more useful[12].

The negative side of agile research methods, in this context, would be that a researcher could easily modify the questions being asked to those for which the answers being given are the ones preferred. In that way, results inconsistent with the conceptual scheme being presented could be covered up[13].

Tight engagement with practitioners

Agile software methods require tight involvement with users because users drive the direction of development. A system that is not used is a waste, and agile methods hate waste with a passion.

Generalizing this to research, we have two potential user groups: other researchers and practitioners. I will assert that for any research whose questions revolved around improving the fitness of practice, practitioners must be cast in the role of users. This is not all of our research[14], but it is a great deal of it.

Obviously, field studies employing case method research tend to include, if not require, tight engagement with practice. Unfortunately, that tight relationship with practice may provoke concern among those more comfortable with the traditional research lifecycle. It is common to refer to research in which the researcher is an active participant as "action research". Short of full involvement, however, researchers may occasionally become involved through offering advice. Suppose, for example, you were doing educational research and you happened to know a technique that was particularly effective in dealing with a problem facing the research participants, such as a disruptive student. Would it be appropriate—or even ethical—to withhold such knowledge from the participants for the sake of maintaining the objectivity of the research? Let me hasten to add that I do not believe there is necessarily an easy answer to this question. But issues such as this will nearly always arise in case method research projects that incorporate field observations.

There are two particularly strong arguments for high levels of researcher engagement with the actual participants[15] of the research project. The first is that such engagement will tend to build trust. In the presence of such trust, freer and more accurate information exchange between researcher and participant can be expected. The second argument is that where the researcher is actively involved in the situation being researched, a measure of research impact is assured—more or less as a matter of definition. More broadly, however, the relationships built through such engagement establish a channel through which future knowledge can diffuse (in both directions, I quickly add).

Are Agile Research Methods Rigorous?

Before leaving the subject of agile research methods, the question needs to be asked: Are they rigorous? Quite honestly, it is a difficult argument to make (and one you will need to make if you want to justify your case method research). Picture yourself standing in front of an audience of your peers. Then imagine yourself asserting the following:

> We should be doing our research as quickly as possible, change research questions when it suits our needs and become heavily involved the processes that we are researching even if doing so threatens our objectivity.

I can almost guarantee that the reception you get will not be enthusiastic. Indeed, I would likely encourage you to wait until you are tenured before you try it.

Having stated the opposing side let me now offer another perspective. "Are agile research methods rigorous?" is the wrong question to ask. The better question is as follows:

> When the environment being studied is complex, are agile research methods likely to be more rigorous than traditional research methods?

In a debate framed in this manner, I would gladly take the side of agility. Traditional research methods, when applied in complex settings, have two serious weaknesses:

1. Traditional research methods for establishing rigor, particularly statistical methods, rely on a number of assumptions that do not make sense when the underlying environment is complex. This horse has pretty much been beaten to death in Chapter 2 and, particularly, in *Informing Business* (Gill, 2010).

2. We cannot really tell if the theories of traditional research are rigorous if such research rarely makes its way into practice. This is particularly a problem in business research, which nearly never makes its way into practice (Pfeffer, 2007; Hambrick, 2007). Absent diffusion of academic research to practice, where do the practical tests of the predictive capacity of business theory come from?

With agile research methods, such as case method research, the seriousness of these two issues is greatly reduced. Furthermore, in conducting the research, there are a number of techniques that can be applied to enhance the rigor of our findings. We now turn to the subject of validity.

Building Case Method Research Validity

Promoting case method research validity serves two important purposes. First and foremost, it keeps the investigator focused on acquiring results that are as true-to-life as possible. Second, it provides a story line that will help the case study navigate the review process. We begin by reviewing the types of validity normally considered in behavioral research. We then consider how proper case method research protocols can contribute to validity.

Types of Validity

In social science field research, validity is typically divided into four categories (Cook & Campbell, 1979; Yin, 2009):

1. *Reliability:* The degree to which measurements and observations of the same phenomenon produce the same outcome each time they are performed.

2. *Construct validity:* The degree to which the constructs being employed can be shown to exist using multiple sources (convergence) and are distinguishable from other constructs (discriminability), as described by Kerlinger (1986).

3. *Internal validity:* The degree to which a causal or explanatory relationship can be supported by evidence.

4. *External validity:* The degree to which results are expected to generalize beyond the observed situation.

In empirical studies, the first two of these validity types are frequently demonstrated using statistical techniques, such as Cronbach's alpha (reliability) and factor analysis (construct validity). The lack of multiple observations needed for such tests obviously presents a problem for case method researchers. There are, however, design decisions that can be made to address the issues that reviewers are likely to raise. We now turn our attention to these techniques.

Validity and Case Method Research

There is good news and bad news with respect to the likely validity of case research. The good news is that the presumed external validity is likely to be high as a consequence of the observation being taken in a field setting. Ironically, if you believe the underlying landscape being investigated is complex, you may be less sanguine about the generalizability of your findings than the reviewers.

The bad news is that every other type of validity will require considerable justification if it is to be convincing to a reviewer or reader. In another irony, case method research has the potential of being far stronger in all three areas (reliability, construct validity and internal validity) than its statistical counterparts under conditions of complexity. The problem is that of weighing objective and subjective evidence.

Support for reliability

Objective techniques for assessing reliability often involve asking the same question more than once on a survey, perhaps using slightly different or inverted phrasing, and considering how responses correlate. While such statistical evidence can be useful in sniffing out problems with questions, it does not determine if the respondent actually interprets the question as it was intended. Consider the following example, taken from the description of a multi-case study I performed described in *Informing Business* (Gill, 2010).

Example: Expert System Phone Questionnaire

The study involved examining the status of a collection of expert system "success stories" that had been published in the late 1980s. The interview portion of the data gathering is described as follows:

> In preparation for each interview, I wrote up a preliminary description of what each system did—based upon the public descriptions we were able to find in the first phase of the project—and tentatively scored where I thought the system would end up on the task change portion of the questionnaire. During the course of the actual interview, if a respondent provided a value substantially different from what I had anticipated, I would ask about the response. In most cases, the explanation led me to better understand the precise nature of the task change brought about by the system; in some cases it turned out the respondent had either misinterpreted the question or did not understand it, in which case he or she was given the opportunity to revise the response.

This particular protocol allowed me to verify the reliability of my questions in a very direct ways: when an answer did not seem to make sense, I asked the respondent to explain it. This, I would argue, made the methodology strong with respect to preventing respondents from reliably interpreting questions in the wrong way.

Such an approach came with a cost, however. Through the process described, the data gathering process was tainted by my subjective determination of whether or not an answer made sense. Here the obvious question a reviewer would need to know is whether I possessed the expertise to make such a subjective judgment in a sensible way. Unfortunately, the purported anonymity of the review process makes it very difficult for investigators to present their credentials in a manner that reviewers can assess[16].

In this particular example, the reviewers eventually accepted my justification for the approach. As noted in a chapter describing the research (Gill, 2010), however, their initial response was a split decision. The practitioner reviewers were very content with the research; the academic reviewers felt the entire project should be scrapped.

Support for construct validity

What the case method offers is the ability to employ many different types of evidence to support construct convergence. This evidence will likely include the ideas of the participants themselves. Participant involvement in construct development is particularly important where the desired outcome of the research is impact on practice. Traditional approaches to demonstrating construct validity include statistical techniques such as factor analysis. The motivation for these techniques is to show that certain responses load together on specific constructs, implying that the constructs are not just contrived by the investigator. Unfortunately, this technique tells us little about whether or not these constructs are meaningful to clients. From an informing standpoint, on the other hand, ascertaining the nature of the constructs clients employ within their own mental models likely to be more beneficial. These are the constructs that will either serve as the scaffolding for future informing, or will act impediments to informing that we need to overcome.

Example: What is the purpose of a case study?

Informing processes can often be derailed when a client holds different perceptions about a construct or activity from the investigator. I developed a particular appreciation from this while developing a case study of an expert system as part of my dissertation in the late 1980s. The client, a faculty member from MIT who had launched an artificial intelligence startup company, had agreed to let me (and my advisor) observe the development and deployment of a gate scheduling expert system that was to be installed at various airports. When we mentioned that we might eventually publish a case study about the project, the faculty member emphatically stated:

I hope not!

When pressed on the subject, it became clear that his view of what constituted a case study was entirely different from our own. In fact, what he thought of as a case study was more akin to an "incident report"—a document specifically intended to lay out the details of a failure or departure from approved procedures[17]. Thus, he imagined that a "case study" would be appropriate only if the installation proved to be a disaster of publishable proportions. When we explained the reality of the situation, his attitude towards a case study changed completely. I

---

can only imagine the long term complications that could have arisen had that misunderstanding not been corrected early in the investigation.

Working closely with a client, it is possible to ensure that misunderstandings relating to the meaning of constructs are resolved, and that whatever constructs are proposed are consistent with prevailing client mental models. These represent the utilitarian side of construct validity, a side often not considered in traditional research protocols that distance the investigators from the client.

Support for internal validity

As described earlier, internal validity focuses on the evidence for cause and effect. In traditional research, the strongest evidence is provided through experimental manipulations and controls. Such techniques are much more difficult to employ in a field setting, since controls are often absent and the ability to manipulate key variables is often limited by practical and ethical concerns.

There are two general responses I would make to these concerns. The first is that evidence for cause and effect is not nearly as valuable for complex landscapes as it is for decomposable ones. Although the general justification for this assertion can be found in Chapter 2, it is worth looking at the issue specifically here with an analogy.

Example: Adding garlic to a recipe

When trying to sort out complexity, I particularly like to use the domain of cooking, since we all tend to share an intuition that it is the combination of ingredients that is most important in assessing the fitness of a particular recipe, as opposed to the independent contributions of each ingredient.

Suppose, then, we add garlic to a recipe and discover that it improves the resulting taste measurably. We might then be tempted to say that the improvement is taste was *caused* by the addition of garlic.

In fact, this is not precisely true. We can all agree that the improved taste value was the result of the new combination of ingredients (that contained the added garlic). In other words, it is the particular combination that *causes* a particular taste, not the presence or absence of a par-

---

ticular ingredient. The fact that adding garlic led to an improvement in taste is only true because we happened to be in a garlic-deficient combination that was less fit than its garlic-abundant close cousin.

Why this is important is its implications for generalizability. In a highly decomposable environment, the fact that adding garlic improves fitness in one situation is likely to have important implications for many (if not all) garlic deficient combinations. In a complex environment, we can make no such generalization. Unless the particular garlic-deficient combination we started with is widely observed, our conclusion that adding garlic caused increased fitness is not terribly useful—since the absence of garlic in a recipe does not necessarily mean that its taste will be improved by adding garlic.

The second response more directly deals with validity itself. In case research generally, some support for internal validity may be demonstrated through quasi-experimental measures. Longitudinal changes to fitness that are observed as changes are made to a situation (as discussed in the Ism3232.A course described in Appendix E) can be an acceptable source of evidence. An even better source of evidence, however, may be the opinions of individual participants regarding causality.

Using opinion data of this sort moves us far into the domain of subjectivity. Subjectivity, in turn, tends to be confused with lack of rigor. To this criticism I make two responses:

1. The demands of rigor typically *require* us to consider evidence from as many sources as possible. Ignoring opinions is therefore as great an affront to rigor as relying upon them exclusively.

2. If we are ever going to produce research that resonates with practice, we must understand the nature and diversity of existing client mental models.

In *Informing Business* (Gill, 2010), I write a great deal about the barriers to informing a client. Nearly all of these result from the absence of suitable client models upon which we can build, or the presence of conflicting models. If we do not understand what client models already exists, we cannot expect to properly inform.

Given that cause and effect is not as important as it first appears (in a complex environment) and that we need to work with existing client conceptual schemes, client notions of cause and effect should play an important role in the conceptual schemes that we devise. Does this move us towards the unattainable and continuously changing "truth" that underlies the system we are studying? Perhaps so, perhaps not... Does it increase the likelihood that the conceptual schemes we develop will be put to use? Definitely...

The Case Write Up

The question of how a case research project is best written up is likely to be so situation specific that useful rules will be few. Nevertheless, for researchers new to case method research, I will venture to offer a few suggestions in the area of organizing a case research report and some comments on practical matters.

Case Research Report Organization

I tend to view writing up any research activity as a complex task. By this point in the book, you should recognize what that means: many fitness peaks consisting of different combinations. In writing up my own case method research, I have found three combinations to work reasonably well, the traditional research organization, the example-explanation organization and the case appendix. Each is now described.

Traditional research organization

The traditional research organization endeavors to make the case research appear as much like other social science research as possible. It employs an organization along the following lines:

I.   Introduction

II. Literature review

III. Relevant theory and research questions/hypotheses

IV. Data gathering protocol

V.   Case write up

VI. Analysis & discussion

VII. Conclusions

This particular organization is likely to resonate particularly well with a researcher audience. It will be familiar, with each section arriving as expected.

There are a couple of disadvantages to this organization. First, its large emphasis on review, theory and methodology means that there is often little room left for descriptive material related to the case. For this reason, the case presentation tends to be driven by the theory section with details adding to the richness of the case omitted. That is fine when the reader buys in to whatever conceptual scheme the paper advocates. The case itself tends to be less useful for other purposes, however, since its presentation is so highly focused.

The other disadvantage, particularly when used to report case method research, is that the presentation is often misleading with respect to how the research was actually conducted. If an agile research method is employed, for example, it is likely that the development of the preferred conceptual scheme *actually* followed the observation, or was heavily influenced by it. To frame the write up as if the research involved a hypothesis test may cause it to appear rigorous to the reader, but if the hypotheses you are "testing" are actually derived from what you observed, then the fact that they were supported could hardly be considered a rigorous test[18].

My own view is that this organization is best employed when either a traditional research method was actually employed (making it unlikely that it fits my criteria for case method research) or when the purpose of the case is to contrast alternative theories (conceptual schemes) using the facts of the case. The fact that different theories are being considered forces the case portion of the write up to be less directed in its presentation. I would also tend to use this approach when the case or cases being considered are the result of a literature search rather than first hand observations (as was true for the "High Tech Hidebound" example that I described in previous chapters). Here, the reader can be referred to the source references, reducing the potential benefits of having the researcher to describe the case or cases in complete detail.

Example-explanation organization

The example/explanation organization is radically different from the traditional research organization. In this organization, the case material is presented as close to the beginning as possible, after which analysis is performed and conceptual schemes are developed.

The advantages and disadvantages of this approach tend to be mirror images of the traditional approach. Reviewers and readers who are used to looking for theory and hypotheses may well be disturbed by the fact that the report organized in this fashion reads a bit more like a detective novel—keeping the reader in suspense until the end. Its effectiveness also depends on the author's ability to make the case interesting—which is often harder if the cases being profiled have been extracted from the literature.

On the positive side, this particular organization will tend to be consistent with the typical case method research sequence—the case observation coming first, followed by an attempt to synthesize it into an existing or novel conceptual theme. It is also unlikely to incorporate contrived hypothesis tests precisely because the reader with see the inconsistency of proposing and testing hypotheses after the observation has been made. As justification, the researcher may also refer to a large literature in the sociology field that refers to *grounded theory*[19].

A variation on the example-explanation organization involves using an example case to motivate a conceptual scheme or to communicate an idea more effectively. Journals with a practitioner audience, such as the *Harvard Business Review*, use such an approach extensively (e.g., Rynes, Giluk, & Brown, 2007, p. 999). I have found leading with a case to be helpful in introducing complicated conceptual schemes such as individual client resonance, where I generally begin with the previously presented example of the obstacles faced in the diffusion of naval gunnery techniques. Here, of course, the objective of employing the case is informing rather than knowledge creation. As you may have guessed, however, I treat that distinction as being less important than others do, since I view informing as an integral part of research.

Case appendix organization

The case appendix organization is a hybrid of the two previous organizations. It places the case study or case studies in an appendix, employing a more traditional organization for the body of the report. Appendix E is an example of this organization.

Using an appendix allows you to present the case as a coherent narrative while, at the same time, allowing you to present the research analysis and theory in a manner that is familiar to scholars. Its principle disadvantage, as I see it, is that the appendix will tend to be ignored by reviewers and readers. That may not be a problem, however, if the materials are being presented principally for the unusual reader interested in greater detail. It may also make sense where the research has dual purposes: one theory-focused and one practice-focused. Pedagogical research, for example, is often designed both to test a conceptual scheme and to provide a practical example that other instructors can follow (as was the intent of the research presented Appendix E).

A variation on the case appendix organization would be to publish the case description itself—either as a research case or a teaching case—as one publication, citing it within a subsequent theory-focused research article. In fact, this was done to some extent in Appendix E, where previous articles written on the Ism3232.A course were referenced as supplements to the appendices included in the article. While this can be an effective approach to keeping the length of the articles manageable, it more-or-less ensures a lack of anonymity that is likely to be criticized.

With this observation, we turn to some practical considerations related to writing up case research, including both length and anonymity.

Practical Considerations

Presuming you have adopted a suitable organization for your case research report, there are still a number of issues that seem to surface more frequently in case research than other research methods. In my own experience, the particularly common practical issues are writing style, length and anonymity.

Keep it engaging

One of the particular advantages that the case study medium offers is the ability to engage the reader. In the context of a research case, however, there is the temptation to present the case description using the particular jargon of the theory or discipline guiding the research. Based on my own experience, I would urge the reader to resist that temptation whenever possible. The fact that readers are willing to tolerate academic prose does not mean that they have to like it. Indeed, some readers may actually revel when given an article to review that tells an interesting or unusual story in clear prose. Consider the peculiar example that I now relate.

Example: The Cruelest Experiment

Sometimes I submit a manuscript just for the fun of shocking reviewers. That was the case back in the spring of 2004 when, a few days before the deadline for the *Decision Sciences Institute* (DSI) conference, I had a whimsical idea for a research question. What would happen if you had to submit a course design to the same Institutional Review Board (IRB) that reviews research designs for the protection of human subjects? Obviously, I thought to myself, it would never be approved—since virtually everything we do in a typical course design potentially violates at least one or more of the human subject rules (e.g., informed consent, privacy, minimizing harm to subjects). Equally obviously, there was no safe way to research this topic. So, just for the fun of it, I created an imaginary case study (using the example-explanation format) one Friday afternoon (and part of Saturday) and submitted it to DSI. The piece began as follows:

PREAMBLE

Not so many years ago, I had a nightmare. Or, if I didn't, I should have. In the dream, I was called before my university's institutional review board (IRB) and asked to justify an experiment I had proposed. I begin this paper by describing that hellish encounter.

THE NIGHTMARE

The nightmare opened with me, sitting in a seat designed for elementary school students, facing a three member IRB panel, resplendent in academic robes. To preserve the sense of anonymity, so critical in achieving rigorous academic review, I will refer to the members of the board as Drs. Torquemada, Sixtus and Carafa, although these were not their real names. Dr. Torquemada led the panel. Dr. Sixtus appeared to be sleeping. The proceedings were as follows:

Dr. Torquemada: Professor, we have called you in to testify before us as a result of a most peculiar experiment that you have proposed. Before passing judgment, we wanted you to speak on your own behalf.

Me: Thank you, members of the panel. *[I find myself squirming uncomfortably in my miniature chair. Who would not be fearful when facing the wrath of the IRB?]*

Dr. T: Before we begin, I'd like to get the basic facts straight. The experiment you propose will last approximately four months and will use student subjects. Presumably, they all volunteered to participate.

Me: Not exactly volunteered. Participation in the experiment is required if they are to graduate.

[At this point, Dr. Sixtus emits what sounds like a loud raspberry, although it is still not clear that he is awake.]

Dr. Carafa: We'll return to that later. For now, I'd like to see how you justify your experiment in light of the guidelines promulgated in CFR Title 45, Part 46, dealing with the protection of human subjects. As you doubtless know, the document stresses sound research design, informed consent, and minimizing risks to experimental subjects. Let's start with the research design, shall we?

The full nightmare sequence went on for 11 pages, and ended with one IRB member morphing into a capybara and the remaining two dancing the Lambada. After that, I provided another dozen or so pages of analysis, during which I unsuccessfully attempted to reclaim my lost dignity.

Needless to say, I expected the outcome of my submission to be some angry reviewer condemnations. Imagine my surprise, therefore, when I learned a few months later that it had been named the "Distinguished Paper" for the Innovative Education track at DSI (which normally has about 30-40 submissions).

I relate this incident for two reasons. First, you can never be sure precisely how a reviewer will react. Second, if you try to make what you are writing entertaining, chances are that at least some readers will appreciate it[20].

Length

The case study format tends to be lengthy. The reason for this is that a case, if done properly, can serve as a source resource for future researchers as well as providing a basis for whatever conceptual scheme its author happens to be advancing. To be a resource for future research, however, it needs to offer sufficient detail so that subsequent researchers are not limited to the original author's point of view.

I have not found any universal solution to the problem of case study length. I tend to gravitate towards three solutions:

1. Seek publication in outlets that do not have hard and fast length limitations. This particularly tends to be true for online journals.

2. Break case research into two papers, one largely descriptive and one that more focused on analysis. The latter can then reference the former.

3. Develop a discussion case that covers the rich details of the case situation, after which a research case referencing the discussion case is written. This is feasible because discussion cases—lacking the literature review, theory, methodology, hypotheses and other research-focused sections—tend to be much richer in their observational detail than research cases.

The problem with the last two of these approaches is that they run headlong into another practical issue: preserving anonymity.

Anonymity

The conventional wisdom in research is that submissions should be anonymous. In *Informing Business* (Gill, 2010), I point out that this wisdom has a sound basis. There is plenty of evidence from other fields, such as music, that knowing someone's identify (or gender, in the case of music) can exert a powerful influence on a judge's decision.

Having conceded that there is a strong argument to be made for anonymity of authors and reviewers, I must also assert that maintaining anonymity can be a real obstacle to many types of case method research. For example:

- It may force you to disguise the organization being presented. This is particularly true in case research involving higher education, since knowing the course, department and institution involved will almost always give clues to the identity of at least one of the authors.

- It can prevent you from referencing other research related to the situation described, such as teaching cases written by one or more of the same authors.

- It makes action research less practical, since the researcher's role as a participant needs to be disguised.

In effect, these compromises all involve trading off rigor for anonymity. In my opinion, this should not be a close competition. Rigor should always win[21].

Conclusions

The central theme of this chapter has been differentiating what I call case method research from case research in general. Whereas "classic" case research, as described by experts such as Yin (2009), tends to meticulously planned and rigid in its conduct, case *method* research tends to be conducted by applying principles similar to those of agile software development. These include:

1. Close engagement with the client

2. Flexibility of methods and objectives

3. Rapid completion

The degree to which these principles offer acceptable rigor heavily depends on the complexity of the environment being studied. For stable environment that are not particularly complex, "classic" methods are doubtless more suitable. For rapidly changing complex environments, speed is required, adaptability on the part of the researcher is a plus and the client's own expertise, despite its obvious subjectivity, may be the most valid source of insights available.

Chapter 6 Notes

---

[1] Oh happy days!

[2] Excluding dissertation credits and non-credit seminars, my doctoral classes involved 50 credits. Of these, 26 were in computer or cognitive science (20 at Harvard's Graduate School of Arts and Sciences, 6 at MIT), 8 were in statistics, and only 16 were in topics related to business research at HBS.

[3] As it turns out, all three issues that I observed in my dissertation but did not address at the time became central themes in my later research. The third item was the inspiration for the multi-case expert study I performed after I arrived at my first academic job. The question as to how preexisting conceptual schemes influence choice and perceptions are central to my research in informing.

[4] As a result of the dissertation topic I chose, I got to rewrite completely the first chapter of my dissertation seven times at the insistence of my chair. At issue was that the theme of the chapter (in an HBS dissertation) was justifying why managers and executives should be interested in what I had written. Of course, it was clear to any idiot that they would not be (a point that I had explicitly asserted in my first draft, provoking considerable disapproval from my chair).

[5] Many versions of the SDLC place feasibility analysis at the beginning and maintenance at the end.

[6] Consider the agile manifesto (Agile Manifesto, 2001), copied from the website of the *Agile Alliance* as follows:

We are uncovering better ways of developing software by doing it and helping others do it. Through this work we have come to value:

Individuals and interactions over processes and tools

Working software over comprehensive documentation

Customer collaboration over contract negotiation

Responding to change over following a plan

That is, while there is value in the items on the right, we value the items on the left more.

[7] To address problems of long term integration, agile developers often employ component oriented development and standards based connec-

tivity approaches (such as web services) that facilitate later uses that are not visualized when an application is developed.

[8] Probably not coincidentally, agile research methods also bear a strong resemblance to effectual leadership, discussed in Chapter 10. All of these, in turn, tend to be highly constructivist in their philosophy.

[9] When I refer to case *method* research "as I have defined it", I wish to very explicitly distinguish it from case research in general, as described by Yin (2009) and others. If you were to follow all of Yin's excellent suggestions for building rigor into the design and conduct of case research, you could quite easily extend the time it would take to conduct and disseminate such research into years and possibly decades. This delay represents a serious problem only if both:

a) The phenomenon you are describing is expected to change over the same time period, AND

b) The results of your research are likely to be used.

Naturally, as long as (b) is false, there is no compelling practical need to streamline our research even if (a) happens to be true.

[10] As described on its website (SSRN, 2010):

Social Science Research Network (SSRN) is devoted to the rapid worldwide dissemination of social science research and is composed of a number of specialized research networks in each of the social sciences…

Each of SSRN's networks encourages the early distribution of research results by publishing submitted abstracts and by soliciting abstracts of top quality research papers around the world.

[11] As an example of the "not being motivated to answer a research question accurately" condition, suppose you happen to be studying a firm that sells new air conditioners. They may well not be interested in the research question "under what conditions does it make rational economic sense to replace an air conditioner", even though it would appear to be relevant. That attitude might change, however, if you could demonstrate that their customer base happens to include a large number of economists and experts in financial analysis. Thus, if you really want to ask the question and make it of interest to the practition-

ers involved, your case research design might need to be modified to include a survey of customer occupations.

[12] For example, in an educational context you might be asking the question for a particular set of course content: "Which leads to better outcomes, distance learning or classroom teaching?" You might later discover, however, that the institution requires the material be offered in both ways—making the practical importance of that particular question moot. The question you should then be asking might be better framed as "What characteristics distinguish those students who will do better in distance vs. classroom settings for the specific set of material being studied?"

[13] It should be noted that omitting results inconsistent with research propositions is not a threat to rigor that is limited to agile research methods. Using the statistical tools of modern behavioral research, it is nearly impossible to avoid doing some tuning to highlight significant findings. Normally this is done with the intention of getting to the truth, not for some nefarious purpose. Unfortunately, few of us in the behavioral sciences using these tools are sufficiently conversant with the underlying mathematics and assumptions they incorporate to be completely confident of the implications of our analytical adjustments. Instead, we justify our actions based upon general rules presented to us in course work, articles, books and help systems. If we were honest, we would acknowledge this fact as a threat to rigor.

[14] For example, both this book and *Informing Business* (Gill, 2010) are directed at the practice of research and teaching, which means its users would be other academics. For my earlier research into expert systems, on the other hand, the "users" were intended to be practitioners. For that reason, I would judge it largely to be a failure since I saw little evidence that it diffused to anyone besides other researchers.

[15] Notice that I refer to "participants" in a case method research study, not "subjects", the term commonly used in experimental research. This is to emphasize the fact that in agile research methods, the creation of knowledge it a collaborative activity between the researcher and the individuals who will become the ultimate users of that knowledge. As soon as we start to go into a research project that assumes the researcher knows more about what's going on than the participants, we start moving back towards traditional views of research.

[16] The inability to convey detailed information about the investigator's credentials is one of the two reasons that I object to the requirement of anonymity in case method research (although I would always allow it as an option). My other objection stems from the fact that case method research, particularly in education, is often action research. This means that in order to preserve anonymity for the purposes of review, the report may be forced to omit relevant details of the case that would identify the case writer(s).

[17] Incident reports were frequently part of Navy requirements, a fact that I was well aware of based on my five years of experience as a nuclear submarine office.

[18] One approach to making hypothesis testing appear rigorous is for the researcher to go to the literature and find prior research that proposes the same or similar hypotheses. That allows the researcher to argue that the hypotheses did, in fact, precede the research. The fact that you have found others who have proposed the same hypotheses you are "testing" does little to make the situation more rigorous. On a complex landscape that has been studied many times, you can expect to find research that advances nearly any plausible proposition—and a great many implausible ones as well—if you search long enough and hard enough.

[19] In fact, grounded theory has many elements in common with what I refer to as agile research methods. It is described by the *Grounded Theory Institute* (Rhine, 2009) as follows:

> Grounded Theory is an inductive methodology. Although many call Grounded Theory a qualitative method, it is not. It is a general method. It is the systematic generation of theory from systematic research. It is a set of rigorous research procedures leading to the emergence of conceptual categories. These concepts/categories are related to each other as a theoretical explanation of the action(s) that continually resolves the main concern of the participants in a substantive area. Grounded Theory can be used with either qualitative or quantitative data.

Because it some definitions of grounded theory are quite specific, and different schools of grounded theory exist, I chose to use "agile research methods" as an alternative. Nevertheless, the researcher seeking to justify an agile design would do well to explore and reference the large grounded theory literature.

[20] Ironically, it was that silly little conference paper that also first got me involved with the Informing Science Institute, since I figured I'd try to publish it somewhere. Eli Cohen, then the Editor-in-Chief of *the Journal of IT Education*, indicated that I could resubmit it to the InSITE conference. I didn't like the idea of submitting the same article twice so I created another version with a similar theme called "The Peer Reviews and the Programming Course" (Gill, 2005c) where I imagined what the reviews might look like if a course were submitted to a refereed journal as a research project. That became my first ISI journal publication.

[21] I am especially vexed with heroic efforts to preserve anonymity at the expense of rigor because, as a practical matter, final editorial decisions on a manuscript that sits on the cusp of acceptance and rejection are nearly always made by an editor who knows the identity of the author(s) (Gill, 2010). As a practical consequence, true anonymity guides only those decisions that are pretty obvious to begin with.

The problem here is that as an author, you may not always win by taking the most rigorous route: disguising information where it does not matter and leaving self-identifying content in the manuscript that is material (without explicitly stating who is who). On more than one occasion, I have received back reviewer complaints regarding anonymity in my own work, including one AE who actually suggested that I should try to make the revision more anonymous. Talk about trying to stuff the genie back into the bottle!

T. Grandon Gill
Informing with the Case Method
Santa Rosa, California: Informing Science Press.

Chapter 7

Writing the Discussion Case

Writing a discussion case offers many joys that cannot be matched by a research case. Rather than observing participants, you find yourself jumping into the decisions that are of greatest interest to them. Rather than constructing an argument, you are writing a story. Rather than seeing your role in the process end once the case reaches the printed page, you can look forward to engaging your students with the product of your efforts. It is good that such benefits are available, since the career benefits of such efforts today are likely to be negligible for the typical research faculty member; a travesty to be sure, yet a truth that needs to be acknowledged.

In this chapter, we consider the factors motivating an instructor to write a discussion case as well as the motivation for choosing a topic. We then turn to the desirability of case writer involvement in the situation being profiled. From there, we consider how cases may be tailored to the needs of the student and participating organization audiences, leading into the approval process. A brief discussion of teaching notes follows. Finally, outlet categories for teaching case publication are identified and contrasted.

Inspiration for Discussion Cases

The inspiration for discussion cases tends to be quite different than the corresponding inspiration for research cases. Whereas a research case offers the potential for a career-advancing publication—even at a research-focused institution—the publication of a discussion case normally adds little to a research academic's CV. Thus, the motivation to write such a case needs to come from other sources. In this section, we consider that motivation and the process of selecting a topic.

Why Write a Discussion Case?

There are many excellent reasons for writing a discussion case. Just be aware that if you are at a research institution, career advancement potential is unlikely to be one of them. Fortunately, I have *always* found four benefits accompany writing a discussion case. In addition, other benefits sometimes accrue.

Benefit #1: Energizing a case method class

If I never facilitated case method classes, I would never write a discussion case. It is as simple as that. When you incorporate a case you wrote (or co-authored) into a class you are teaching, it motivates the students to better prepare. It allows you to offer insights that simply are not available in other cases that you use, but did not write. In many cases, it provides the opportunity to bring the case protagonist or protagonists into the classroom to watch the discussion and later to critique it. Collectively, my experience has been that these lead to energetic discussions even when the case itself is far-from-perfect.

Benefit #2: Increases knowledge of practice domain

Most fields where the case method is warranted have an associated domain of practice (e.g., business, education, law, social work, medicine). As we have already noted in Chapter 2, the best evidence (in business, at least) is that a substantial amount of domain knowledge is actually created in practice, and then flows to academia. This being true, the researcher would do well to spend time observing practice to find out what is happening there. There is no better opportunity to observe than while writing a discussion case.

Leading us to the next benefit...

Benefit #3: Provides practice in observing

Academics, as a rule, tend to prefer to deal in conceptual thinking rather than trained skills. This is natural, since concepts are generally in a form that can be communicated to other researchers and to students. Trained skills, on the other hand, tend to be highly automated; while they can lead to remarkable performance (e.g., watch the hands of a virtuoso pianist), even the performer cannot explain *how* they are doing *what* they are doing. Not to mention that emphasis on trained skills can lead to the "trade school" label so despised by scholars.

The problem with preferring to deal entirely in concepts is that some concepts cannot be learned until precursor skills are acquired. Daniel Willingham (2009), in his superb book, *Why Don't Students Like School?*, explains this by pointing out that our working memory capability is generally the most important limiting factor in our problem solving. Typically, it allows us to attend to only 5-7 chunks of information at any given time (Miller, 1967). Tasks that are practiced require less and less working memory until, by the time they become fully automatic, they require none at all; i.e., they can be performed without conscious thought. As a result of this, practiced knowledge and skills can be applied to a new concept without overloading working memory. Without that practice, there is simply not enough room for the old concepts (the prerequisites) and the new concepts[1].

Working memory has important practical implications for the case method researcher. Anyone walking into a new case site for the first time is all too familiar with the feeling of "drinking from a fire hose" that accompanies the visit. There is always far too much information to digest; too many details to attend to; too much background knowledge that the researcher is missing.

Like any other skill, however, the ability to be an effective observer improves with practice. There are many opportunities for a researcher to acquire such practice—including consulting and, of course, doing case research[2]. There are few opportunities that are as easy to find and as low in cost as developing a discussion case.

Benefit #4: Builds network for future informing

Throughout this book, I repeatedly emphasize that the case method is a tool for informing—practice, students and colleagues. I also point out that most complex informing occurs through a network of relationships, not through documents (see Chapter 12). When you write a discussion case relating to a practice community, you are necessarily building or reinforcing relationships to that community. Stated another way, you are developing a network that will enable future informing into that community. Because informing networks attenuate with time (e.g., individuals retire, get promoted and move into other professions), it must be replenished with ongoing activities. It may also be further strengthened by bringing practice into the classroom (Benefit #1), helping students join the network.

What is interesting about the four benefits I have just presented is that, with the possible exception of the first, all can serve to make the case writer a better and more impactful *researcher*. That is one of the many reasons that I dispute the wisdom of treating discussion case development as being the black sheep cousin of developing research cases.

The benefits of writing discussion cases do not end here, however. There are others that arise with surprising frequency.

Occasional benefits of discussion case writing

The other benefits that I have experienced from writing discussion cases have been situation specific. The first—and this specifically relates to business cases—has been unexpected opportunities to consult. As well as offering monetary compensation, consulting is another mechanism for moving research into practice[3]. The second—and this specifically relates to education cases—is the opportunity to acquire knowledge that I could directly apply to my own practice area: teaching. In both cases, I have found these benefits to be material, sometimes even huge.

Choosing a Site and Topic

Once you have established the underlying motivation, the next stage of discussion case development involves choosing a site and a topic. My own experience suggests that everyone has an interesting story to tell and decisions that need making. All you need to do is listen carefully enough to find them. This observation has practical implications for both choosing a site and choosing a topic for a discussion case.

Choosing a site

Choosing the proper site can make the development of a discussion case much easier. A good site will be open in sharing information, willing to allow some weaknesses be exposed for the benefit of the students, will be eager to see the case completed and will be dismissive of the potential legal implications of being the subject of a case. A bad site will have none of those qualities. There are doubtless deep and insightful approaches to choosing a good site. Since I have never applied them, and remain unaware of them, I will limit my remarks to what my own experiences have been.

I have personally used three approaches to selecting a case site[4]. The first, and by far the most common, has been opportunism. I meet an individual—typically a manager or an educator for the type of cases I write—and we talk about what is going on in his or her professional life. Based entirely on that conversation, I can determine if the likelihood of a "bad site" is high. If so, the conversation ends. Otherwise, I raise the issue of case studies and see if he or she seems receptive. If so, site selection ends; topic selection begins.

The second and third mechanisms are both proactive. They differ from the first only in that I initiate contact with the individual—often someone I have never met—to start the process, typically using the means discussed in Chapter 3. In the case of the second mechanism, my reason for contacting the potential site is that I am personally interested in learning more about the particular domain: perhaps a type of business or some new teaching technique. In the case of the third mechanism, it is because I have a hole I want to plug in the collection of cases I am using for some class I will be offering. Given my experience that everyone has an interesting set of decisions being made at all times, I normally feel comfortable selecting a site without knowing the specifics of what the case will be about.

Selecting a topic

Research cases, particularly those following the admirable protocols set forth by Yin (2009) and others, tend to be inspired by gaps in the research literature. While I argued, in the last chapter, that case method research tends to be more flexible in its topics, the fact remains that you normally go into a research case with an idea of the topics of greatest interest to you. I am convinced, however, that the best discussion cases are inspired by the challenging decisions currently facing the participants involved. As a discussion case writer, you only hurt yourself by coming in with your own agenda.

Identifying the interesting decisions will not always be as easy as it sounds. Much of the time, participants will be most eager to present a decision that: a) has already been made, and b) they are proud of. This is a perfectly natural (and healthy) desire. It will not, however, usually lead to a good discussion case. Followed to its logical conclusion, it will develop into a showcase (as per Chapter 3) for the decision.

Challenging decisions may be hard to surface. They often will not emerge until the client develops a high degree of trust in the case writer. The reason for this is simple. Challenging decisions tend to be those where there is not enough information, where none of the options are without flaws and where the entire subject is sensitive. They often represent decisions where, on the whole, the decision-maker wishes that he or she could put off the decision. In other words, they represent the very type of decision that the client would prefer not to have profiled in a case study.

The very factors that make challenging decisions uncomfortable also make them particularly interesting topics for discussion cases. With patience and trust, however, they may be developed. Later in the chapter I present the AFN (A) and (B) case study pair as an example of this. These cases profiled a situation involving two individuals, an employer who was considering firing a particular programmer and an employee—the very same programmer—who was considering quitting at the very same moment.

My experience has been that case sites will *sometimes* let these situations be explored in a case study. Where I have succeeded, it has required me to: a) become involved in helping resolve the situation, b) act as a trusted confidant to all the parties involved, AND c) continually emphasize the benefits that future discussion participants (i.e., my students) will derive from the topic. This leads naturally to a final aspect of getting started on a case writing project: deciding on your level of involvement.

Case writing vs. consulting

The difference between case writing and consulting can easily become blurred when the domain of the case is business-related. This is particularly true where a discussion case is being developed, since these tend to revolve around decisions that are actually being made as the case is written. As mentioned in Chapter 6, a reasonable argument can be made for not becoming actively involved in decision making for a research case; some will find the argument for objectivity compelling, others may not. For a discussion case, on the other hand, I find rigor-based arguments for non-intervention to be mainly self-serving. Many case writers object to giving away their advice for free.

In business case writing scenarios, case writing often leads into consulting opportunities for the case writer. I have found that to be a fact of life and generally one that I applaud. While writing a case, however, I tend to be very free in offering advice—but only when asked—and would not dream of charging for it. When the case development is over, should further requests for advice be made by the client, I *still* would not turn the billing meter on unless the time demands appear to be substantial.

My rationale for this easy-going attitude is as follows. Every time a client allows me to develop a discussion case around his or her situation, I have been granted a great boon. Anything that I can do to reciprocate is therefore welcomed. I believe it is important to convey this attitude, which is genuinely held, because in developing a discussion case I am attempting to nurture an informing relationship that I hope will continue for a long time. I would be very reluctant to introduce into that relationship the notion that I was in it for the money.

Naturally, my views on this subject have been heavily influenced by the fact that only once (out of all the cases I have developed) have I ever felt a client was trying to take advantage of me. Much more common is situations where clients ask far less of me than I would have gladly offered for the privilege of being allowed to observe the inner workings of their organizations. In fact, when the subject of consulting does come up, it is nearly always the client that raises the possibility.

I suspect the situation is quite different at institutions such as HBS, where companies frequently line up for both the case writing and consulting services of many faculty members. Obviously, this book is not meant as advice for that audience; they face a different landscape and seem to be doing quite well enough without my thoughts on the matter.

Common Case Plotlines

If you are not used to writing teaching cases, getting started can be a daunting task. In Chapter 3, the mapping between the intelligence-design-choice framework (IDC) and case design was presented. Three basic designs for discussion cases were recommended at that time: discussion/choice, discussion/sense-making and discussion/design. In this section, I get a bit more specific and introduce a number of common plot lines for cases within those categories that I have encountered. I would emphasize both that the list is neither complete nor an attempt to limit the creativity of potential case writers. I just happen to find them to be a (sometimes) useful way to think about getting started.

Discussion/Choice

Nearly all discussion/choice case designs revolve around a particular decision. What make these choice cases is that the alternatives being considered have been enumerated.

The Difficult Decision

One the most common forms of case discussion involves choosing between alternative courses of action. As mentioned in the previous section, to be a useful discussion, the choice must be a difficult one.

This particular case plotline usually provides a reasonably clear set of options as part of the case. Thus, its focus tends to be on the choice aspect of the IDC model. That does not make such cases simple, however. Even a decision with two straightforward options—e.g., fire an employee or keep the employee on; fail a student or give the student another chance—may require considerable deliberation. Moreover, decisions may also require proposing a sensible action plan, permitting a hybrid difficult decision/action plan plotline to be developed.

I will nearly always employ the difficult decision plotline when creating a case in a complicated setting—frequently the situation in MIS cases, since they tend to involve a lot of technology. By providing clear options and explanations, you help the reader understand the context, as well as the possible solutions. In settings that are more familiar—such as higher education cases—I am more confident with designs that require the use of tacit knowledge held by the student; this will nearly always be necessary for discussion/design plotlines.

Generally, a good difficult decision case will include elements that are both relevant and irrelevant to the decision being made. This encourages the development of observational skills, although it necessarily adds to the length of the case. Many of the criticisms leveled against the case method by individuals such as Mintzberg (2004) stem from the fact that cases do not model the complexity of real world decision. If the case contains only relevant information, such criticism becomes particularly valid, since identifying what is most relevant and what is not is central to any real world decision.

Discussion/Sense-making

Sometimes, the best you can do with a case is analyzing what an organization did "right" or what an organization did "wrong". Personally, I normally avoid these "post mortem" cases since hindsight always renders decisions consequences clearer than they were at the time they were made. Nevertheless, these types of cases appear fairly regularly and can sometimes lead to a good discussion, depending upon how it is managed by the facilitator. Two such plotlines—both emphasizing the intelligence aspect of the IDC model—spring to mind.

Underlying Forces

It is possible to build a case such where actions and plans are documented; the participant's job is then to explain the underlying forces that led up to the situation and justify the choices that were made. Such cases can be useful when you are trying to help students develop conceptual frameworks. When I try to illustrate the strategic potential of information technology, for example, I often assign one of the most widely used MIS cases of all times: Frontier Airlines.

Example: Frontier Airlines

Set in 1983, the Frontier Airlines is still in use after nearly three decades after being written[5]. What is interesting about the case is that while it appears to be a discussion/choice or discussion/design case, it should not take very long for the reader to become convinced that every option available to the company at the time was bad. Thus, the case discussion moves towards understanding what happened.

In essence, the case goes as follows. Frontier Airlines, in the early 1980s was a large regional carrier operating out of Denver, Colorado. Its competitive climate had changed dramatically in the previous few years as a consequence of the deregulation of the U.S. airline industry that had occurred in 1978. Prior to that time, airline routes and pricing had been heavily regulated, and government subsidies for low volume routes were commonplace. Subsequent to deregulation, prices and routes could change rapidly, and route subsidies were being rapidly phased out. As a consequence of this deregulation, many new carriers had entered the industry, and many others (such as Frontier) had expanded rapidly. Hub-and-spoke patterns also became commonplace,

---

with Denver serving as the hub for two airlines in particular: Frontier and United.

The central focus of the case is airline reservation systems. Prior to deregulation, these systems were little more than an internal convenience, used to book seats and generate boarding passes for flights whose timing and prices almost never changed. After deregulation, however, they became indispensable to travel agents. Only through a reservation system could up-to-the-minute information on schedules, fares and seat availability be obtained. As a result, airlines that owned reservation systems—such as United (Apollo) and American (Sabre)—had a huge competitive advantage over airlines that had to exist as guest hosts on these systems, such as Frontier.

By the time of the case, Frontier was in desperate shape. In large measure, this was a result of United's aggressive—and sometimes dirty—use of its reservation system. Through screen bias, it could delay the display of Frontier flights when travel agents were looking to book[6]. With full access to Frontier's pricing and availability, United could (and did) rapidly respond to any Frontier marketing promotions. It could also delay or prevent such promotions through amorphous "technical issues". Using a highly coercive incentive system, United ensured that nearly all travel agents in the Denver area used Apollo and not the competing reservation systems. Largely as a consequence of these tactics, a close reading of the case suggests that Frontier was unlikely to survive in its existing form[7].

The case offers a variety of options that Frontier could pursue. It could continue with ongoing legal challenges, it could build its own reservation system (either by itself or as part of a consortium), it could seek a stronger airline partner, and so forth. The problem with the options is that none of them are workable; this becomes very clear during the discussion. Essentially, the company was doomed in its existing form and no managerial action seemed likely to save it.

Where the case adds value, then, is in illustrating how changes in the environment (e.g., deregulation) can dramatically change the importance of an information system and how an information system can make or break a company. In addition, United's use of its information systems as a weapon provides a valuable platform for discussing the boundary between valid competitive and ethics. Thus, judgment regarding the best course of action becomes secondary in the discussion to understanding how forces shape an industry and to surfacing questions of morality.

Writing a case to be a tool for building an understanding of underlying forces—including forces such as ethics, regulation and globalization—tends to be appropriate where the decision to be made is either obvious or seems to be relatively immaterial to the outcome (as was largely true for the Frontier Airlines example). I would quickly add here that *all* discussion cases tend to have some decision element and some underlying forces that need to be understood. Thus, rather than focusing on writing a case to be either a choice or a sense-making case, it is better to view the decision as one of which type of skill to emphasize.

The Detective Story

Sometimes a case can appear to be a "post mortem" case where ill-considered decisions were made and yet, with careful dissection, the approach taken can be justified. Writing such a case is hard to pull off, but the result can be a wonderful discussion opportunity. The Tektronix case, presented as an example in Chapter 3, is the best example of such a case that I know of. In that case, as you may recall, a series of peculiar decisions are reconciled once the idea that the company might be preparing to sell off its divisions is introduced.

Discussion/Design

Discussion/design cases emphasize the design aspect of the IDC framework. They tend to require some background knowledge or assumptions on the part of participants, since it is hard to put everything relevant to creating a new set of alternatives into a single case.

The Action Plan

One of the most common types of design challenge presented to students in a case is coming up with an action plan. Even at HBS, this activity often seemed to stump students early in the program. Students in case method classes often come to think of participation in terms of sound bites. Action plans require the construction of a consistent set of interrelated items; a truly complex cognitive activity and one that benefits considerably from practice.

Example: Action Plan in EMBA 2002 (A) Case

As has already been noted in a previous example, the EMBA 2002 (A) case, presented as Appendix G, describes a case method course I taught that does not appear to be going very well. In preparing to discuss this case, students are only given the (A) case. This case emphasizes that the instructor needs to take action, but provides only two extreme choices (ignore the student protests or cave into them completely). The principle objective of the discussion of the case is to surface better options.

When writing the case—something I *did as the situation was unfolding*—I recognized two things. First, because the setting was going to be very familiar to participants (who would themselves be students enrolled in a similar class), it was reasonable to assume they would have a lot of tacit, pre-existing knowledge they could apply to the situation. Thus, a design problem, rather than a simple choice of options, seemed appropriate. Second, I anticipated that participants might have trouble coming up with options. To address this, I included a vignette about a similar confrontation that I had experienced at a previous institution and outlined the solution I employed at that time. Typically, a small percentage of participants pick up on this as part of their original preparation, but I have only seen one (in seven years) who initially came up with a plan that resembled what I actually did, described in the (B) case.

Based on many discussions of this particular case, I believe the reason that students have a problem coming up with workable designs stems from the fact that they are too inclined to take student complaints about workload and other issues at face value. I wrote the case specifically to encourage this—minimizing those suspicions that I had at the time that my grading might play a greater role than the student emails included in the case suggested. I provided some hints, to be sure, but do not emphasize them.

By writing the case in this way, I increase the likelihood that students will experience a transformation in their thinking as a result of the classroom discussion. Also, by pointing out the hints I dropped (such as a student comment that showing me to the program office was not an attempt to "brown nose" on her part), I reinforce the notion that careful reading and re-reading of each case is required for a successful analysis. Since this is the first case they discuss in any class where I use the case, I use this as a means of setting expectations for future discussions.

The "Outside the Box" Option

A hybrid of the action plan and difficult decision case structures, some cases present a set of obvious options—none of which are particularly good. Beneath the surface, however, lurks an option that diverges greatly from the others; one that the participants must discover on their own through thinking outside of the constraints suggested by the case itself. The EMBA 2002 (A) example just presented illustrates this somewhat. My favorite example is the well-worn Concordia Casting case.

Example: Concordia Casting

Concordia Casting is the only discussion case that I have used in my classes that I also discussed while I was an MBA. The highly disguised case has been rewritten from time to time to update the technologies in order to make them appear more realistic[8]. Specific technologies, however, have little or nothing to do with the case.

The case describes a manufacturing company that has multiple divisions. These divisions are tied together by a home-grown ordering and production systems (called CAPS) that is literally decades old. Within the case, three particularly relevant facts are included:

1. The hardware necessary to run the system is about lose all support from its vendor.

2. Attempts to create a new version of the system have stalled, after proving much more expensive and difficult than originally anticipated.

3. In the event the system were to fail, the company's production lines would need to be shut down.

Much of the case focuses on the organizational changes that the company's head of MIS is making to try to improve its MIS activity and expand its scope. He expresses particular frustration with the CAPS project because it is draining his time and energy. He is also angered by the fact that the "old-timers" who built the original system and know how it works are dragging their feet and are making it difficult for the "newcomers" who understand the technologies that will be employed in building the replacement system.

Of all the cases I have facilitated, this is the sole example where I would strongly assert that only one line of solutions is possible. That approach, however, is not suggested by the case. The reason is simple. The first action the company needs to take is to fire the case protagonist—the MIS director—in a very visible way. Based on what was presented in the case, he does not have a clue as to how to manage the CAPS development effort, nor does he understand that the "old-timers" are the only ones with the knowledge necessary to give the project any chance of success. By virtue of his extreme misunderstanding of the situation and willingness to alienate the company's most experienced employees, he has put the entire company at risk[9].

My experience has been that as students extract what is relevant from what is irrelevant during the discussion, a light bulb eventually goes on and the solution becomes clear. I hope they gain two insights from this. First, that analysis can lead to insights—not all solutions are equally meritorious! Second, that it pays not to be constrained by the options presented in the case. Generally, I feel these lessons have been conveyed because Concordia discussions were always lively and the case was among the most popular I used despite its age.

As a side note, I would add that this case only works with students lacking executive experience[10]. More experienced executives quickly consider the firing option and the decision then seems obvious.

Discussion Case Outlines

Suggesting that a general outline of presentation applies to discussion cases would be like proposing that all novels be written the same way. Unfortunately, for nearly any general rule I could propose, there will be more exceptions than situations consistent with it. Thus, the best advice I can offer is:

> Attempt to organize the case, or collection of cases, in a manner similar to how you would like to see it presented.

This advice particularly applies to situations where the students are relatively new to discussion cases. My experience has been that students asked to open a case will generally do so following the case organization—no matter how unsuitable it is for opening. Thus, your best bet is to help them get into the habit of opening in a sensible way. Naturally, when dealing with students experienced with the pedagogy, this advice is less applicable. In fact, you may want to present the case in a manner that forces them to reorganize it—since that is an important skill to master. Unfortunately, the skill of reorganization is unlikely to develop before students have acquired a sense of what constitutes a good organization.

Topic Organizations

There are two general approaches to organizing case topics that are reasonably common. One involves drilling down to the question through a successive series of context layers. The other involves relating the case as an uninterrupted narrative. It is important to emphasize, at the outset, that the two organizations are not mutually exclusive. Even within a drill down organization, the decision situation itself is likely to be presented in narrative format. In addition, most case studies will have separate exhibits that provide source material.

Drilling down to the issue

My favored outline for a case involves spending about a page presenting the issue as an introduction, then introducing the broadest topic I plan to cover, followed by drilling back down to the issue. For a business case, you can visualize this as a series of subsystem relationships, as illustrated in Figure 7.1. Using that illustration, for example, the outline would become:

I.   Introduction
II. The Industry (including key competitors)
III. The Company (or Organization)
IV. The Business Unit (or Department)
V.   The Specific Situation

The advantage of this particular organization is that it encourages the participant to take a broad perspective of the setting before narrowing down to the specifics of the case.

While this organization seems straightforward, it can only rarely be applied in practical settings. The problem is that systems overlap, cross boundaries and, in some cases, seem almost orthogonal to each other.

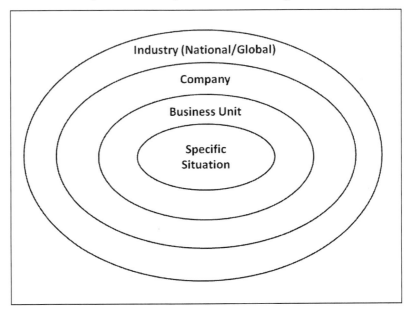

Figure 7.1: Subsystem relationships leading to discussion case outline

Consider, for example, the type of relationships we might find in a higher education setting, illustrated in Figure 7.2. Here we have an educational system consisting of both institutions and research/subject matter disciplines. The issue being examined likely occurs in the context of a program offered by the institution to which a department contributes some, but not all courses. The instructor probably teaches courses within that department (which is grounded within a particular research discipline) but the instructor may well teach courses within the program as well. Then we have the course which—in the illustration— is taught by a single instructor but might also be taught by several. Finally, we drill down to the issue or decision associated with the case. This actually represents the situation described in the EMBA case series (Appendix G), which could have equally well followed many different patterns of organization while nevertheless remaining faithful to the drill-down philosophy.

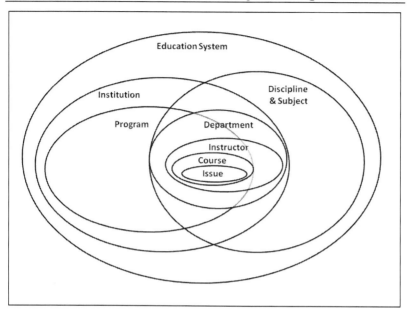

Figure 7.2: Subsystem relationships in a typical higher education case—the simplified version.

It should also be relatively self-evident that not all systems can be covered in detail, if at all. Here, the case writer's assessment of the situation will be important. Personally, I would disagree with sticking to the bare bones of facts relevant to the case, however. As I have already emphasized a number of times, distinguishing what is relevant from what is not is an important skill for participants to practice.

The narrative case

There are times when a drill-down approach to case topics is simply not suitable. A good example might be a heavily disguised case that deals with a universal issue. For example, a case study might focus on an individual's response to grief caused by the death of a loved one. While some aspects of work or school might be relevant, such as the external demands they are placing on individual, it may well be that factors such as industry, product or subject matter are not driving the situation. Under such circumstances, it probably makes sense to omit them from the case.

Where a drill-down approach is not used, the situation and context tend to be blended. The result is a narrative that flows more naturally and reads like a story. While this can lead to a presentation that is more pleasant to the reader, it makes it harder to digest and locate the details necessary for analysis of the decision or situation. It also tends to encourage participant openings that are, in essence, little more than a précis of the case situation. For this reason, I would generally employ this topic structure mainly for short and simple cases.

This, of course, leads to one of the main advantages of pure narrative cases: they can be quite short. Many of the discussion cases that I have read in the education area, for example, are just a few pages long. Obviously, such a short presentation cannot begin to cover all the areas that could *potentially* impact the decisions or actions that could be contemplated in the case. There may be rare times, however, when the essence of a particular decision situation can be captured so concisely[11].

More commonly, however, the best use of a narrative case is to bring to the surface differences in the tacit assumptions of discussion participants. When necessary information is not stated within a case, participants need to supply the missing pieces based on their own experiences. When the diversity of the participant group is great, so may be the diversity of these assumptions. Seeing how these differ as the discussion progresses can be a very informative experience.

My own preference has always been to embed these mini-cases in the context of a broader discussion of a more comprehensive case study. For example, when discussing Frontier Airlines (mentioned in an earlier example) and the topic turns to ethics, I always take a few minutes to describe what American Airlines was doing with its reservation system during the same time period in an effort to undermine Braniff Airlines (American's chief competitor at its Dallas airport hub). Very quickly, substantial differences in participant assumptions regarding what is, and is not, ethical behavior emerge. Recognizing that such diversity of perspectives exists in one's peers is the lesson that I am trying to help participants learn; that is far more important knowledge than any situation-specific ethical rules or guidelines that might be derived from the examples presented.

Case exhibits

A common supplement to discussion cases is a set of exhibits. These usually contain source material or supplementary information that can help the participant to acquire a more cohesive picture of the case situation and can serve as the basis for further analysis. In business cases, these supplements might include financial information, newspaper clippings, tables or graphs of statistics, selected slides from presentations, memos, resumes, and so forth. In education cases, they might include course syllabi, material from web sites of institutions involved in the case, biographies, and so forth. The selection is limitless.

Generally, exhibits are placed at the end of the case as opposed to being inserted in the case narrative. In the event exhibits are limited in size and mainly consist of graphics, a reasonable argument can also be made for embedding them within the text for convenience of reading.

I have heard two arguments made with respect to what should and should not be used as an exhibit. One line of thought is that every exhibit should make a material contribution to the case. This is the more common view and helps keep case size down. Its principal disadvantage is that it provides students with a useful heuristic to use in analyzing a case—if you are not using the exhibit, then you are missing something. If such a heuristic had a real world analog, teaching it to students would be an undeniable benefit. Unfortunately, few situations I have encountered allow for such straightforward determination of what is and is not relevant.

The other argument is that exhibits should be allowed to contain both highly relevant and less relevant content. This tends to force the student to engage in the more realistic task of distinguishing between what does and does not matter. This approach comes with its own risk. If students fail to recognize that exhibits often contain information that is critical to the analysis of the case, they may choose to ignore them as a general practice.

I tend to write cases that oscillate between the two extremes. In a normal case, I will add exhibits that I think are interesting but not critical to the key issues of the case. If the case starts becoming too long or complex, however, I will remove them.

The Case Sequence

A fairly common case organization that allows plotlines and topic outlines to be mixed involves creating a sequence of cases. The EMBA 2002 (A)-(C) cases illustrates this particular strategy:

- The (A) case employs a Discussion/Design-Action Plan plotline and a drill down topic outline. Students learn about the case context and have to devise an action plan.

- The (B) case employs Discussion/Sense-making-Underlying Forces plotline and a more narrative topic outline. In this case, handed out in class, students are asked to predict the student response to the particular strategy employed by the instructor and explain the instructor's rationale for his decision.

- The (C) case simply presents the outcome and is rarely used for discussion.

Case sequences offer the case writer the opportunity to provide a number of different options for using a case. For example, by handing out the (A) and (B) cases just described at the same time, the nature of the classroom discussion could be transformed. It would, for example, become much more focused and could probably be completed in a much shorter time. In an entirely different context, the (A), (B) and (C) cases collectively could be cited in research as evidence of the efficacy of the strategy employed.

There are three disadvantages I can see to using the case sequence approach:

1. If the later cases in the sequence are to be handed out in class and read, they can place very serious demands on class time. That constrains them to be quite short if intended for that purpose (or the class needs to be very long…)

2. Once sequenced cases are written and published, there is always the possibility that diligent students will be able to locate these subsequent cases on the Internet and allow themselves to be unduly influenced by them.

3. Telling participants how a particular course of action succeeded or failed tends to place more importance to outcome than it deserves in a complex environment. What we are trying to

convey to participants is a process of analysis and a toolbox of actions they might consider when a similar situation arises. The nature of complexity is such that it is probably not in the participant's best interest to induce that a particular action will or will not work in a general way.

Naturally, the fact that I create sequenced cases for my own purposes from time to time implies that I do not consider these obstacles to be insurmountable[12]. Rather, they simply need to be considered.

The Case Cross Section

A challenging structure to implement, yet one that tends to be well received when you can pull it off, involves presenting multiple cases that relate to the same topic or the same case from two different perspectives. My most vivid experience with the latter involves the AFN (A) and (B) cases, presented as an example later in the chapter. Constructing a case by embedding multiple cases is illustrated in the example that follows.

Example: Classroom response units in human sexual behavior

For a number of years, I participated in a summer teaching workshop, sponsored by the USF *Center for 21ˢᵗ Century Teaching Excellence*, that was intended to encourage faculty members to incorporate appropriate technologies into their teaching activities. As part of that workshop, participants were required to implement a technology in a course they taught in the following fall semester, then report back on the outcome in the spring.

I attended first as a participant in the summer of 2004. During that time, I noted a distinct tendency among participants to be more interested in the technologies than in the unintended consequences that would invariably accompany adding a particular technology to a course. Thus, I suggested that we develop a series of discussion cases that profiled the decisions facing instructors using technology. We would then make the discussion of the cases an important element of the workshop. The idea approved and, ultimately, nine new cases were developed as a consequence of the project.

The first round of cases included a case study on the implementation of audience response technology (a.k.a. "clickers"). The particular setting

---

was an undergraduate course in human sexual behavior that, to put it bluntly, had not gone very well for a variety of reasons (Gill, El-Rady & Myerson, 2006). The decision to be made was therefore whether to continue with the project or to abandon it. And, if the project were to continue, what changes needed to be made?

The difficulty writing this case presented was that it would be hard to justify continuing without sounding like a marketing brochure for the technology. Actually, it was hard to make an argument for continuing at all, given the technological and organizational problems the instructor faced. Needless to say, I was not particularly enthusiastic about a case that highlighted only the weaknesses of the technology.

The way we addressed this—both in the write up and in reality—was to put the instructor together with two other instructors who had used the technology successfully (one of them was me, the other an instructor in Biology). We then looked at how the implementations had differed and what paths the original instructor might take if she chose to continue. In the case study itself, this was accomplished by writing sections on all three implementations within the same case. Not only did this provide a broader cross section of how the technology might be used, it also provided a basis for discussion participants to propose suggestions as to how the human sexuality course might be modified to make the use of clickers more effective.

Writing for Your Audiences

The purpose of a discussion case is to facilitate learning on the part of participants in later discussions. When you are writing a case, however, it is important to recognize that you are writing for at least three potential audiences: your students, your client organization and other researchers/instructors. We now briefly consider the needs of each of the three.

The Student Audience

Since much of what I have already said about case topic selection and organization has obvious implications for the student audience. I limit my remarks here to two topics: writing style and assuming background.

Writing style

Write in whatever style will best help your students understand the case.

This hard and fast rule will typically force you to abandon all the pretensions of academic writing that you have likely learned. The good news is that they will not be missed. So as not to dilute the message, I shall say no more on this topic.

Assumed background

Nearly every discussion case, whatever the domain, assumes that participants will have some background in the subject of discussion. Over the years, I have come to find that the less background we assume the better[13]. Even supposedly basic knowledge is often lacking. For example, Jeffrey Pfeffer and Christina Fong (2002, p. 82) report the following:

> Recently, an investment bank was horrified to find that an MBA graduate it hired from a leading business school, an individual who had apparently taken a number of courses in finance, could not calculate the net present value of a future stream of payments[14].

The problem is not that basic materials are omitted from our curricula. Rather, it is that we assume coverage in a course is sufficient to assure retention. In doing so, we fail to recognize the critical role that repetitive practice plays in knowledge formation (Gill, 2010; Willingham, 2009).

Case studies actually provide a reasonable venue for acquiring the type of repetitive practice that can lead to retention of basic analytical skills and concepts. Somewhat paradoxically, however, this only works if we are prepared to walk our students through a particular analytical process every time it comes up in a case.

Normally, I choose to embed whatever instructional material I deem necessary into the case itself. Another sensible approach to handling the issue of insufficient recall on the part of students is through developing an accompanying *technical note[15]*. Such notes can also be used to offer instruction on new concepts introduced by a case[16]. A particular advantage of this approach is that the same note can then potentially be used in other non-case method courses.

The Client Organization Audience

Whenever I facilitate a case discussion class, I warn students that they should be aware of the case writer's need to satisfy the requirements of the case client organization. This is most likely to be reflected in embellishments to the case and in how difficult topics are covered. Sometimes, however, the demands of accuracy and the demands of the client diverge so greatly that the only ethical alternative is to walk away from the case. These three aspects of writing a case that satisfies the client are now discussed.

Forgivable embellishments

There may be times when the case writer may need to express enthusiasm for a situation that he or she may not necessarily feel. In truth, I have found this happens relatively rarely. More often, I find myself being caught up in the client's enthusiasm. This is good, since I would generally prefer not to write about a business or teaching situation where I felt the protagonists were not exhibiting at least some dimensions of excellent behavior.

Where embellishments are most likely to occur is where client statements about the present situation or past situation go unchecked by the case writer. A business client may indicate that his organization is a market leader; an educator may report that a past offering of a particular course was highly successful. Quite often, clients do not have a factual basis for making such statements. At least in my own case writing efforts, I have been reluctant to question such assertions too stringently.

I am of two minds with respect to how a willingness to accept the client's version of the facts impacts the rigor of the case. On the one hand, stating as fact something that is wrong is clearly invalid. On the other hand, decisions are made on the basis of what the client perceives to be true. That perception may be in error, yet it nonetheless drives the decision. Since discussion cases are fundamentally about learning to make complex decisions, the fact that some client assumptions may be in error should not necessarily invalidate the process—although it could certainly invalidate the conclusions drawn by the client.

Regardless of your views with respect to the need to verify those facts presented by the client, you can avoid taking a position on the accuracy of a set of facts by presenting them in a quote within the case. For example, rather than asserting that the client produces the highest quality products in an industry, you can write words to the effect:

J. P. Cruikshank, the firm's marketing director, stated "we believe our products are the highest quality in the industry..."

Instead of asserting that students uniformly enjoyed a particular course, you could write:

C.W. Jamieson, the course instructor, said: "Students love the course! If you read the evaluation comments, they positively gush over the new format..."

I use this technique extensively in my own case writing. To ensure the validity of the quotes, when interviewing case clients who make a statement of this sort, I usually try to get the precise wording at that point in time[17]. Once again, I do not view this approach as necessarily being inconsistent with the demands of rigor. It is our beliefs that necessarily guide our decision making, not the underlying truth of those beliefs. And, of course, it avoids the need to confront the client with evidence that their products are not as high quality as those of competitors, or that a particular course is not nearly as excellent as they think it is.

The sensitive topic

It is a rare case situation where the case writer does not make one or two observations that the organization would prefer not to see disclosed. Earlier in the chapter, I argued that it is often possible to get such situations included in the case if you have established a sufficiently good rapport with the client. There still remains the problem, however, of writing it up.

The philosophy that I have always employed in these situations is to write about the sensitive topic entirely from the client's perspective. What I happen to think about the matter is immaterial. When the area is sensitive, I try to get inside the client's head and describe precisely what he or she tells me he or she is feeling. Moreover, I would never let anyone else see what I have written until the individual being interviewed has seen it first and has informally approved it. Where more than one individual is involved, each individual gets to look only at those parts relating to his or her thoughts. A particularly vivid example of how sensitive certain situations can become is provided by the AFN cross sectional cases.

Example: American Financial Network (A) and (B) Cases

The AFN pair of cases profiles a difficult decision being made by the CEO and founder of a mortgage company in the mid-1990s. I developed it for use in my own classes, but it was later included in the short-lived *Prentice Hall* MIS case series (Elam, 1997).

The protagonist in the (A) case was an HBS alumnus who had become a friend of mine through the local HBS club. He had suggested that I come in to do a case study on a new information system he was developing that was intended to automate a number of aspects of the mortgage origination process. The company was a small one and the project was an ambitious one. As it happened, their lead (and only) full time developer was a former student of mine, one that I had recommended to the company.

As I began the case development, it became increasingly clear to me that the scope of the information system being developed was growing far out of proportion to the number of developers assigned to it—which, as I mentioned, was one. Moreover, tensions between the protagonist and the developer were mounting. This culminated when the protagonist sent an extremely ill-advised email to the developer that consisted of little more a laundry list of criticisms. He then came to me, outlined the episodes that were leading to his frustration, and asked my opinion as to whether or not he should fire the developer.

During the time period that this was occurring, the developer also sat down with me and, in confidence, told me he had another opportunity and wondered if he should quit. He also described many of the same episodes, but from an entirely different perspective.

Thus, I found myself with, not one but two, interesting decisions that happened to be completely interrelated: whether or not to fire, whether or not to quit. Compared with these, the original case topic—involving decisions regarding features to be included in the system being developed—was entirely uninteresting. Indeed it was irrelevant, since any functionality questions needed to take a back seat to the personnel issues involved.

As I came to understand the nature of the conflict, I allowed myself to be used as an intermediary between the two parties and, finally, got them into the same room talking with each other. The result was a surprising amount of consensus and forgiveness. Seizing on the moment, I suggested that I write a two part case on the situation. The first case would be written from the manager's perspective; the second, from the developer,s. Both agreed and my friend even went so far as to let me include the offending email as an exhibit to the case.

Over the next 5 years, I used the AFN (A) and (B) cases many times. I could always count on them to produce an active discussion because a typical class would split almost 50-50 between the two perspectives, leading to lively debate. In addition, the two central characters—who parted ways shortly after the case was written—could nearly always be counted on to come to the class and comment after the discussion. When I taught the case a couple of times online, using an asynchronous format (see Chapter 11), they did more than that. Owing to the uninhibiting effect of being online, they actually entered the discussion and posted numerous comments, much to the amusement of the students who were supposed to be discussing the case.

Whatever happens, should someone involved in a sensitive situation become uncomfortable with what I have written, I rewrite it or simply move on to another topic if I cannot. I cannot imagine a worse breach of case writing ethics than to punish someone for sharing their private thoughts with me through including an unapproved version of those thoughts in the final case.

Very rarely, however, after profiling someone's thoughts it is I who become uncomfortable, not the person involved. That leads us to the next topic, when to walk away from a case.

When to walk away

In almost any field where the case method is appropriate, students can find ample examples of bad practice on their own. They do not need my help in doing so. Thus, I have little motivation to write a case study demonstrating bad practice. In fact, I quickly lose interest in a potential case site once I begin to get the sense that it is unlikely to yield any evidence of exemplary practices along some dimension. Usually, this determination can be made well before actual case writing begins. On a very few occasions, however, it was not until I became involved in the actual case writing process that I began to question the wisdom of the case. Just once, I decided that the case should be abandoned after it had already been developed and used once[18].

There are at least three specific circumstances where it probably makes sense to walk (if not run) away from a case writing opportunity. These are as follows:

1. When a real decision cannot be profiled

2. When it becomes clear that the truth of a situation will never make an acceptable (or approvable) case

3. When the individual with final authority for approving the case cannot be identified

We return to the last of these topics later in the chapter, when we consider the case approval process.

The Researcher Audience

When writing a case for discussion that you plan to publish, you should always recognize the real possibility that it will serve as an observation for later research. I have argued in previous chapters that a well written discussion case can and should be as rigorously written as a research case. Both types of cases necessarily make some concessions to reality, however. In the research case, the concessions usually revolve around presenting the case in a manner that allows it to be mapped to whatever theory or theories are being tested. Imagining that the case description in a research case is not being molded in such a way is simply naïve. Indeed, Graham Allison's (1971) previously mentioned *Essence of Decision*—one of the most well-known case studies ever published—demonstrates this perfectly by relating the same case in three different ways.

In the discussion case, the most likely threats to rigor come from the previously discussed need to write the case in a manner that is consistent with the client's desires. To maximize rigor in the event the discussion case is subsequently used for research, the case writer should strive to:

- Disguise as little as possible.

- Clearly identify where disguising has taken place.

- Discuss any liberties taken within the case in a not-for-public-distribution teaching note (or research note).

The last of these would not generally be covered in a release document, particularly if distribution is controlled. That leads us to the subject of getting a discussion case approved.

The Case Approval Process

Research cases typically require approval to commence, but do not require the organization to sign off at the end. On the other hand, I have never participated in writing a discussion case where a formal approval from the participating organization was not required.

Human Subjects Issues

The old adage goes, "it is easier to ask for forgiveness than to ask for permission." Case studies present an interesting challenge in this regard when it comes to the protection of human subjects (in the U.S. at least). How a case is intended to be used plays an important role in this context.

Case method research approval

Where a case is intended for research, the situation starts out relatively straightforward. Case studies involve human beings so, for the most part, we would anticipate institutional review would be required. When case research is conducted as case *method* research, the situation may become a bit less clear cut for two reasons:

1. The types of research design documentation that would be expected for other types of research—such as experiments or clinical trials—may either be unavailable or so nebulous that an institution's review board will have a difficult time passing judgment.

2. The co-mingling of participant roles—both in the activities being observed and in writing up the research—that is common in case method research may obscure the researcher/subject distinction to such an extent that it becomes impossible to tell which is which.

Both these issues were previously noted in Chapter 5. As a general rule, however, it certainly makes sense to contact an IRB member directly for guidance, as Yin (2009) suggests.

Discussion case approval

Where discussion cases are being developed, the waters become even murkier. This lack of clarity is the consequence of two further issues:

1. Many academics do not consider the development of discussion cases to be research.

2. Specific exemptions are granted for research directly related to normal classroom activities.

As should be evident by now, I consider the first of these issues to be a product of academic narrow-mindedness, hardly worthy of comment. Since practice, students and the researcher all become better informed as a result of discussion case development, the only justification I can see for failing to treat the activity as research would be if we defined research as being the creation of knowledge devoid of all possible use. While an outsider might easily be convinced that we, in the social sciences, are using precisely such a definition as the guiding principle for our research, I'm not sure that even we would want to define research quite that narrowly.

The second of these issues needs to be considered a bit more explicitly. In the U.S., the document governing human subjects research is the *Code of Federal Regulations* (CFR), specifically Title 45 Part 46 (45 CFR 46). This code lists activities governed by the code, then asserts the following (paragraph 101b):

(b) Unless otherwise required by department or agency heads, research activities in which the only involvement of human subjects will be in one or more of the following categories are exempt from this policy:

(1) Research conducted in established or commonly accepted educational settings, involving normal educational practices, such as (i) research on regular and special education instructional strategies, or (ii) research on the effectiveness of or the comparison among instructional techniques, curricula, or classroom management methods.

These exemptions, while not specifically applying to the development of course materials are part of a series of exemptions that relate to educational methods. Discussion cases are generally accepted to be educational tools. Thus, the general consensus—at least at my institution—is that they are exempt from IRB approval, whether or not they are considered research[19].

Once a discussion case has been developed, its later use for research purposes is protected by another exemption in 45 CFR 46 101b, which exempts:

> (4) Research involving the collection or study of existing data, documents, records, pathological specimens, or diagnostic specimens, if these sources are publicly available or if the information is recorded by the investigator in such a manner that subjects cannot be identified, directly or through identifiers linked to the subjects.

I would encourage discussion case writers at other institutions to determine their own institution's policy on these matters. I also include, as Appendix I, a document that I submitted to the USF IRB for a research proposal to develop discussion case studies as part of an NSF grant; although I did not ask them to do so, they ruled it exempt.

Case Release Document

For many organizations, participating in a case study can raise significant concerns. The same is true for individual protagonists described in a case. Some of these issues were addressed earlier, in Chapter 5, since they apply to nearly all case settings. These involve establishing processes that ensure individuals get the chance to see what is written about them before it distribution of case drafts becomes widespread. For discussion cases, however, at the end of the case development process, the client organization will normally sign a release document. The same would be true for a discussion case profiling an individual (e.g., an instructor in an education case) provided that individual is not listed as a co-author, which would imply a release has been granted.

Purpose of the case release document

The explicit purpose of a case release document is to formalize the organization or individual's agreement that the case study may be distributed. The implied purpose is to give the organization participating in the development of a case study considerable leverage in ensuring that the resulting case is consistent with its expectations. Because of the leverage that the release/non release authority provides, this process is much more likely to pertain to discussion case development than to research case development (where giving client's excessive control over the final product could justifiably be considered a threat to rigor).

In addition to making the release formal, the release document will often include a number of clauses detailing subsequent handling of the case. These include:

- Revision rights

- Distribution rights

- Withdrawal rights

We now briefly consider each of these issues.

Revision rights

As a case writer, you really do not want to go through the approval process again if there is a typographical error or small fact that needs correcting. As a consequence, I always try to ensure that there is provision for making small revisions to correct obvious errors without requiring a new release document. On the other hand, it is important for the client to feel protected against substantive changes that the case writer might be inclined to make to the case after the release has been signed.

Right to distribute and copy

Copyright is, in essence, the right to copy and to specify who can copy a piece of written work[20]. In the U.S., at least, copyright is automatically assigned to the author of a work—with or without the © notation—and the author can then choose to reassign it or give explicit permissions to copy.

Depending upon what the final case product looks like, an organization may want to distribute it to selected stakeholders, post it on a web site or make the copy available in some other way. I always give the client that right in the release document. Not only does this make the client happy, it gives me justification for a specific exclusion should I choose to publish the in a journal or at a conference that requires me to transfer the copyright. I have never had a problem getting such an exclusion after providing the publisher with a copy of the signed release document[21].

Although I have yet to have an organization request to hold the copyright to a case, such a situation could arise. In that case, I would request the rights to copy the case for my own purposes. Then, in the event that we (the organization and I) agreed to submit the case for publication or to a conference, I would need to ensure that the publication/conference did not insist upon copyright transfer.

The only other copyright issue that a case writer needs to be concerned about in creating a case is to be sure that the copyrights of others are not inadvertently infringed upon. The greatest danger here occurs when images and other artwork (e.g., logos) are included in a case. Often, these works—particularly photos—are not even owned by the company that is using them[22]. Sometimes, the use of these in a local case can be defended on the basis of "fair use", which offers academics some rights in course materials not generally available to others. In the U.S., however, fair use law is sufficiently vague so that a sensible publisher would not take the risk of publishing a case with such content unless proper permissions have been obtained.

Right to withdraw the case

What happens if a client organization decides a particular case no longer serves its purposes? A few decades ago, this could be handled by preventing further distribution of the paper copies of the case. For the most part, doing so was tantamount to making the case disappear.

Today, it is much more difficult to put that particular genie back in the bottle once it has been released. Even removing a case from a web site does not necessarily clear all the copies that have been cached by various search engines. Furthermore, if a case study has been published, it is very unlikely that you would be able to convince a journal or conference to remove it because its protagonist suffered from second thoughts. Thus, once a case is released, it is likely to stay released.

What I will often do for a client is ask if we can delay the release until after the first time it has been used for a class discussion. For local cases, that means that the client is likely to be there, watching the discussion. Sometimes, this leads to changes in the case. It could, conceivably, also lead to the client's refusal to release the case—although I have yet to see that happen.

I would also be willing to commit to best efforts to withdraw a case after its release should the client demand it. As just noted, I suspect those efforts could not be entirely successful. Nevertheless, I would be willing to try if my offering to do so made the client more comfortable.

Sample release document

Appendix D provides a template for the case release document that I typically use. In addition to covering the points just mentioned, there are two key features that I would point out. First, it is very short. Second, it describes a process of attempts at amicable resolution followed by arbitration in the event a dispute arises. Both of these represent my attempt to make the release something that the individual protagonist feels confident in signing without the need to involve legal counsel. The goal here is to streamline the case release process.

If a client were to indicate that he or she planned to involve legal counsel as part of the release process, I would insist (to the degree that I could) that legal counsel be given a draft of my intended release agreement template as soon as possible—well before the case itself was written and ready for release. If counsel raised any objection, I would attempt to negotiate a suitable template prior to doing anything else. If an agreement on an acceptable form for the release agreement could not be reached, this would strongly indicate that the case would never be released. I would then be inclined to stop the case project, since it would leave a bad taste in everyone's mouth—including that of the actual client—if the case were written and could not then be used.

Ethical Issues

In developing a case study, a strong bond of trust typically forms between the client and the case writer. In my own experience, I have many times been asked for my advice with respect to what should and should not be included in the case. Oddly enough, this includes areas where I would have thought that the client should be more knowledgeable than I—questions such as: Is this piece of information of competitive value? Would revealing this aspect of my teaching raise eyebrows in the administration? And so forth…

Being asked for advice from a client about issues where you are obviously self-interested creates a serious potential for ethical breaches. For my part, I look at these issues in the broader context of my ultimate goal for every case writing activ*ity: establishing an enduring informing rela-tionship with the client.* This particular perspective greatly reduces any temptation I might otherwise feel to tell little lies, such as "Developing a case will hardly take any of your time at all…" or "Even after a case is released, you can recall it if you want to…" or "Revealing to the world the strategy you use for negotiating with customers won't be of any use to them…" or "Nobody will care that you grade papers using a Ouija board…"[23].

My view is that asserting something that later turns out to be untrue will quickly erode whatever trust I have managed to build up. That means that the long term informing potential of the relationship with the client will be correspondingly diminished. Personal ethics aside, there are few issues that come up in a case writing situation to make such a risk worth taking. Thus, I have always found the best policy is to be completely candid. That includes being willing to admit "I don't know" when I am asked for advice on issues where I cannot be sure of the implications even though I know what I would like the client to do.

The Teaching Note

If you decide to get a teaching case published, you will probably need to write a teaching note. In this section, we will consider the basic ele-ments that should be incorporated into these notes[24].

Resources in a Teaching Note

The purpose of a teaching note is to help an instructor better facilitate a case discussion. This can be done by providing the instructor with a number of different types of resources. These most commonly include:

1. Learning objectives

2. Examples of analytical frameworks

3. Information not available to students that can help clarify the case

4. A road map for the case discussion

5. Possible study questions for students

6. Key points for the discussion summary

In addition to these resources, it is increasingly common for supplemental teaching materials, such as interview videos, to be made available to facilitators. These are discussed later, in Chapter 8.

Every resource provided to the facilitator has its own advantages and disadvantages. Broadly speaking, the teaching note tends to encourage a rather directive approach to the case discussion. For those finding this approach consistent with their facilitation style, the resources can be very useful. For individuals who prefer a less directive style, the benefits are less evident.

Learning objectives

The learning objectives of a case study, often combined with synopsis, highlight the key lessons the case was designed to instill. By identifying these up front, the facilitator is given guidance on where to focus. The problem I occasionally find with these is by emphasizing very specific lessons that should be "learned" from the case, they ignore the bigger picture of why we use cases in the first place, which is to build more general skills of problem solving, communication and cooperative learning.

Learning objectives can also be particularly useful when a course designer is trying to decide what cases to include in a course without fully preparing the actual cases themselves (or in some circumstances, even reading them). While this sounds like a backhanded criticism, it actually reflects a real need. Preparing a case in sufficient detail to even begin to recognize its strengths, weaknesses and potential value takes a long time (I typically devote 4-6 hours to my initial preparation of a case). As it happens, such time is often hard to find when revising the collection of cases listed in a syllabus being prepared for an upcoming semester. Concise information that helps determine if a particular case should be included can be very helpful.

Examples of analytical frameworks

If you have been reading the chapter notes as they are encountered, you will know by now that I am not a particular fan of teaching notes. Given that a teaching note is a practical necessity for publishing discussion cases in many outlets, however, the type of materials that I find most useful is presentations of suitable analytical frameworks.

An analytical framework includes conceptual schemes useful in understanding the case. Every domain has these schemes. In business cases, they might include growth-share matrices, SWOT (strength, weakness, opportunities, threats) presentations, competitive forces models, value chain diagrams, and so forth. In education cases, Bloom's taxonomy and Perry's Stages may be used, among a myriad of others. Where the teaching note can assist facilitators is in identifying which conceptual schemes—from the vast array of options available in a given field—will fit most naturally to the particular case. The note may also provide illustrative figures that could be developed on the board by the instructor under the direction of participants.

Analytical frameworks are not limited to conceptual schemes, however. They may also include novel ways to present case material that highlight important points, without necessarily interpreting them. For example, when a case contains multiple alternative options to choose from, I frequently end up creating a table on the board with the options presented as columns and distinguishing features of the options presented as rows. This presentation helps students better understand where the options differ and where they are similar.

Analytical frameworks may also identify specific analyses that ought to be considered. Particularly in a case with a lot of numeric exhibits, a common occurrence in business cases, there is an unbounded number of analyses that could potentially be performed. The teaching note can help the facilitator identify what analyses are likely to be most beneficial for understanding the case.

Example: What is the meaning of 42?

I still recall, from my first year MBA marketing class, a professor demanding to know the importance of the number 42^{25}. For 15 minutes we debated this—every attempt to resolve the question failed (including my own, dismissed without comment). It turned out to be the percentage of the organization's sales that were attributable to a single customer, a number that we *should have* computed from the case exhibits but did not. That proved to be absolutely critical to the understanding of the case. And, to this day, it is always an issue I check whenever I look at a company.

Additional information

Teaching notes often include additional information that the students are not privy to. Most commonly, this information relates to what happened after the case. Sometimes, however, it may also include useful background on the context of the case. In a case that has been disguised, for example, the note may explain what aspects of the case have been disguised (or if the case is a major transplant, such as the Concordia Casting case, mentioned in an earlier example).

Personally, I prefer to avoid providing facilitators with too much information that could be material to the case. While it can make the instructor appear to be an "insider", if the information is truly material to understanding the case, my choice would be to embed it in the case itself.

Roadmap for case discussion

The resource most commonly found in a case teaching note is a roadmap for organizing the discussion. This roadmap normally identifies a sequence of topics, the rough amount of time to be allocated to each, and comments about the types of reaction to expect and issues that may be confronted in each topic. Naturally, this means a roadmap should *never* be prepared prior to having facilitated the case.

The potential problem with a roadmap is that it can easily turn into inflexible marching orders. It certainly would for me. This may be a personal problem, but when I develop a well-defined plan, I tend to follow it to the letter[26]. For individuals with a different predisposition, such as my wife Clare (who is nearly my opposite in this respect), having a specific plan in hand could be a godsend, since it would serve as an organizing tool and would not be taken overly seriously. The point I am making is that the suitability of the roadmap—as well as nearly everything else that might be incorporated in a teaching note—depends on how well it fits the needs and personality of the particular facilitator using it rather than on any objective "right" or "wrong".

Student questions

Another nearly universal component of case teaching notes is study questions that can be provided to students in advance. Coming up with good specific questions can be hard, so the experienced facilitator's advice is on this topic is generally welcome.

Many facilitators swear by providing students with these questions. They conclude, quite rightly, that it encourages students to think about these important issues more carefully. As a result, when these issues come up in the discussion, they are likely to be better prepared. In this respect, they perform a function similar to a review session before an exam. When you get specific about the topics that students should study then limit your questions to those topics, you get better performance. The danger here is concluding that this better performance is proof of better learning.

Personally, I almost never provide students with questions about the case. This is just another example of how fit with the facilitator's instructional strategy impacts what is and is not used. Since I tend to be very non-directive, teaching note tools such as roadmaps, study questions and canned summaries hold little appeal for me. Facilitators who prefer a more directive strategy, on the other hand, may use all of these to great effect.

What I particularly encourage the reader to recognize is that anyone who asserts that one approach is objectively better than another either: a) is too committed to his or her own philosophy, or b) simply has not acquired a broad enough exposure to the diversity of the craft.

I return to this topic at greater length when considering case facilitation in Chapter 10.

Discussion summary

Teaching notes often include summary points that can be made at the end of the discussion. These would be particularly useful for those facilitators who conduct a discussion according to the lock step roadmap that was most likely included earlier in the same teaching note, developed based upon experiences with students who had all prepared discussion questions also included in the note. As for me, I would be loath to summarize the key points of a class discussion that has yet to take place. This is true even for cases I have facilitated dozens of times.

Organization of a Teaching Note

Teaching notes tend to be organized according to one of two patterns that closely mirror the two general topic patterns used for the case itself. These are the resource organization and the roadmap organization.

Resource organization

In this organization, the more common, the teaching note is divided into sections that correspond to the resources provided. For example, a typical note organized along these lines might include:

I.   Synopsis/Introduction
II. Learning objectives
III. Analytical framework
IV. Roadmap
V.   Discussion Questions
VI. Summary & Outcome

Full coverage of all these topics is unlikely. Many outlets limit the size of teaching notes and when notes start to become longer than the case themselves, they lose value to facilitators hoping to save time by using them.

Roadmap organization

The roadmap organization corresponds to the narrative organization of a discussion case. Rather than separate out analysis and outcomes from the proposed discussion roadmap, it blends the areas into a continuous narrative of the expected progress of the discussion. This, I would argue, is the more directive of the two teaching note organizations, since its effectiveness tends to depend upon leading the discussion down a particular path.

Publishing the Discussion Case

I am perfectly content when a discussion case that I write is only used locally—often only by me in my own classes. This is fully consistent with my view that the principle goal of writing cases should be to establish enduring informing channels. Nevertheless, it is possible to get high quality discussion cases published. In the "real world" of academia, it is probably important to do so.

There are a variety of potential outlets for publishing discussion cases. These vary considerably by discipline, so I will focus on general categories, outlining the pros and cons of each. All of these outlets are available for business cases. I have found examples of each category for some areas of education. Other disciplinary areas would require the reader to do some individual research.

Conference Discussion Cases

One of the best outlets for discussion cases is conferences. The reason I make such an assertion is that the attendees of the conference become the most likely initial users of the finished case. Unfortunately, it is relatively easy for discussion cases to get lost in the huge amount of content available on the Internet. In a conference setting, you get to market your case and, in the process, establish reciprocal informing with instructors who may use your case and who may have written cases of their own.

There are a couple of disadvantages of publishing conference cases as well. First, of course, is a practical matter: in many disciplines, a conference publication is considered less valuable than a journal publication. This may be less of an issue than it first appears. My only discussion case published in a ranked research journal within my field (Winter & Gill, 2001) was invited after my co-author, Susan Winter, presented it at a conference. The other disadvantage is that conferences frequently place severe restrictions on the length of submissions. Particularly in cases that include a rich set of exhibits, this can be problematic unless it is known—before the case is written—that such limits exist[27].

Case Repositories

A particularly suitable outlet for discussion cases is case repositories. The biggest advantage of this channel is that individuals looking for case studies will invariably start looking at these sources first.

In business, there are a number of different types of repositories for discussion cases. The most prominent is the one maintained by HBS Publishing, which claims to be responsible for 80% of the cases actually used[28]. (The Harvard Graduate School of Education maintains a similar repository of cases in the area of educational leadership). The problem with these repositories, and other university-sponsored repositories I have encountered, is that they generally are not open to submissions from outside the institution or, if they are, those submissions need to be invited.

In business, there are also case repositories that will accept submissions. These include *Ivey Publishing* (out of the University of Western Ontario) and the *European Case Clearing House* (ECCH). Both these outlets review submissions for suitability and send out newsletters to faculty members to publicize their cases. These major case repositories seem peculiar to business.

Discussion cases can also sometimes be found in general repositories of educational materials. A good example of such a repository is Merlot (http://www.merlot.org), where I found a variety of special purpose collections of discussion cases in fields related to education and the social sciences. The *National Center for Case Study Teaching in Science* (http://sciencecases.lib.buffalo.edu/cs/teaching/) maintains a large repository of science-focused cases, although most represent exercise and walkthrough cases (rather than discussion cases). These tend to be quite short and are often constructed—which is to say made up examples.

As may be expected, the problem with repositories is that you do not necessarily get much academic credit for publishing in one. Also, they tend to be created with great enthusiasm and then subsequently abandoned as submissions cease to arrive. I can personally attest to that, as illustrated in the example that follows.

Example: *Informing Faculty*

In several earlier examples, case studies were profiled that were published in the journal *Informing Faculty*. This journal was launched by the Informing Science Institute, at my suggestion, to serve as an outlet for discussion cases of teaching situations in higher education, with a particular emphasis on the use of technology. Its inspiration was the cases that had been developed for the summer institute for *Increment and Transformations* offered by the USF *Center for 21ˢᵗ Century Teaching Excellence*.

The initial volume of the journal, published in 2006, consisted of nine discussion cases and one research case (profiling the *Increments and Transformations* program). Despite a vigorous attempt to publicize the journal, including presentations at four different conferences, not a single additional submission was ever received by the journal. In 2007, the decision was made to reposition the journal as a repository, its current status. Even so, it has yet to receive an outside submission[29].

The main source of the lack of interest in the journal has been obvious. At a research institution, faculty members are typically encouraged to avoid publishing in unranked journals. Discussion cases are often not

---

classified as research. And, outside of schools of education, publishing on pedagogical issues tends to be of lower status than publishing on disciplinary issues. Thus, *Informing Faculty* managed to achieve the triple threat:

- Unranked

- Focused on teaching cases

- Directed towards pedagogical issues

Sadly, no prizes are awarded for coming up with the most improbable publication outlet ever developed. Still, it sounded like a good idea at the time. No wonder so many discussion case repositories seem to have a short lifetime.

Journals and Book Collections

In many business fields, certain journals will publish discussion cases and collections of cases are often published in book form. Such collections published as books also exist in many other fields, acting as specialized repositories of limited duration.

The career advantage of placing a discussion case in a refereed journal is obvious. You can just list the reference on your CV, omitting the fact that it is a case. The disadvantage is that relatively few instructors will search refereed journals for teaching cases. The likelihood of it being found and used is therefore limited. In selecting a research journal outlet for a case, should one become available, I would pay close attention to whether or not it has a policy of allowing copies to be made for educational purposes. If it does, that will make life much easier when making copies available to students.

Publishing discussion cases as chapters in books makes them easier to find. A major problem here is that the books can be so expensive that only libraries can afford to buy them—once again reducing the likelihood that they will be found by other instructors. The aforementioned comment about choosing outlets that allow copies to be made continues to apply here.

In business, we also have some journals that publish collections of discussion cases periodically. These typically resemble a hybrid of a book and a journal. The comments relating to both outlets apply. My sense is that publishing in these may offer greater career benefits than publishing in a repository or conference—but only at the cost of reducing the likelihood that the case will actually be used outside of its authors' own classrooms.

Conclusions

The most important thing to remember when writing a discussion case is that you are not writing a research case. The two approaches differ in a number of ways. The research case writer typically chooses the problem or situation being studied. It pays to be more flexible when developing a case for discussion. The research case writer must maintain objectivity. When writing a discussion case, it is okay (and often necessary) to take a tone favorable to the protagonist. The research case writer (who hopes to be published) needs to anchor the case analysis to theory. Discussion cases are not similarly constrained. The research case writer is interested in cause and effect. The discussion case writer is interested in finding an intriguing situation—one where there is a decision to be made and there are many alternatives to be considered.

Having said all this, when writing a discussion case it is a serious mistake to casually assume that its potential value is limited to the classroom. Discussion cases tend to offer a much richer view of the situation being studied than a research case. As a result, they can be excellent source materials for research and can, from time to time, even serve as a substitute for direct observation (although direct observation is *always* preferable). Thus, the same standards for accuracy that are observed in research should be maintained when writing for the classroom. Indeed, I would argue that the classroom case will have greater direct impact on practice than the typical published research case. Thus, it should probably be held to even higher standards.

With respect to writing and disseminating a discussion case, it is very important for the case writer to recognize that the principal benefits of the activity are not likely to be short term career enhancement. The best reason to write a case for discussion is to develop enduring relationships with practice, to energize your own classroom and to learn about the real world applications of the subject you teach. While publication of quality discussion cases is possible—indeed likely—in many disciplines, I would encourage case writers not to become overly enamored with that particular goal. In most cases, the enduring benefits of writing the case will not flow from an entry on your CV.

Chapter 7 Notes

[1] Understanding working memory has very practical implications. It has helped me to understand why, for example, I can give the simplest programming logic example that I can possibly devise to students in my introductory course, yet they still draw a complete blank. Until they have enough practice looking at the notation itself, they will be completely unable to simultaneously attend to the logic I am trying to teach.

[2] I believe that even the act of facilitating new discussion cases can be a source of practice in observing, although the typical discussion case does not offer the richness of details (particularly irrelevant details) that on site observations provide.

[3] On the subject of consulting, consider the following, that I quote from *Informing Business* (Gill, 2010, p. 485):

> After I had completed the first semester of my doctoral program, I started to develop a picture of the nature of academic research in business[3]; it was not a pretty picture. Being confused as to why we were conducting so much research that seemed (to me) to have no purpose, I began pestering the late Jim McKenney, the department chair, for examples where our research had made an impact on practice. Every time I did so, he began to describe his consulting activities. Each time he responded in that fashion, I explained that I was *not* asking about consulting—after all, I had been a professional consultant and was aware that impact could be exerted through that channel—I was talking about our actual research. After that exchange, a pattern of discourse we engaged in *several* times, we usually agreed to change the subject. Unfortunately, it took me decades to recognize that two quite profound points were being made in these conversations. First, that *consulting is research*. Second, that *consulting offers the researcher one of the most effective channels for achieving impact*.

[4] Actually, there is a fourth approach to case site selection I have experienced: being told to write a case on a particular site. That, of course, was the principal means by which I "selected" sites as a doctoral stu-

dent at HBS. As I have indicated several times in this book, however, HBS is not the best model for most of us to use, since many faculty members literally have organizations lining up to become case sites. That would be a very unrealistic expectation at virtually any other institution.

5 Normally, I avoid discussing cases by name that are still in use since it is possible that a student searching for a case might find this book on the web and have his or her thoughts unduly influenced by my analysis. For Frontier Airlines, however, I make an exception. It will not take the average student long to figure out that all the alternatives available to the company at the time of the case are bad. The case then becomes the vehicle for conveying a particular conceptual scheme: the strategic potential of information systems.

6 Delays in display could lead to huge drop off in bookings. A similar phenomenon today occurs when advertisers do not appear on the first Google page.

7 Students looking the case up on the Internet quickly find out that the company did go bankrupt, though it was later reorganized at least once.

8 Since it has not been updated since the early 1990s, however, the case has become too obsolete even for my own use. Thus, as was the case for Frontier Airlines, I feel comfortable discussing it here.

9 In addition to these sins, the Concordia protagonist also buried bad news about project status deep within memos to the company's executives, thereby ensuring that they would not be noticed.

10 The comment on Concordia Casting only working for less experienced students was initially made to me by an HBS faculty member experienced at facilitating the case.

11 Cases used as examples are entirely different from the short universal cases I am describing, of course. The example case, which can be quite short, is intended to present a particular perspective in short, concrete manner. Thus, the context of the example is often ignored when the lesson to be conveyed does not heavily depend on it.

12 When I facilitate the EMBA 2002 case, for example, I feel it is that the participants complete the class with the sense that the situation worked itself out to everyone's satisfaction. It would not be a good start

to the course to have them all concluding that I was completely clueless with respect to my teaching (and excessively arrogant, to boot). Such a conclusion might easily be drawn from the (A) case by itself.

[13] For example, I have far-too-often been shocked by how little some students in my capstone MS-MIS class know about general IT topics such as information systems architectures. Originally, my assumption had been that there were serious holes in our program (since the capstone course is generally taken in the last semester). Over time, however, I have come to realize that the topics *are* being covered; they simply are not being practiced. As it turns out, that is as bad as not covering the topics at all.

[14] Coincidentally, I once had to walk a recent graduate of MIT's Real Estate master's degree program through precisely the same net present value calculation.

[15] Just to be clear here, a technical note is not the same as a teaching note. Technical notes are provided to students as a supplement to case studies by providing background information useful to the case. For example, while at HBS I wrote two technical notes: "A Note on Farm Supply Channels" and "A Note on Expert Systems".

[16] In business cases, technical notes are also sometimes used to provide background on a particular industry. I have mixed emotions about this, particular where HBS is involved. There used to be an excellent note, for example, on the evolution of airline reservation systems. That note was typically assigned as a companion to the Frontier Airlines case. The problem is that they discontinued publishing the note, and the case suffered as a result. Generally speaking, if a note is integral to the case, I would keep it in the case.

The other problem with HBS notes is that they double the price tag of the case for students. Since HBS cases are already quite costly, and students cannot usually resell the packet at the end of the semester, I find that they rather resent the extra cost.

[17] I further discuss the art and science of acquiring quotes in Chapter 4.

[18] In that particular instance, I read in the local paper that a protagonist of one of my cases—the owner of the firm, a small business specializing in selling used computer equipment—had been arrested after alleg-

edly chasing one of his employees around the office while brandishing a machete. At that point I felt only two alternatives were open to me: 1) abandon the case, or 2) write a best-selling business book titled "Cutting Edge Management".

[19] The matter of exempting discussion case development from IRB approval needs to be revisited when developing discussion cases under a federal grant. Appendix I, which led to an exemption from the USF IRB, was my first effort in this direction. Unfortunately, throughout the document is a line of argument to the effect that case studies do not qualify as "research". Writing those words left a cold, hard knot in my stomach.

[20] Other types of work besides written work can also be copyrighted. This might be applicable in situations where a case includes multimedia (such as video of client interviews).

[21] In fact, when I provided one publisher with a copy of the release document I was using at the time (similar to Appendix D), they then asked if they could use it for other cases.

[22] While developing a recent discussion case, the client related how they had recently been forced to take down a model's web site because the photo of her that she had posted were actually still copyrighted by the photographer, meaning she could not use pictures of herself without paying royalties.

[23] The examples presented are for illustrative purposes only. They do not represent actual situations.

[24] I probably should point out that I never use teaching notes myself and am therefore possibly the worst person in the world to provide guidance about writing them. My personal objections to teaching notes are threefold:

1. *They promote laziness on the part of the facilitator.* My own view is that the facilitator should first approach a case from the student, perform his or her own analysis at a level of detail far deeper than the student would normally attempt and unbiased by preconceptions of what the solution "should" be.

2. *They encourage a particular view of the case, often promoting a "right" solution.* I view the case method as exploratory. Most teaching

notes tend to direct the facilitator down a particular path, or at least encourage a particular direction. Once you have a map with the trail marked, the tendency is to follow it.

3. *They are very often inconsistent with my analysis of the case.* I will not go so far as to assert that these teaching notes are "wrong"; I suspect that depends on how the facilitator choreographs the case. I will say, however, that a great many teaching notes on cases that I have used for many years seem to miss the point of the case entirely, based on how my discussions typically proceed. Paradoxically, I did not discover this until I was writing this book and actually looked at the teaching notes for some of the cases that I profiled and used.

With respect to last point, let me again emphasize that there are many different paths down which a case discussion can proceed. I am far from asserting that mine is the best path. I am comfortable with saying that the paths I have evolved to on certain cases are almost certainly *better paths for my discussions* than the paths promoted by the teaching notes—which were, of course, designed for discussions involving a vastly different group of discussion participants than my students.

[25] Readers of the Douglas Adams' *Hitchhiker's Guide to the Galaxy* will recognize it as the "the Answer to the Ultimate Question of Life, the Universe, and Everything." Sadly, that had nothing to do with its use in the case.

[26] For example, a couple of times my family and I took seven week road trips of the western U.S., typically involving about 30 different hotel stays in as many as 20 different states on each occasion. Both summers, we did not vary one iota from the initial itinerary—even when it would have probably made sense to do so. Given this personality quirk, I am reluctant to get too specific in planning my discussion classes.

[27] For example, as I was writing this book, I developed a discussion case that I submitted to the ICIS conference. For that reason, even before having written a word I could assert that it will be precisely 14 pages long and written in the font that they require.

I will refrain from relating the past experiences that allow me to express the above with such certitude. They revolved around cases prepared *before* I knew the limits. The thoughtful reader can doubtless imagine the plot lines of these stories.

[28] I presume that the HBS repository measures use by counting the number of student-case use instances, rather than by the number of cases. I suspect, however, that the actual "measurement" applied to produce the 80% statistic was rather limited, at best. In fairness, the only basis upon which I make such a skeptical conjecture is my experience trying to verify other similarly vague marketing statistics.

[29] My current plan is to begin another project once this book is completed that could lead to a replenishment of the *Informing Faculty* supply of cases. It would seem that I have a tough time taking a hint.

Chapter 8

Beyond the Paper Case

The practical considerations that mandated most case studies to exist in the form of paper documents are rapidly disappearing. Technologies for creating, editing and distributing multimedia content have become much more widespread and accessible. It has become vastly easier to access information on organizations that is not contained in case studies. New tools for displaying mixed media—such as the cell phone, IPod and web—have become almost universally available. And the pace of change in all these areas does not appear to be slowing. If anything, it is speeding up.

In this chapter, we briefly review some alternative ways in which discussion cases are being delivered. We begin with the multimedia case, versions of which have been in use for nearly two decades. We then consider the web based real-time case—where public information is used to frame a case discussion on issues of current interest as they unfold. We then look at emerging developments in the area of display technology, such as tablet-based computers and readers. Finally, we consider how gaming and AI based technologies might further change the nature of the discussion case.

Of particular interest in this chapter is the construction of the cases themselves. The complementary topic of the challenges and opportunities presented by facilitating and participating in technology-enabled discussions is considered in Chapter 11.

Multimedia Case Studies

Multimedia case studies incorporate a variety of different types of content (e.g., photos, film clips, source documents, interviews) into the presentation of the case. Originally distributed on read-only media such as computer CDs, today they are more commonly distributed over the web. Public video sharing sites, such as *youtube.com* make the process relatively painless. If the case writer does not know how to create and upload such video, his or her children or younger students most certainly will be able to render assistance.

Example: AucNet USA

AucNet USA is one of a series of multimedia case studies developed by the *Laboratory for Innovative Technology and Engineering Education* (LITEE; www.litee.org), a center working mainly out of Auburn University that received much of its initial funding from the *National Science Foundation*. The case study has been distributed in CD form, in PDF form (text only) and online. It features the company AucNet, a Japanese firm originally established to conduct dealer-to-dealer online auctions of used cars. Unlike an earlier HBS case (Konsynski, Warbelow. & Kokuryo, 1996) that featured the same company, the multimedia case included extensive technical decision-making content—making it particularly suitable for engineering students—in addition to business and strategy content.

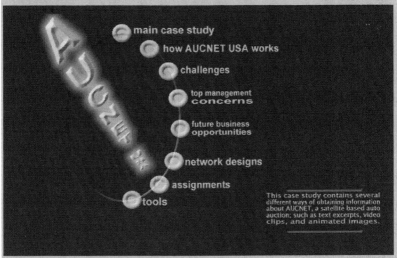

Figure 8.1: Main screen for AucNet USA case study

The web version of the AucNet USA case is available on the LITEE site. As illustrated in Figure 8.1, the main screen provides access to a variety of static content that is organized in hierarchical fashion, meaning that the student will typically drill down through a number of menu layers before reaching the actual content—consisting of text, PDF files, video, animations and slide shows.

In a research study that presented the case, the authors described the case and how it was used as follows (Halpin, Halpin, Raju, Sankar & Belliston, 2004, pp. T2F-13-14):

> AUCNET USA was auction house selling used automobiles. The buyers, however, were in their offices across the country, and the automobiles were still on the sellers' lots. The auctioneer was in a suburban office building in Atlanta, Georgia. In the Network Control Center Yuki Oana, CEO of AUCNET USA, was pleased that the company was selling many vehicles using digital satellite technologies to operate the real-time on-line auctions.
>
> He and others in top management were not sure how long AUCNET USA would remain competitive. They were considering changes in network design to include low-orbiting satellites or even the Internet. What could they do to be a technology and market leader? They even wanted to know about other business opportunities the company might pursue.
>
> Student assignments with this case include having a group research and discuss marketing challenges and ways to keep the company successful. Other groups (a) describe information technologies used in the past, (b) discuss issues in modifying technologies used by the Japanese parent company, and (c) suggest new technologies that could be used by AUCNET USA. The task for yet another group is to make recommendations related to company expansions, including the auction of heavy earth moving equipment and even the flower auction business.

Components of a Multimedia Case

As illustrated in Figure 8.2, a multimedia case typically consists of three components:

1. *Content collection*: A location where multimedia content—which can consist of text, video, audio, data and programs—is stored.

2. *Content server*: A system or application that provides access to content on demand.

3. *Presentation platform.* A system or application that presents the content to the user, typically in the form of text, video and/or audio, or as an interactive experience.

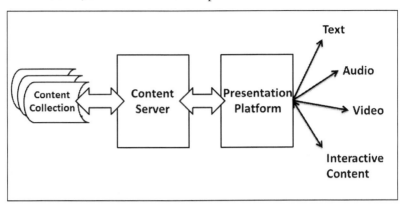

Figure 8.2: Elements of a multimedia case

The actual components of Figure 8.1 can range from the very simple to the highly complex. At the simple end, a multimedia case study might consist of static (i.e., unchanging) text and video files delivered on a CD (content collection) that is accessed through a web browser (content server) on a student's laptop (presentation platform). At the other extreme, the content collection might be stored on a computer in "the cloud" and could consist of static files, data bases that interact with the user of the case, and software applications. The content server might consist of a web server interacting dynamically with the student's web browser that could alternatively reside on a computer, cell phone or tablet-based display system.

Development of Multimedia Cases

Over the past few decades, the challenges facing developers of multimedia case studies have diminished rapidly. In 1990, for example, such a case would have demanded extensive technical expertise in order to overcome obstacles such as:

- Lack of a suitable common software platform for delivering the content

- Low penetration of graphic-capable computers among the targeted students

- High requirements for audio and video storage relative to available storage on most systems (e.g., 100 MB drives vs. today's 1000 GB drives)

- Impracticality of centralized storage of media as a result of low (dialup) download capabilities

- High cost of equipment to capture and edit multimedia.

Today, such technical obstacles have largely fallen by the wayside. A web browser provides a solid platform for delivering basic content and higher end tools—such as Adobe Flash—are readily available for creating customized interactive content. All computers—and most mobile devices—boast graphics capabilities equivalent to the high end systems of two decades ago. Storage problems have largely disappeared both as a result of larger installed media and improvements in compression algorithms (e.g., MP3, MP4). Broadband Internet and cheap web servers have made storing centralized content easy. Finally, the equipment needed to capture video—even high end HD video—has dropped to the point that it is readily affordable even for individuals, with sophisticated editing tools now available for a low price, and even for free.

Although I have not seen any studies to this effect, I also suspect that some of the social obstacles to developing a multimedia case may be dissolving, particularly among younger case protagonists. It is frequently remarked that the new generation entering the workplace is much more willing to share itself electronically (e.g., Facebook, YouTube) than prior generations. For such individuals, a case writer's request to set up a video camera to record an interview, or even to request a few comments be made into a camera-enabled cell phone, would seem perfectly natural.

Just because it has become much easier to develop multimedia cases does not mean that we should *always* set out to develop multimedia cases. As with every tool and technique described in this book, multimedia cases have their advantages and disadvantages. We now consider some of these.

Advantages of Multimedia Cases

The multimedia case differs from its paper-based ancestor in three important ways: i) the flexibility it provides in choosing the sequence of how content is to be displayed to the reader, ii) the richness of the content that can be provided, and iii) the degree of interactivity associated with the process of preparing the case.

Flexibility of Display Sequence

A paper-based case presents its content in a particular sequence that cannot be altered. Obviously, the student preparing the case is free to flip around, e.g., jumping back and forth from text to exhibits. The author, however, has no control over how that material is accessed unless a sequence of individual cases is distributed, such as the (A), (B), etc. cases discussed in the previous chapter.

Once a case is deployed as a multimedia case, on the other hand, the ability to control presentation order can be built into the case. This can be done in any number of ways. If the content server being used is a sophisticated course management system such as Blackboard, content can be hidden until a specific date/time has been reached (it can also be hidden at some point in time, to prevent student procrastination). Alternatively, features provided under the general heading of *"adaptive release"* can be employed to expose content based upon student progress through previously displayed content.

Even where a multimedia case is provided using a simple web server or a CD/DVD, it is possible to exert some degree of control over content. For example, when I was teaching a virtual MBA class using a number of cases that I developed, I arranged interviews with case protagonists where they talk about the decisions that they had actually made after the case was written, captured using a simple webcam. This being in the year 2000, a time when consumer broadband Internet access was rare, I mailed a CD containing all these interviews to the students. To prevent early access, I compressed each interview in a password protected .zip file. Then, after each online discussion, I provided students with the password they needed to view the video.

Richness of Content

One of the big advantages of a multimedia case study is the richness of the content that can be provided. Some types of information—such as the behavior of a product when it is used, the body language of individuals making a statement, or the nature of a production facility—are much easier to convey using full motion video or animations.

The multimedia also case offers few practical limitations on the amount or size of documents that can be included with the case. Unlike a paper case, including additional documents on a web server or CD does not add measurably to cost. An argument for including such background material is that in the "real world", information does not come nicely packaged as exhibits containing relevant summaries of important information. The important process of determining what is, and what is not, useful information can therefore be made far more realistic in a multimedia case study.

Interactive Content

An area where multimedia cases particularly shine is in their ability to offer the reader an interactive experience. For example, a case may provide the user with pre-developed spreadsheets containing information and formulas that can be used to perform sensitivity analysis. It may provide access to programs such as simulations—a common component of many of the multimedia cases developed by HBS. It can also include self-tests and forms that can be used for assessment and feedback to the instructor. Such content can make case preparation a true vehicle for active learning, rather than the more passive reading experience that students often take it to be.

Disadvantages of Multimedia Cases

The seductive flexibility offered by the multimedia can easily hide some important disadvantages of the approach. Three of these, in particular, are likely to limit the degree to which such cases dominate the discussion case arena: 1) Development time and skills, 2) Preparation time, and 3) Discussion dynamics.

Development Time and Skills

The first disadvantage of the multimedia case is the time and skills that are required to develop such a case. A typical business case can be written and released in 40-100 hours by one or two individuals, depending on the experience of the case writers and the complexity of the situation. Education-related cases can often be written even more rapidly, in my experience, because the relevant materials for such cases tend to be located more centrally and fewer interviews are required. Creating and proofing the multimedia for a case will doubtless take much longer. It is also more than likely to impede the release process for the case, particularly if an organization's legal department becomes involved.

Even more of a challenge is the skills needed to develop such a case. Whereas the text case can be written by the case writers and, if desired, made more readable by a good editor, the quality multimedia case could, in theory, require all the skills necessary to produce a film (and associated video game), including author, director, cinematographer, actors, editors and programmers. Very few existing case writers individually possess this full suite of skills. Thus, such cases will nearly always involve a team effort that includes both domain experts (i.e., traditional case writers) and instructional technology experts.

Preparation

While I was at HBS, the student rule of thumb to prepare a 20 page case for discussion was around two hours. Obviously, such a rule goes out the window where a multimedia case featuring 6 hours of video, a few thousand pages of text, and interactive exhibits is supplied to the student. In the previously mentioned *Aucnet USA* case example, the normal protocol was to have different student teams explore different aspects of the case. Where a case revolves around a complex key decision, however, such a divide-and-conquer approach seems inadvisable. Moreover, workload complaints were the most commonly voiced in the course that featured that particular case (Halpin, et al., 2004).

That a case study takes a long time to prepare should not necessarily be viewed as a negative. It does, however, mean that a course that emphasizes the case method will need to make a tradeoff between the richness of each case included and the total number of cases covered in the course. This is a depth vs. breadth question that is unlikely to have a general answer.

Discussion Dynamics

The final drawback of multimedia cases is specifically related to their use as a tool for classroom discussion. Assuming that the case provides lots of material that must be actively accessed, it may be assumed that students will not come uniformly prepared. It may also be assumed that information provided in non-text form (such as interviews or animations) will be very hard to locate during the rapid-fire exchange that typifies a case discussion. As a result—and this is a speculation on my part rather than being based on actual experience—the discussion of a multimedia case is likely to be very tricky to facilitate.

Based upon this conclusion, the multimedia case might best be used as a tool for generating student presentations, such as those that typify student case competitions, rather than as a tool for inspiring discussions. This observation is not intended as a criticism. I believe that both approaches to the case method have value, and therefore have a place in a well-rounded curriculum.

Public Real Time Cases

With the large amount of publically accessible content on the Internet, is possible to construct case studies that present a topic for discussion over the web as it unfolds in the real world. Such cases potentially provide the student with access to thousands of pages of documents and, of course, guarantee that he or she will not be able to look up what was actually done. A pioneer in this arena was the *Yale School of Management* (SOM) as discussed in the example that follows.

Example: Raw vs. Cooked Cases at Yale

In 2006-2007, began producing web-based multimedia cases, referred to as "raw" cases (Elias, 2011). The first such case was "Equity Office Properties (EOP) Trust.", described as follows by Jaan Elias, the Director of Case Study Research at Yale:

> The EOP case website drew together various "raw" materials concerning the buy-out of Sam Zell's real estate investment trust by the private equity firm Blackstone. The site included videotaped interviews, deal documents, analysts' reports, and links to newspaper articles. This new "raw" format for a case study proved to be quite a hit with students and faculty, and we have continued to add web-based, "raw" cases to the inventory. Over half of our case production (17 cases) this year were entirely web-based or had a significant web component. These web-based, "raw" cases represent more than a move to a different medium. They open up pedagogical opportunities consistent with Yale SOM's new integrated curriculum. Traditional cases (what we have come to refer to as "cooked" cases) inevitably simplify a management situation because a narrative requires an understandable beginning, middle, and end. Therefore,

---

the cases are told from a single point of view and focus on a set of questions that tend to fall into one or two disciplines. However, a website is a more flexible format, allowing a number of points of view or story lines to be considered simultaneously. This creates the opportunity for a single case to be analyzed from multiple perspectives. For example, a web-based case study of General Electric's Ecomagination Initiative was taught this year in Professor Fiona Scott Morton's Competitor course, but the class session also brought Professor Ravi Dhar to discuss the case from the Customer perspective and Professor Doug Rae to look at GE from the point of view of State and Society.

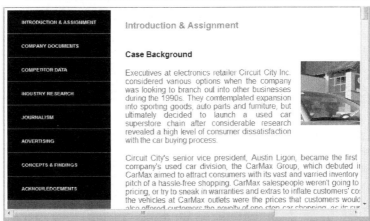

Figure 8.3: CarMax case from http://cases.som.yale.edu/carmax/

As illustrated in the CarMax example case provided on the Yale SOM web site, the "raw" case is presented to students with an interface not unlike that of the earlier Aucnet USA multimedia case. Presented in this fashion, these cases can include "cooked" elements, such as interview transcripts with organizational decision-makers provided by case writers.

Elias (2011) summarizes the difference between raw and cooked cases in the table, included here as Table 8.1. Many of the strengths of raw cases that are listed closely resemble those of multimedia cases in general.

Table 8.1: Comparison of "cooked" and "raw" cases (Elias, 2011)

Cooked, narrative case	Raw, multimedia cases
Linear narrative with a privileged point of view	Multiple points of view of equal weight
Focus on a single discipline	Multiple foci within one package
Separate explanatory notes	Explanatory notes embedded in package
Clean, boiled-down fact pattern	Messy, original documents
An artificial construction (real world problems don't come in cases)	More realistic presentation of information
A story line that presents a set of facts	Preserves real-life uncertainty as to the "real" facts and story line
Students read, then work	Students work as they are navigating through the website
At least six-month lag between an event and the production of a case	Recent events, with the possibility of adding more information as it becomes available
Limited number of black and white exhibits	Colorful, even animated exhibits and graphics, limited only by the imagination of the case writer

Discussion Cases of the Future?

There are a number of technologies that could greatly change the attractiveness of the technology-enabled multimedia case. These are evolving on two fronts: presentation platform and content servers.

Emerging Presentation Platforms

Within the next decade, it is quite possible that we will see a revolution in how we display and read content that will rival the printing press. Should this revolution take place—and there is considerable debate on this, with opinions ranging from "it's inevitable" to "I will never give up the smell of books"—it will be the result of a convergence between three technologies:

- *eBook reader:* For more than a decade, it has been possible to buy relatively compact systems that allow text to be displayed and read in a window. This technology began to gain real traction with the advent of Amazon.com's *Kindle*, which combined easy download and purchase of content with a high quality, paper-like display.

- *Cell phone*: Smart phones now account for half of new cell phone sales. These phones allow users to browse the web and perform a variety of tasks using special-purpose applications known as "Apps". Apple's iPhone revolutionized this space, turning the smart phone into the multimedia platform of choice for many users.

- *Tablet PC*: Fully functional computers that can be operated as slates using a stylus or, more recently, a touch screen instead of a mouse. Microsoft's Tablet PC (Gill, 2007) dominated this space since its introduction in 2002.

The initial convergence of these technologies led to devices such as Apple's iPad, introduced in 2010, and, most recently, the *Kindle Fire*, being launched just as this book went to press.

The significance of this convergence for the future of case studies is great. In the past, a major drawback of multimedia cases has been the need to switch between paper (for easier reading) and the computer screen (for playback of multimedia). The hybrid tablet technologies eliminates this problem, being suitable both for reading[1] and multimedia display.

Along with the new presentation platforms are content standards, such as PDF and EPUB, which make it very easy to incorporate multimedia within text, as illustrated in the example that follows.

Example: A PDF Portfolio eTextbook

To get a sense of the current art-of-the-possible with respect to what can be accomplished with electronic documents, it is instructive to look at the features of an eTextbook that I recently developed for an undergraduate programming course. The "book" incorporated all the materials for the course within a single portfolio PDF file, created with *Adobe Acrobat Professional Extended Edition.*

Flowcharting

Clicking box activates
a narrated video

In introducing constructs, we will--from time to time--use diagrams called flowcharts. In the 1960s and 1970s, developers were often required to flowchart entire applications. Over time, however, it was discovered that flowcharts were mainly useful to those learning how to program. For experienced programmers, they were tedious to prepare, huge in size and offered few real benefits for code design. Thus, they fell out of favor, replaced by less detailed diagramming techniques such as UML. Nonetheless, as noted, these charts can be useful in learning to write code and for illustrating constructs.

We will use a tiny fraction of the flowcharting symbols, including those shown in the table below:

↓	Flow of control
◇	Decision points (flow comes in and goes out along two or more paths)

Figure 8.4 Example of text with embedded video from programming eTextbook

A "portfolio file" is a single document that binds together multiple other documents. In the case of the programming text I prepared:

- Over 450 pages of text with embedded video (roughly 25 hours in total), as illustrated in Figure 8.4.

- Dozens of interactive practice quizzes

- MS-Word forms that are filled out as part of each assignment

- Roughly 70 practice quizzes

- Source code and other files that can be extracted in order to complete exercises.

The splash screen displayed upon entering the book is presented as Figure 8.5.

At the present time, to take full advantage of all the functionality of the programming eTextbook, it must be read on a PC (regular or tablet) or an Apple Macintosh. This restriction is the result of the use of Flash technology to create interactive effects. In the near future, however, we can reasonably expect that similar capabilities will be available for nearly any platform.. Even today, the blend of text and video incorporated in the portfolio can be achieved in the standard EPUB format supported by the iPad.

Figure 8.5: Splash screen for programming eTextbook

The fact that it is becoming increasingly easy to blend text, graphics, video and other interactions into a single document does not change the inherent strengths and weaknesses of multimedia. It does mean, however, that the obstacles to developing multimedia cases are rapidly diminishing.

Tools for Embedding Content

As we look to the future, it may be prove that the next logical step in the evolution of the paper case study is not replacing it with static multimedia, but rather attempting to build an immersive experience. An obvious model to use here is the computer game, either operated by a single student or involving a group of students in role playing mode.

There is little doubt that today's young people are conditioned to game playing experiences, and that they perceive these games to be engaging. There is every reason to expect that game-based cases (built to a standard similar to that of today's commercial games) would prove to be a valuable educational tool. Unfortunately, commercial games today take tens (or hundreds) of thousands of hours to develop. Moreover, if such game-based cases were to become highly popular, it is likely that a market for "cheats" would develop, just as it has for popular games today. Such a development would effectively limiting how long a case could remain in service. Thus, the investment required to create such cases is unlikely to justify their use today. Assuming tools continue to advance, however, we are probably a decade or so away from being able to develop such cases economically. Nevertheless, it is interesting to imagine what such a tool for developing such cases might look like.

Example: A Prototype AI Tool for Case Study Development

In 2008, I had the idea of attempting to build a prototype for a relatively simple to use tool for creating interactive case study games. I spent about three weeks developing the tool—which was written in Microsoft's Visual C# programming language—and, as an assignment, I required my MS-MIS capstone course students create a simple real world case study using the tool. I located for companies/individuals willing to act as case sites and the project took about 8 weeks to complete (in addition to the other class assignments).

The most important lesson I took away from that experience is that it is excessively optimistic to expect students to be able to operate a hastily constructed, undocumented and rather buggy tool that I provided to them. Indeed, only one group actually succeeded in bringing its case materials into the tool. Despite this indifferent outcome, my feeling is that the tool probably offers some useful hints regarding what such a case development environment might look like (if created by others, more competent than myself).

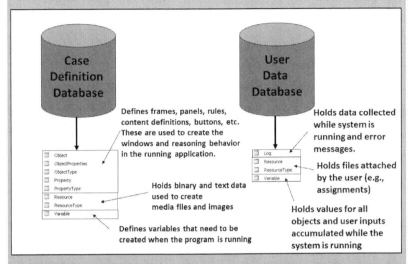

Figure 8.6: Database architecture of AI-based case study development tool

An important aspect of any interactive case study experience is the ability to configure what the user sees based on what the user has already done. As shown in Figure 8.6, I implemented this by using a separate database to hold the case definition (locked down) and information related to the user, which changes as the case study is run.

The case definition database contained a number of different types of information:

1. Definitions of the window layouts used to display case information.

2. A collection of rules that controlled the behavior of the system. For the system, I developed a rule language similar to that used in expert systems, an application category developed within the field of artificial intelligence (AI).

3. Storage for file images of various types (e.g., HTML documents, Word documents, Excel spreadsheets, PowerPoint presentations, plain text, video formats, audio formats and image formats). These were retrieved from the database when needed.

4. Variables that held the state of the system.

The use of rules to define system behavior was particularly critical to the system design. For example, there might be a collection of inter-office memos within the database. Rather than allowing the user to simply browse through them, however, a rule might be established of the form:

IF JaneInterview.Viewed == TRUE

THEN

ACTION JanesMemo.Accessible = TRUE

Assuming JaneInterview was a video clip in which someone named Jane mentioned a memo and JanesMemo was a document file holding the memo, what the rule would accomplish would be to keep the memo inaccessible until the user had actually viewed the JaneInterview clip.

In addition to allowing a case to be created, the system interacted with the user using standard web forms. This allowed questionnaires, quizzes and other information to accumulate as the user progressed through the case study. Since that information could be incorporated into rules, it was possible to make content contingent upon a user's behavior. For example, access to interviews with the president of the company might be made contingent upon a certain score on a quiz being achieved. In addition, the system could be configured to collect documents (e.g., a summary of an interview in an MS-Word document) and store them in the user's database. Upon completing the case, the user-generated information could then be transmitted to the instructor, providing a complete profile of how the user went about interacting with the case.

Based upon my experience developing this tool and using it in a course, I have little doubt that a less user-hostile version could be developed. I also believe that such a tool could provide a valuable complement to existing self-contained case studies. I further believe, however, that a lot more work would need to be done in order to assess just how useful such cases would actually be, and how hard they would be to develop (problems with buggy tools notwithstanding). In particular, I am not sure how easy it would be to:

- Create reasonable rules for controlling content in order to create a realistic experience, and

- Interpret, in an educationally meaningful way, the vast accumulation of data that would be acquired for each student using the tool.

Conclusions

Most of the technical issues that plagued the development and delivery of technology-augmented cases in the past—such as lack of accessibility, inconsistent performance and the need for extensive multimedia expertise—have already been resolved, or will be resolved shortly. That does not mean that we will soon see these cases everywhere. User acceptance demands far more than technical feasibility, a lesson the MIS field has repeatedly had to learn at considerable cost.

There are many challenges that must be overcome if the technology augmented case study is to gain the respectability of its paper cousin. For the most part, however, the technology-based challenges are likely to be the easiest to overcome. What will be more difficult is figuring out how such cases can best be employed. The traditional paper-based case has a long history of successful use as a basis for discussion. The value of the multimedia case has yet to be proven. It seems highly likely that the richness of presentation, the variety of media and interactive capabilities of such cases will lead to positive learning outcomes. We need more experience in figuring out precisely how these capabilities can best be leveraged.

Chapter 8 Notes

[1] There will, of course, always be some debate regarding the merits of reading on a tablet/eReader vs. using paper. My own experience—using a Tablet PC (I'm currently on my fourth)—comes down squarely on the technology side. I have not printed out an article for my own use in nearly 5 years, finding it infinitely more convenient to store and read them in their electronic form (with the added benefit that they are

searchable on my hard drive, except when they are created from scanned documents).

This said, I still tend to buy my books as hard copy. There are three key reasons for this: 1) the Tablet PC has two major weaknesses—weight and battery life; my experience with the iPad suggests that these will rapidly cease to be an issue, 2) I have a large existing inventory of books and my "filing system" (if what I have can be dignified as such) involves a loose arrangement by topic on my bookshelves, and 3) many books that I purchase—particularly older ones—have not been formatted for eBook display. What I anticipate, however, is that one day I will reach a tipping point—as I did in changing from vinyl to CD music and from VHS to DVD movies—where I suddenly cease acquiring paper content and go entirely electronic for all new purchases.

Chapter 9

Designing a Case Method Course

Nowhere is the dividing line between art and science more blurred than in the design of a case course. No one disagrees that both designing a case method course and preparing individual cases for discussion benefit greatly from the effort you expend. The precise direction that effort should take is what seems to be in dispute.

In this chapter, we consider the instructor's role in designing a case method course, selecting the cases and preparing an individual case for discussion. I then conclude with some thoughts on evaluation. Throughout the chapter, I emphasize that there are few hard and fast rules that can be followed. The experience and personality of the instructor necessarily interacts with the experience and personalities of the discussion participants; the nature of the cases impacts the mixture as well.

Designing a Case Method Course

There is quite a mystique associated with case method course design. During my time at HBS as a student, I have met any number of instructors who extolled the virtues of a particular design (often their own). Generally speaking, there seem to be three views that apply to case course design:

1. It is a science

2. It is an art

3. It probably matters less than we think it does

I suspect there is truth to all three positions. If I had to bet on one, however, it would be the last. I believe this is important to acknowledge since I would hate to see instructors discouraged by the fact that they do not "know" how to design a case method course. I don't know either, and have been doing it for years. There are, however, some common sense rules that I generally try to follow in designing my own courses.

Include Cases as Part of a Mix

If you look at a course design in the broadest possible way, what you have is a problem of fitting together four different pieces: the characteristics of the instructor, the characteristics of each individual student, the nature of the content and the approach to delivering that content. There is every reason to believe that these will interact and be subject to dynamic forces—that is a key conclusion of "A Tale of Three Classes", presented as Appendix E. In other words, when you are designing a course you are working on a rugged fitness landscape. That, in turn, means that there will be many combinations that exist on local peaks. Where do case discussions fall in this mix?

Portfolio of pedagogies

Let us assume, for the moment, that the content being taught is suitably complex to justify case discussions, that appropriate discussion cases are available, that the venue for the course is a classroom and that you—as the instructor—feel comfortable applying the methodology. What is then left is the student component of the puzzle. If you happen to teach at a case method institute populated by high achieving students who applied to the program knowing what they were getting into, it may then be a great idea to base your course entirely on case discussions. While this situation may reflect a few institutions[1], their number is small in proportion to those institutions that are not committed to a particular pedagogy. Thus, if we are going to attempt to match our instructional efforts with the preferences of all of our students at least some of the time, we would be well advised to use the case method as part of a portfolio on instructional techniques[2].

Portfolio of case styles and delivery

Characterizing all discussion cases as equivalent in style, context and impact is about as valid as treating all novels as being the same. Dimensions across which cases differ include:

1. *Specific vs. universal interest.* Some cases delve very deeply into a specific problem area (e.g., business industry, educational context) whereas others present more universal situations. Both

types of situations are encountered in practice, so both can be valuable.

2. *Choice vs. design vs. sense-making emphasis.* As described in Chapter 7.

3. *Level of decision-making.* Some cases involve policy decisions whereas others involve localized issues at a much lower level (e.g., line manager, instructor). Even if participants are all at a particular level, there is often value to having cases that include higher level decisions, since that may well be what participants aspire to and because it is often useful for individuals at a given level to be familiar with the issued faced by those at higher levels.

4. *Degree of resolution.* Some cases lead to conclusions that a particular course of action is best, others present situations where many of the options could be viable and still others provide situations where no decision alternative seems attractive. Mixing these cases prevents students from assuming that all discussions should end in a particular form of conclusion.

In addition to variations in the case itself, it is often beneficial to provide variety in how cases are delivered. In Chapter 11, for example, we discuss how different forms of delivery (e.g., online asynchronous, online synchronous) can lead to changes in the discussion dynamic. Since each dynamic tends to favor a particular subset of students, mixing them enhances the likelihood that every student will find some area where he or she excels.

Example: Ism6155 Design

Appendix F presents an example of case course design that incorporates many of "principles" discussed in this section[3]. Among these:

1. A mixture of three different activities in the course: case discussions, debates and a research exercise (mentioned in an earlier example).

2. A broad range of types of cases, featuring both local and global issues. Particular attention was paid to tying together case topics with debate issues.

3. A range of delivery approaches, with online class days providing the opportunity to discuss cases both synchronously and asynchronously.

Since the course was described in the appendix, it has continued to evolve. Cases have been swapped in and out of the class. The online activities have been expanded to include discussions that take place in a virtual world (see Chapter 11).

One of the most important aspects of the course has been the process of continuous redesign that has taken place. This has involved continuous experimentation with new approaches. Clicker technology was replaced by ink-based responses using Tablet PCs, acquired as part of a grant from Hewlett Packard. This approach, in turn, was replaced by the pre-case and post-case questions uploaded to Blackboard, my institution's course management system, discussed later in the chapter. Some experiments have been successful. For example, I concluded that many of the student presentations developed for the debate exercise were not of professional quality. I therefore began requiring students to read Chip and Dan Heath's (2007) *Made to Stick* and made students assess each other's debates on the dimensions of stickiness proposed in that book. As a consequence, the number of 56 slide "presentations" filled with text composed in a 10 point font has dropped from an alarmingly high percentage to zero. Other experiments did not appear to add sufficient value to justify their continuation. One example was the multimedia case development exercise described in Chapter 8.

Despite the continued tweaking—or, perhaps, because of it—the Ism6155 has remained among the most popular in the MS-MIS program. This assertion is confirmed by both student evaluations and comments made in exit forms. I consider this positive reaction particularly noteworthy because of another aspect of this course that would normally provoke a highly negative reaction, which is how students are graded. Specifically, at the beginning of the course I explain to students:

1. I grade using a curve—but I do not specify what that curve is going to be[4].

2. I do not tell students what their grades are (excepting for minor exercises) throughout the semester.

3. I assert that my grading is entirely subjective and, in all likelihood, I will make a number of mistakes in my subjective assessments. And students will just have to live with that.

Candidly, I am almost shocked that students let me get away with these policies, which I specify mainly to remove grades from the table as much as possible[5]. Unfortunately, the last of these items (subjectivity) tends to be the rule rather than the exception in case method courses, although I am sure there will be facilitators who deny it.

Be Sure There Are Enough Cases

Having earlier argued that a course consisting of *all* case discussions may not be optimal at most institutions, it is also probably true that we need *enough* case discussions in a course if we are to make the pedagogy effective. There are two main issues here. First, there is a learning curve for both instructor and student associated with a case discussion. Even in programs with a lot of case discussion courses, this applies to some degree since the pattern of interaction between a particular group of students and a particular instructor takes some time to settle. Thus, I am not sure that one or two case discussions over the course of a semester would be worth the setup cost.

The other argument for having enough cases derives from the methodology itself. Participants tend to construct their own conceptual schemes that are based upon the cases they discussion. If too few cases are included, these conceptual schemes may be overly weighted towards the available observations. While this may not be any worse than presenting a particular theory as fact (as is often done in lecture courses), neither approach does justice to a complex landscape.

Selecting Individual Cases

I have found selecting case studies to be an inexact process, to put it gently. To really determine the worth of a case, hours and hours of preparation are required. Even then, a substantial number surprise me once the discussion begins.

Build an Ecosystem of Cases

In the previous section, I discussed creating balanced portfolio of instructional techniques. A portfolio is a collection whose membership exhibits a targeted level of diversity. When thinking about inserting individual cases into that portfolio, an ecosystem might be a better metaphor. Where an ecosystem differs from a portfolio is in the interrelationships between components. Portfolios succeed because the individual elements behave differently when the same external force is encountered, reducing the risk that the entire system will fail. Ecosystems depend on synergistic relationships between the diverse elements of the system. Properly nurtured, the total value of the ecosystem exceeds the sum of the values of its individual parts.

In Chapter 6, we discussed some of the designs for case research. Many of these involved collections of cases. It can be useful to conceive of your students as "researchers" and the cases you select as their source material. Applying this conceptual scheme, two particularly important aspects of the ecosystem you want to create involve relationships between cases that either conflict or link together; these relationships justify narrowing or generalizing behaviors observed in a single instance. The other critical aspect of creating a case ecosystem involves developing a sensible sequence. We now turn to the practical implementation of these ecosystem design elements.

Illustrating conflict where it matters

One of the greatest potential weaknesses of case method instruction is that students learn from induction, meaning that the validity of the lessons learned is only as good as the cases discussed. One particular problem is overgeneralization. The participants engage in a resonant discussion of a particular case. Principles useful in the analysis of that situation are induced. The ill-founded conclusion that we would like to avoid is that these principles are universally applicable.

Just as is true in research design, the most compelling remedy to excessive generalization is choosing cases that are superficially similar, yet lead to different outcomes. This type of pairing encourages students to look for small details that can dramatically impact results of their analysis of each case. In complex environments, case pairs of this type should be easy to find. In less complex environments, on the other hand, you may be hard-pressed to find such cases; that might lead to the question of whether or not the case method is the best approach to instruction. Where principles are universal and the details do not matter much, why not just teach the principles themselves?

Providing cases that can be linked together

The complement to conflicting cases is linking cases. If the environment we live in happens to be chaotic, such linkages—in the form of common principles that apply across many cases—would be nearly impossible to find. Fortunately, the environments for which the case method is most appropriate tend to be complex, not chaotic. Thus, we should always be looking for common behaviors or outcomes across cases.

By the same reasoning that conflicting cases should be as similar as possible, linkages are most compelling when the cases are as different as possible. I already provided several examples of this in Chapters 3, 4 and 5. The High Tech Hidebound example is particularly instructive in this regard. Noticing a large number of similarities between two superficially dissimilar cases—one involving a cookie chain, the other involving a financial management company—I constructed a conceptual scheme that helped to explain both outcomes.

It would be nice to assert that linkage between cases *should* be designed into a course before it is ever offered. Unfortunately, that would require a level of prescience far beyond anything I possess, so I am reluctant to demand it from the reader. To the contrary, I believe that linkages are more likely to be discovered as a consequence of the experience of using the cases rather than as a result of brilliant design. I hold this belief for two reasons. First, the best linkages emerge as a result of overlooking the superficial structure of a case and seeing its deep structure. In my own experience, it is very rare that I fully understand the depth of a case at the time when I first select it for a course[6]. Second, I find that the strength of case linkages varies each time I facilitate a particular course. That is because I tend to land on the less directive end of the facilitation spectrum—meaning that discussions of the same case can vary considerably from semester to semester. That, in turn, means that linkable topics may be very evident between two cases in some semesters, while being secondary at best in others. There always will be an abundance of linkages that can be made. It is just the subset of those linkages most salient that will change.

Sensible sequencing of cases

The sequencing of cases is yet another area of case method course design where concrete and straightforward principles rarely apply. Here are some rules of thumb that I generally follow:

1. *Lead with cases that help participants better understand the case method itself.* These tend to be shorter cases, involving more familiar contexts, require fewer participant assumptions and allow the facilitator some opportunity to discuss the case method itself. I take this principle to extreme. Where students are unfamiliar with case method, I always lead with the EMBA 2002 (A) case (Appendix G) which is a case about the case method[7].

2. *Early cases that are organized in a manner that parallels how openings should be prepared will improve later openings.* My experience: early openers in a class nearly always go through a case linearly, no matter how much I warn in advance that they should not simply regurgitate the case facts. Given that observation, I tend to start with cases offering a resource organization (see Chapter 7) similar to what I would like to see in an opening, rather than a narrative or other organization.

3. *Keeping cases with strong links and conflicts as close together as possible will increase the likelihood that the relationships will be recognized.* Participants will tend to have the best recall for recently discussed cases, so if you want them to identify the relationships (conflicts, links) that are present, it is best that the cases involved be adjacent or nearly so.

4. *If you want participants to read cases in detail, be sure that the details really matter in some of your early cases.* In some case studies, "big picture" issues drive the discussion. In others, observing a particular detail or two can produce a major impact on analysis. By offering sufficient detail-driven cases early, you encourage participants to look carefully at the details in their analysis.

5. *By ensuring that cases with critical auxiliary issues are sprinkled uniformly throughout the course, you make it more likely participants will attend these issues.* In every subject, there are going to be some issues that you want participants to think about, even where the case does not directly address them. For example, in business two such important issues are ethics and the effects of globaliza-

tion; in education they might include diversity and assessing learning. Retention demands practice, so if these issues are truly critical, they should surface in cases throughout the course.

In Appendix F, Figure F.1 shows how I attempted to blend a number of these principles into the Ism6155 course mentioned in an earlier example. I would also caution the reader, however, that it will likely be *impossible* to incorporate all these rules-of-thumb into a course design that also provides a sequence of topics that participants can comprehend. So, as I so often conclude in this book, what makes the most sense is to choose what is most important to you and try to incorporate that. And do not expect all your outcomes to follow your expectations, as the following example illustrates.

Example: Cape Cod Potato Chips

As I write this book, I am continually struck by how often exceptions to the very recommendations I am making have occurred in my own experience. Nowhere is that more the true then in the *Cape Cod Potato Chips* case that I wrote in late 1984. Although it was only the second case study I ever wrote, it was my most successful without a doubt. Immediately after it was written, it was used as an examination in the Agribusiness course at HBS and, shortly thereafter, it was used in executive HBS Agribusiness Seminar, where it was discussed by many of the top executives in global agribusiness. Starting the next year, it was used as the opening case in the MBA Agribusiness course. It continued to be used for that purpose for well over a decade—an unusual achievement in a course where the typical case has a life of 2-3 years. About five years after I wrote the case, I met the then current agribusiness program research assistant, who greeted me with the words:

> I've always wanted to meet the man who wrote *Cape Cod Potato Chips*.

So what prompts me to heap such immodest accolades on myself? What I find particularly intriguing about this case is the means by which it was written. You might have guessed that I, being so inexperienced at the case writing business at the time, would have meticulously followed all the guidelines for case writing presented *ad nauseum* in Chapters 4 and 7. In fact, it would be hard to describe a process that was further from the actual reality.

What actually happened was the following. That year, the professor who ran the agribusiness program at HBS[8] had reluctantly dismissed his research assistant, who had been unable to keep up with the pace of case development required by the program. That meant that he needed other assistance in getting cases completed. At the time, I happened to be a consultant working for a firm that the professor had originally founded, and where he still sat on the board. As a result, he called me on a Friday and asked me if I would mind writing a case for him over the weekend. I agreed (gladly, since the professor was a close personal friend as well as being my mentor), went over to his office and was handed a box full of reports, newspaper clippings, some random interview notes and other miscellaneous bric-a-brac.

I finally got around to writing the case on Sunday morning. Knowing no specifics, and having no way of learning them, I read the materials, tried to put myself in the shoes of the manager running the company. In addition, I inserted a number of "big picture" issues involving the sourcing of potatoes and other commodity related issues since these are nearly universal in agribusiness settings. The resulting case was much shorter than my usual effort—it had to be, since I had access to few details—and was completed by Sunday night. I brought it to the professor's office the next morning, with strict instructions to pass it on to the company's manager so that my misperceptions could be cleared up. Shockingly, the manager was pleased with the case and all modifications were entirely cosmetic.

So why am I presenting this example here?[9] The reason is that although the case study itself would not necessarily measure up to other cases I have written in my own mind, it was very well suited to its particular role in the course as the leadoff case. The reasons for this fit include:

- It embodied, and made reference to, the commodity systems analytical approach that had defined agribusiness since the late 1960s[10]. As a consultant working for a firm that was built around this approach, I was reasonably well qualified in that area.

- It was structured the way a good agribusiness opening should be organized; as a recent graduate of the MBA program and the agribusiness course in particular, I was in a good position to make that assessment.

- Its lack of details, brought about by ignorance rather than desire on my part, made the case unusually sparse. That made it a good choice for emphasizing the conceptual scheme to be used in the course, rather than the specifics of the case itself.

Thus, although I have my doubts about its quality as a case, its fit within the ecology of the course was indisputable.

Motivating Preparation

A good case discussion almost never emerges from an unprepared group of students. Designing appropriate tools for motivating preparation into a course can help ensure adequate preparation. At the outset, let me assert that I believe the best motivation for good preparation is having interesting and engaging classroom discussions. When students feel that their classroom time is well spent, and look forward to contributing to the discussions, the level of preparation is generally quite good. There are, however, some additional ways that preparation can be encouraged. I have seen all of these used. Some I am comfortable with, some I am not.

The Pre-Case Analysis

One way of ensuring that students come in prepared is to have them write up their analysis of the case and hand it in before class. This is an example of an approach that I am not comfortable with. I have four problems with it:

1. It sends the message to the students that you do not trust them to prepare without a coercive measure.

2. It puts too much emphasis on pre-discussion learning; it is what students have learned *by the end of the discussion* that is of greatest interest to me.

3. The write-ups are a punishment for students to write.

4. The write-ups are a punishment for the instructor to read.

Where I could see value in this exercise is if the instructor painstakingly corrects the spelling, grammar and logic in each write-up. While that would increase the pain associated with (3) & (4), it would provide students with a valuable learning experience—although not one that is actually related to the case studies being discussed. It is, however, an experience that they could certainly benefit from.

What I have seen some instructors do is to require that each student analyze a certain percentage of the cases. I find this practice particularly abhorrent since, in my opinion, it would likely guarantee that those students not assigned to submit an analysis of a particular case would prepare for the subsequent discussion hardly at all.

The Pre-Discussion Quiz

Another way to ensure preparation is to quiz the students before beginning the discussion of each case. I have done this with clicker technology (see the Ism6155 description in Appendix F) and it works reasonably well[11]. It does not take too long to administer five or so multiple choice questions about the case to the class this way. The protocol I used was to make a game out of it. The top scorers on the 5 question quiz would be given one or more nearly impossible to answer "challenge questions" (e.g., the phone number of a manager listed in a particular exhibit). The winning student would then call the result of a coin toss. If the winner got the choice right, he or she could choose to open or could ask me to click the "choose a random student" button provided by the clicker software. If the student got the toss wrong, I would automatically press the "choose a random student" and the name that came up would open the case. The particular advantage to this process was that most of the time openers would be randomly selected, giving everyone a strong motivation to prepare.

The weakness of this particular approach to ensuring preparation is that although it is easy to create questions that test case facts, knowledge of such facts should be the byproduct of careful preparation, not the object of it. On the other hand, it is nearly impossible to test analysis using this mechanism, since most cases are too complex to have a simple right answer. The danger therefore becomes that by putting too much weight on knowing case facts, participants will emphasize learning facts in their preparation at the cost of devoting less time to analysis. That is why I chose to turn the clicker exercise into a game.

The Pre-Discussion Question

The technique that I have been using in recent years is to present a "big picture" question on the case to students at the very start of the class and making them write a brief essay before the discussion starts. Typically, I give the class 20 minutes to prepare the essay, which I have them upload to Blackboard (our course management system) using laptops (although an entirely paper-based approach would work nearly as well)[12]. I grade these each week on the same Weak-Satisfactory-Excellent scale I use to assess participation, providing students some feedback. I decline to tell them how it impacts their grade, beyond saying "not very much". In fact, I use the results of this measure the same way I used to employ the clicker scores, as an indicator of level of preparation for those students who do not participate aggressively in discussions.

The advantage of this approach over the previous case quiz is that the questions I ask can be quite conceptual and being able to answer them can only be assured through careful preparation of the case. I do not ask questions about case facts. As discussed later in the chapter, it also provides the basis for a pre-test, post-test analysis of the discussion results for each case.

The main disadvantage I have seen for this approach to motivating preparation is the issue of class time. Subtracting 20 minutes from the beginning of the class and another 10 for the post test at the end means less time for discussion. Given that it is hard to conduct a substantive discussion of a complex case in under an hour, it would be hard to follow this protocol in a class period of under 90 minutes[13]. For the technique to work, however, it must be employed during class time. Otherwise, it is simply a weaker cousin of the pre-case analysis.

The "Cold Call"

The favorite (and principal) technique used to ensure students come in prepared at HBS is to select a student to open the discussion without prior warning. It is not unusual for facilitators to badger unprepared participants unmercifully under this technique. Once this happens a time or two, the average level of class preparation improves dramatically for the rest of the semester.

Perhaps as a captive to my own experience, I have always employed cold calls as a means of encouraging class preparation. To avoid the bullying aspect, when I encounter the unprepared student I vary my technique according to the student. If the student has not been an exemplary participant, I generally move on quickly, perhaps expressing regret for the lost opportunity to excel. Where the student is a strong participant—and, in my experience, these individuals tend to come in under-prepared *at least* as often as the weaker participants—I go at the individual with considerable gusto and make it clear to the class that I am enjoying the inquisition every bit as much as they are. I particularly relish these episodes when they occur near the beginning of the term, since they are an investment in better participant preparation for months to come.

There are two problems with relying on cold calls. First, and most significant, is their potential to produce hurt feelings. As already mentioned, I try to avoid this by being selective in whom I roast. What I also try to do is to talk privately to students who have really blown an opening after class. The purpose of this is not to counsel them on the need to prepare better; if they haven't figured this out from the experience, my telling them is not going to make it any clearer. Rather, my goal is to assure them that: a) I do not take their failure personally and I am therefore not "mad" at them, b) that they have not destroyed their chance of getting a good grade in the course as a result of one bad opening, and c) to offer some suggestions about how they might better organize their thoughts in the future. In doing so, I can also determine if it would make sense to call on them to open in some future session. I genuinely believe that the chance to open is an opportunity, not a threat. In fact, I think most of my students feel the same way, although they might not admit it.

The other problem with cold calls is that it is nearly impossible to predict what a participant will say. Unless you are willing to terminate an opening immediately when it goes off track, an unexpected opening can totally throw off any plan you might have for the discussion. I have much more to say on this topic in Chapter 9.

Policy towards Outside Preparation

In the days of my MBA, preparing 15 cases a week in the absence of computers, we never even considered augmenting our preparation with outside sources. It would have been far too much work. Today, the situation is entirely different. Where real world cases are involved—particularly business, government or public policy cases that are not disguised—motivated participants will definitely try to look up what happened as part of their preparation.

As part of your course policy, it might make sense to specify whether facts outside the case are allowed or disallowed. It might also make sense to simply ignore the issue, which is what I usually do. My reason for this unwillingness to specify policy is my belief that the merits of the alternative policies are so evenly matched that I have been unable to decide.

In favor of allowing outside research are a number of factors. First and foremost, anything that encourages our students to do outside research at their own initiative is beneficial from a learning standpoint. Learning to search for hard-to-find information is a valuable skill in almost any context. I would also hate to do anything to discourage curiosity. A secondary factor is my personal aversion to specifying rules that I am unable or unwilling to enforce. My fear is that if I promulgate enough of these rules, students will start ignoring the rules that I really care about.

The argument for not allowing outside research is just as strong. Where students can determine the outcome of a particular decision, the discussion case becomes transformed. Instead of discussing alternatives, participants lean towards a discussion of the case as if it were an experiment; the case facts being the cause, the outcome being the effect. Unfortunately, in a complex environment I feel this is too simplistic. While discussion cases are certainly richer than theories, it is a mistake to assume that they contain all the information necessary to explain a particular outcome. Other factors, not listed in the case, could well have determined what actually happened as part of an interaction. Thus, it is better to under-emphasize the actual outcome of a particular case and focus on the quality of the analysis. This is much harder to do when the outcome is known and has been injected into the discussion.

As a facilitator, it is possible to "disallow" certain facts that enter the discussion. Thus, my own policy has been to say nothing about outside preparation unless asked, thereby neither encouraging nor discouraging it explicitly. When a fact is introduced that is not contained in the case, I usually ask the contributor of that fact if he is advocating that the organization involved drop all other projects in favor of inventing and constructing of a time machine to aid the decision maker. I then follow up by asking if this would be the most profitable use of such a time machine. That usually distracts the discussion from the outcome just described and indicates that I am not wild about pursuing outcome information at the moment. This generally returns the discussion to the case protagonist's time frame.

Designs for Assessing Learning

Perhaps the greatest obstacle to widespread acceptance of the case method is the frustrating inability to measure what participants have learned from the process. This is not unexpected. The greatest benefits of the case method arise from its ability to develop core communication and problem solving skills in a context of collaborative learning. Not only are these devilishly hard to assess under the best of circumstances, there is also the problem of not being able to separate what is learned from what was already there are the beginning of the process. In this regard, the case method suffers mightily compared with methods that attempt to instill a large quantity of factual and conceptual material that can be tested readily and that students were unlikely to know prior to taking the course[14].

Assessing Discussion Contribution

There are elements that must be considered in evaluating performance in the case method: 1) How the participant contributed to the discussion, and 2) How much the participant actually learned from the discussion. While neither is particularly easy to measure objectively, the first is *observable* by the facilitator and encouraging it almost certainly enhances the classroom learning for the group as a whole. Thus, it makes considerable sense to weigh participation very heavily in any grading scheme.

In the field of psychology, there is a tendency to fit performance to bell curves. Unfortunately, in all my years facilitating case discussions, I have never seen a class where individual participation fit such a distribution. Instead, I would characterize the typical distribution of participation as looking like a power law[15], such as the 80-20 rule (i.e., 80% of the good comments come from 20% of the participants). For this reason, numeric totaling of quality comments rarely tells a useful story; or at least not one that you would care to put in a grade book.

That being said, there is a continuum, with two extremes, through which classroom discussions can be assessed. We now consider the pros and cons of each extreme, recognizing that a sensible approach will almost certainly exist in the middle ground.

Tracking all contributions

Some really great case facilitators do a spectacular job keeping track of each contribution made by every student. I recall one professor from my MBA days who not only seemed to be able to keep count—a prodigious accomplishment in a section with 78 students—but who also seemed be able to play back the content of every comment made. At least he was able to do so for my comments, most of which seemed far from memorable[16].

A very useful side-effect of this particular approach, which conveys the sense that every participant remark is carefully assessed, is encouraging extremely high levels of participation, even among students who were generally reluctant to participate. I do not recall a single instance in that class where several hands were not raised at the same time; usually it was dozens. What this allows is for the facilitator to choose who will participate, thereby transforming the earlier mentioned 80-20 distribution into a more conventional type of curve. That, in turn, can enable greater rigor in assessment.

While I admire the remarkable feat of memory involved, and feel guilt that I am so far from being a master that skill, I also believe that there are drawbacks to being extremely systematic in assessing contributions as well as benefits. While it is motivating to think that every contribution you make counts, the flip side is the sense that if you take a risky position and it fails, that will also be remembered and will count against you. For natural risk takers, as I was, the classes where I made the contributions that I would most like to forget also happened to be the classes where I made the contributions for which I would most like to be remembered. This is no coincidence. If you feel you are continuously being judged, your incentive to go out on a limb is very limited.

The other weakness of tracking all contributions becomes evident when applied outside a program where the case method is widely accepted. Whereas in an 80 person MBA section at HBS, being tracked may lead to universal participation, I am not the least bit sure that it would work as effectively in a smaller section dominated by students for whom the case method is an unexpected, and not necessarily comfortable, pedagogy. I always have some students who do not seem willing to participate voluntarily unless forced to do so—usually with a cold call. I am not sure it would be effective to do anything that would add to their nervousness about participating.

Loose groupings

At the other extreme from keeping a meticulously accurate record of all contributions, it is also possible to assess overall participation more loosely. My experience has been that in any given class, it is relatively easy to identify 10-20% of the students as truly standout participants. Similarly, unless you force the issue by cold calling students who do not otherwise speak, 10-20% of the class will have said absolutely nothing that you can remember. Thus, as long as you are only worried about breaking participation into three groups, you can usually come up with a reasonable breakdown that will not produce great objections. As I mentioned earlier in the chapter, one of the things that has surprised me about my current case method class is how few objections I have heard about a grading scheme that is so vague.

The greatest danger of loose the groupings philosophy, in my opinion, is that it can lead to laziness on the part of the facilitator. Specifically, if you are not tracking students, you are unlikely to be proactive in encouraging weaker participants to join in the discussion. You may not even recognize them soon enough to cold call them so that they have their chance. As a facilitator, I feel it is part of my mission to help participants develop their communications skills. If I am too relaxed about who participates and who does not, I miss an important opportunity to help students improve on this particular dimension.

Learning from Discussions

Determining what each student learned from class discussions, individually and collectively, is the other key area of assessment. Unlike participation, however, there is no immediately observable knowledge or behavior change that is a natural byproduct of the case method. Thus, you need to design specific activities for these purposes. In my experience, this represents the most frustrating aspect of case method course design.

Summative assessment: Case analysis exams

The most widely used approach to estimating actual learning is to give students a case to analyze as an examination. HBS has done this for just about as long as the school has existed; most other case method courses employ the same approach. Such exams may either be take home or given during an exam session. They do not necessarily have to be summative[17], but usually are (i.e., used as midterm or final exams).

On the surface, having students prepare an analysis of a case would seem to be a pretty good tool for assessment—certainly a lot more rigorous than a multiple choice clicker test! After using these exams for many years, however, I stopped. My problem was that I was not at all sure what I was measuring. What I *wanted* to measure was how much students had learned in attending my class. As far as I can see, case analysis exams have three weaknesses in this regard:

1. *The analyses students submit are, on average, not very good.* This observation used to depress me. Then I realized that this is as it should be; if our students could analyze cases well without discussing them, there would be no point in discussing them. The case method not only serves to hone individual problem solving skills, it also should reinforce the value of collaborative problem solving.

2. *The case method targets core skills.* The problem is that students come in with a huge diversity of these skills and leave any given course with those skills (acquired over many years) only slightly altered. Our analysis of skills at the end of the course does not therefore measure learning—even assuming that it is accurate—it measures the sum of learning plus pre-existing skills. Given that the variance in the latter is likely larger than the former, our measure is highly suspect if learning is what we are hoping to assess.

3. *Participants bond with each case differently, and the variance is huge.* Sometimes, a sensible approach to a case just jumps out at you, sometimes you can only find one if it is pointed out to you. After over 30 years analyzing cases, this remains true for me. I find it hard to imagine that the variance is much smaller for other people. This variance in bonding, however, means that a reliable assessment probably would require dozens of cases before an acceptable error level was obtained.

These three factors are much less of an obstacle if a particular course is designed to instill the application of a particular theory or method into its participants. The ability to apply theory and methods is something that can be tested and is much less subject to the problems described. Such a design is, however, generally in opposition to the constructivist philosophy of the case method.

Formative assessment: Post case reflections

Because, as just noted, I am not confident that case analysis exams are a particularly good estimator of learning, I have developed a technique that I particularly like for assessing what students have learned from each discussion. It involves having a student fill out a form (see Exhibit E of Appendix I for an example) with just two questions at the end of each discussion:

1. What are the three most important things you learned from preparing and discussing this case?

2. How did discussion of this case change your original analysis of the case?

The first of these questions allows me to assess if the students have seen the "big picture" of the case. The second question allows me to assess the degree to which the discussion of the case added value. Because I can compare the second answer with the student's response to the earlier-mentioned pre-case question, I can also make an assessment of the degree to which the reflection is accurate (versus being an attempt to feed back to me what I want to hear).

Typically, students take about 10 minutes to fill out the post case reflection form. In my class, I have them create their responses on their personal laptops and then submit them to Blackboard. As was true for the pre-case forms, there is no reason that the same process could not be accomplished with pen and paper.

Conclusions

I have taken great pains in this chapter to avoid seeming overly dogmatic about how a case method course *should* be designed. Perhaps my own uncertainty regarding the approach that is "best" will encourage new instructors to experiment and find out what designs work for them. My firm belief is that the best designs will be those achieving a fit between:

- *The content being presented.* Courses where quantitative analytical techniques are being taught—such as introductory finance— will probably benefit from designs that provide a lot of similar cases, giving students the opportunity to practice these skills. Courses that emphasize exploration, such as entrepreneurial management, might do better by providing a large range of case settings and decisions, reflecting the immense variety of the entrepreneurial environment.

- *The personality and instructional philosophy of the instructor.* Some instructors like to maintain tight control over class discussions and, as a consequence, may prefer to use cases that are organized such that discussions follow a predictable path (matching the order in which the case is presented). Others may be comfortable with cases where the decisions and assumptions are hidden, and discussions can therefore flow in many directions. Some instructors may dislike ambiguity, and will therefore benefit from cases where there is a set of decisions that are clear winners. Others may actively seek out complexity, being completely comfortable with the notion that many collections of decisions may be acceptable—with finding a good fit between recommended actions being far more important than the actions themselves.

- *The experience of the class.* Students with extensive experience in the case method pedagogy are far less likely to be phased by cases lacking a clearly specified decision point than students participating in a case method course for the first time. Students with limited work experience are more likely to seek the "right" solution than students who have spent a lot of time in the "real world". The design needs to take into account such differences if the method is to achieve maximum effect. This can affect both the choice of cases and their sequence.

- *The nature of the course setting.* Questions such as "how many cases should be included" will likely depend on how the course is delivered. For example, my experience has been that participation in asynchronous online case discussions take 2-3 times as much time as classroom discussions. Thus, while I might use

25 cases in a pure case method classroom MBA class, I would reduce that number to 10 for a pure online class covering the same material (see Chapter 11) while, at the same time, demanding much deeper discussions of each case in the online forum. Similarly, when I have a class that meets twice each week for 90 minutes, I am comfortable with assigning a case for each session. When the same class meets once a week, for 3 hours each session, I tend to use half as many cases and develop other activities for the second half of each class. My experience with my students has been that discussions tend to flag when two cases are handled back-to-back. Class size makes a difference as well. At HBS, a typical first year section of a course might be 80 students and might discuss 40 different cases or more. With a 20 person class, on the other hand, the same individual participation opportunities might be afforded with 10 cases.

The predictable conclusion is, therefore, that there are no hard-and-fast rules for proper case method course design. Rather, the designer must seek his or her own best fit. The good news here is that the effectiveness of the course will not be judged against a standard of perfection. Rather, it will be judged against more traditional lecture courses. In my experience, even an imperfectly designed case method course can do quite well in such a comparison.

Chapter 9 Notes

[1] At HBS, for example, potential students apply knowing it is a case method institution and that their classes will consist almost entirely of case discussions. If an applicant felt uncomfortable with that situation, he or she would probably not apply.

On the other hand, even if all the classes at HBS were taught using the case method (which they are not), it would still be a mistake to assume that all learning is based on case discussions. A full time program, particularly one with a large group of residential students (as HBS has), promotes a great deal of learning outside of the classroom, though social contacts, clubs, organizations and other activities (both organized and disorganized). As I pointed out in *Informing Business* (Gill, 2010), when I surveyed the Harvard MBA class of 1982 for our 25th reunion and asked them to identify the greatest strength of the HBS MBA Program, the top choices, accounting for over 90% of all 143 responses, were:

1. The case method (34%)

2. The quality of my classmates and what I learned from them (while in school) (32%)

3. The networking opportunities it afforded me after I graduated (14%)

4. The quality of the faculty (11%)

The second place winner, chosen by almost as many respondents as the case method, highlights the importance of interactions outside of class in the minds of students. The faculty themselves did no better than fourth place.

[2] Another reason to rely on a portfolio of techniques is to avoid diminishing returns, a.k.a. case discussion fatigue. At HBS, for example, my own experience was that of being highly stimulated by the discussions during the first year of the program, and being rather bored with them the second year. During my first year, I prepared each case with considerable diligence. During my second year, I considered giving each case a casual read quite sufficient—a fact that annoyed my roommate to no end. Ironically, I got the same grade point average, to four decimal places, during both years. I can only attribute this to the fact that I was not the only student experiencing a similar fatigue and so, given the HBS firmly specified grading curve, the playing field remained relatively level.

[3] I'm not sure that the loosely constructed advice snippets offered here actually rise to the level of principles, hence the quotes.

[4] See Appendix G for an explanation as to why I am a bit reluctant to specify grading curves too specifically.

[5] Another reason for specifying these unusual grading policies at the outset of the course is to ensure that if protests are made to my department chair, they get made early enough so that there is time to

address them. The fact is that after seven years of teaching the course twice a year, I have yet to hear a single such protest. That surprises me.

[6] At institutions, such as HBS, that write nearly all of their own cases and where case writers also tend to be facilitators for the same cases, the depth of knowledge when a case is selected for a course might be greater. I would be hesitant to assert that because I never saw a case abandoned before being used as a result of non-linkage during my time there. After you write a case, you naturally want to see it used.

Where HBS may have a true advantage in detecting linkages is in their multi-section courses (mainly taught in the first year). For these courses, instructors get together and pre-discuss each case, as well as develop a common teaching plan.

[7] I would not necessarily encourage other facilitators to employ this particular case. Every facilitator needs to develop his or her own style; having students critique my own idiosyncratic approach may not help them understand their own facilitator that well (although it is certainly okay by me if that case is used). What I would encourage facilitators to do is to develop their own case as soon as an appropriate situation evolves, then discuss that. In fact, you could even write a case about the design of your course, and have students discuss that.

[8] A more complete full description of the Agribusiness program at HBS is provided as an example of what I believe business research *should* be doing in *Informing Business* (Gill, 2010) and in Chapter 12.

[9] Perhaps a better question would be: Why am I presenting the Cape Code Potato Chips example at all, given that it pretty much seems to contradict every guideline for case writing I offered earlier...

[10] For business readers, to understand the commodity systems approach, just imagine what it would be like if value chain analysis had been discovered 30 years earlier and immediately been put to work. That is commodity systems in a nutshell.

[11] For those not familiar with "clicker" technology, more correctly called audience response systems, each participant gets a remote control with buttons that correspond to the answers available on a multiple choice question. The question is projected on the screen. Each participant presses the button corresponding to his or her response, and the

results are tabulated. Cumulative scores for a particular set of questions and for an entire semester are maintained, so it is possible to see how well students performed on average. Some instructors use these scores directly in calculating a particular student's overall grade. I used them mainly as an additional source of information to deal with the hard cases of students who had participated little. Here, cumulative scores provided a weak indicator of whether lack of participation was a result of lack of preparation, or of other factors.

[12] Examples of the pre-discussion and post-discussion forms I use are included as Exhibits in Appendix I.

[13] As it turns out, at USF, the college of business went to a 12 week schedule for its graduate courses. Since the classes generally meet in the evenings, that means 4 hour classes. I usually use the first 2 hours for the case discussion cycle, including pre- and post-case questions.

[14] A sample evaluation plan for a case method course that I developed for an NSF grant—both for our own purposes and for the IRB—is included as Appendix I.

[15] See *Informing Business* (Gill, 2010) for a more substantive discussion of the ubiquitous power law.

[16] The professor even made some remarks that led me to suspect that he still remembered many of our comments when he dropped by our section party during our 25th Reunion—the only one of our former professors to do so. My only reaction to this is… Yikes!

[17] Before I started at HBS, the school used to require weekly case analyses from each student. These analyses were slid down a chute that closed promptly at a specified time (5 PM on Saturday, as I recall). It left quite an impression; alumni from that era are quick to recall nightmares about just missing the chute closing.

Chapter 10

Facilitating a Case Discussion

The most useful advice I can offer on facilitating case discussions is to adopt a style that fits your personality. During my time as a student, I experienced outstanding facilitators who were very directive and, at least by appearance, simply let discussions flow. I have seen the same in ineffective instructors. I have observed pre-class preparation effectively motivated through fear, but also through fostering a strong desire to ensure that a good discussion takes place. I have seen grades play a huge role in motivating participation, but have also seen participation motivated almost entirely by the joy of the discussion. I suppose, in theory at least, we should be striving to make our discussions as constructivist and intrinsically motivated as possible. I cannot recall having seen any hard evidence that such an approach leads to better learning outcomes, however. My conclusion, therefore, is that whatever approach feels right to the instructor—so long as it leads to active engagement in the classroom or online—is probably a sound approach.

Having conceded that I am unwilling to specify a "best" approach to facilitating a classroom discussion, in this chapter I will focus on describing some of the techniques that I have observed (and in many case tried). I begin by looking at what can be done to ensure appropriate pre-class preparation. I then look at launching the discussion, referred to as the opening. The conduct of the main discussion is then examined, followed by the summing up process (with and without visitors from the firm). Finally, we turn to the tricky process of evaluating the case discussion and individual participation.

Preparing to Lead a Case Discussion

Before facilitating a case discussion, an instructor must prepare the case. For some instructors, preparation may rely heavily on a teaching note. For others, the process may be more similar to that experienced by students. No matter how well you prepare, there will always be surprises when the discussion takes place. The only real surprise would be if the discussion succeeds if you are not sufficiently prepared.

Preparing With a Teaching Note

If you read through the section on writing teaching notes in Chapter 7, my suspicion of these documents should have become apparent. The root of my distrust stems from the fact that most teaching notes tend to promote a "right" way to facilitate a case. I *might* even be convinced that such a right way exists provided:

- The instructor has a nearly identical personality and teaching style to the case writer.

- The instructor's students have the same profile as those of the case writer.

- The case writer is a first-class case facilitator.

- The case writer's viewpoint has not been unduly influenced by his or her contact with the protagonists and other stakeholders encountered while writing the case.

With the possible exception of the third of these—which is likely true for *some* of the HBS cases I have used—I think it highly unlikely that any of these criteria are routinely met in my world[1]. Moreover, what I have found with the cases that have led to my most successful in-class discussions is that the teaching notes *never* describe a discussion even remotely similar to mine. In fact, more often than not, my discussions end up coming to conclusions diametrically opposed to what the teaching note recommends[2].

My own reservations aside, use of a teaching note can dramatically compress case preparation time, not only helping the instructor identify salient facts of the case but also allowing the preparation and planning phases of facilitation to be combined. Most case method instructors I know eagerly utilize teaching notes. And, as noted in Chapter 7, it is rarely possible to publish a case study without one.

Preparing as If You Were a Student

The alternative to relying heavily on a teaching note while preparing a case study for discussion is to prepare the case as if you were a student.

Predictably, however, there are few general rules regarding how "best" to prepare a case. My own attempt to provide students with a handout offering guidance in this area is included as Appendix H. Its key points are summarized in Table 10.1.

Table 10.1: Steps in preparing a case study (see Appendix H)

Step	Comments
Step 0: Do an initial reading of the case	Need to get "big picture" prior to analysis.
Step 1: Determine the goal of your analysis	Figure out if the case is focused on a decision to be made or if it has some other objective.
Step 2: Determine your units of analysis	Unit types are "environments" (e.g., systems establishing the context of the case situation) and "stakeholders"
Step 3: Assemble and organize facts	Facts should be grouped by units and classified according to usefulness.
Step 4: Analyze how the protagonist is likely to fare in the present and future	SWOT analysis could be used here, as could many other analytical frameworks depending on the case.
Step 5: Identify possible alternatives	In the event a case is not based around a decision, this might be modified to "Possible lessons learned".
Step 6: Broaden the analysis to include all stakeholders	Use a "balanced scorecard" in making a decision—it is easy to become obsessed with the protagonist and to forget what the other players may do or feel.
Step 7: Develop a concise "solution" that addresses the goals of the case	*The last two steps are specifically for students. When the facilitator reaches this point, it is time to start planning the discussion.*
Step 8: Develop an opening outline	

While there would certainly no harm in peeking at the teaching note once analysis "as a student" has been completed, there are definitely advantages to waiting until that point. The most significant of these is empathy—you get to share the student's joy or pain associated with making sense of the case. My typical students, for example, come to case discussions with very little experience in the pedagogy. If I cannot make reasonable sense of a particular case after a casual first read, it is highly unlikely that it will make any sense to them and, in my opinion, another case should be selected. On the other hand, I would have no reservations employing such a case with second year MBA candidates at a case method school; I would expect them to have the experience to rise to the challenge.

The second, somewhat less significant, factor that motivates me to prepare cases before looking at any available instructional aids is that I enjoy preparing cases. It can be argued, I suppose, that the purpose of education is not to provide a pleasant diversion for instructors. I would, however, assert that if you do not derive any enjoyment from reading and analyzing a case study, then the case method paradigm is probably not a good fit with your instructional style (and that you should look elsewhere for your pedagogical innovations).

Planning the Case Discussion

After preparing a case, an instructor typically develops a plan for facilitating the discussion. In my experience, there is a wide range of plans that can lead to successful discussions. Others, particularly those favoring the "detailed plan" side, often disagree with that conclusion. For that reason, I will consider a continuum—inspired by studies of entrepreneurial decision-making—that ranges from *goal-driven planning* to *effectual facilitation*. After describing each approach, I identify some of their likely strengths and weaknesses.

Goal-Driven Planning

In the goal-driven planning style of facilitation, the instructor begins with a clear set of goals to be accomplished over the course of the discussion. He or she then develops a plan that describes:

- The sequence of discussion topics, often with approximate time estimates (to ensure everything gets covered)

- The questions to be used

- A diagram showing how the board is to be constructed as the discussion progresses

- An outline of the summary to be given at the end of the session

Stated another way, the plan covers precisely the same ground as a well-constructed teaching note. That is, perhaps, why many facilitators do not share my suspicion of these notes.

Through nearly 900 case studies during my MBA, I had always assumed that student comments largely drove a case discussion. To be sure, some of my less experienced instructors seemed as if they were trying to force topics according to some plan, as evidenced by jarring changes of subject that were occasionally initiated by the instructor during the middle of the discussion. But the really experienced facilitators seemed as if they were going with the flow of the class. Thus, when I heard how first year instructors spent hours as a group preparing each case that would be taught across all 9 sections, I was not convinced that such preparation was actually accomplishing anything. That perception changed considerably once I became a doctoral student, as illustrated by the example that follows.

Example: Two Sessions Facilitated by Warren McFarlan

Looking back at my MBA at HBS, I would have to say that the class I most enjoyed was a ½ credit course in the Management of Information Systems (MIS) facilitated by Professor Warren McFarlan. This is no small compliment, by the way. His class took place during the highly undesirable second semester of our second year, a period when our perspective on courses had fully transitioned from "opportunities to learn" to "obstacles in the way of graduation".

What made McFarlan's class particularly enjoyable was his facilitation style. He used humor extensively. He asked good questions. He did not allow students who spoke without a point to waste our time. As I recall, the 75 minutes of his classes literally flew by. Several years later, I mentioned to him how entertaining I had found his classes to be. His response was a rather suspicious "I hope you learned something too..." He need not have worried. If he wanted a concrete indicator of his impact, all he needed to recollect was the fact that I chose to do my doctorate in MIS and, when I was making that particular decision, the first person I contacted was him.

It was four years later—when I first entered the doctoral program—that he changed my perception of the nature of case facilitation at HBS. During the summer before I started taking doctoral classes, the MIS department ran a week-long case-based seminar for practitioners and academics. The number of participants, well over a hundred, meant that two sections were required. Since many new cases were being debuted in that seminar, incoming doctoral students were told to sit in on both sessions for a particular case and to take notes that could ultimately be used as the basis for a teaching note.

The case assigned to me happened to be facilitated by McFarlan. I enjoyed myself, as always, during his animated first session in the morning. That afternoon I sat in on the second session. What I discovered, to my complete astonishment, was that the two sessions proceeded in a sequence that was virtually identical. Even the notes on the board ended up being as close as photocopies. What I had thought was beautifully improvised evolving discussion instead proved to be a carefully choreographed plan.

When I pointed this out to McFarlan after the second session, he nodded and indicated that I had understood the point of the exercise. Thinking back on that experience, I find it somewhat paradoxical that the individual whom I most admired as a facilitator employed a planning approach that is almost the polar opposite of my own.

Strengths of Goal-Driven Planning

Goal-driven planning has much to recommend it. Among its many advantages:

1. It ensures that what the instructor feels should be covered gets covered.

2. It keeps discussions from degenerating into collections of aimless comments

3. It provides opportunities for the instructor to introduce theory or conceptual schemes at specific points in the discussion

4. It provides a lifeline for the facilitator, much the way a lesson plan does for a traditional lecture.

For these reasons, I would recommend that instructors new to case facilitation *always* try out this approach (as I did during my early years as an academic). As the previous example suggests, it can be particularly successful if you are able to direct the discussion according to plan *without* making what you are doing immediately evident to the discussion participants.

Weaknesses of Goal-Driven Planning

I would also caution the reader against those who assert that goal-driven planning is the *only* way to organize a discussion. The very strengths of the approach lead to corresponding risks:

1. Keeping to a firm plan often motivates the facilitator to exert too much control over a discussion. One of the benefits of the case method is its constructivist philosophy.

2. It encourages the misperception—so common in today's education—that what you are covering maps directly to what students are learning.

Taken to an extreme, a highly planned "discussion" can easily degenerate into a lecture about the case on the part of the facilitator. This risk will be particularly severe when participants are new to the case discussion pedagogy but are (all too) familiar with lectures. Such students are far too willing to sit back and listen if the instructor is willing to talk.

Effectual Facilitation

One of the challenges of presenting the polar opposite of "goal driven planning" is that it is hard to come up with a description that doesn't sound awful. What is the opposite of goal driven…aimless, perhaps? What is the opposite of planning…disorganized? Somehow, I am not convinced that describing the planning approach I tend to favor as "The Aimless, Disorganized Facilitation Strategy" would cast it in the best light.

While I was preparing this chapter, a colleague forwarded an article from *Inc. Magazine* (Buchanan, 2011) that employed the term effectuation in describing how entrepreneurs reason. I immediately recognized that process as being highly similar to the process I employee in planning and facilitating a case discussion. The example that follows describes effectuation in greater detail.

Example: How Entrepreneurs Think

It has long been recognized that entrepreneurs often make decisions and plan differently from executives in established organizations. Working with the late Nobel laureate Herbert Simon, Saras Sarasvathy (2001) set about to examine the differences in reasoning approaches. As described in an article published in Inc. Magazine (Buchanan, 2011), the upshot of her research was as follows:

> Sarasvathy concluded that master entrepreneurs rely on what she calls effectual reasoning. Brilliant improvisers, the entrepreneurs don't start out with concrete goals. Instead, they constantly assess how to use their personal strengths and whatever resources they have at hand to develop goals on the fly, while creatively reacting to contingencies. By contrast, corporate executives—those in the study group were also enormously successful in their chosen field—use causal reasoning. They set a goal and diligently seek the best ways to achieve it. Early indications suggest the rookie company founders are spread all across the effectual-to-causal scale. But those who grew up around family businesses will more likely swing effectual, while those with M.B.A.'s display a causal bent.

One of the major distinctions between "effectuators" and "planners" involves their perception of the future. The distinction is as follows:

> Corporate managers believe that to the extent they can predict the future, they can control it. Entrepreneurs believe that to the extent they can control the future, they don't need to predict it. That may sound like monumental hubris, but Sarasvathy sees it differently, as an expression of entrepreneurs' confidence in their ability to recognize, respond to, and reshape opportunities as they develop. Entrepreneurs thrive on contingency. The best ones improvise their way to an outcome that in retrospect feels ordained (Buchanan, 2011).

Sarasvathy summarizes the distinction between causation and effectuation in a table, presented here as Table 10.2.

Table 10.2: Causation versus Effectuation (from Sarasvathy, 2001, p. 251).

Categories of Differentiation	Causation Processes	Effectuation Processes
Givens	Effect is given	Only some means or tools are given
Decision-making selection criteria	Help choose between means to achieve the given effect	Help choose between possible effects that can be created with given means
	Selection criteria are based on expected return	Selection criteria based on affordable loss or acceptable risk
	Effect dependent: Choice of means is driven by characteristics of the effect the decision maker wants to create and his or her knowledge of possible means	Actor dependent: Given specific means, choice of effect is driven by characteristics of the actor and his or her ability to discover and use contingencies
Competencies employed	Excellent at exploiting knowledge	Excellent at exploiting contingencies
Context of relevance	More ubiquitous in nature	More ubiquitous in human action
	More useful in static, linear and independent environments	Explicit *assumption* of dynamic, nonlinear and ecological environments
Nature of unknowns	Focus on predictable aspects of an uncertain future	Focus on the controllable aspects of an unpredictable future
Underlying logic	To the extent we can predict the future, we can control it	To the extent we can control the future, we do not need to predict it
Outcomes	Market share in existent markets through competitive strategies	New markets created through alliances and other cooperative strategies

Applying the idea of effectuation to a case discussion involves the following premises:

1. Every case study has some fairly large number (say 5 to 20) aspects that are worth discussing[3]. These become *possible goals.*

2. Participants learn best when they are actively engaged in the topic being discussed.

3. It is naïve to imagine that students will remain equally engaged throughout the course of a 75 minute discussion.

4. It is nearly impossible to predict or control what topics will resonate with a particular set of students. (This is, perhaps, an overstatement; some topics nearly always work—but you typically do not recognize these until you have facilitated the case a number of times).

5. While you cannot predict what topic will engage a particular group of students, as a facilitator you do have considerable control over what topic is being discussed.

6. When a topic is engaging students, keep discussing it until it becomes less engaging. When a topic fails to generate interest, move on.

7. If you succeed in engaging students with several topics (possible goals) over the course of a discussion, the discussion has been a success. *It does not matter how many possible goals did not get discussed or failed to generate expected interest.*

Broadly speaking, what distinguishes the effectuation approach from the goal driven approach is what determines the sequence of discussion. In the goal driven approach it is the lesson plan. In the effectuation approach, it is a process of experimentation with the actual direction being determined by what appears to be working and what does not.

Strengths of Effectual Facilitation

The principal strength of effectual facilitation is that it is driven by student engagement; specifically, by what seems to be working. This aligns the approach closely to the constructivist goals that underlie the case method. With effectual facilitation, students truly are constructing their own knowledge. With the goal-driven planning approach, they may think they are—if the facilitator is sufficiently skilled, as in the previous "Two session" example—but, ultimately, it is the instructor who is driving what is learned.

Weaknesses of Effectual Facilitation

The weaknesses of the effectual facilitation approach are closely tied to the instructor's own view of the subject being taught. If the instructor believes that the content being taught conforms to a rational model and is governed by rules that are largely invariant, then effectual facilitation is likely to be unsatisfying. Students will rarely learn the model in the way the instructor intended and there will always be critical pieces that never get covered. Discussions will seem unpredictable and disorganized; transitions between topics may seem awkward. And, of course, measuring learning outcomes—always a concern with the case method—will be nearly impossible.

These drawbacks may seem less serious to the instructor who believes that the real world is disorganized, unpredictable, violates rational principles at least as often as it follows them, and that individuals always face situations with incomplete information. Thus, how "good" or "bad" effectual facilitation seems is likely to be in the eye of the beholder.

Choosing a Planning Approach

The key point of this discussion of planning approaches is that a wide continuum of approaches can be employed successfully. What is critical is achieving a fit between the content, the students, and the instructor's personal style. The reader should bear this in mind when hearing someone pontificate about the "right" way to facilitate a case. It may way be the right way for that individual's field, students and personality. That does not make it right for you. You should never feel guilty about employing an approach that is different from that recommended by an expert…just so long as it works for you and your students.

As a final conclusion, I would note that I see little evidence that we are "hard-wired" to favor one planning approach or the other. I've certainly tried a variety of points on the planning continuum and have found I can make all of them work reasonably well. I would also add that if you look at the descriptions of the two courses I taught in Appendix E, you would find one—the programming course—to be planned out in meticulous detail whereas the other—the case method course—is far more effectual in the way it is taught. Both courses were highly successful. But fit was achieved in very different ways.

The Facilitator Persona

My simple recommendation is to be as authentic (to your actual personality) as possible while facilitating a case study. Nevertheless, most of us behave a little differently when in front of a crowd than we do one-to-one or on our own. Thus, a few comments about what you might, and might not, want to convey as a facilitator may be in order.

Competence and Warmth

Often the challenge facing the facilitator is not what he/she would like to convey, rather what gets conveyed unconsciously. HBS social psychologist Amy Cuddy and her colleagues have studied the underlying factors associated with stereotypes for a decade (e.g., Fiske, Cuddy, Glick, & Xu, 2002) and have found that two key dimensions are particularly critical in our classification scheme: competence-incompetence and warm-cold. How we classify someone, in turn, impacts our dominant reaction to that person, summarized in Figure 10.1.

	Competent	Incompetent
Warm	Warm/Competent *Admire*	Warm/Incompetent *Pity*
Cold	Cold/Competent *Envy*	Cold/Incompetent *Contempt*

Figure 10.1: Reaction to stereotype dimensions (Lambert, 2010, p. 50)

I believe it is useful for the potential case facilitator to consider these dimensions carefully for two reasons. First, I do not recall every having a positive reaction to a facilitator who did not appear to be competent. Those few instructors I encountered who lost my respect in this area were quickly dismissed from my thoughts. Fortunately, Cuddy suggests that competence has a halo effect (Lambert, 2010), meaning that once we clearly demonstrate our competence in one context, competence in other contexts is assumed until proven otherwise.

The warm-cold continuum is quite different. Warmth is defined on a scale that includes "good-natured, trustworthy, tolerant, friendly, and sincere" (Cuddy, Fiske & Glick, 2008, p. 65) and is evoked by behaviors such as "Appropriate self-disclosure, the use of humor and natural smiles" (Lambert, 2010, p. 51). Eye contact is great as well. Because warmth can be faked, however, a single act that is interpreted as being cold can color our overall perception of an individual indefinitely[4].

Example: The Late Student

I was taught by one of the best known professors at HBS during the first year of my MBA. It would be hard to recall a professor more dedicated to the craft and more demanding. There was scarcely an instant during his typical class where 5-10 hands were not raised. And I cannot recall a single professor who attempted to catalog our participation more accurately and fairly. Moreover, he is the only one of my former professors who, for 25 years and counting, managed to drop by our section's reunion gatherings for a few minutes to say hello.

Despite his extraordinary competence and attentiveness, the day I best remember from his class involved a woman student who came in a minute or two late (and, quite possibly, not for the first time). In front of the whole class, he came down on her so hard that she burst into tears. That single act altered my perception of him for the remainder of the course. Did it impact my learning? Hard to say… Did it impact my enthusiasm for that particular course over the remainder of the semester? Without a doubt!

As the previous example suggests, it is not necessary to be perceived as warm in order to be an effective facilitator. I would propose, however, that with classes inexperienced in case method discussion, it is generally better to motivate with warmth as opposed to fear. These students will be scared enough already without the facilitator appearing to be intolerant of mistakes.

Body Language

Another area of non-verbal communication explored by Cuddy and her colleagues (e.g., Carney, Cuddy & Yap, 2010) is that of body language. As it happens, posture and bearing provide powerful signals of power and confidence. This can be significant in case facilitation because, in my observation, confidence is similar to competence. In other words, I cannot recall a single master of the case discussion who did not project confidence.

The non-verbal cues that project power and confidence typically involve opening up your stance to make you seem larger than you actually are. Cues include striding purposely around the classroom, making your gestures sweeping while standing. As suggested by the stick figures in Figure 10.2, when using furniture to lean on, you spread out as if you own it. You would never allow yourself to be trapped by a podium.

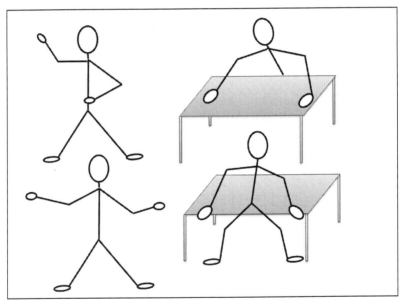

Figure 10.2: High power poses involve are animated and spread out.

Low power poses, in contrast, seem defensive. Limbs are held close to the body, motion around the classroom is limited and tentative. Furniture—particularly the podium—is used as if it were a shield. Some of these poses are illustrated by the stick figures of Figure 10.3.

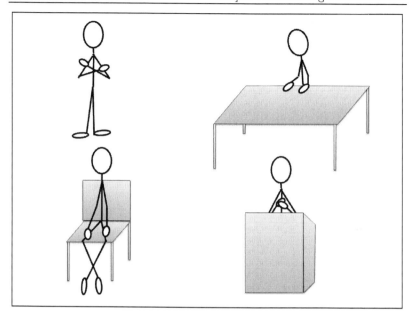

Figure 10.3: Low power positions are less animated and mainly involve trying to look small and to put as many barriers as possible between you and the participants.

Candidly, before I began researching this chapter, I would have viewed body language as a matter of personal style; the fact that my antics as a facilitator are practically a caricature of the Figure 10.2 examples would not have caused me to recommend them. What the research suggests, however, is that assuming high power positions actually causes hormones to flow that induce a feeling of power and confidence (Lambert, 2010). Let me state that again, for emphasis:

Assuming positions that make you appear to be confident will actually make you more confident.

Thus, I would encourage facilitators to be bold in their personal presentation, even if it does not feel completely natural at first.

Using the Board

A final area in which non-verbal communication can take place is in the use of the board. In a classroom case discussion, the facilitator typically stands close to the board and writes points that help to organize what students are saying. Board use tends to mirror the facilitator's choice of goal-driven planning or effectual facilitation. The goal-driven planner tends to have the board mapped out in advance. Sometimes, rather than asking a question to move on to a topic, the instructor simply writes a new heading on the board—signaling his or her intent to the class.

The effectual facilitator uses the board to summarize comments. Sometimes the writing reflects an accurate summary of what the participant has said. Sometimes it offers a challenge to the participant. For example, a student might suggest that an organization's legal department approve a contract before the protagonist signs it. If the facilitator does not feel that needs additional discussion, he or she might write:

Get approval from legal

If additional discussion seems warranted, the facilitator might write:

Turn the management of the organization over to legal

Either the student speaking or other participants will jump quickly on such a rewording, and the discussion will commence.

The other way the effectual facilitator can use the board as a signaling device is by the position of what is written. When a participant gives a disorganized opening—something that happens far too often with inexperienced students—I will typically place headings across the entire board and then run, in a very visible way, between them each time a student makes a comment. I have found that this communicates my message every bit as well as chiding the student for not spending more time organizing his or her opening.

Leading With Questions

Because the case method is built on constructivist principles, asking participants questions plays a much greater role in the pedagogy than it does in teaching techniques that involve less active participation. There are two types of questions that may be employed: study questions to help the student prepare for the case and questions asked during the discussion itself.

Study Questions

If there is one area where even experienced facilitators have agreed to disagree, it is on the matter as to whether or not it is a good idea give students study questions to use in preparing the case. The pro side of the argument is essentially:

Students will focus on the wrong thing in preparing the case if they are not given questions to direct them.

Those who object to study questions will respond with the following argument:

Students will focus on the wrong thing in preparing the case if they are not given questions to direct them.

If these arguments look suspiciously similar—identical, in fact—then the real difference becomes clear. To the best of my knowledge, *no one questions the fact that if you give diligent students study questions, they will focus their preparation in the directions the questions suggest.* If you believe that students are wasting their time when they study the "wrong thing", then it follows that you should give them study questions. If you believe, in contrast, that allowing students to discover that they have been distracted by the "wrong thing" is an essential part of learning, then you want to give them that opportunity and will therefore *not* give them leading questions.

Although I have no empirical evidence to back this up, I would speculate that facilitators who adopt a goal-driven planning approach would do better to provide study questions. Doing so will make it easier to keep to the plan. Those of us favoring effectual facilitation, on the other hand, are probably less likely to see the benefits of such questions. Since such questions are an essential part of any teaching note, making them up is rarely an issue. Their use is really a matter of personal choice.

In-Class Questions

The ideal case discussion would probably involve the facilitator doing nothing but asking questions of participants, gently nudging the discussion into areas of interest. With a top notch facilitator and a class full of highly motivated students with a lot of case discussions under their belts, it is possible to come close to achieving this. Most of us will fall considerably short of this ideal, however. With inexperienced students, a certain amount of hand-holding and explanation is inevitable. Sometimes, a gentle nudge does not get the job done—a forceful push in a particular direction is required. My own view is that it is best to be pragmatic about what works, just so long as you do not lose sight of the ideal and turn the discussion into a lecture about the case.

A Typology of Questions

Perhaps the most legendary case facilitator and proponent of the case method at HBS was the late C. Roland Christensen. In a chapter on facilitating case discussions that is well worth reading, he proposed a typology of ten questions that he had found useful in leading discussions. These are summarized in Table 10.3, with examples I have provided.

It is certainly possible to ask questions without have categorical labels such as those provided in the table. What is useful about Table 10.3 is that it serves as a reminder of the range of questions that the facilitator has available. Experienced facilitators will, in all likelihood, employ most if not all of these question types during the course of a single discussion. Doing so provides welcome variety to the discussion, keeping it from becoming too predictable.

Thinking about the types of questions you are asking can also help in diagnosing problems. Christensen (1991, p. 153) relates the following story:

> One distinguished educator...who chose early retirement because he felt his classroom magic had disappeared, said "The students would just sit there and answer my questions politely, but I couldn't get them stirred up anymore. No zip!" A colleague of his saw the situation from a more detached perspective: "'Why' questions had disappeared from his repertoire and 'what do you think?' was replaced by 'don't you think?' It was as if he had forgotten to listen."

That quote underscores a critical point about facilitation. It does not matter how good your questions are if you do not pay careful attention to the answers.

An interesting aspect of Table 10.3 table is that it does not identify a class of questions asked specifically for the purpose of directing the discussion. I call these "leading questions" and will now turn to their use.

Table 10.3: Types of questions used by case facilitators (Christensen, 1991, p. 159-160).

Question	Example
Open ended questions	e.g., What are your reactions to the case? Would you care to start us off?
Diagnostic questions	e.g., How is the productivity of the organization trending?
Information-seeking questions	e.g., What is the protagonist's background?
Challenge (testing) questions	e.g., What does the case say about the competition?
Action questions	e.g., If you were the protagonist, what immediate steps would you take?
Questions on priority and sequence	e.g., Given that both of these alternatives are desirable, which would you do first?
Prediction questions	e.g., How do you think the other staffers might react to the decision you propose?
Hypothetical questions	e.g., If the organization had made this decision two years ago, how would the current situation be different?
Questions of extension	e.g., Do you think other organizations are facing similar situations to the one we just discussed?
Questions of generalization	e.g., Which of the lessons we have learned from this case study are likely to apply to other situations?

Using Leading Questions

It is pleasant to imagine that the purpose of asking a participant a question is to elicit a thoughtful response. Nevertheless, a good deal of the time there is a pragmatic reason for asking—such as moving on to a new discussion topic. As mentioned in the earlier "two sessions" example, this can sometimes be done subtly. For example, the facilitator can listen closely to answers until a word or two related to the next desired topic is mentioned and then jump on those words so as to suggest the change in topic was actually the participant's idea. In the hands of a master facilitator, participants may not even be aware of what is happening. But, if you are trying to maintain the trajectory of a goal-driven plan, happen it must.

A somewhat more interesting case is that where the disciple of effectual facilitation starts to ask leading questions. I, for example, delight in asking a sequence of questions in a manner that encourages students to reach a desired conclusion. While this hardly sounds like a constructivist approach, the twist I provide is that when doing so the conclusion I am teasing them towards is invariably a bad one.

Why encourage participants to reach a bad conclusion? What I have found is that in many cases, linear thinking leads participants towards analysis and plans that closely align with the status quo. (The same trend takes place in the thinking of most large organizations.) For some cases, this is a sensible approach; for such cases I would *never* lead the group towards a particular consensus. For other cases, however, details within the case—if spotted by the reader—clearly indicate that the status quo and linear thinking will not lead to an acceptable outcome. For such cases, unless a brave participant thinks outside of the box, building a consensus is easy.

Then I drop the bomb...

In no uncertain terms, I make it clear to the class that they have come up with an entirely unsuitable analysis or set of solutions. Then, I make them "fix" it. The example that follows provides an illustration.

Example: I drop the bomb…

My most memorable bomb drop took place in an EMBA class where the case discussed—Concordia Casting (mentioned in an earlier example)—lends itself to a predictable, but entirely unworkable, conclusion. Once the class jumped on that solution I moved close to the first row and said:

> Well you seem to have the case wrapped up. I really have only one remaining question… WHAT F*****G CASE DID YOU READ?

Personally, I think profanity in class is vulgar, so I surprised even myself with the stridency of my remark—entirely staged, of course, since my leading questions had been responsible for helping them to reach the false consensus. I hope that I will never be that coarse again. Once my outburst subsided, however, the case discussion proceeded with

---

considerably renewed vigor. Within about 30 minutes, a vastly more sensible solution was reached—one that involved the unlikely step of firing the protagonist immediately.

My evidence that the outburst was useful comes from what happened later. During the final dinner for the class cohort I was awarded the "Most Memorable Professor Award". In the course of the comments made about my class, one student remarked that my particular outburst on that day—a day that had occurred more than a year before—was the most significant thing he recalled from the entire program.

The pedagogical justification for the approach I have described is built upon the power of the unexpected in learning. The unexpected is a key element to what is interesting (e.g., see Davis, 1971). If students are interested and engaged, the odds that they will recall the lessons being discussed are vastly higher. Thus, occasional theatrics (even the occasional descent into crudity) may serve an educational purpose. It may also put you on the cover of the local paper, and not in a good way, if carried too far[5]. So I'd recommend knowing your students and yourself before going too overboard along these lines.

Summarizing the Discussion

Summarizing the discussion tends to serve a dual role: highlighting key topics and covering important issues that were missed in the discussion. In addition, it may provide the facilitator with the opportunity to pass on information regarding the outcomes of whatever decisions were actually made and, where a case study was locally developed, even provide case protagonists with a chance to talk about what happened.

Differing Summary Styles

Helping participants reflect on what they learned from the case is an important objective of the summary portion of the class. The nature of the summary, as might be expected, is likely to vary with the facilitator's planning style. Where the goal-driven planning approach is taken, the summary is likely to be planned as well. In a sense, it will constitute the "lecture" portion of the discussion. This should, in no way, be viewed as a criticism. While not necessarily a constructivist approach, such a summary provides the facilitator the chance to help students reflect upon what they have learned. It is also the point at which analytical frameworks, such as the Five Forces model (Porter, 1980), are often introduced. Backed by a completed discussion, such tools are much more meaningful.

For the effectual facilitator, no such canned summary is possible. Instead, the facilitator must—to the greatest extent possible—tie together the discussion threads that engaged the class. Rather than being an opportunity to summarize the case itself, it is an opportunity to summarize the most meaningful contributions in the discussion. To the extent that the facilitator is also able to recognize and acknowledge the role that specific individual students played in building the discussion, it will be very much appreciated by the students and will serve as motivation for future participation.

Discussing Issues That Were Missed

Unless a facilitator is very directive, there are almost certain to be important issues in the case study that were not discussed. This is particularly true when the instructor leans towards effectual facilitation, but even the best laid goal-driven lesson plans frequently do not proceed precisely as expected.

The first comment I would make—and this repeats statements made earlier in the chapter—is that it is nearly always a mistake to rush through the later stages of a case discussion simply to ensure that all critical areas are covered. Worrying that every possible point is touched upon as opposed to ensuring understanding is achieved is a common flaw in lecture-based courses. There is no merit to carrying that flaw over to case discussions.

What I will say is that there are sometimes interesting issues that are important to touch upon that may not naturally come up during the discussion. Sometimes when they do, they even interfere with the flow of the discussion. I find that this is often the case with critical concerns such as ethics, sustainability and globalization. Because these are general issues that apply broadly—while the case situation is often focused on a very specific situation—forcing these into the discussion itself can seem very artificial. I feel that participants can become suspicious when they feel that I have pushed them on to a topic because I am "obligated" to do so. If the students involved are business students, they are likely to chalk it up to political correctness.

What I typically do with these topics is to jump on them during the discussion if a student raises them naturally, without any prompting from me. If these issues are not raised in this way, however, I close down the discussion a little bit early and then, after we've reached whatever conclusion the case allows for, I raise the issues as an "aren't we forgetting something?" topic—adding an element of the unexpected. Then, I re-open the discussion and we mutually consider if and how placing greater emphasis on these areas might alter our decision making. This seems to work reasonably well, though there are doubtless other approaches to these types of issues that work as effectively.

Relating What Happened After the Case

For older large company cases, participants may well have determined what happened after the period of the case from the Internet. If they have not, however, they will nearly always be very interested in what decisions were made and the associated outcome. As a result, information of this sort often is included as part of the summary.

Personally, I recommend underplaying actual outcomes for a number of reasons. First, we do not know what would have happened if the protagonists made another choice. So we can never know how a particular decision compares with other alternatives, even when the actual outcome is known. Second, no matter how long the case write-up, it will necessarily be a simplification of reality. In complex systems, very small details can make a very big difference, so it may be a fact unknown to the discussants that heavily influenced what happened. Finally, the "success" of a particular approach depends heavily on the goals of that approach. Unless the participants fully buy in to what the protagonist wants—in the unlikely event that it is fully disclosed in the case itself—differing goals could sensibly lead to differing decisions.

The bottom line is that case discussions are used to build reasoning skills and to act as an admittedly weak substitute for experience when actual experience is too expensive to obtain. Knowledge of actual case outcomes does little to advance this learning goal.

Providing Guests an Opportunity to Participate

One of the greatest benefits of developing your own discussion cases is the opportunity it provides to have case protagonists sit in on the discussion. I find this venue to be infinitely more satisfying than the typical executive guest speaker engagement, which often ends up as a combination of personal experience and platitudes presented as if they apply to all situations. After having listened to a discussion, on the other hand, both students and protagonist are primed with meaningful questions and comments.

The main challenge that I have found with the guest protagonist is keeping him or her from participating too actively in the actual discussion. The issue here is not one of my losing control of the discussion (sad to say, the effectual facilitator never feels that much "in control"). Rather, as soon as a case protagonist begins to suggest conclusions, participants—particularly inexperienced students—will immediately tend to lock into a state of consensus that will be nearly impervious to subsequent analysis.

What I do to reduce the risk of this is two things. First, I explain the philosophy of the case method to the visiting protagonist. Second, I encourage him or her to limit remarks during the discussion to clarification of facts. This briefing approach seems to work with about half the visitors I have had in my classes. The other half more or less ignores my suggestions and jumps right into the discussion[6]. Even so, I feel that the benefits of having the tangible proof that the cases are real far outweighs the risk that the discussion gets derailed.

Conclusions

Let me end this chapter where I began it: effective case facilitation is more likely to be a matter of fit than one of following a prescribed set of rules. Were I—after 19 years of working with students who were complete novices in the case method—to suddenly find myself facilitating a second year class at HBS, I have absolutely no doubt that the students would eat me alive. I am equally convinced that were the icons of case facilitation at HBS suddenly transported to one of my classes, they would quickly discover that they needed to modify their time tested techniques rather quickly—or find themselves dealing with a lot of "dead air". In some cases, they might also find themselves fielding calls from upper administration officials in response to threats of legal action initiated by students or, equally likely, their helicopter parents.

What I would provide as two relatively immutable rules is that the best case facilitators share two characteristics:

- Competence, and

- Confidence

Competence is achieved through systematically preparing the case, having command of the broader subject matter associated with the case, and is greatly amplified by having participated in the case writing experience. Confidence tends to come with time and experience. It can, however, be mimicked with bold body language that will, in itself, help to build confidence as well as convey it.

Chapter 10 Notes

[1] As I noted previously in the book, in a typical case method class that I facilitate, by the time we discuss our final case my students have as much experience in case discussion as an HBS MBA candidate has by Thursday of the first week of a 2 year program.

[2] For an example of how my experience diverges from that described in a teaching note, see the earlier Tektronix example.

[3] If a case study does not have a substantial number of interesting topics to discuss, the time has come to select another case.

[4] The Jane Austin fans among the readership of this book might recall, from *Pride and Prejudice*, Mr. Darcy's memorable line: "My good opinion once lost is lost forever." Indeed, most of the book revolves around the extremely tortuous path that Darcy endured in his gradual transition from the cold/competent quadrant to the warm/competent quadrant, thereby gaining the admiration of Miss Elizabeth Bennet.

[5] That classroom antics may lead to a local paper cover story is speculation on my part—I don't yet have an example from own life to relate on this score. Whew…!

[6] In Chapter 11, I provide an example of an asynchronous case that went completely haywire when the two main case protagonists started debating each other right in the middle of the student's online discussion forum.

Chapter 11

Case Discussions beyond the Classroom

The case method is not limited to the classroom. In fact, case discussions can be conducted effectively online in a number of ways. These online discussions do not necessarily proceed in the same way as their classroom counterparts, but this is not necessarily a bad thing. In fact, what I have found is that the group of students who are the most effective participants in class often differs considerably from those who are the most effective online. Thus, my own preferred approach to designing a case method course involves building in a mix of discussion types.

When moving outside of the classroom, there are two key dimension of flexibility that can be achieved:

1. *Flexibility of time.* Rather than requiring students to interact during a specified class period (synchronous), participants can be given a longer window of time for their involvement (asynchronous).

2. *Flexibility of place.* Rather than having students meet at a particular location, participation may be achieved from a location of the individual's choosing. This may further be broken down by instructor and student freedom of place (e.g., the instructor may be constrained to a particular technology station while the students can connect from anywhere; students may to come to a classroom to interact with a televised instructor).

In this chapter, I relate my own experiences with three types of online case discussions: asynchronous discussions (using an online discussion forum), synchronous discussions (using an audio/visual conferencing tool) and discussions in a virtual environment (Second Life). Not surprisingly, I find merits and drawbacks with each approach.

Online Asynchronous Case Discussions

Until about a decade ago, when broadband Internet started to gain some real traction, the only real alternative to classroom discussions was to hold text-based asynchronous discussions using tools such as threaded discussion boards[1]. Between 1999 and 2003, I facilitated courses that made use of asynchronous case discussions to varying degrees. The description of these experiences that follows draws heavily on two articles, one describing the protocol I used (Gill, 2005) and one that specifically looks at learning outcomes (Webb, Gill & Poe, 2005). These are, of course, heavily supplemented by my recollections.

The Context

During the period from 1991-2001, I was a faculty member *at Florida Atlantic University.* During my final two years there, I found myself in a variety of teaching situations all of which employed the case method. These consisted of the following:

- A traditional MBA class that met twice a week, where we discussed a total of 18 cases in the classroom, supplemented by other activities.

- A weekend MBA class that met only 12 times, where we discussed 11 cases in the classroom, supplemented by 4 asynchronous online case discussions.

- Two sections of an Environmental MBA class that met only 4 times, where we discussed 3 cases in the classroom supplemented by 9 or 10 asynchronous online case discussions.

- A virtual MBA class, conducted over a 10 week summer session, where we conducted 10 asynchronous online case discussions, supplemented by other activities.

As it happens, the overlap between the cases discussed in each of these courses was high, and—being the same course—the course objectives were identical. Thus, these courses provided a unique opportunity to contrast asynchronous online to synchronous face-to-face applications of the case method.

Protocol for Online Case Discussions

The protocol employed for the asynchronous discussions varied from that of a typical classroom discussion in a number of ways. Highlights of the differences, adapted from the protocol article (Gill, 2005), are now explored.

Case Openings

The first significant variation from the classroom protocol involved the initiation of the discussion. Rather than calling upon a single student to "open" each case, 4-5 students were each assigned a different topic to discuss and were given 24-48 hours to open a discussion thread on that topic (see example that follows).

Example: An Actual Opening Request Email (Gill, 2005, p. 148)[2]

Sent: Sat 3/22/2003 3:09 PM

Congratulations!

You have been selected to open the Xerox case (as per the revised schedule):

I would like each of you to prepare an opening on the following topic:

1. Karl: Should the outsourcing agreement proceed, or would you recommend pulling back?

2. Karleen: What are the benefits of the outsourcing arrangement to both sides (Xerox, EDS)? Does either side appear to be realizing a disproportionate share of the benefits?

3. Mark: What does it signify that hundreds of person-weeks were devoted to drafting the outsourcing agreement between EDS and Xerox yet the breakup provisions were handled in a single morning? Do you view this as a good omen or a bad omen?

4. Robert: What are the potential benefits and drawbacks of the strategy whereby EDS manages existing (legacy) systems while Xerox focuses on developing the systems of the future? Can you see any implementation issues that are likely to be addressed.

---

5. Jason: Why does EDS feel it can make a profit running Xerox's IT processes for less money than Xerox is currently spending?

By Tuesday, 3/25/03 at 7PM I'd like each of you to post an opening to the Xerox discussion group, opening a new thread. Please choose your own title for the thread, but try to focus on your assigned topic. After you have posted your opening, feel free to participate in the discussion, just like every other student.

Thanks, and good luck!

Regards,

Grandon

From this example, it is clear that my attitude towards posing specific questions to assist in preparing the case changes dramatically when the medium is asynchronous. Assigning multiple topics allows discussion themes to develop in parallel, rather than sequentially. It also enables more complete coverage of the issues related to the case study. This is another example of how changing the medium of discussion can affect the instructor's planning and facilitation style.

Instructor Intervention

A second change involved the nature of instructor intervention. As described in Chapter 10, my view is that the "ideal" case instructor does not lecture using the case as a backdrop. Instead, he or she uses subtle feedback (e.g., smiles, body language, stern glances) to direct the discussion—acting as a conductor rather than a soloist. In online asynchronous discussions, the ability to provide such subtle direction is almost entirely absent. Thus, the instructor is left with two choices: respond directly to student posts (with an assessment, argument or leading question) or sit back and watch, in the hope that other students will do so.

My experience was that the "respond directly" technique proved to be both impractical and inconsistent with the premises of the case pedagogy. When I attempted it (during one of the first Environmental MBA sections), what emerged was a series of independent but concurrent dialogs between me and individual students—much as if the discussion had been conducted by email. Not only did the process place unsustainable time demands on both the student and me, it also violated the constructivist learning premise of the case method. Classroom case discussion leaders are often warned against being too directive (Barnes et al., 1994, p. 25):

> If the instructor lays out a step-by-step outline for the discussion—orally or on the blackboard—the class picks up a clear signal: follow my lead or be lost! Any partnership between leader and followers is clearly a limited one.

> In contrast, when the instructor invites students to set the agenda for the day's discussion, the openness of the invitation conveys a different message: you, the students, bear the responsibility for this discussion. It belongs to you.

What I found was that if student "ownership" of online discussions were to be established, the immediate convergence of opinion that tended to occur after I expressed an opinion had to be avoided.

To avoid stifling discussion, I therefore established a policy that I would not reply to, nor comment upon, any individual student post until at least 24 hours had passed. From the point of view of the students—being graded on participation—the advantage of the policy was that it gave them time to make their own observations before the I effectively coerced diverse opinions into convergence by posting the "right answer" (whether by intent or not). 24 hours also proved to be enough time so that most posts that warranted a response got one before I became involved. The approach also had an unfortunate side effect, however. My online "monitoring" activities tended to be invisible to students. A student could therefore conclude that the instructor had disengaged from the discussion, even when I was diligently examining posts several times a day.

Summarizing the Discussion

The final modification to the discussion protocol involved the procedure for bringing the discussion to a close, presented in Figure 11.1. As noted in Chapter 10, in the classroom the process of reaching closure varies considerably. Some instructors use the end of the class as an opportunity to lecture about the case. Others prefer to continue the peer-oriented process, attempting to coax closure out of discussion participants. Interestingly, asynchronous discussion technologies make it possible to do both.

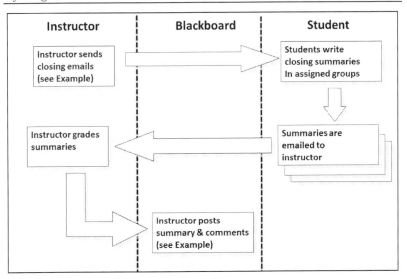

Figure 11.1: Procedure for closing a case (adapted from Gill, 2005d, p. 145)

In order to ensure some peer-to-peer interaction as part of the asynchronous discussion, I assigned students to groups of 3-5 randomly for each case. Each student was then sent an email identifying the other members of his or her group, along with instructions for closing, as per the example that follows.

Example: Closing Instructions Email (from Gill, 2005, p. 149)

Sent: Mon 3/31/2003 7:00 PM

[List of student names—randomly generated for each case—omitted]

Congratulations!

You have been randomly selected to close the Xerox case as Group 1. I would like to have the closings done and sent to me using *private* email by Wednesday, 4/2, at 7PM.

You should endeavor to include your key recommendations and/or lessons learned in your summary. Be sure to identify the key elements of the case and/or your analysis leading to your conclusions. Outline form is fine.

Ideally, your summary should be an MS Word attachment. Please keep your summary under 250 words and include the names of all participants in the body of the summary (the names are not included in your word limit). Also, try not to use exotic formatting, that Blackboard won't be able to handle.

Finally, please do not include the name of anyone who did not participate, even if they were assigned.

Regards,

Grandon

After receiving the responses from the various closing groups, I would then present my own summary of the case and short critique of each group's effort, as per the example that follows.

Example: Instructor Closing (from Gill, 2005d, p. 149-150)

[Instructor summary of the case, about 4 paragraphs, omitted]

With respect to the groups, I could abide with recommendations either for or against continuing the arrangement. The central thing I needed to see, however, was the clear recognition of the level of risk involved.

My ranking is as follows:

Rank #1: Group 1

In addition to recognizing my preference for recommendations that jumped out at you, the group clearly recognized the strategic realities of the case. They appeared to proceed from the assumption that it was too late to back out of the agreement, so the company's focus needed to be on mending it. I think this is a very reasonable position (although it would have been nice if they'd stated the assumption explicitly). Overall, as good as it gets on a Xerox closing.

Rank #2: Group 4

Also a nice job. Their "lessons learned" really captured the heart of the case. Their recommendations were okay, but suffered a bit by comparison. I just don't know how you'd implement them given the nature of the arrangement with EDS.

Rank #3: Group 3

The recommendations of this group were among the best. My main complaint was that their issues seemed to totally disregard long-term concerns and their lessons learned section looked as if it had been written by the author of the Xerox case. I'm sure it must have some meaning, but darned if I can figure out what that meaning is. (And even if I could, I doubt it would be even remotely actionable).

Rank #4: Group 5

My main problem with this group's summary is I wasn't sure whether or not they were recommending dissolving the current arrangement or not. The recommendations, on the one hand, seemed to suggest EDS in more of a consulting role (implying dissolution) yet they also seemed to suggest the agreement would continue to remain in place. That's a bit much hedging for my taste.

Rank #5: Group 2

This group focused on the problems leading to Xerox's decisions to outsource, rather on the risks of doing so. In doing so, I feel they stuck too close to the words of the case, rather than looking deeper at what those words actually meant. The recommendations were also pretty generic, such as "make sure the agreement is fair and equitable", "get buy in from the existing IT workers", "hire a consulting group" and "give the head of IT the power to implement these changes". Moreover, they suggested the company learn from its past outsourcing arrangements. Holy mackerel—you mean they've outsourced their entire IT function before???

One very nice aspect of this particular procedure was the fact that I could critique all groups in the open, without singling out individuals. This was possible because the groups were randomly constituted (as noted earlier) and therefore participants only knew the membership of their own group. This allowed for my grading approach to be become more transparent than has ever been possible in a classroom setting.

Assessment

In theory, assessing participation in asynchronous forums should be more rigorous and easier to do than is possible in the classroom. After all, the student comments are all posted—there is no need to figure out who said what.

In practice, I found assessing participation to be the most daunting aspect of the asynchronous discussion approach. Among the many challenges I encountered:

1. Discussions of an individual case tended to get very long—typically over 100 posts translating to 30-50 pages of single spaced text.

2. It seemed as if every post needed to be read and assessed 2-3 times. First, I had to read them soon after they were posted and consider what, if any, reply I needed to make. Next, I had to assign a grade to each post when the discussion was closed. Finally, I often found that posts repeated what other students had said (possibly because the poster did not read the other discussion thoroughly prior to posting). That meant I often had to compare posts to determine who posted first.

3. Because students could not tell when I was reading but not responding to the discussion, I needed to compile grades and provide individual feedback early to demonstrate that their participation was not simply being ignored or being determined by a count of posts.

To be fair, students faced a somewhat similar set of challenges. The individual who waited 2-3 days before making his or her first post had to read a huge volume of posts before adding comments.

To keep students motivated while, at the same time, attempting to keep my own workload manageable, what I did for each of the classes was to write a program that compiled all the student posts into a database. I would then grade each post on a 0 to 10 scale, where:

- 0 was used for posts such as "I agree" or for administrative questions

- 1 was the default

- 2-10 were used for posts that were distinguished in some way

Using the database, it was then possible to generate a report for each student along the lines of Figure 11.2.

[Name Hidden]				
Comment Total	114			
Class Average Total	84.6			
Comment Count	67			
Class Average Count	50.9			

Photo

Total Distinctions	27			
Class Average Distinguished Comment Total	11.7			
Count of Distinctions	13			
Class Average Distinguished Count	5.5			

Total Opening Comments	12	Total Closing Points	32
Class Average Opening Total Opening Points	12.8	Class Average Closing Points	27.4
Average Per Opening	6.0	Average Per Closing	3.2
Class Average Points Per Opening	6.4	Class Average Points Per	2.8
Opening Count	2	Closing Count	10

Figure 11.2: Participation grading summary (from Gill, 2005, p. 146)

Learning Outcomes from Asynchronous Protocol

When, back in 1999, I realized that I was going to be facilitating such a wide range of case discussion classes, I decided it would be prudent to try to assess the relative merits of the techniques I was employing. Lacking any validated tool for assessing case method learning, I decided to triangulate using three types of measures:

1. A factual identification quiz, measuring if students recalled details from the cases covered

2. A concept grouping quiz, where students attempted to identify key thematic elements of cases and judge their relative importance in the class. An example is included in Appendix I (Exhibit F).

3. Self-reported student perceptions of the class in response to a variety of questions.

A detailed analysis of these findings is provided in Webb, et al. (2005). Table 11.1 presents a summary table of these findings. In brief, we found that:

- Score on the identification section rose uniformly as we moved from full in-class to full online. Personally, I consider this result to be rather unimportant both because answering simple ID questions is not a key skill associated with the case method pedagogy and because it may reflect a smaller number of cases.

- Concept grouping scores all fell within a range that made them indistinguishable from a practical standpoint.

- Self-assessed perceptions that the case method would make them better managers were strongest for the hybrid treatments.

- The self-assessed role played by peers vs. instructor in learning rose uniformly and significantly as the treatment moved from the classroom to online. This I view as an important finding, since peer-to-peer learning is central to the case method.

Table 11.1: Summary of Results

Value	MBA: All in class	WMBA: Light Online	EMBA: Heavy Online	VMBA: All Online
Number of sections	1	1	2	1
Number of classroom cases	18	11	3	0
Number of online cases	0	4	9.5	10
Score on ID quiz (out of 20)	4.53	6.62	7.91	10.95
Mean score on concept grouping test (out of possible 100%)	29.0%	35.3%	41.4%	39.8%
Felt participating in case discussions would make them a better manager*	4.37	4.88	4.82	3.95
Felt they learned more from peers than from professor*	1.47	2.38	3.12	4.25
Felt professor should have been more active in case discussions*	1.37	1.77	2.12	3.9
*Scale: 0=strongly disagree to 3=neutral to 6=strongly agree				

Overall, then, my assessment is that we do students no harm by incorporating some asynchronous discussions into our case method classes. Given the final result regarding peer-based learning, it is quite reasonable to argue that the asynchronous discussion is even more faithful to the case method pedagogy than the traditional classroom discussion.

Another advantage of incorporating asynchronous discussions—particularly into a blended course—is that the pattern of participation tends to be different from that of the classroom. While there will certainly be students who trend towards heavy or light participation in both, I have also found, purely as a qualitative observation, that there are some individuals whose participation diverges considerably across the two channels. Of particular interest, individuals who are shy in class or who are uncomfortable with their personal command of English often participate much more frequently and thoroughly when given the opportunity to do so asynchronously. This can be particularly beneficial in programs where diversity is high.

I have also found that asynchronous discussions make it particularly easy to bring protagonist guests into a discussion, since it eliminates both scheduling issues and travel time. Also, with multiple threads of discussion evolving simultaneously, it is generally the case that active participation on the part of the protagonist is less disruptive than it would be in a face-to-face classroom discussion. I say "generally" here because I have experienced at least one situation, described in the example that follows, where protagonist involvement most definitely had an impact on the flow of an asynchronous discussion.

Example: AFN Participants Go At It…

First mentioned as an example in Chapter 7, the AFN (A) and (B) cases were rather unique in that they presented the same situation from the perspective two different protagonists: of a small business owner (who happened to be a friend of mine) and a programmer (a former student of mine, recommended to the firm by me). Both of them enjoyed sitting in on face-to-face discussions of "their" case and were popular with the students for their keen insights and humor.

When I invited them to participate in an online asynchronous discussion of their case, they both eagerly agreed. I had not anticipated that there would be much of a difference. I was wrong…

In my MIS classes, I frequently mention the fact that individuals tend to be less inhibited when communicating online. Indeed, that is probably one of the reasons that shy and international participants often participate much more actively when a discussion goes online. I can now say—based on experience—that case protagonists can be similarly affected. In the case of that particular AFN discussion, what quickly evolved was an online dialog between the two protagonists in the middle of the student discussion. Suffice it to say, many repressed resentments were released; to my mind, quite a number of them might have done better remaining repressed. Before long, both the students and I were mainly cast into the roles of spectators as the exchange between the two protagonists grew more and more strident.

I do not regret what happened. One lesson the students clearly learned was that these cases we were discussing were not just academic exercises. They were, in fact, very real to the individuals involved and the decisions made impacted them at a deeply emotional level. Nevertheless, on subsequent online offerings of that particular case, I alternated between which of the two protagonists that I invited.

Despite these advantages, I have found that overall student preference always leans towards synchronous discussions (whether face-to-face or online) rather than asynchronous. Since their preference mirrors my own, I now generally avoid this particular type of discussion in my classes. I recognize, however, that I may be losing some learning advantages by doing so.

Synchronous Online Discussions

With the near-ubiquity of broadband communications that has emerged over the past decade, it has become increasingly practical to implement discussions with shared audio and video. Using this technology, synchronous discussions can much more closely resemble the classroom discussion than their asynchronous counterparts just described. My own experience has involved three different configurations, each of which is described after a brief foray into the technology.

Capabilities Required for Synchronous Case Discussion

Before describing my experiences, it is useful to outline the capabilities required in order to conduct a synchronous discussion online[3]. Basically, I see three main features as being necessary if an online case discussion is to come close to its classroom counterpart:

1. *A shared audio channel.* As I mentioned in an earlier footnote, I am a weak typist and would therefore not want to facilitate a discussion that depended solely on text chat. The channel can be full-duplex (more than one person can speak at a time) or half-duplex (only one person can speak into the channel at a time, similar to a CB radio).

2. *A mechanism for signaling the desire to speak.* Particularly if a half-duplex channel is used, it is critical that participants have the ability to let the facilitator know that they want to speak.

3. *A shared white board.* Just as is true in the classroom, the discussion will be enhanced if the facilitator can jot down notes as individual participants are speaking.

While it would be nice to have high quality full motion video of the participants and the facilitator, I have found that the absence of these does not necessarily detract much from discussions.

The tool that I most commonly employ for online case discussions is called *Elluminate.* As shown in Figure 11.3 (taken from an actual case discussion, with student names blurred out) the tool offers:

1. Shared audio, either half-duplex or with a specified number of simultaneous talkers.

2. A shared whiteboard, supported with a variety of drawing tools and the ability to upload PowerPoint slides.

3. A participant list, with the ability to raise your hand electronically.

4. A text chat window that operates in parallel with the audio channel.

In addition to these "must have" features, it also provides some "nice to have" capabilities that include:

5. The ability to display a participant's desktop

6. A survey and quiz feature that allows tests/surveys to be created and results displayed

7. One or more video windows for webcam display.

8. Multimedia streaming

9. The ability to take participants on "web tours", so that each participant's browser is synchronized to the same web site.

10. A session recording feature that allows users to replay a class at a later date.

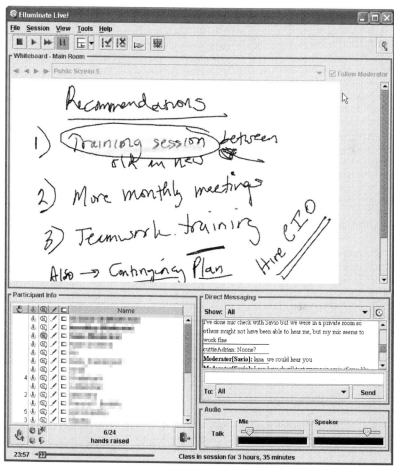

Figure 11.3 *Elluminate* screen taken from an actual case discussion

Elluminate is by no means the only tool that offers a similar bundle of capabilities. But it happens to be the tool that my university provides and is therefore what I am most comfortable discussing.

Discussions with Flexibility of Place

For over six years—since access to the tool *Elluminate* was first acquired by my university—I have been including an "online class week" in my case method capstone course. When I first started, the week would consist of an asynchronous discussion of one case and a synchronous discussion of another. When it became clear that the synchronous online discussion was vastly preferred to the asynchronous, I got rid of the asynchronous case and added a second week where the discussion took place in *Second Life*, a virtual world to be described later.

The *Elluminate* discussions offer the students nearly complete freedom of place. As long as they have their own computer and a broadband connection, the setup works fine[4]. The same applies to me, as I nearly always connect to those sessions using a Tablet PC laptop in my living room.

What I have found, after having conducted nearly two dozen such discussions, is that the protocol for online and face-to-face discussions is so nearly identical that the differences are not worth describing. To be sure, there is the occasional setup problem on the part of students. (For that reason, I normally offer a session before the class where they can test their connection.) But, with the exception of being able to communicate with body language, the discussions strike me as being nearly identical in character.

Discussions with Quasi-Freedom of Place

In summer 2010, I got to try a slightly different type of online discussion. I had been offered the opportunity to teach a case method course to MBA students at the *University of Osnabruck*, in Germany. Previous professors from my institution who had taught a similar course had given the students projects to do and then, after our summer semester ended in July, they would travel to Germany for 2-3 weeks of intensive sessions. What I proposed was that we run 8 sessions in May, June and early July using Elluminate, then finish up the class in Germany with a smaller number of face-to-face sessions.

To make this approach work, a significantly different configuration was used. First, all the students gathered in their Osnabruck classroom for each discussion session. A single computer in the classroom was then set up with Elluminate and two video windows were opened: one showing me to the class, and one showing the class to me.

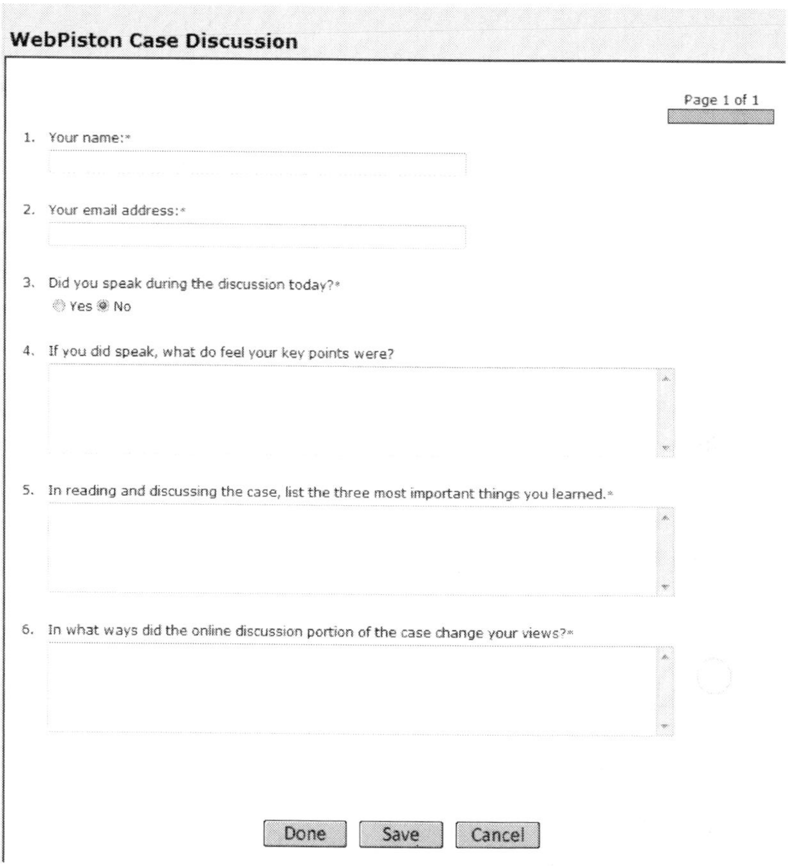

WebPiston Case Discussion

Page 1 of 1

1. Your name:*

2. Your email address:*

3. Did you speak during the discussion today?*
    ○ Yes ● No

4. If you did speak, what do feel your key points were?

5. In reading and discussing the case, list the three most important things you learned.*

6. In what ways did the online discussion portion of the case change your views?*

[Done]   [Save]   [Cancel]

Figure 11.4: Form used to capture contributions from students in Osnabruck

When students in the class wanted to speak, a wireless microphone was passed to them so that I would be able to hear. At my end, the session worked almost identically to the previously described sessions with one important difference: I was almost never sure who was talking—the video window was too small, the lighting was not conducive to clarity and I had never met the students face-to-face. This is obviously a serious problem in a case method discussion course. We resolved it by having my host, the professor who had invited me to offer the course, sit in on the discussions and keep track of who said what. Naturally, this was not a very efficient use of resources, but it was a workable one. What I also did was to have students fill out a form, shown in Figure

11.4, at the end of each discussion that required students to summarize their own contributions,. Had my counterpart not been present, these would have allowed me to better map responses to students.

As it turned out, having freedom of place proved to be an important advantage to me. The first session of the class conflicted with a case competition that required me to travel to Las Vegas; thus I introduced the course from a hotel room in the Mandalay Bay Resort. A session in later June conflicted with the InSITE 2010 conference that was being held in Casino, Italy. Both my German colleague and I hosted that session from a spare dining room in a local restaurant whose wireless connection was "iffy" at best. Despite these obstacles, the discussions were generally rich and the class was quite satisfied with the experience.

My own assessments of this particular case discussion configuration are mixed. On the one hand, I found broadcasting to a classroom to be inferior to both face-to-face and pure Elluminate discussions where each student logs on individually. On the other hand, it may not be fair to make that comparison. Instead, I should perhaps be comparing it to having no such experience at all—in which case I would evaluate it as a resounding success. If we are to prepare students for a global work-force, there is considerable merit to the idea of sharing discussions electronically across continents. The logistics can be challenging—time zones are always a looming problem when such exchanges are planned. But we are increasingly reaching the point where even free technologies, such as Skype, may be used to set up discussions that are more than passable.

Discussions in a Virtual World

Once I abandoned asynchronous discussions in my case method course, I introduced a new venue: the virtual world known as *Second Life*. My rationale for this choice was similar to the reason I initiated my first online class week: we need to better prepare our students to inter-act in electronic environments, as their use will become increasingly important as more and more of our management becomes global.

As illustrated in Figure 11.5, *Second Life* offers an imaginary environment where each individual has his own avatar and screen name (mine is *Grandon Loon*). It is free to non-premium users and is gigantic in size, with millions of enrolled users and tens of thousands of users typically online at any given time.

Educators have flocked to *Second Life* because it offers users the ability to build their own items within the environment. Unlike massive Multi-player online role playing games (MMORPGs), it has no preset goals or quests. Instead, it has a currency (the Linden) and many locations within the world where you can buy things—most often, "things" that have been created by other users. In fact, shopping and socializing are the two most common activities of *Second Life* community members.

Second Life is definitely not the world's best case discussion environment. It does offer passable, and sometimes excellent, audio channels. It also provides instant messaging and gesturing that allow participants to signal they want to say something. What it lacks is a built-in whiteboard (although some user has probably developed one). If a whiteboard were available, however, it would to detract from the scenery.

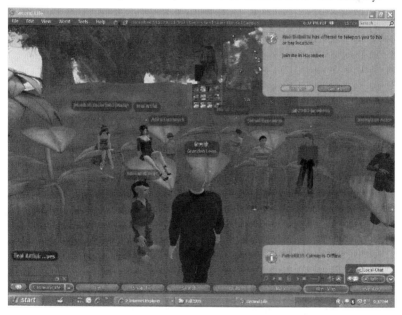

Figure 11.5: My students starting to assemble for a case discussion in Second Life

As suggested by the example that follows, I have a love-hate relationship with *Second Life*. Overall, I have concluded it to be a valuable experience…but once a semester is quite enough. I would also add that its popularity seems to be declining and that over the past year more technical glitches have emerged. So its value as a venue may be declining.

Example: Second Life Scares Me (from Gill, 2010, pp. 444-445)

Lest it seems as if I am waxing euphoric about Second Life, let me also add that there are currently a number of drawbacks to its educational use. In fact, I positively dread my Second Life class as it approaches each semester. To being with, the environment currently demands more computing power than some of my students have; that means I have to figure out ways of accommodating them. In addition, no matter how many practice sessions we hold, there will always be a few who lose audio or experience other problems. There is also the problem of being a relative newcomer; I would guess that it takes several days of practice to become really smooth at navigating. As for myself, I am continuously bumping into things and people. Just a week before writing this, I had to endure several students ribbing me about the fact that it had taken me over a minute to jump up on the tree stump from which I planned to facilitate the case discussion.

These inconveniences pale, however, when compared with my biggest fear. The first time I conducted the exercise, in spring 2009, after the case discussion I sent my students out into the broader Second Life world for an hour to explore. After that, they were to come back and report what they found. Nearly every female student in the class, and at least one of the males, reported that they had been propositioned by a stranger at some point during the excursion (the most common pick-up line being "do you want to cuddle?"). All it would take would be one student lacking in *either* a sense of humor or a sense of perspective—it is, after all, only a "virtual" environment—and I would probably need to curtail the exercise forever. Interestingly, since that time Linden Lab instituted some new policies intended to segregate the X-rated crowd[5] from the PG participants. When I ran the exercise in fall 2009, not one student reported being propositioned.

Evaluating Synchronous Discussion Outcomes

When I informally compare the actual synchronous discussions that take place during online class week with those of the regular face-to-face classes, I see few qualitative differences. To get a bit more feedback, I always survey the class after the *Second Life* session to gain their

---

reaction. I list three cases that we have discussed (one discussed face-to-face, one discussed on *Elluminate* and one discussed on *Second Life*) What I have found, over about 8 of these surveys, is the following:

1. The face-to-face case I list for comparison purposes always edges out the *Elluminate* case by a small margin. The Second Life case falls behind by a larger margin.

2. When asked where they want to hold the next class session (I give them a choice between the three venues), they always choose to go online—typically by a 3 to 1 margin. Seven times the choice has been *Elluminate*, once it was *Second Life*.

I believe these results to be important, suggesting that flexibility of place can be decisive even when the quality advantage is with face-to-face. This is of significant because we can expect the quality advantage of face-to-face to decline over time as technology improves, the topic of the next section. When that happens, we could suddenly find many students *demanding* online discussions. Such demands will probably not be felt at institutions featuring full time, cohort-based programs (such as HBS with respect to business and most elite undergraduate institutions). These students need to be around anyway, and have few travel or schedule conflicts. But for students who are enrolled in part time programs or who work full time, schools that do not offer online options could become far less attractive than their competitors.

The Online Discussion in the Future

In considering the future of the online case discussion, there are two dimensions worth considering. The first is the evolution of technologies to support such discussions. The second is the evolving needs and expectations of students.

Emergence of Telepresence

With respect to technologies that support discussion, the future is already here, and it is called *telepresence*. It is just too expensive for most schools. But that will change, and soon.

My optimism about telepresence springs from two sources. First, I read an article in a recent *Bloomberg BusinessWeek* describing the technology, which allows individuals in different conference rooms to communicate with each other's live images on big screen TVs. The reporter describes the experience of using the technology as follows (Bennett, 2011, p. 55):

> As advertised, I found I could look into people's eyes as they talked to me, and they could look into mine. I could gauge their facial expressions when they were bored or discomfited, interested or surprised. Watching people's reactions as they listened to others talking, I could get a sense of the mood of the "room". Because there's no transmission lag, it's easy and natural for people to interrupt each other. Comments can be cushioned or emphasized by body language and small gradations in tone. And, inevitably, from time to time I found myself distracted by a strange bump on someone's lip, or the size of a person's wristwatch, or by trying to make out what someone sitting on the other side of the country was writing in his notebook. In short, it felt very much like the many hours I've spent attending meetings in person.

Once we start achieving this level of richness in our media, I see the advantages of traditional face-to-face classrooms diminishing rapidly, particularly for smaller classes. And, as I noted in the previous section, students—at least my students, who include a fairly large number of working professionals—are already willing to sacrifice a certain amount of richness for a lot of convenience.

The second source I use to gauge the likelihood that telepresence technology will be feasible for case discussion is the fact that the *CA International Case Competition*—which for two years ran regional competitions that involved participants and judges travelling to a central location—is now planning to run these competitions using Cisco telepresence technology.

The obvious question is this: how long before such technologies become affordable to institutions and then individuals? It is always risky to make predictions, but a reasonable rule of thumb is that the price of a given unit of IT capability tends to decline by a factor of 10 every five years[6]. Given that existing units cost around $300,000 according to the article, we can expect to see classroom-appropriate units going for around $3000 by 2020. Another way of looking at the situation is that today's systems—once again, according to the article—require 20-40 times the bandwidth of a typical Skype connection. Assuming the same rate of progress, in 8 years or so we should be able to harness comparable bandwidth in free, or very cheap, consumer systems.

Moving images and audio is, of course, only part of the problem. To provide the anyplace freedom that makes synchronous online discussion attractive, a telepresence conference room will not provide a total solution. Better applications that, for example, automatically enlarge the image of an individual who is speaking and provide tools for whiteboard and classroom management will be required. I would, however, be far more willing to bet that these solutions will be developed within the next decade than to bet against such development.

The Online Student

Much has been written about our future (and present) students being digital natives. Being comfortable with recreational technologies (e.g., MMORPGs) or social technologies (e.g., Facebook) does not necessarily mean that our students will embrace online technologies for learning.

There are, however, a number of reasons for believing that the role of online education will explode in the coming years. The first involves a growing need for non-traditional education. The twin forces of globalization and technology have both increased the complexity of modern life and reduced the number of years an individual can expect to do the same job. This creates a strong market for life-long education. As a consequence, the part-time student is likely to become the greatest area of growth in education. In business education, we have already seen this trend over the past decade. The twenty most elite business schools continue to have over half their MBA students enrolled in full time programs, often residential in nature[7], and the percentage is relatively constant. Move to the next tier down, however, and we see a very different story. Between 2000 and 2008, full-time enrollments dropped from 54% to 38% of total MBA enrollments. Part-time enrollments, on the other hand, rose from 31% to 45% of the total (Datar, Garvin & Cullen, 2010, pp. 25-26). At schools such as my own, at least one further tier below, virtually the only full-time students are international, facing restrictions on working. And, as noted earlier, my students *always* opt for online, when given the choice.

The second reason for believing that online education is likely to experience a major upswing in popularity involves changes in both experience and attitude. In the excellent book *Disrupting Class* (Christensen, Horn & Johnson, 2008), the authors propose that online education and technology assisted learning environments represent disruptive technologies. According to Christensen's theory, such technologies tend to emerge when two conditions are met:

1. A mainstream organization tunes itself to a particular large group of clients, who dictate the direction of progress for that organization.

2. Technologies exist to serve other clients with somewhat similar needs but, for a variety of reasons, these technologies are not suitable for the main client base.

Where these conditions exist, entrepreneurial companies will move it to support the second group of clients using the alternative technology. What will often happen is that the second technology will advance rapidly such that, at some point in time, its capabilities surpass those offered by the mainstream organization. At that point, a rapid disruption occurs, as mainstream clients flock to the new technology.

In the book, the authors suggest that the traditional model of public education represents a mainstream approach. For various reasons, such as the complex relationship between unions, administrators and school boards, it is extremely difficult to change the focus of this system. Over the past few decades, however, these institutions have chosen to ignore the small home schooling market. That led to the development of online educational competitors, such as the *Florida Virtual School* (se example that follows). Over time, these competitors will provide a viable alternative to traditional public education. Increasingly, not only will they attract non-traditional students, they will also attract the best students who—for various reasons—feel that they are not realizing their full potential by limiting themselves to a traditional public school. Once it is clear that the best students are learning online, we can expect to see a rapid increase in both the reputation of these programs and their enrollments.

Example: The Florida Virtual School

The Florida Virtual School (FLVS) was founded in 1997 and is the probably the largest and best known online provider of online education to middle school and high school students. Enrollment is free to students residing in Florida. The state also has rules that allow students to substitute FLVS courses in place of face-to-face courses even if they are attending a public school. Because of the wide range of courses

---

offered by the FLVS and the fact that counties compute GPAs in a manner that rewards the number of courses taken, many—if not most—of the state's top performing public school students take FLVS courses even while enrolled in public school. In fact, such course taking is particularly common in prestigious *International Baccalaureate* programs.

My own experience with FLVS comes mainly from my two sons, both currently enrolled in high school and both taking FLVS courses on the side. Of particular note is my oldest son Tommy, who took the FLVS Computer Science AP course while in the 9th Grade. Looking over his shoulder from time to time as he took the course, I was very impressed with its design. I was even more impressed by the outcome. According to an email from the instructor, on the order of 70-80% of the class scored 3 or better on the AP exam and something like 40% received the top score, a 5[8].

To provide a basis for comparison, the year after Tommy took the course, the same course was offered by his local high school. Tommy served as a TA for that class. All 20 or so student in the class took the AP exam. Not one scored higher than a 2.

More generally, FLVS students reportedly have a substantially higher pass rate (scoring 3 or better) on AP courses and also have substantially higher averages on state mandated achievement tests (FCATs) according to a report issued by Florida's *TaxWatch Center for Educational Performance and Accountability*. This difference in averages is particularly significant since—in addition to getting the best students—FLVS also gets certain incorrigible students for whom a face-to-face program has been deemed unacceptable. Thus, the distribution has a bi-modal character.

Unfortunately, many professors today regard online learning as the substandard, low cost option for education. With experiences such as the example just described, however, it is hard to imagine that students leaving high school today will have the same attitude. Thus, in the long run, it strikes me as inevitable that a vastly higher proportion of our education will be delivered with technology. I see no reason to believe that case discussions will be exempt from that trend.

Conclusions

Surprisingly little has been written about the use of the case method online. In this chapter, I have therefore relied heavily on relating my own experiences. To summarize some of my key conclusions:

- Asynchronous online case discussions appear to be effective, but can place a heavy burden on both facilitator and participant. They probably make sense as part of a portfolio different discussion approaches, but a class or program built entirely around them could become quite tiresome.

- Synchronous online case discussions are slightly less engaging than face-to-face discussions but the difference is small enough so that students will often opt for them over face-to-face by virtue of their flexibility of place.

- The gap between online and face-to-face settings will grow substantially narrower in the coming decade.

Perhaps the most important conclusion of the chapter is that online approaches to case discussion cannot be ignored. With both technology and student preference moving towards online—a trend that I predict with accelerate rapidly as a tipping point is reached—if we do not work on improving our online delivery of the case method, the method itself is likely to fall into disuse outside of elite, full-time, residential programs.

Notes for Chapter 11

[1] This is, perhaps, an overgeneralization since synchronous tools for text chatting (such as Internet relay chat) were available throughout the 1990s and before (using BBS technology). I have never tried to facilitate a case using such tools—being a lousy typist the results would be predictably awful—and therefore cannot comment on them. My general sense is that technologies best suited to short bursts of text (such as IRC and today's popular text messaging and Twitter) are probably not a good fit with the case method as I have described it.

[2] Names and dates are disguised on all materials taken from actual courses.

[3] If push comes to shove, I would argue that only one capability is actually required: a shared audio link. In fact, I did hold one case discussion in the 1990s using a standard conference call line. It actually went more smoothly than I expected.

[4] Even a broadband connection is not strictly necessary. I had one student, who had to return to India during the middle of a semester, come in over a cell phone modem from a village where there was no broadband and somewhat unreliable electric power. The result was a little ragged, but still understandable.

[5] Did I mention that you can purchase naked body parts of nearly every type on Second Life?

[6] A factor of 10 every 5 years is roughly equivalent to a factor of 2 every 18 months—the well-known Moore's Law.

[7] At an elite university, it makes considerable sense to enter a full time residential program since the development of lifelong professional connections is a major advantage of such programs. Thus, these programs are likely to have little motivation to engage in extensive experimentation with online education, however much lip-service they pay to the concept. This is perhaps why the whole issue of online education was almost completely ignored in the otherwise comprehensive book *Rethinking the MBA* (Datar, Garvin & Cullen, 2010).

[8] Tommy was happily among the group that scored a 5.

Chapter 12

The Case Method and the Informing Institution

A central thesis of this book is that separating the activities of case writing, case research and case facilitation diminishes the overall effectiveness of the case method. Part of my argument is based upon the similar types of expertise required for the three activities. Part of it builds upon the fact that coping with complexity is a common theme for the three. The final element of the argument is based upon situations I have observed in my decades as an academic. In this chapter, I turn to that final element.

I begin the chapter describing what I mean by the "informing institution", followed by two examples—both originally introduced in *Informing Business*—that illustrate the challenges of balancing informing activities. The first, examining the forces that led to the closure of a well-respected MIS department, illustrates the serious consequences of failing to balance informing activities. The second, the Agribusiness program at HBS, illustrates how a strong commitment to the case method can fundamentally transform a program. It also illustrates the potential costs of such a commitment in the absence of strong institutional support.

I conclude the chapter by proposing that the area where a strong institutional commitment to the case method would provide the greatest benefit is in diffusing our ideas to practice. In *Informing Business* (Gill, 2010), I described the business flavor of this challenge as "the informing crisis". What I have found, however, is that nearly every applied discipline claims to be facing similar problems. My goal here is to convince the reader that such commitment would lead to an "informing institution" that would be far more resilient to the ever-more-frequent shocks that accompany today's turbulent environment.

The Informing Institution

An informing institution is any organization whose principal purpose revolves around informing. In this chapter, our main interest is in academic institutions and their subsystems (e.g., colleges, schools, departments and individual faculty members). We should not imagine, however, that such institutions are limited to universities. Indeed, the world today is increasingly dominated by organizations whose main activities are achieved by way of information flows (e.g., financial institutions, governments, consulting firms, etc.).

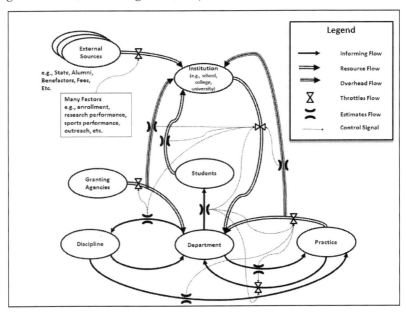

Figure 12.1: The informing system representation of a typical departmental unit within an informing institution

Because informing cannot take place in a vacuum, informing activities will nearly always need to be matched by complementary resource flows (e.g., money, facilities, capital equipment, consumables). Where such resources are not available, the informing activities are unlikely to be sustainable. A diagram that illustrates how such high level flows[1] might look for a department within a university is provided as Figure 12.1.

To provide a brief explanation for the illustration, the solid arrows represent flows of informing. For example, the solid, line between the

Department ellipse and the Discipline ellipse means the department (e.g., through its research faculty) is informing the overall discipline (e.g., through papers and conferences). The returning arrow reflects the fact that the discipline also informs the department's researchers, most likely through the same channels.

Hollow lines indicate resource flows, such as budget dollars or facilities. Hollow lines with a stripe inside indicate overhead resource flows; such flows are frequently mandated for institutional support.

The triangles laid out like an hourglass represent throttles on the flow of either resources or informing activities. These throttles are controlled by the source of the resource using control signals (dotted arrows) from flow estimators (two curves facing each other). As an illustration, in the illustration the dotted lines from the flow estimator on the Department-to-Discipline informing flow goes to two throttles: the resource flow from Granting Agencies to Department and the resource flow from Institution to Department. This would imply, in the example, that granting agencies award grants to the department based, to some extent, on the agency's overall assessment of the department's resource productivity and that the institution uses its own estimate of the department's research productivity as one factor in determining what resources are provided to the department. In the diagram, there is no assumption made that the estimates of departmental research productivity are the same for the agency and the institution; the estimates may, indeed, be very different. The fact that estimates of a particular informing flow can be quite different depending upon who is interpreting it will play an important role in the examples that follow.

Case 1: MIS at the University of Central Florida (UCF)

The first case study I present involves the MIS department at the *University of Central Florida* (UCF), which was recently disbanded. It illustrates the problems that can occur when informing flows are judged insufficient to match needed resources. To understand it, we first need to look at the MIS research discipline more generally.

Evolution of MIS Research Discipline

The management information systems (MIS) discipline emerged in the 1970s, as it became clear that the challenges presented by rapidly changing information technologies had important managerial consequences.

By the early 1980s, the discipline had established significant outlets for published research, such as the journal *MIS Quarterly* (MISQ). Moreover, there is some evidence that the discipline was actively engaged with its practitioner clients. For example:

1. The field's leading journal, MISQ, was established as a joint publication of academia and the *Society for Information Management* (SIM), a practitioner organization.

2. In 1980, over 40% of the articles in MISQ had at least one practitioner co-author.

3. When a symposium on the MIS research challenge was convened at Harvard in 1985, practitioners were invited and actively participated (McFarlan, 1985).

Table 12.1: Industry and academic author contributions to MISQ at 5 year intervals

Year	Count of Articles	Academic Authors	Industry Authors	Total Authors	Percent of Authors from Industry
1980	18	16	11	27	41%
1985	23	32	8	40	20%
1990	23	45	11	56	20%
1995	24	60	3	63	5%
2000	23	55	3	58	5%
2005	28	66	0	66	0%

In the decades that followed, the MIS research discipline changed dramatically. The evidence of academic-practitioner collaboration that was so striking in the early 1980s largely reversed itself. In the 1990s, the *Society for Information Management* essentially divorced itself from MISQ by eliminating the free subscription that had previously come with membership—at which point most members dropped their subscription (Benbasat & Zmud, 1999). Practitioners became almost entirely absent from the discipline's most prestigious conferences. Perhaps most striking is the pattern of academic-practitioner contributions to MISQ. Over a quarter of a century, it fell from 41% (in 1980) to 0% (in 2005), as shown in Table 12.1.

The MIS discipline's failure to inform its practitioner clients was highlighted in the *AACSB International's* (AACSB, 2008) attempt to list areas where MIS research has exerted an impact on practice. The report's authors, a group of business school deans, were able to identify only two areas. The first involved applying a model actually developed by a marketing professor and the second involved a researcher whose principal impact has been through consulting, rather than published research. Talk about being damned with faint praise![2]

It is reasonable to attribute part of the change in MIS research philosophy to wildly fluctuating enrollment patterns. For example, in the mid-1990s, student interest in MIS began to skyrocket. Undergraduate MIS major enrollment increasing by a factor of three between 1994 and 2001—as happened at my university—was the rule rather than the exception. For example, by the time I joined the USF in 2001, MIS had just become the largest business department, with around 1100 majors. By acting as a magnet for students, MIS was serving the informing needs of the institution's single most important client. As a consequence, resources—in the form of new faculty lines, salary increases, and reduced teaching loads—were lavished upon MIS departments around the world.

Shortly after the Internet bubble burst in the 2000-2001 time period, the enrollment situation reversed itself. Students left the MIS major in droves. At USF, for example, we saw an 80% decline in major enrollments during the period from 2001 to 2007. We went from being the largest department in our college, based upon the number of majors, to the smallest. MIS faculty salaries lagged behind those of almost every other business discipline and hiring dried up.

Another particularly interesting aspect of the MIS research discipline is the degree to which its research became distinct from its teaching. An assessment of overlap between teaching and research interests, compiled from the *Association for Information Systems* (AIS) database, is presented in Figure 12.2[3]. It takes four core course topics that are widely taught at both the undergraduate and graduate levels and compares them with faculty research interests. The figure presents a paradoxical picture. On the one hand, those faculty members who research a given area are very likely to teach it. For example, 74% of AIS members who research telecommunications also teach that subject. On the other hand, most of the AIS members who teach a particular subject are not doing research in that subject. For example, 85% of the individuals teaching programming are not doing research directly or indirectly related to programming.

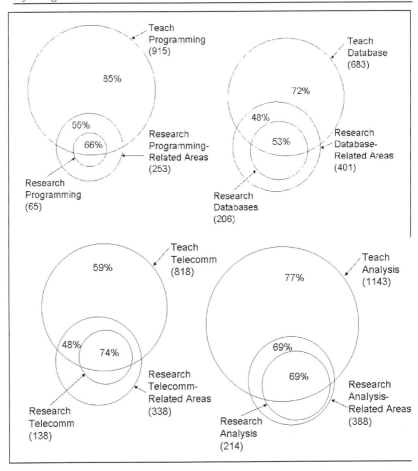

Figure 12.2: A comparison of teaching and research interests for AIS members. Numbers in the non-overlapping portion of the large circle represent percentage of faculty members who teach in a particular area but do not research in that area. Numbers in the smaller overlapping circles represent the percentage of faculty who perform research in the specified area (or related area) and also teach in it. (Adapted from Gill and Bhattacherjee, 2009)

The explanation for this situation derives from the nature of the research conducted within the disciplinary informing system. Specifically, MIS has always engaged in research in two areas: the behavioral and the technical. Over time, however, that research has increasingly favored the behavioral. MIS educational programs, however, have retained a large technical component. Thus, a mismatch has developed between what MIS teaches and what it researches. If a researcher happens to engage in technically-focused research, opportunities to teach the same content are readily available. On the hand, if the researcher studies behavioral topics, he or she is likely to have to teach some technical courses since there just are not sufficient technical researchers available to support the teaching demand.

MIS at UCF

The MIS department at UCF[4] provides an interesting example of the failure of an informing system. UCF is a large state university located in Orlando. During the late 1990s, that university decided to make its MIS department a high priority. Towards that end, it hired some of the most respected and productive researchers in the field—including the soon-to-be Editor-in-Chief of *MISQ*—raised its promotion and tenure standards and expanded its doctoral program. Doing so required substantial institutional resources but resulted in a department whose research reputation was international in scope and far beyond what was typical for that particular institution.

Not long after the new departmental focus was established, the rapid drop in MIS enrollments experienced by virtually all business schools began. Despite the department's stellar research reputation, administrative concerns regarding the high cost per student were expressed. Soon, even relatively strong assistant professors were denied tenure, an expression of the department's extremely high research standards and also its declining need for instructional faculty. By 2008, the institution's focus gravitated entirely towards minimizing the resources required by the department. First, the department's doctoral program was discontinued. In the summer of 2009, the university then announced that it was disbanding the department as of spring 2010 and terminating the employment of departmental faculty, irrespective of their tenure status.

Analysis of UCF MIS

Obviously, the main culprits in what happened to MIS at UCF were: a) the decline in enrollments impacting all MIS programs, and b) the economic recession that jeopardized funding for all state universities after the global financial meltdown that occurred. Nevertheless, the priorities set by the department and college for its MIS department contributed to the debacle. To understand this, Figure 12.3 adapts the Figure 12.1 informing system diagram by using shading to characterize informing and resource flows for the department by 2008.

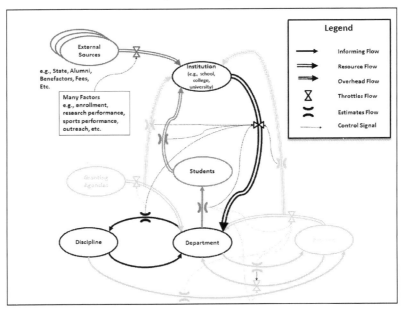

Figure 12.4: Informing and resource flows for USF MIS Department by 2008.

What the diagram shows is that—consistent with what was typical for MIS research at the time—informing and resource flows between the department and practice/granting agencies were minimal. Thus, the department was almost entirely dependent upon resource flows from the institution. Research flows in both directions remained strong between department and discipline. At the same time the student informing flows were down (owing to lack of enrollments) while the overall flows of general resources to the institution were down as a result of the economic situation—which hit real estate dependent Florida particularly hard. Faced with this situation, the institution chose not to maintain the resource flow to the department based totally on the department's continuing strong research informing activities. Had the department had strong resource flows from other clients, such as practice or granting agencies, the outcome might have been different. To illustrate such a situation, we now turn to the Agribusiness program at HBS.

Case 2: The Agribusiness Program at HBS

If there was ever an informing system that demonstrates the power of the case method, it is the Agribusiness program at HBS. What makes it a particularly interesting example for this chapter is the way its informing system evolved to a state that was nearly the exact opposite of that reached by the UCF MIS example. We begin be describing what is meant by "agribusiness" then consider the specific program offered at HBS.

What is Agribusiness?

Agribusiness describes the system through which agricultural products, food and fiber in particular, are produced, transformed, and distributed throughout the world economy. Rather improbably, given its geographic location, the term was coined by Harvard Business School professors John H. Davis and Ray A. Goldberg in 1957. The term was needed to capture "the closeness of interdependence and manifold interrelationships of agriculture and business" (Goldberg, 1968, p. v).

The philosophy driving agribusiness is that individual participants in the system cannot manage effectively without considering the overall behavior of the system in which they participate. As described by Dr. Ray Goldberg (1968, p. 3):

> if managers, private and public, are to develop effective strategies and policies, they must be fully aware of the total commodity system in which they participate, and they must understand the interaction of its parts.

Goldberg's assertion that agribusiness behaviors are best viewed through the lens of commodity systems quickly justifies itself when you look at the unusual nature of many agribusiness entities. For example, the farmer—the producer—often serves as a supplier of one or more inputs: selling seeds, equipment, and other production necessities on the side to neighboring farmers. Such is also true of some of the largest firms. For example, *ConAgra*—one of the world's largest food processors—owned *United Agri Products*, once the largest farm inputs supplier in the U.S. until it divested it in 2003.

The inherent price volatility and yield volatility of farm production—the latter largely attributable to weather but also a result of biological factors such as disease and pests—led to a wide range of agricultural risk management tools emerging well before their use was widespread elsewhere. For example, commodity exchanges in agribusiness could— potentially—exist without major speculator participation. The needs of farmers to reduce the price exposure of their existing crop makes it sensible for them to "go short" (i.e., sell contracts on the futures markets) in the commodities market; the need for producers to ensure they can acquire future supplies at a predictable price gives them an incentive to "go long" (i.e., buy contracts on the futures markets). In addition, even the most laissez-faire government makes exceptions in the case of its agricultural industries; price supports and centralized attempts to manage agricultural supply have long been in place. Needless to say, this process often produces unintended side effects. For example, when Coca-Cola was studying the possibility of building a corn wet milling plant to produce high fructose corn syrup (HFCS) plant in the 1980s, an important issue to be considered was the likelihood of further or reduced government price supports for ethanol, since that use of corn would compete for inputs and production facilities[5]. At the same time, it was trying to grapple with the expected impact of a new sweetener, aspartame, that had the potential to transform consumption (as saccharine had done previously) yet was also potentially subject to regulation—as had been the case when the U.S. banned of cyclamates in 1969.

There are few competitive landscapes where global effects are as large and as rapid as agribusiness. In the 1960s and 1970s, for example, wheat farmers in states like Kansas suddenly found themselves critically impacted by production failures in the Soviet Union. It is virtually impossible to understand commodity behaviors when considering them from a local perspective.

In the research context, the commodity system concept seems refreshingly contemporary in light of the emphasis current business research places on supply chains and value-added networks. This should not be surprising. Throughout its history, agribusiness has tended to surface important phenomena well before they are re-discovered as areas of interest in disciplinary research. Since the 1950s, for example, we have recognized that it is nearly impossible to develop a clear vision of any commodity system without considering *all* of Porter's (1980) five forces, along with the effects of government; collectively, these forces have probably been experienced in more strongly in the agribusiness sector than in any other sector of the economy.

Even in the area of business research, agribusiness has played an important role. For example, Everett Rogers (2003), whose *Diffusion of Innovations* is the seminal work in the field, began his career studying the introduction of crop control chemicals in Iowa. It built upon findings regarding the difficulties in getting farmers to adopt hybrid corn seed in the 1930s and 1940s. Much of the early work in applied statistics took place in agribusiness settings. William Sealy Gosset, the developer of Student's t-test worked for Guinness Brewery, an agribusiness concern. Analysis of crop yields also proved to be a popular domain for developing new statistical techniques.

The widespread availability of higher education in the U.S. can also, to a great extent, be credited to agribusiness. Starting in the middle of the U.S. Civil War, a series of federal laws (e.g., the Morrill Acts of 1862 and 1890) established a system of "land grant" colleges specifically intended to further agricultural and mechanical education. Many of today's public universities owe their existence or size to the funding and other resources made available through these efforts. Later, government funding for agricultural experiment stations and the Cooperative Extension Service—both operating under the supervision of land grant universities—allowed farmers to observe, initiate, and participate in agricultural research projects, as well as having access to researchers. In other words, these institutions—established nearly a hundred years ago and earlier—sought to inform farmers through establishing enduring relationships with them in the field.

Agribusiness at HBS

When I first encountered agribusiness at Harvard, the program had been active for nearly 30 years[6]. By that time, Professor Davis had retired and the program was directed by Ray Goldberg, the George M. Moffett Professor of Agriculture and Business. Goldberg's research record is impressive by traditional academic standards; according to his HBS biography, he authored, co-authored, or edited at least 23 books and 110 articles. What is *really* impressive, however, is the fact that he has authored or supervised the development of over 1000 HBS case studies. This accomplishment—representing about 20 case studies a year over the course of his entire academic career—is a feat that I would guess to be unparalleled in the annals of HBS.

Goldberg's extraordinary success in case development was inextricably linked to his impact on students and on practice. With respect to practice, the appetite for cases was almost inexhaustible. Each year, continuing to the present day, HBS offered a three-day agribusiness seminar for executives[7] that consisted almost entirely of case discussions. Because the same people—including many, if not most, of the world's top agribusiness executives—came back year after year, the cases to be discussed needed to be renewed annually. As a result, Goldberg would usually choose one or two students from the second year MBA agribusiness elective class to act as research assistants for the following year. While some of these students went on to get doctorates, most did not. Instead, they delayed their entry into the MBA job market for a year in order to get the experience of working with Goldberg. Although he was known to be relentless task master in the area of case development, his later involvement in helping to place these students in highly desirable positions more than compensated for the hectic year they had experienced.

I would characterize the late-1970s and early-1980s as the peak of the agribusiness program at HBS. Part of this can be attributed to the environment; the Russian grain deals and price spikes of commodities such as sugar in the 1970s had brought agribusiness to the forefront of the nation's consciousness. More importantly, the intellectual climate within HBS still welcomed the applied nature of the agribusiness research program. Agribusiness at HBS was never oriented towards the pursuit of rarified theory. Rather, it was unashamedly focused on building knowledge through case studies.

If agribusiness had an Achilles heel at HBS, it was its lack of clear ties to the research stream of single discipline. Although technically part of the Marketing Department, the focus of agribusiness was on a competitive landscape not a discipline. An agribusiness case could just as easily focus on issues of finance, strategy, government, technology, or operations management as it did on marketing. For most of HBS's 100 year history, such a focus was not a problem. In its early days, for example, much of the school's research output consisted of industry reports. Beginning in the 1960s, however, notions of what constituted acceptable business research had started to change, as described in Chapter 1.

By the time I started my MIS doctorate at HBS, agribusiness had already been displaced from its easily accessible offices in Loeb Hall and relocated to a site within the labyrinthine recesses of the school's Baker Library[8]. More significantly, the school chose not to recruit an agribusiness research specialist as a successor to Goldberg. Instead, upon

Goldberg's retirement, leadership of the agribusiness was first given to Professor Warren McFarlan, the internationally renowned MIS researcher whose discussion facilitation I profiled in Chapter 10, and subsequently to Professor David Bell, a faculty member with a very distinguished research record in the decision sciences whose publication record, aside from case studies, was nearly devoid of agribusiness-related research.

To handle the day-to-day activities of the agribusiness program, a Director of the Agribusiness Seminar position was established in 2005. As of this writing, that position is occupied by Mary Shelman, who completed the HBS MBA program in the late-1980s and then served as Goldberg's research assistant for a year and established a reputation as an exceptionally talented case writer. Her key responsibility is the continued development of the case studies needed for the three day Executive Agribusiness Seminars, which still attracts 200 executives a year at a current price of $7500 per person and remains oversubscribed. A rotating international version of the seminar, recently held in Paris, Shanghai, and Mumbai, has also been instituted. Goldberg, as a professor emeritus in his early 80s, continues to participate in these seminars, and also does some teaching at Harvard's Kennedy School of Government.

On the surface, then, the agribusiness program at HBS looks much as it once did. The agribusiness seminar continues to generate the type of financial contribution that would make it the crown jewel of most business schools. A dozen or so cases continue to be written each year, directed by one of the most respected case-writers in the history of the program. Its titular head is an academic of international reputation whose contributions to the decision sciences are familiar to anyone doing research in that field.

Despite these apparent signs of health, I find what I observe—entirely as an outsider—to be troubling with respect to the future of the program. While a passion for agribusiness still guides the case writing activity, evidence that other forms of academic research are being conducted by the school are not visible to the outsider. The attention of the academic researcher in charge of the program is divided among many interests, both research and administrative. There are no current agribusiness doctoral students. At an institution whose focus is increasingly being directed towards traditional research productivity measures[9], being separated from the central research mission of the school in this manner would not bode well for the status of the area within the broader institution.

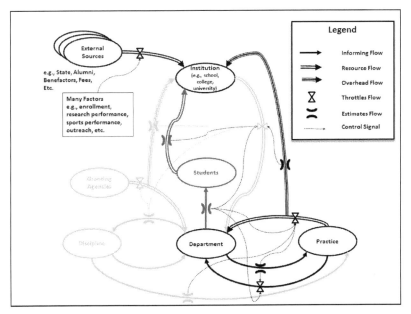

Figure 12.4: Informing system diagram of HBS Agribusiness program as of today

Analysis of HBS Agribusiness Program

As shown in Figure 12.4, an informing diagram of the HBS Agribusiness program looks very different from that of the UCF MIS department. The key differences are as follows:

- Whereas the UCF/MIS system showed little apparent involvement in informing practice, the HBS Agribusiness system maintains an extremely rich set of bi-directional informing channels with practice, both through case development and through the Agribusiness seminar.

- Whereas the UCF/MIS department was a net user of institutional resources, the HBS Agribusiness program actually brings it more revenue (through its seminar) than its operations require.

- Whereas the UCF/MIS system involved a rich informing engagement with its disciplinary system built around disciplinary paradigms, the HBS Agribusiness system was quite unique in its case-based research approach; quite different from the agricultural economics paradigms commonly observed in land grant programs.

My somewhat negative prognosis for the long term survival of the HBS Agribusiness Program stems from the fact that institutional resources consist not only of money, but also of long term commitments—such as the commitment made when tenure-earning faculty members are hired. Based upon my observations as an outsider, this type of long term commitment seems lacking. Thus, as long as the program continues to generate net contribution to the institution, it is in little danger of being discontinued. While its productivity flow is judged using the metrics of traditional research paradigms, on the other hand, it will never be allowed to reestablish the pre-eminent position that it held a few decades ago.

To summarize, the HBS Agribusiness Program represents a superb illustration of the power of the case method as a tool for ensuring engagement with practice. In addition, it demonstrates that such activities can become self-sustaining in terms of resources (at least at a prestige institution such as HBS). It also highlights a danger, however. Once the development of case studies—whether they be for instruction or other purposes—is viewed as an activity that is somehow distinct from "real" research, its days of being taken seriously are numbered. Even at HBS, the institution where the case method got its start in business and where it is still practiced actively today, the stature of the case method as a research tool seems to be on the decline. How is the case method then to survive and flourish at institutions where it is less established?

The Case for Cases

The lesson from the two examples just presented is as follows:

Applied disciplines that do not place informing practice high among their research goals risk their long term survival. On the other hand, heavy reliance on the case method without tying case development into an established disciplinary research stream may not be all that viable as a long term strategy either.

In this section, I present the argument that an integrated program of case writing, case research and case method pedagogy could contribute greatly to an institution's ability to inform its clients, both students and practice.

The core of the argument involves taking a broad view of what constitutes research. I have argued elsewhere (Gill, 2011) that for an *applied* discipline, such as business, education, medicine and even engineering, in order for research to impact practice it must have three components:

1. *Discovery*: It must tell us something we did not know.

2. *Documentation*: It must be archived in a form that makes it available to clients.

3. *Diffusion*: It must be communicated through appropriate channels in a form that is suitable for clients.

The first two components are a central focus of nearly all research—having a novel idea and rendering it in a publishable. With respect to case studies, these elements of research have been given ample coverage in the earlier parts of this book. What many researchers seem to forget, however, is that applied research that never diffuses cannot really be called applied. We will therefore consider this specific topic for the remainder of the chapter. We begin by outlining what is known about diffusion. We conclude by considering how the nature of the case method makes it particularly well suited for diffusion—both in terms of the cases themselves and as a means of setting up a system for diffusing other research findings.

The Diffusion Challenge

When I began my research in the informing science transdiscipline, a large part of my motivation was better understanding why business academic research was so divorced from practice. As I researched the field further, however, I came understand that the same concern is experienced in virtually every applied discipline. This message was reinforced when I joined an "implementation science" task force at my university, only to find that nearly all of its members came from health sciences and engineering. Ironically, these were the very disciplines that I was using as examples of research that was impacting practice! Even more ironically, when I was working on a research proposal with a professor from health sciences, she commented on how my discipline must be "incredibly practical".

Much of *Informing Business* (Gill, 2010) was specifically devoted to understanding the challenges of moving research into practice. Probably the best single source of theory and examples can be found in the literature relating to diffusion of innovations. As I summarized in my earlier book (Gill, 2010, pp. 231-232), by 2003, an estimated 5200 publications had addressed that particular subject (Rogers, 2003, p. xvii). The seminal book in the field, *Diffusion of Innovations* (now in its 5th edition), was written by the late Everett Rogers, a researcher whose pioneering studies of diffusion were conducted in the 1950s after patterns started to become apparent in the adoption of farming technologies during the 1930s and 1940s. Some of the key findings from this research stream, as summarized by Rogers, are as follows:

- Certain characteristics tend to make some innovations easier to diffuse than others. Examples of these are simplicity, compatibility with previous models or ideas, relative advantage compared to previous ideas, trialability (the ability to try out the innovation prior to adopting it), and observability (Rogers, 2003, p. 222). Ideas lacking these characteristics take much longer to diffuse.

- Diffusion does not occur immediately but, instead, through a gradual process of adoption within the client community. Two forces that are particularly important for this process are mass media (i.e., any communication where a single sender provides information to multiple clients concurrently) and interpersonal communications within the client network. In general, mass media communications are more important in the earlier stages of communications, while interpersonal communications dominate later stages (Majaran, Muller, & Bass, 1991, cited in Rogers, 2003).

- Diffusion processes often have to reach a "critical mass" after which diffusion starts to take off at a very rapid rate (Rogers, 2003, p. 349).

- Individuals within client communities are not homogeneous. Rather, they exhibit different characteristics with respect to their willingness to adopt innovations. These may be modeled in terms of thresholds (Rogers, 2003, p. 355). Idealized categories of adopters are often classified as: innovators, early adopters, early majority, late majority, and laggards (Rogers, 2003). Individuals may also exhibit different degrees of influence on other clients in the community (e.g., opinion leaders; Rogers, 2003, p. 300), awareness of the social nature of the community (e.g., key informants; Rogers, 2003, p. 310), and willingness to venture outside of their community and cumulative past experience (innovators; Rogers, 2003, p. 282).

The critical insight from these findings is that *we can expect that interpersonal client-to-client communications will play an increasingly critical role in idea diffusion as the complexity of an idea grows and in informing the less receptive members of the practitioner client community.*

We now consider some of the ways in which the case method may be employed to facilitate the diffusion of complex ideas to practice.

Case Writing as a Tool for Relationship Building

Far too often, academics look at case writing in terms of the artifact produced, instead of the relationships established. As the earlier HBS Agribusiness Program example illustrated, however, a network of relationships may be one of the most powerful tools available for diffusing ideas. An active case development program—whether for discussion cases or research cases or both—forces faculty members into close contact with their relevant practice community. Most of these contacts will blossom into more enduring relationships, at least in my experience. They may evolve to consulting relationships, friendships or mutually beneficial professional relationships (e.g., practitioners seeking students to employ). But these are precisely the type of relationships through which ideas—even complex ideas—can move.

As noted in previous chapters, the development of discussion cases involving local protagonists also allows the formation of direct relationships between practitioners and students. I have yet to find a case protagonist who was reluctant to meet with an engaged student after class. These relationships are illustrated in Figure 12.5.

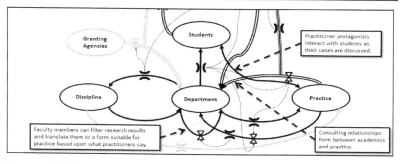

Figure 12.5: Informing relationships that evolve as the case method is widely employed at an institution

Cases as a "Sticky" Medium

Malcolm Gladwell (2000) uses the term stickiness to refer to the likelihood that a message will be received and retained. As I first noted in Chapter 2, the story format has been singled out as being unusually sticky (e.g., Heath & Heath, 2007). The fact that case method research is nearly always presented in narrative story format makes it particularly well suited for later diffusion to practice.

Cases as a Tool for Exploring Diversity

When theory drives our research and teaching, we focus on those principles common to our observations, since a theory that is not generalizable is not much of a theory. In a complex environment—such as business or education—there are three problems with this. First, there are not many of these common principles; the logical consequence, if not the definition, of complexity. Second, practitioners are well acquainted with these principles and are generally well able to pass them on to others, such as new employees. Third, exceptional situations often tend to be the most interesting; the "next, best thing" is rarely presaged by widespread, prevailing practices.

Based upon an individual observation, rather than a survey, case development—whether for research or discussion—tends to be attracted to unusual situations. Protagonists, in particular, are much more motivated to document the results of novel actions that they have taken or high-risk successful decisions that they have made. As Davis points out in *That's Interesting!*, it is precisely such situations that depart from the expected that best capture our attention.

There is, of course, the potential danger that by documenting mainly unusual cases, we could paint a false picture of how the environment we are studying actually behaves. As researchers, we particularly abhor Type 1 error (asserting something that is not actually true). The response to this concern depends upon the nature of our clients. Particularly for research cases, our best audience is—or, at least should be—experts in practice. If we strive for less, then we could hardly describe our research activities as "leading edge". But, if our audience is experts, they have their own base of knowledge through which they can sensibly filter our findings. We need to view them as partners in discovery, not as receptacles for the knowledge we offer. They may find a particular case, or aspect of that case, potentially applicable to their own situation or they may reject it. They bear considerable responsibility for this choice. No matter what they decide, however, it will be far easier for them to pick and choose lessons learned from a narrative than it would be from the general prescriptive guidelines that typify "evidence-based research".

Opportunity to Build Expertise in Practice

Our brains are wired such that what psychologists refer to as expertise can only be achieved through repetition. If you look at what tasks today's academic business researcher performs repeatedly, you would find activities such as teaching lecture classes, performing data searches, rapidly distilling the contents of journal articles, designing survey instruments, and so forth. What you would be unlikely to find—at most business schools, at any rate—is academics routinely working with practice to solve their problems. Ironically, this would seem to be the skill where we should be most eager to see our faculty acquire expertise.

A particularly valuable side effect of the case method, particularly case development, is that it forces academics to spend a lot of time in the field and in contemplation of the types of decisions that practitioners must make. Too often, today's academics have embarked on a career of teaching and research with little exposure to the pressures and demands of practice. Even those who started out in practice (e.g., working as business professionals, teachers, practicing engineers) may be decades out-of-touch with today's environment. While writing a case or engaging in a subsequent consulting assignment is never quite the same as engaging in practice, it certainly provides a first-hand opportunity to observe what practice is like. Such experience cannot help but improve the individual's teaching effectiveness and research relevance.

Building an Informing Institution

Adoption of the case method will not, by itself, cause an institution to undergo an immediate transformation into a paragon of informing. Establishing an informing network is a time consuming process. Nor would we expect the process to be an easy one. There are many institutional barriers that typically need to be overcome. Among these:

- The relative scarcity of expertise in case discussion facilitation within most institutions.

- The peculiar notion that writing discussion cases is not a form of research.

- The absence of criteria for measuring and rewarding research impact on practice within most disciplines.

- The challenge of measuring case method learning in an era where "assurance of learning" has become a key goal for most accrediting bodies.

Most of these issues have been discussed in prior chapters. And this list leaves out the 900-pound gorilla in the room: motivating faculty members—especially tenured faculty members—to make radical changes in their teaching and research. It is the rare academic institution, at least in the U.S., that has the power to force such changes from the top down. Deans can, however, encourage bottom up motivation through the system of goals and incentives that they establish. For the remainder of this chapter, I will offer examples of the types of policies and goals that an institution might establish to encourage a culture favorable to the case method, both in instruction and research.

Take a Broader View of Research as a Mission

At least in business, accrediting bodies are increasingly taking an agnostic view as to what a school "should" do. Instead, they start from the school's mission statement and strategic plan and ask three important questions:

1. Are the activities and policies of the school consistent with that mission and plan?

2. Are the desired outcomes specified in the mission being measured?

3. Are there mechanisms in place to use these measurements as a basis for continuous improvement?

If a professional school explicitly describes research in the broad terms used by this chapter—as a process entailing discovery, documentation and diffusion to practice—a robust case development activity will be easy to justify. Indeed, it is hard to imagine how a research or teaching case could be developed *without* some diffusion of ideas occurring. This applies to institutions focused mainly on teaching as well as those whose central mission is research.

Treat Consulting Projects as Grants

As I have mentioned before, case writing is a gateway drug that, almost invariably, leads to consulting. If consulting is viewed as being distinct from research and if the revenue received by the faculty member involved is treated as a private transaction, then such consulting will tend to take place in the shadows.

Particularly in disciplines that do not have a well-established tradition of external research grants, such as business schools, the current situation strikes me as inefficient on many levels. For example:

- Consulting, as noted previously, is an excellent way for faculty members to develop professionally. It should be encouraged for that reason. Instead, most schools tend to have a formal or informal policy limiting such activities (e.g., to 1 day per week).

- Institutional affiliation often helps to establish the faculty member's credentials; institutions should be compensated for that role.

- Institutions supply facilities, such as an office, that would normally represent costly overhead for a private consultant; again, there should be compensation for this.

- Private money, such as that derived from consulting, typically comes with far fewer strings and restrictions than funding from other granting agencies.

With respect to the last three of these, the argument that I have typically heard is that since faculty members tend to be compensated less generously than their counterparts in practice (certainly true in business), unconstrained consulting allows them equalize the gap somewhat without costing the university anything.

My own view is that a much more sensible approach to consulting would be to treat it very much the same way that research grants are treated in disciplines that rely heavily on external funding, such as medicine and engineering. This would involve a tradeoff for the faculty member along the following lines:

- Consulting would be subject to the same type of institutional overhead costs as grants (e.g., 40-50% of revenue goes to the institution)

- Consulting fees could be used to buy course release time, just as is commonly done with grants.

- Revenue brought in from consulting would be viewed as equivalent to grant monies for the purpose of promotion and tenure decisions.

The last of these becomes particularly important where junior tenure-earning faculty members are concerned. At most institutions, at least in the U.S., the pressure to "publish or perish" is growing ever more intense. Since case development—particularly discussion case development—counts for little under the prevailing view of "publish" (see comments in the example that follows), few junior faculty members have the time to spare on what P&T committees might view as a frivolous pastime. For consulting, the situation is even worse, since it often results in no subsequent publication. The attractiveness of the case/consulting combination would be dramatically altered, however, if consulting revenues carried the same weight with P&T committees as grants. In such a world, junior faculty would have a tremendous incentive to go out into the practice community. As a side effect of doing so, they would acquire the seasoning that would, in the long run, make their contributions to disciplinary research all the more valuable.

Example: GIS for McDonald's Latin American Division

As a junior faculty member at Florida Atlantic University (FAU) in the early 1990s, I was afforded the opportunity to take the lead on a consulting project that was, in fact, run through the school much like a grant. The client was McDonald's Latin American Division (headquartered in Boca Raton, Florida). The project involved building a Geographic Information System (GIS) that could be used to help locate restaurants in Mexico.

The project involved a number of challenges. The first was that the data required (from the Mexican Census) was not in a format that was easily used. Thus, I found myself needing to create a considerable amount of code simply to do things such as accessing the database and drawing maps, all of which would be trivial in today's world. Even more challenging, it had only been a couple of years since *MS Windows* had become the clear winner in the operating system battle. Thus, I needed to learn how to program in *MS Windows* in order to complete the project. Finally, no one was exactly sure what such a system would look like. Thus, we needed to use a process of successive prototyping to build the application, an approach that was new to me (and to programming) at the time.

From an institutional standpoint, I was encouraged to take on the project—which generated $40,000-$50,000 contribution to overhead (the actual project was well in excess of $100,000). At the time, the Dean of the College of Business assured me that my successful participation would be treated as the equivalent of "at least one top tier publication".

The project turned out to be a great success for everybody except the client. We got the program working, with functionality exceeding what we initially promised, nearly on time. The school got paid promptly. Based upon what I learned, I transformed our programming project course to include an exercise where each student created a similar but simpler mapping application that used U.S. census data. I also learned a great deal about organizations—while the client was delighted with the software, their MIS department refused to allow them to deploy it because they did not want to support a 3rd Party application developed by a university.

Once I completed the project, I embarked on my first active case writing project, developing cases on three local companies to use in my MBA and Executive MBA classes. Two of these three cases led to subsequent consulting assignments, while the third led to a lifelong connection that I still maintain.

About a year later, however, I discovered the "rest of the story". At that time, I went up for promotion and tenure at FAU. This also happened to be the first year for our new Dean. At the department level, two of the faculty members abstained owing to the fact that I had not met the five paper guideline (I had four, plus about 10 case studies). At no time during the process was my involvement in the McDonald's project even mentioned. Had it not been for the fact that two of my papers were in the MIS discipline's top research journal (MIS Quarterly), my continued employment at that institution could have been in serious doubt. The lesson I learned from this was that if I was to get no credit for my case writing and consulting, there was little point in offering the institution any portion of whatever revenue stream I might realize from these activities.

I feel no bitterness with respect to the process I describe; after all I was promoted and I was never made to feel like I was a "close call". Nevertheless, had I realized how little my consulting and case writing would count towards an assessment of research, I am not at all sure I would have devoted my time to them until getting tenure—by which time I could have easily lost the urge to engage in such activities. The lesson here is that for case writing and consulting to be attractive to junior faculty members, they must be viewed as research by the institution. *And the institution must mean it!*

Treat Networking as an Element of Research

Complex ideas diffuse through networks of individuals, not through publications. An active case development program will, over time, build a network of contacts that cannot help but enhance the institution's ability to inform both practice and students.

Case development is not the only way networks linked to practice can develop. Participation in professional organizations is another common example. Even today, many institutions include such faculty activities under the heading of "service". What is different about my perspective is that I propose such activities really need to be considered under the "research" category (or "teaching", depending upon where the institution sets its highest priorities), since building a network plays such a critical role in the diffusion of knowledge.

Encourage Collaboration across Disciplines

The case method does not play well with functional specialization. Any institution truly devoted to informing practice will, therefore, seek to encourage collaborations across disciplines and even across schools or colleges. If part of the purpose of a case development effort is to build a network through which ideas diffuse, it is best that all disciplines be represented within that network. Similarly, attempts to develop case studies that describe a single function or discipline will nearly always result in an artificial end product.

Here, once again, a rethinking of traditional institutional priorities may be required. While it is common, and practically mandatory, to pay lip service to interdisciplinary activities at most institutions, it often proves difficult to credit such activities in practice. Interdisciplinary teaching requires considerable coordination across departments; such efforts often fail as a result. Interdisciplinary research suffers from the manner in which publications are usually evaluated, which is to say rankings developed by faculty within a particular discipline.

Revisit Evaluation Systems

Ultimately, all of the ideas presented in this section depend upon re-thinking current systems for evaluating faculty and students. As long as faculty members are evaluated on traditional research productivity measures and standard student evaluation instruments, we can count on a high degree of attachment to the status quo. As long as student learning is assessed based upon content knowledge (as opposed to higher order skills such as judgment under uncertainty) instructors will be reluctant to abandon content-focused teaching methods such as lectures.

If you want to drive the system towards the case method and building an informing institution, you need to evaluate performance based upon measures that capture activities involved in building networks and interacting with practice. Items of this type might include:

- Provide examples of how your research is used in your classroom.

- List the members of the practice community who have participated in your class over the past year.

- Describe how your research has impacted practice over the past year.

- Describe the off-site activities you engaged in with the practice community over the past year.

- To what professional practice organizations do you belong? List the events sponsored by these organizations that you attended over the past year.

- Describe the consulting engagements that you conducted under the auspices of your department; include figures

In my experience, similar items are often included in today's evaluation forms for faculty members. Unfortunately, they represent the part of the form that is typically ignored (much the way only the overall rating of the instructor gets much attention on student course evaluation forms, no matter how many other questions are asked).

It would be foolish to underestimate the resistance that will be encountered in making the types of changes to evaluation systems that would be necessary to redirect an institution towards the case method and informing practice. Aside from inevitable attachment to the status quo, a variety of sincere objections are likely to be raised. First, that moving away from established publication requirements towards more flexible standards that credit case writing and network formation would represent a drop in standards. It is certainly true that it can be very hard to achieve publication in an elite academic research journal; just because it is hard, however, does not necessarily make it valuable. But difficulty is a lot easier to gauge than value. On a similar vein, many individuals will argue that existing evaluation systems, whatever their flaws, are more objective than systems requiring judgment of research quality and thoughtful assessment of student learning. Once again, while objectivity in a measure is certainly desirable, a measure that objectively drives us in an unwanted direction may be worse than none at all.

Cultivate Institutional Independence of Spirit

The very same issues that act as obstacles to adoption of the case method and other informing-focused practices by individual faculty members are likely to plague the institution as a whole. This is particularly true in the area of research, where aggregated individual productivity measures (e.g., elite publication counts) become the basis for departmental and college rankings. If case studies, particularly discussion cases, fail to count towards the individual productivity metrics, outcomes are likely to look even worse when these same metrics are summed across a group of faculty members and all explanatory justifications are lost. For an institution that pays close attention to these types of measures, the short-term effects of emphasizing case development could be a sudden drop in conventionally measured research output. It would take a brave administrator to venture down such a path knowing that a short-term decline was going to be nearly unavoidable.

To be sure, pockets of case method activity can exist within any institution; my own activities at non-case method schools provide living proof of that. That path, however, takes unusual training (e.g., an MBA and DBA from HBS). It also helps when the individuals involved are willing to act in ways that do not maximize personal career advancement. On the other hand, to establish the critical mass of individuals necessary to achieve the "informing institution" goal set forth in this chapter is likely to require a paradigm shift on the part of the organization.

The history of science tells us that achieving a paradigm shift is never easy (Kuhn, 1970). At a minimum, it requires two key elements:

1. A growing certainty that the prevailing paradigm is wrong, and

2. An alternative paradigm that can be adopted.

In the absence of either, the prevailing paradigm will be retained. Much of my last book, *Informing Business* (Gill, 2010) was devoted to explaining why the way we do research and teach does not make sense in a world made up of complex systems (i.e., item 1). Much of this book, on the other hand, is built around describing an alternative approach to these activities (i.e., item 2).

The challenge facing the institution contemplating such a paradigm shift is not only the short term disruption it can cause. It is the long term pressure to return to the status quo. Maintaining goals that are very different from those of peer institutions is hard. There be external pressures to change, such as institutional ratings that are based on criteria that you are not attempting to maximize.

Even harder to resist, there will be pressures from within. Each new faculty hire will be operating according to the assumptions of his or her previous institution; if those involve lectures and traditional approaches to research, you will need to effect changes in these individuals' attitudes. Existing faculty members, concerned about their own personal marketability, may resist institutional priorities that discourage what is most valued by the marketplace (e.g., refereed research in top journals) in favor of using case studies to build relationships with the local practice community. At research institutions, doctoral students may worry if their training will serve them well in the broader marketplace. As the example that follows illustrates, these worries may be well founded.

DBA Program at HBS

It is fitting that for my final example I, once again, return to my alma mater, HBS. For decades, it was unique in its commitment to the case method. If there is anywhere in the world that comes close to the ideal of the "informing institution" that I have attempted to describe, it is probably HBS. In fact, if you can overcome your aversion to the smugness that permeates every nook and cranny of that venerable institution, it remains a pretty decent place to get an education to this day.

Even HBS, where self-satisfaction is a required element of every program and all other business schools are routinely dismissed as "lesser institutions", is not immune from external pressure to change. Where this appears most evident is in its doctoral programs.

I first got an inkling of these pressures in 1980, after I had been accepted by the HBS MBA program. During my application process, I had applied to a number of other schools including a doctoral program (in Marketing) at the University of Illinois. I was accepted by that program but before I even got the letter (which took 4 months to find me after I left the Navy) I got a call from the chair of the program wondering why I had not replied. I explained my mail situation and that I had decided to go to HBS. He was positively horrified, and went into a long speech about just how bad the doctoral program at HBS was. After a few minutes of this, I indicated that I was actually getting an MBA. He immediately retracted his statements and assured me that HBS was a great place to get an MBA, after which the call ended.

As someone who later received a DBA from HBS, I have heard a similar refrain on several occasions. On some level, the concerns with respect to an HBS doctorate were justified. Although the DBA I received was far more similar to a PhD than DBA programs at other institutions (see Gill & Hoppe, 2009), the HBS DBA was unusual in that it:

- Required considerable breadth of coverage but not very much depth in my field

- Emphasized case writing, particularly discussion cases

- Strongly discouraged me from publishing *any* traditional research articles while in the program

- Repeatedly lectured me that anyone who counted papers or worried about journal rankings was a little more than a bean counter

- Was so informal in its requirements that, to this day, I'm not convinced that I ever did a dissertation defense or completed comprehensive exams[10].

Personally, all these differences from more conventional programs suited me to a tee. Nevertheless, they did cause me some confusion when I found myself being asked to take an active role in doctoral programs at other institutions.

Part of the reason for the unique design aspects of the HBS program resulted from the special needs of the institution when I was in attendance. First, HBS has an almost insatiable appetite for new cases; at the time, doctoral students played an important role in supplying that need. Second, unlike nearly anywhere else, HBS was perfectly content to hire its own doctoral graduates as assistant professors. That made sense, since HBS DBAs were among the few academics actually trained to hit the ground running at a case method school[11].

This background is important because it represents a strong contrast to what I observed when I attended a doctoral program reunion in 2009.

While the institutional self-satisfaction at HBS had certainly not diminished, it was also clear to me that HBS had been stung by criticisms of its doctoral programs and was rapidly moving towards becoming much more traditional. Among the changes I observed:

- Professional case writers have taken on a much more central role in case development

- HBS now avoids hiring its own doctorates directly from the program. This conclusion appears to be supported by the schools recent hiring. For example 6 of 7 HBS hires at the Assistant Professor level were not from HBS in 2010. Moreover, according to the director of the program speaking the reunion dinner, they tell students to take a job at a top institution elsewhere and then to apply back to HBS after staying away for 3 years[12].

- Students are strongly encouraged write refereed research papers during their doctorate. In fact, many are staying an extra year or two (i.e., taking 5-6 years to graduate) in order to get 3 acceptances before applying for a job. This appears consistent with the 2010 HBS Annual Report data, which reports that there were 130 active doctoral students, while approximately 25 were admitted each year. Assuming some attrition within the program, that suggests an average duration per student of well over 5 years.

- Junior faculty members have now become obsessed with getting top journal "hits"[13].

What all these changes have in common is that they represent a transformation of the HBS DBA into a much more conventional doctoral program. This is combined with an increasing tendency within the school to move beyond the case method—now representing less than 80% of its curriculum (down from virtually 100% in the early 1980s). Such a shift is not necessarily bad. HBS still has a long ways to go before it becomes like every other business school. But I strongly doubt these changes would have occurred in the absence of external pressure to become more like its peers.

These changes should not be taken as evidence that HBS is losing its commitment to the case method. Indeed, its case sales have been rising—up to 9.7 million in 2010, representing an important revenue stream for HBS Publishing—and the school just opened another international research center (in Shanghai), adding to those in Europe, Latin America, Hong Kong, Mumbai and the Silicon Valley, California. These centers act as staging areas for case development. HBS is all too aware of the important role played by cases in establishing and maintaining its unparalleled network of connections to practice. What does appear to be happening, however, is that discussion case development is moving from being a—and perhaps the—principal research activity conducted by faculty members to an activity that they can choose to participate in, with full-time case writers taking on a greater share of the case development slack. In my view, by gradually moving cases away from the central research thrust of the school, they risk eroding what had been the key dimension across which they were distinguishable from their competitors. But such a state of affairs could be a very long time in coming and could still be reversed through a conscious effort.

If an institution can resist the power to conform, the long term rewards of a strong commitment to the case method will be high. By bringing practice into the classroom every day (both through case studies and protagonist visits), a program will never find itself mincing words when the question of relevance is raised. By interacting with practice continuously, examples of research impact will be abundant. When funding from the university (or government) becomes scarce, practitioners will become a powerful advocate for the school or college. They are also likely to become important sources of funds—for educational services rendered, for consulting and in the form of grants. In the very long term, satisfied practitioners are among the most likely candidates to provide the institution with large bequests and gifts. They have the money and, through informing them, the institution has given them the motivation. None of these benefits will happen quickly. But I am convinced they will be realized by the institution that has the confidence and independence of spirit to stay the course.

Conclusions

Building an informing institution that relies heavily on the case method is a long term strategy. The key to implementing that strategy is recognizing a basic truth: the main benefits of a strong institutional commitment to the case method is not the "documents" it produces (a stream of case studies whose research value is likely to be heavily discounted) or even the (hard-to-measure) educational impact of classroom discussions. Rather, what a strong institutional commitment to case development activity and case discussion offers is a pathway that will lead to a genuine partnership relationship between academics and practitioners. In such a relationship, neither party views itself as the "informer" or "client". Rather, both groups work together to advance both practice and education.

For over a hundred years, HBS carved out a distinctive place for itself in business research and education through precisely that type of institution. But a school does not have to be HBS to proceed down that route. A regional institution can mine its local service area for case study sites. HBS considers its "region" to be the globe, and it is probably justified in its view. But, for most schools, employment and business opportunities are heavily influenced by the local landscape. For state-supported institutions, that is nearly always the case. Thus, such schools do not need to travel the globe to build these relationships, although I would certainly not discourage such international case development when the opportunity presents itself. Instead, institutions can develop a local focus and set of relationships that no competing institution, and certainly not an HBS, can match.

By a similar reasoning process, there is no reason that the case method should be limit to business settings. Throughout this book, I have asserted that what makes the open, authentic case an attractive option is complexity. Evidence of an appropriate setting for cases includes:

1. For most problems, a diversity of possible approaches can be successful

2. The best practitioners often lack extensive formal training

3. It can be very hard to evaluate the success of a particular course of action

4. Many theories, often contradictory in nature, co-exist

5. Dramatic shifts in the environment occur unpredictably, but often enough so that they cannot be ignored. Such changes may be brought on by technology, regulations or, in some circumstances, may appear to occur with no obvious cause.

As it turns out, many applied disciplines outside of business—such as education, public administration, social work, architecture, engineering, and medicine—have communities of practice that exhibit many of these qualities. By making the initial investment required to establish the case method as a respected component of their research and educational portfolio, an institution can establish itself as a major contributor to the local practice community. In time, it can expect that initial investment to be paid back many times over.

Chapter 12 Notes

[1] I use the term "high level flows" here to acknowledge the fact that in a typical "real world" institution, every informing flow could conceivably impact (i.e., throttle) every resource flow and, quite possibly, every other informing flow as well. Including these would make Figure 12.1 look even more like a plate of spaghettis with elliptical meatballs than it already does, and would do nothing to make it any more understandable.

[2] I am unwilling to reject the possibility that alcohol was involved in AACSB's identification of areas of MIS research impact. The very fact that a bunch of deans had to stretch so far to come up with anything useful that MIS has done is, in itself, significant to my mind.

[3] After eliminating doctoral and service courses from the mix, what remains are MIS-specific courses that are taught at the undergraduate and graduate level to students whose principal goal is NOT to become MIS researchers. Because of the highly dynamic character of IT in general, we would expect that cutting edge findings from MIS research should rapidly make their way into the classroom to the extent that what we research overlaps what we teach.

[4] The mini-case describing the elimination of the MIS department at the University of Central Florida was developed through personal sources. I first became aware of their newly developed research focus when I considered applying for a faculty position there in late 2000. The subsequent elimination of their doctoral program followed by the laying off of their tenured faculty was widely reported in the media throughout Florida. This was confirmed by one of their faculty mem-

bers, a personal friend, who learned of her termination, effective 2010, in a brief email from the university.

[5] I am aware of Coca-Cola's deliberations in the area of sweetener acquisition since I was project manager for the consulting team that conducted one of these studies.

[6] Bertrand Fox, the HBS Division of Research Director in 1967, placed the official starting date of the *Program in Agriculture and Business* at December, 1952 (Goldberg, 1968, p. v).

[7] In the 1980s, HBS would routinely run two agribusiness seminars, one in Boston and one in London.

[8] Although Goldberg never mentioned any feelings with respect to being relocated, his secretaries were not reticent about expressing their displeasure to me. This situation was made more awkward by the fact that the department that had displaced them was, in fact, the same MIS department from which I was getting my doctorate.

[9] My assertion that HBS is increasingly driven towards traditional research productivity measures is my subjective interpretation of a number of observations I have made over the years. Most recently, at the doctoral reunion held in 2009, I heard a remark from a recently hired assistant professor about how important it had become to publish in the top tier journals of the field; during the 1980s while I was a doctoral student, such words would have never been uttered—even though they might have been thought. It was always supposed to be the quality of the idea, not the quality of the outlet that mattered. The increased importance of outlet seemed to be supported by comments made by the current director of the doctoral program, who observed that many doctoral students were delaying their completion, staying in the program 5 or even 6 years, in order to publish the requisite three articles that would ensure them placement at another top institution. While I was doing my doctorate, I was actually urged *not* to publish, lest it distract me from the more important task of getting through.

[10] Let me assure the reader that I did, in fact, complete everything that was required in order to get my degree. HBS simply gave them different names or had different requirements than seem to be the norm for more conventional programs.

[11] I also suspect that the willingness of HBS to hire its own was symptomatic of the institution's high regard for itself. Nearly every school seeks to hire from peer institutions or, preference, aspirational peers. Since HBS was convinced that it has no peers, it felt compelled to hire its own.

[12] There is something about the "stay away for 3 years and then we'll hire you back" policy that gives me a slightly queasy feeling in the part of my stomach that responds to ethics, but I may just be oversensitive. The rationalization given was that HBS did not want to be accused of keeping its top students for itself. I'm not entirely convinced, however, that the HBS doctorates now applying for jobs elsewhere make it clear to their potential employers that their fondest desire is to turn their new institution into a 3 year mandatory pit stop before returning to the job they want.

[13] The obsession with top journal hits was made clear to me in conversations with HBS junior faculty attending the reunion.

Appendix A

Three Little Pigs

This is a series of case studies I use in my case writing workshop to illustrate alternative case study designs.

THREE LITTLE PIGS (A)[1]

"Poor dumb porkers", Charlene the pig muttered under her breath as she surveyed the wreckage around her. Her siblings had lost everything they owned, blown away by a seriously deranged rogue wolf. That wolf was now on life support in a prison ward with a pair of collapsed lungs. And Charlene's two siblings were in her guest room, ready to go out into the world without a single possession to their name.

Background

Charlene's story had begun a few months before, immediately after the sale on her parents' homestead had closed. After commission, the sale had netted $300,000 to be split between her and her two brothers—Alan and Brian. As the oldest, she had been responsible for getting her former home ready to sell after her parents had died in a freak barbeque grill explosion. By the time the deal had closed, her two siblings had already gotten loans from the bank and spent their share of the money. Charlene had been in no such hurry, however. She recognized that she might have to live with what she purchased for a long time.

The Decision

Charlene has spent a considerable amount of time analyzing how to spend her inheritance. A variety of factors had weighed into the decision. As a given, there was her job—like her two brothers, she worked at a factory in Pigston. Second, there was housing. A number of factors had come into play here. The greater Pigston area could be very expensive—with the cost of land depending on proximity to the factory. There could also be substantial variation in construction costs—ranging from low-cost straw to mid-cost wood frame to high cost brick. There had also been the issue of transportation (e.g., walking, biking, automobile, etc.). Naturally, that choice could not be made independently of housing—since walking to the factory from the Pigston exburbs was not an option.

By the time Charlene had begun to study her choices in detail, her two brothers were already settled. Although she respected their choices, she chose a very different direction. Rather than spending big bucks on travel or a foreign prestige car, she had chosen to invest nearly all her money ($95,000) on a brick house with many safety options, spending the remainder on inexpensive furnishings purchased from Sties-To-Go and a moped to get her back and forth to work without the slightest pretence of style. Charlene and her brothers' choices are summarized in Exhibit 1.

A number of factors had entered into Charlene's decision. Her choice to spend so much on the house itself was motivated by the fact that brick homes had traditionally depreciated at a much slower rate than straw or wood and that Pigston was in an area that could potentially be frequented by a rare species known as the "bellows wolf"—capable of generating Category 5 winds (on the Saffir-Simpson scale) when they blew with their enormous lungs. Such a blow would immediately flatten a straw dwelling and would, if continued long enough, lead to eventual catastrophic structural failure of wood frame homes. Even brick houses (see Exhibit 2) were not guaranteed to withstand an encounter with a bellows wolf unless they were specially reinforced. Citing safety as her top priority, Charlene had opted for every construction safety feature available—leading to a home that far exceeded all known building codes.

Having chosen the house, the remaining elements of her decision fell into place naturally. She built the home on a lot in a family neighborhood close to Brian and about a mile from the factory and had minimized transportation costs by purchasing a moped. As she put it:

> It's not as if I wouldn't prefer to be driving a luxury pen-on-wheels like Brian, or even a flashy pigup truck like Alan. But sacrifices had to be made. In the long run, I felt I'd be better off with a nice house in a great neighborhood that I could sell at a profit some years down the road.

Little did she realize how soon her life-style choices would impact her very chances for survival...

The Big Bad Wolf

It had been just a week ago that the big bad wolf had blown into Pigston. An unusually large rogue bellows wolf (canis gasbagus) who had been cast out of the peaceful colony to the north, his first stop had been the unincorporated area known as New Pigston, home of Charlene's brother Alan. Hearing a crash, he had looked out and seen—to his dismay—the wolf outside his neighbor's house, which had just collapsed. Even with advance warning, he had just barely been able to outrun the wolf in his chrome-detailed pigup truck as he headed towards his brother's house in Pigston. Once there, the two had laughed about the whole experience, dancing and singing the then-popular "Who's afraid...?" when Brian's stick house began to quiver. In terror, they realized the big bad wolf had caught up with Alan, and that they were trapped.

Just moments before they became dog food, divine providence intervened. As Brian's house collapsed—destroying his "sow magnet" German sports car and Alan's pigup—a single large branch separated from the rubble and started to fly away in the breeze. Some deep instinct within the wolf then appeared to take over, and it sprinted after the flying stick, temporarily forgetting the two trapped pigs. Extricating themselves from the rubble, Alan and Brian quietly sneaked away from the house, then sprinted over to the next block, where Charlene lived.

She opened the door and let them in. A few minutes later, there came the terrible noise. The big bad wolf had regained his senses and had picked up their trail. Louder and louder the sound grew, like a freight train running through the solidly built brick structure. And then, all at once, it stopped. Cautiously peering through the curtains, they saw the huge bellows wolf lying on his back, his tongue hanging limp out of his mouth and his eyes rolled up into the back of his head. Within seconds, a squad car arrived and nets were tossed over him. The danger was past.

Lessons Learned

As Alan and Brian sadly walked out the door, their entire inheritance squandered, Charlene pondered what she had learned from the experience. Living for the moment has its pleasures, she decided, but how much greater is the pleasure when you're not living in fear that each of those moments will be your last.

Exhibit 1: Inheritance Allocation of Pig Siblings

Item	Alan	Brian	Charlene
Housing	**$25,000**: 5000 sq. ft. straw house **$5,000**: Mud Jacuzzi	**$40,000**: 1600 sq. ft stick-frame house	**$50,000**: 1000 sq. ft. brick house (basic) **$10,000**: Tile roof with hurricane straps **$15,000**: Electric hurricane window shutters
Lot	**$15,000**: 10 acre mini-estate in unincorporated Pigston exburbs	**$40,000**: 1 acre double golf course lot in Pigston proper	**$20,000**: ½ acre lot in Pigston proper
Furnishings	**$25,000**: "Party Hearty" complete set from William Sownoma.	**$10,000**: 5 rooms of exotic furnishings from Pig 1.	**$4,000**: 3 rooms of furnishings from Sties-to-Go
Transportation	**$35,000**: P150 pickup truck with chrome detailing	**$40,000**: Porkhe sports car	**$1,000**: Moped
Travel	**$10,000**: 3-week vacation in Europe	**$10,000**: 3-week vacation in Europe	N/A
Mortgage	**($15,000)**	**($40,000)**	**($0)**

THREE LITTLE PIGS (B)[2]

"Who's afraid of the big bad wolf?", Charlene the pig asked her two brothers Alan and Brian as they danced around, almost mocking her. "Well, I am, just to name one!" And she had reason to be. Her siblings had lost everything they owned, blown away by a seriously deranged wolf. That wolf was now wandering around her neighborhood. This very moment, she had to make the most important decision of her life. Should she evacuate to the safety of the local market or should she stay at home? Or was there some other option that she might consider—such as laying a trail of roast beef to lead the wolf away to some other neighborhood? The lives of everyone in her family were at stake.

Background

Charlene's story had begun a few months before, immediately after the sale on her parents' homestead had closed. After commission, the sale had netted $300,000 to be split between her and her two brothers—Alan and Brian. As the oldest, she had been responsible for getting her former home ready to sell after her parents had died in a freak barbeque grill explosion. By the time the deal had closed, her two siblings had already gotten loans from the bank and spent their share of the money. Charlene had been in no such hurry, however. She recognized that she might have to live with what she decided for a long time.

Charlene's House

Charlene had spent a considerable amount of time analyzing how to spend her inheritance. A variety of factors weighed into the decision. As a given, there was her job—like her two brothers, she worked at a factory in Pigston. Second, there was housing. A number of factors had come into play here. The greater Pigston area could be very expensive—with the cost of land depending on proximity to the factory. There could also be substantial variation in construction costs—ranging from low-cost straw to mid-cost wood frame to high cost brick. There had also been the issue of transportation (e.g., walking, biking, automo-

---

bile, etc.). Naturally, that choice could not be made independently of housing—since walking to the factory from the Pigston exburbs was not an option.

By the time Charlene had begun to study her choices in detail, her two brothers were already settled. Although she respected their choices, she chose a very different direction. Rather than spending big bucks on travel or a foreign prestige car, she had chosen to invest nearly all her money ($95,000) on a brick house with options that went considerably beyond code, spending the remainder on inexpensive furnishings purchased from Sties-To-Go and a moped to get her back and forth to work without the slightest pretense of style. Their choices are summarized in Exhibit 1.

Charlene's decision to spend nearly all her money on housing had been motivated by two factors. First, brick homes had traditionally depreciated at a much slower rate than straw or wood. Second, Pigston was in an area that could potentially be frequented by a rare species known as the "bellows wolf"—capable of generating Category 5 winds (on the Saffir-Simpson scale) when they blew with their enormous lungs. Such a blow would immediately flatten a straw dwelling and would, if continued long enough, lead to eventual catastrophic structural failure of wood frame homes. Even brick houses (see Exhibit 2) were unlikely to withstand an encounter with a bellows wolf without special reinforcement. Citing security as her top priority, Charlene had opted for every construction safety feature available—leading to a home that far exceeded all known building codes.

The Big Bad Wolf

It had been just a few hours before that the big bad wolf had blown into Pigston. An unusually large bellows wolf (canis gasbagus), his first stop had been the unincorporated area known as New Pigston, home of Charlene's brother Alan. Hearing a crash, he had looked out and seen—to his dismay—the wolf outside his neighbor's house, which had just collapsed. Even with advance warning, he had just barely been able to outrun the wolf in his chrome-detailed pigup truck as he headed towards his brother's house in Pigston. Once there, the two had laughed about the whole experience, dancing and singing the then-popular "Who's afraid...?" when Brian's stick house began to quiver. In terror, they realized the big bad wolf had caught up with Alan, and that they were trapped.

Just moments before they became dog food, divine providence intervened. As Brian's house collapsed—destroying his "sow magnet" German sports car and Alan's pigup—a single large branch separated from the rubble and started to fly away in the breeze. Some deep instinct within the wolf then appeared to take over, and it sprinted after the flying stick, temporarily forgetting the two trapped pigs. Extricating themselves from the rubble, Alan and Brian quietly sneaked away from the house, then sprinted over to the next block, where Charlene lived.

The Decision

Once Charlene had opened the door and let them in, she realized that she had to make a decision immediately. Although her house had been designed to withstand typical wolf-blows, Brian's description of the collapse of his house made it clear that this was no typical bellows wolf. Furthermore, unlike wood and straw houses, the collapse of a brick house would likely kill all the occupants—and there would be no flying sticks to distract the wolf. Another option would be to run to the market. Less than three blocks away, it was constructed of steel and also housed a satellite police station. It was unlikely the wolf would dare to follow them there—but they'd be extremely vulnerable for a few minutes. Caught out in the open, there'd be no way to run (wee, wee, wee) all the way home. Alan had also suggested another possibility. Charlene's refrigerator was well stocked with roast beef—a favorite of both pigs and wolves. Perhaps they could use it to distract the wolf, tossing chunks of it into neighboring yards. She felt that time was on her side—the presence of the big bad wolf was unlikely to have gone unnoticed. That meant a squad of the meanest boars you ever saw was probably on its way. Every minute that the wolf was distracted increased their likelihood of survival. But, tossing your meat next door when a wolf came prowling wasn't exactly the neighborly thing to do. Or maybe there were other options—ones she hadn't considered at all.

One thing was certain, however. Whatever decision she made had to be made now.

Exhibit 1: Inheritance Allocation of Pig Siblings

Item	Alan	Brian	Charlene
Housing	**$25,000**: 5000 sq. ft. straw house **$5,000**: Mud Jacuzzi	**$40,000**: 1600 sq. ft stick-frame house	**$50,000**: 1000 sq. ft. brick house (basic) **$10,000**: Tile roof with hurricane straps **$15,000**: Electric hurricane window shutters
Lot	**$15,000**: 10 acre mini-estate in unincorporated Pigston exburbs	**$40,000**: 1 acre double golf course lot in Pigston proper	**$20,000**: ½ acre lot in Pigston proper
Furnishings	**$25,000**: "Party Hearty" complete set from William Sownoma.	**$10,000**: 5 rooms of exotic furnishings from Pig 1.	**$4,000**: 3 rooms of furnishings from Sties-to-Go
Transportation	**$35,000**: P150 pickup truck with chrome detailing	**$40,000**: Porkhe sports car	**$1,000**: Moped
Travel	**$10,000**: 3-week vacation in Europe	**$10,000**: 3-week vacation in Europe	N/A
Mortgage	**($15,000)**	**($40,000)**	**($0)**

THREE LITTLE PIGS (C)[3]

"So many choices", murmured Charlene the pig as the closing agent handed her a check for $100,000—her share of the inheritance left by her parents. Now that her money was in hand, the time had come to decide how it could best be applied. Her two brothers, Alan and Brian, had not even bothered to wait. As soon as the contract had been signed on their old house, they had gone out, borrowed the money from a bank, and spent it. "To each his own", she thought. "But I'd like to spend my nest egg on something a bit more permanent".

"So Many Choices"

$100,000 was a lot of money for a pig. In order to spend it wisely, Charlene felt she had to weigh a variety of factors. As a given, there was her job—like her two brothers, she worked at a factory in Pigston. Second, there was housing. A number of issues were involved here. There was considerable variation in land prices throughout the greater Pigston metropolitan area. Charlene had verified this by making a rough sketch (shown as Exhibit 1) that plotted all land sales that had been recorded in the past month. Another issue relating to location was being close to family—something she desired, but did not require. Finally, although it was possible to buy an existing home in Pigston, she felt that doing so was unlikely to be an attractive option—since, prior to the opening of the factory during the previous year, nearly all homes had utilized straw construction. Would you want to live in a straw house that had recently been occupied by a family of pigs?

Closely related to lot location was the issue of acquiring transportation (e.g., walking, biking, automobile, etc.)—since walking to the factory from the Pigston exburbs was not an option. Unfortunately, the freak barbeque grill explosion that had claimed her parents' lives had also destroyed both their cars. Although her two brothers, Alan and Brian, had both purchased expensive vehicles—Brian referred to his as a "sow magnet"—Charlene had never really been that into cars (except as a

---

means of reliable transportation). Typical transportation option prices are summarized in Exhibit 2.

One of the biggest elements of the decision facing Charlene was how her new house should be built. There were three different styles of construction commonly used in Pigston: straw, wood and brick. The costs of these varied substantially. Straw was the clear winner in terms of cost—with costs roughly 10% of an equivalent brick house. Weighing against it was the fact that it was not at all durable. It was rare that a straw house lasted more than 3 years and the resale value of a straw dwelling dropped precipitously after it was first occupied.

Wood occupied an intermediate position. Pig dwellings relied on stick construction and typically lasted 20-25 years. The price of these dwellings tended to be about 5 times higher than for straw—and about half that of brick. Wood was substantially more durable than straw and wood dwelling resales were not uncommon. Typically, wood dwellings depreciated at a rate of 10% of their original cost for the first 3-4 years, then more slowly (around 2-3% per year). Unlike straw, wooden homes offered substantial protection against violent weather (e.g., gales, which occurred quite infrequently in Pigston owing to its inland location sheltered by rolling hills on all four sides). Nonetheless, they could not withstand extremely high winds or the fetid breath of a bellows wolf.

The final class of construction, brick, was—by far—the most durable and expensive. Having herself grown up in one of the few brick homes in the greater Pigston area, the material held a sentimental attraction for Charlene. Furthermore, unlike the other forms of construction, pig-occupied brick homes had no natural lifespan limits and did not depreciate in value over time. On the negative side, they were much more expensive and they were not guaranteed to withstand the breath of a large bellows wolf—although, with the purchase of expensive options such as roof tie downs, they were probably up to the task. Construction costs and specifications are presented in Exhibit 3.

In considering her various options, Charlene also needed to consider what she could do with any money she did not spend. Saving it, of course, was an option. But another option was travel. Recently, her brothers had returned from a trip to Europe, where they had toured the continent (except for the sausage-obsessed countries of Germany and Poland). She had envied them as they raved about the trip. But the price tag had been steep--$10,000 each. Was she willing to spend that much for memories?

Time to Decide

Whatever she planned to do, the time had now come to make the decision. The nice family of hogs that had purchased her family home wasn't going to occupy it for a month, and offered to let her stay until they arrived. After that, however, she'd be paying $50/night for a bed-and-slop near the factory if she hadn't made up her mind. And there was the problem of timing. While a straw house could be thrown up in a day or two, brick took 6 weeks—and more, if additional options were to be installed.

One source of guidance could be found in the choices made by her brothers—who had borrowed money before the closing to finance their own choices. Their choices are summarized in Exhibit 4. She was not altogether comfortable with their priorities, however. Alan, for example, had built the largest and flashiest straw house you ever saw. After just a few weeks, the parties he threw there practically every night had already started to become the stuff of legends, as had the escapades in his mud Jacuzzi. But would he remain so popular once his house had decayed into a haystack and he had no money to rebuild it? And anyway, Charlene was more of a home body.

Recently, Charlene had developed another concern. About two weeks before, an article in the Pigston Pigayune (Exhibit 5) had mentioned how environmentalists were reintroducing bellows wolves to the north. Fortunately, this species was extremely rare—none had been seen in Pigston for over a decade—and members of a wolf pack were generally well behaved. Less fortunately, the occasional rogue male was sometimes cast out of a colony and, if not apprehended, could pose a serious problem owing to its taste for pork flesh combined with its ability to generate Category 5 (Saffir-Simpson scale) winds by blowing. Charlene's brothers had laughed and taunted her—singing excerpts from the popular hit "Who's Afraid...?"—when she mentioned her apprehensions to them. But she felt uncomfortable ignoring the situation completely.

What made her *really* uncomfortable, however, was the thought of paying a price of $50/night for her indecisiveness. So she gave herself a deadline. By midnight tonight, she would make her decision.

Exhibit 1: Charlene's sketch of building lot prices in and near Pigston

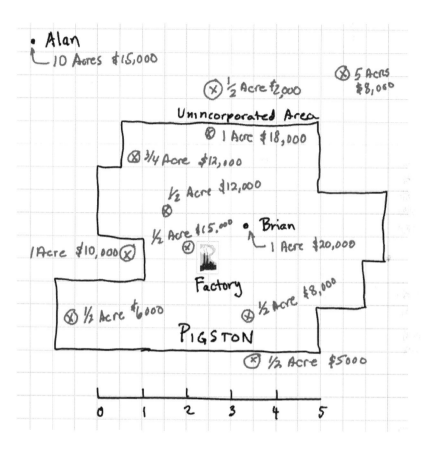

Exhibit 2: Transportation modes and costs

Mode	Description	Cost range	Comments
Luxury sedan	4-6 pig vehicle	$30,000 - $60,000	Foreign models, such as the Porkhe, tend to run $5,000-$10,000 higher than domestic models
Pigup truck	2-3 pig vehicle	$20,000 - $40,000	State laws prohibit pigs from riding in the bed area
Economy sedan	4-6 pig vehicle	$15,000 - $25,000	Version of the sedan for pigs who don't want their pockets picked in order to broadcast their economic status.
Motorcycle	1-2 pig vehicle	$3,000-$5,000	Can provide an uncomfortable ride during cold and inclement weather
Moped	1 pig vehicle	$1,000-$1,200	Motorized bicycle best suited for distances under 10 miles. Can provide an uncomfortable ride during cold and inclement weather
Bicycle	1 pig vehicle	$200-$500	Pig-powered conveyance best suited for distances under 10 miles. Can provide an uncomfortable ride during cold and inclement weather.
Walking	Nature's way	$0	Based on typical pig physiology, best suited for distances under 1 mile. Can be uncomfortable during cold and inclement weather.

Exhibit 3: Building specifications and costs

Item	Description	Key Specs	Costs	Comments
Straw Construction	Straw-built residential single family unit	Life span: 2-5 years Depreciation: 50%(30%)[1] Wind rating: Cat 0 (55 mph)	~$5/sq. ft.	
Wood Construction	Wood/stick-built residential single family unit	Life span: 20-25 years Depreciation: 10%(2%)[2] Wind rating: Cat 2 (100 mph)	~$25/sq. ft.	
Brick Construction	Brick-built residential single family unit	Life span: 100+ years Depreciation: 0% [3] Wind rating: Cat 4+ (160 mph)	~$50/sq. ft.	Wind rating may be affected by options
Popular Options				
Jacuzzi	Mud-filled tank agitated by air jets	Capacity: 6 pigs or 8 piglets	$5000	
Exterior trough	Water and slop trough for parties	Capacity: 16 pigs or 24 piglets	$3000	
Smoke house	Stone-built exterior structure for smoking parties. May also be used as a shelter.	Capacity: 6 pigs/100 sq. ft. Wind rating: Cat 5+ (175 mph)	$100/sq. ft	State law prohibits piglets from attending smokers

Barbeque pit	Circular pit with firewall designed for roasting sides of beef	Capacity: 1 side of beef Fuel: wood or charcoal	$2000 $1000 (propane option)	
Automatic door	Door incorporating voice recognition to provide easy entry	Min DB: 75 Max DB: 150 Freq Range: 400-25,000 Hz	$2000	Owners should not use "wee, wee, wee" as entry phrase
Stucco coating [4]	Cement-based mixture with appearance of mud	Color: brown Sound reduction: 5-10 DB	$1/sq. ft	Primarily for aesthetics and noise reduction
Hurricane roof [4]	Tile roof attached by tie-down straps	Life span: 40-50 years Warrantee: 20 years [5]	$10/sq. ft.	Adds 10-20 mph to wind rating
Hurricane Panels	Hand installed steel panels	Life span: 25+ years	$50/window [6]	Adds 10-20 mph to wind rating
Hurricane shutters	Motor-operated aluminum roll ups	Life span: 25+ years Warrantee: 20 years [7]	$1200/window [6]	Adds 10-20 mph to wind rating

Notes:

[1] Straw Depreciation: First Year (Later Years)

[2] Wood Depreciation: First 3 Years (Later years)

[3] Brick construction does not appear to depreciate, owing to its long expected life span

[4] Available only for brick construction

[5] Warrantee applies only to replacement of roof, not to any structural damage caused by roof failure

[6] Assume roughly 1 window for every 10 feet of perimeter space

[7] Warrantee includes $20,000 insurance for content damage in the event of panel failure

Exhibit 4: Spending by Alan and Brian

Item	Alan	Brian
Housing	**$25,000**: 5000 sq. ft. straw house **$5,000**: Mud Jacuzzi	**$40,000**: 1600 sq. ft stick-frame house
Lot	**$15,000**: 10 acre mini-estate in unincorporated Pigston exburbs	**$40,000**: 1 acre double golf course lot in Pigston proper
Furnishings	**$25,000**: "Party Hearty" complete set from William Sownoma.	**$10,000**: 5 rooms of exotic furnishings from Pig 1.
Transportation	**$35,000**: P150 pickup truck with chrome detailing	**$40,000**: Porkhe sports car
Travel	**$10,000**: 3-week vacation in Europe	**$10,000**: 3-week vacation in Europe
Mortgage	**($15,000)**	**($40,000)**

Bellows Wolf Colony Thriving

Associated Pig News Service– 8/9/2005

For over a decade, naturalists affiliated with the Porcine Conservation Society have been struggling to reintroduce the bellows wolf (canis gasbagus) into northern Hogvale county. Today, it was announced that five breeding pairs, transplanted from other areas of the country—particularly the southwest—had joined together to form a viable wolf pack. With such a pack in place, scientists believe the colony has, at long last, become self-sustaining.

The establishment of a wolf colony has been marked by controversy. Exterminated near the middle of the last century as part of a federally funded eradication program, the bellows wolf has been widely misunderstood within the pig community. "Our view of wolves tends to be formed by the fairy stories we were told as piglets", states noted psychologist Linda Sower. "Wolves do not like to dress up as grandmothers. They do not sound like a bassoon when they walk. And they most definitely do not want to engage in carnal relationships with our young sows. Indeed, they find the very thought as unnatural as we do."

Jim Hammond, the naturalist who has spent his last 5 years living with the breeding pairs, was even more emphatic on the subject. "The wolf pack is one of the most stable communities in the animal kingdom. Wolves mate for life—something we could learn from—and exhibit great respect for authority." Hammond also commented on the benefits of having a thriving wolf population. "Contrary to popular belief, wolves do not crave pig flesh. In fact, the members of a healthy wolf pack focus their hunting on mice, rodents, rabbits and squirrels. In case you didn't notice, those are the very same pests that try to steal our truffles."

Others do not share the community's enthusiasm for wolves. "Sure, a wolf pack is benign enough," shouted Chuck Slopworth at a

(continued on p. 4)

(continued from p. 1)

local community protest meeting in Pigston, "But what about the rogues?"

Pigston's mayor, Mary Carnita, described the city's position on rogue wolves: "First, you've got to understand that the rogue phenomenon is very rare—for a colony to produce a rogue more than once a decade is very unusual. Second, the wolf community has made a commitment to notify us if one of their members develops rogue tendencies. Third, this is not the 20th century and we need to recognize that all sentient beings need to be given the right to live their lives. Naturally, should a rogue problem arise, we will be prepared to deal with it."

Hammond, acknowledging that a rogue wolf could indeed present a problem, made the following observations. "The best thing to do in the extremely unlikely event that a rogue wolf is sighted is to hide. Once a rogue wolf sees you, it will follow you to the ends of the earth, using its highly tuned sense of smell—the most sensitive in the sentient animal community. Also, forget about hiding in your house. Straw, wood, even many brick dwellings, can't stand up to the 175 mile an hour wind that a bellows wolf can produce. Remember, as well, that while a rogue wolf will eat pork—unlike its pack-member counterparts—its preference is still for other foods. In particular, if a rogue wolf is in the area, be sure you don't have any roast beef in the house. This is one circumstance where it's best to be the little piggy who had none!"

Appendix B

Case Writing Checklist

This is a checklist I use to remind myself of the key elements of the case writing process.

Writing Case Studies Checklist[1]

Stage 1: Before the case development begins

Stage 1A: What is the purpose of the case are you envisioning?

X	Type	Comments
	Research	Objective is to examine cause and effect, typically in a situation where phenomenon being observed are too complex for a controlled experiment. May be single case or part of a collection of cases.
	Discussion	Objective is to create a case study that can be used as the basis for class discussion. Typically, such cases present a situation which requires discussants develop and/or evaluate solutions.
	Illustration	Objective is to provide a concrete example of some phenomenon of interest, with the objective of creating a more lasting impression than could be achieved with a more abstract form of presentation.
	Walkthrough	Objective is to provide an example of the analytical process (quantitative or qualitative) that is appropriate for a particular situation, often used within the context of a lecture.
	Exercise	Objective is to present a contextually rich situation that can be analyzed using one or more approaches. It is similar to the traditional word problem in intent.
	Other	*Describe:*

Stage 1B: What is its expected relationship to other cases?

X	Type	Comments
	Independent	The case stands alone and can be meaningfully discussed, presented or analyzed without reference to other cases. It can be used by itself without creating false impressions.
	Comparative	The case is specifically intended to be used with one or more other cases, where it serves as a basis for comparison. It will normally not be used by itself.
	Cumulative	The case is to be developed as part of an inductive framework (e.g., a multi-case class, a multi-case research project) and could be misleading if used as the only example, situation or observation.

Questions: If comparative or cumulative:

1. What is the source of the other cases?

2. What role should the case being developed play?

Stage 1C: How will case material be acquired and presented?

X	Type	Comments
	Reported Observation	Case writer(s) will acquire non-public information from case site (in-person or by electronic means) and public information. Case will be written as description of the actual situation.
	Lightly Disguised	Case will be developed through reported observation. After the case has been prepared, non-material changes to participant, organization and quantitative elements may be made to preserve privacy.
	Heavily Disguised	Case will be developed through reported observation but, after its development, will be changes in such a way such that material elements (e.g., industry, organization) cannot be determined.
	Public sources	Case is developed entirely using sources available to the public (e.g., public Internet, journal articles, government documents). *Permission to release public-source cases is not normally required.*
	Fictional	Case study is based on an entirely fictional situation, organization, individual, etc. Similar to a novel, its sources could include the writer's own experience, imagination and public sources.

Stage 1D: What is the anticipated outlet for the case?

X	Type	Comments
	Local	The case will be used locally, in the classroom or as an exercise. Write up may assume certain common knowledge (e.g., where the organization is located, its size, role, etc.)
	External	The case is designed for use outside the local organization but is to be distributed informally (e.g., web, email, working paper). Should include information relevant to understanding the local context.
	Published	The case is intended for publication as a research case, teaching case or learning object. Similar to local case except publication criteria (e.g., length) must be considered.

Stage 2: After case site has been identified

Explore publicly available sources related to the case situation:

X	Type	Comments
	Search	Google the protagonist and other relevant keywords
	Research	Examine research databases for relevant literature
	Web	Browse organization-department-project/course web sites
	Repositories	Look for similar cases in sites like HBS (business) or MERLOT
	Records	Is topic described in press, reports (e.g., LexisNexis search).
	Other	Describe:

Stage 3: First meeting

Topics for initial discussion:

X	Type	Questions
	Context	• What is the **industry/field** → **organization** →**organizational unit** in which the case is taking place? • What is the historical context of the case? • What are the available data sources? • Where should I look for publicly available data? • Are there any private documents or systems that I can be given access to while I'm developing the case?
	Protago-nist	• What is the background of the individual most directly related to the case? • What are the available data sources?
	Situa-tions	• What do you view as your most important recent accomplishments? • What interesting issues are you currently facing?
	Possible Topics	For each accomplishment or issue identified: • What makes the situation particularly interesting? • What decisions are you currently facing? • What decisions did you (or your organization) make in the past that led up to the current situation? • How might my involvement in writing the case assist you with respect to this situation? • Who else was involved, and would they be willing to talk with me? • What are the available data sources?
	Release	• When the case is completed, would you like to be listed as a co-author? • What, if any, aspects of the case study do you think you may want to disguise? • Who has the authority to release the case, once it has been approved? • When can I speak to that individual?

Items to provide before or during the first meeting:

X	Item	Comments
	Biography	Provide some background on yourself, so they know where your experience lies. Don't just throw in your vita—tailor it to your audience. Compare Exhibit 1 (business version) with Exhibit 2 (NSF version) of same biography.
	Case objectives	Explain why you want to develop the case. First page of Exhibit 3 is an example of a document prepared to solicit business sites willing to participate in case studies.
	Process outline	Outline the case writing process so the site has a clear idea what they are getting into. It is far better to have a potential case site decline to participate early—rather than late—in the case writing process. See Exhibit 3 FAQs for example.
	Benefits summary	Explain what the benefits of participating in the case study are likely to be. Don't assume that "contributing to the world's knowledge" will be enough. Other benefits may include: clarifying a complex situation, access to your unusual expertise, creating a document that can be incorporated elsewhere (e.g., in strategic plan). See Exhibit 3 FAQs for example.
	Sample case	No matter what type of case you're writing, many sites will not be familiar with what a case is. Offer them a sample of a case study similar to what you are contemplating writing.
	Other	*Describe:*

Stage 4: Determine Topic

Stage 4A: For each possible topic, what type of case is likely to emerge?

X	Type	Comments
	Decision-Making	Topic focuses on a decision that needs to be made or the situation leading up a decision that was made in the recent past. Best fits with the "Discussion" objective, though can also be used for "Exercise" objective.
	Knowledge	Topic will serve to convey knowledge to its reader. Such knowledge can include better understanding of the case context or the approach used in some decision-making process. Best fits with "Research" and "Walkthrough" objectives— also useful for cumulative case sets.
	Showcase	Case will illustrate an exemplary handling of some problem or situation, particularly useful when a case is to be used for "Illustration" objectives. *Be aware that most sites are hoping your case will serve as a showcase for their activities.*
	Fable	Case provides an unambiguous narrative tying a particular series of actions to a particular observed consequence. Can be useful for "Illustration" objectives but is best saved for comparative sets of cases if a balanced perspective is to be maintained.
	Mixed	*Describe:*

Stage 4B: What are the sequencing options?

X	Type	Comments
	Complete	The topic can stand alone as a single entity. If outcome information is desired (for a discussion case) it will be provided in a teaching note or informally by the instructor. Typically, however, such outcome information does not critically contribute to the value of the discussion.
	Staged	The topic naturally breaks into a series of stages—typically labeled A, B, C, etc. Normally used for discussion cases, participants will typically get access to later case stage write ups as the discussion progresses. This format allows for discussions of the potential impact of different actions prior to revealing their consequences.

Stage 4C: Emphasis on Intelligence-Design-Choice

X	Type	Description
	Intelligence	Develops knowledge, comprehension and the ability to apply information in a real-world setting. Facts incorporated into the case and techniques described in the case are inherently valuable to students. Cases provide an alternative means of conveying information that would otherwise be presented in lectures.
	Design	Case provides student the opportunity to choose and perform analysis—the form of which must be determined by the reader. Thoughtful preparation of the case may require proposing actions or designing activities not specifically specified by the case. Information in the case must be prioritized with respect to relevance and value.
	Choice	Case presents two or more plausible alternatives, justifying that decision based upon materials presented in the case. Thoughtful preparation includes identifying the strengths and weaknesses of each possibility and using a deep understanding of the case situation to guide the decision process. Assumptions regarding information not presented in the case but relevant to the decision may be required and justified.

Stage 4D: Complete each of the following actions

X	Activity	Description
	Choose the preferred topic	If more than one situation exists, choose the one that you prefer based on your analysis.
	Write opening section	Create an introduction suitable for the case type. For example: • *Research:* Identify the relevance of the research problem being addressed by the case. • *Discussion:* Identify the context of the decision being made and any alternatives that are explicitly being considered • *Illustration:* Summarize the situation. • *Walkthrough, Exercise:* Present a concise statement of the problem being addressed.
	Get preliminary approval	Email the introduction to the protagonist (if applicable) and ensure there is mutual agreement to proceed on the chosen situation.
	Inventory existing data sources	Determine all public and private resources you've been given access to that are relevant to the specified topic.
	Outline case study	Create an outline of the case with the principal objective of determining what data you need to gather.

Stage 4E: If none of the topics seem appropriate, return to the contact and see if there are any other options.

Stage 5: Second meeting

Stage 5A: Establish ground rules for data gathering

X	Activity	Description
Acquiring direct quotes		
	Record	Record interviews as they are conducted
	Paraphrase	Approximate quotes then let individual correct, as necessary, in draft
	On request	Send individual request for quote on a specific topic
Circulating rough drafts		
	Independent	Each individual interviewed for the case is contacted privately to approve relevant materials prior to anyone seeing draft
	Coordinated	The contact point for the case is given all drafts of the case and is in charge of gaining approvals for all participants
	Broadcast	A group of individuals is granted simultaneous access to each draft of the case as it is finished
	Managed	The contact point for the case is given all drafts of the case and determines if other participants need to see it when its finalized
Responsibility got getting permissions for included materials		
	Contact	The contact point takes responsibility, desirable if many of the materials require organizational approval
	Case writer	The case writer takes responsibility, desirable if many of the materials are 3rd party (e.g., newspaper clippings)
	Mixed	Both parties take responsibility, based upon the source of the materials

Responsibility for setting up interview schedules, if needed		
	Contact	Site contact identifies the appropriate contacts and sets up a schedule of interview times
	Site adminis-trator	Case writer contacts an administrative assistant at the site with requests to meet specific individuals
	Case writer	Case writer contacts individuals to be interviewed directly, and sets up appointments as desired

Stage 5B: Conduct in-depth interview of contact

Stage 5C: Create to-do list for remainder of case development

Stage 5D: Determine timing of release document (for teaching cases)

X	Item	Description
	Prior to first use	The case must be released prior to any use in the classroom
	Subsequent to first use	A one-time release is granted for first use, with the formal release made after a "test run" in the classroom

Stage 6: Write the case

Typical organization for discussion and research cases:

Discussion Case	Research Case
Introduction Present the decision setting and motivate the decision being made.	**Introduction** Motivate the research topic by highlighting its importance and demonstrating that it is not fully understood.
Environment Describe the environment (e.g., industry, field, country/culture) in which the case is set, explaining aspects pertinent to the case.	**Literature Review** Review previous literature related to the case situation and frameworks that have been proposed
Organization Describe the organization (e.g., agency, company, institution) in which the case is situated.	**Research Framework** Research questions to be addressed and the analytical framework to be used. Formal hypothesis testing is less common than presentation of arguments relating to cause and effect.
Locale Describe the small group (e.g., department, tribe, neighborhood, subculture) in which the case is situated.	**Data Gathering Protocol** Methods used to gather data related to the case, often emphasizing triangulation (gathering data from multiple sources to confirm the same observation)
Protagonist Describe the individual or small group most directly responsible for any actions or decisions relevant to the case.	**Background & Situation** Description of the case situation and the key elements of the case.

Situation	Analysis
Describe the specific situation to be addressed in any analysis of the case that is to be performed.	Discussion of the case in the context of the analytical framework.
Constraints and Requirements	**Conclusions**
Revisit the case situation specifying all constraints (e.g., time pressure, specific criteria that must be met) and requirements (e.g., alternatives to be considered or important priorities).	Presentation of conclusions from the case, with particular attention being paid to their likely generalizability to other situations.
Exhibits	**Appendices**
Source documents, images and tables relevant to the case.	Source documents, images and tables relevant to the case.

Stage 7: Gain case approval

Stage 7A: Key items in the approval document

X	Item	Description
	Copyright	Copyright could be held by author, author's institution or site organization. This can become a particular issue in the event the case is subsequently published.
	Duplicating rights	If a case is to be used in the classroom, it's a good idea to explicitly provide duplication rights to the author, the author's institution and the site organization.
	Right to recall case	Sometimes an organization may wish to recall a case. Typically, such a clause should be in place only if the case is being distributed or published locally, and never in research cases.
	Non-material changes	It is a good idea to add a clause allowing minor edits, not affecting the overall case, to be made. This prevents multiple rounds of approvals for typos or small changes.
	Consequential damages	Particularly in a commercial setting, it may be appropriate for the site organization and author to agree not to pursue each other if the case leads to unintended consequences.
	Good faith and arbitration	Particularly in a commercial setting, it may be reassuring to the site for you to state that you'll try to act in good faith to resolve any disputes and that you'll submit to arbitration if you can't

Appendix C

10 Frequently Asked Questions

During the process of finding a case site, I often use this list as a tool for introducing managers to the process. You are welcome to copy or adapt these questions for your own use.

Why Should I Participate in a Case Study?
Answers to 10 frequently asked questions[1]

by

T. Grandon Gill
Professor
Information Systems and Decision Sciences
College of Business
University of South Florida

In the course of my experience in writing teaching cases, both for Harvard Business School and for Prentice Hall, I have found that managers who are considering participating start out with many questions. Here are 10 of the most common:

1.   *What is a business teaching case study?*

A business *teaching case study*, as distinguished from a *research case study*, is a description of an administrative situation that is specifically intended to be the basis of a class discussion. Sometimes referred to as *Harvard-style* cases, these cases typically have a number of distinguishing characteristics:

- *Their central focus is some decision that needs to be made.* While many cases (particularly research cases) have been written that document the outcome of some decision, the best teaching cases usually motivate discussion with an agenda that includes deciding what the manager needs to do.

- *The situations examined tend to be complex, and multi-faceted.* Just as few business decisions can be reduced to a single function, few good teaching cases attempt to present a business situation as if it were strictly a "finance" or "marketing" or "MIS" problem.

- *There is rarely a single "right answer" to a case.* As with all business situations, there are certainly better answers and worse answers, but good teaching cases do not come with ready-made solutions that the instructor can announce at the end of class.

In addition, as a practical matter, Harvard-style case studies tend to share a certain physical appearance: 7-12 pages of single-spaced text followed by exhibits (figures) that may range from 1 to 15 pages.

2.   What does it cost my company to participate in a case study?

In terms of dollars, nothing. When you participate in a case study, your firm is doing the educational community a service. Having said that, there can be a significant cost of time associated with the case writing process.

3.   What kind of time commitment will participating in a case involve?

This varies from company to company, and from case-writer to case-writer. Generally, the decision-maker about whom the case revolves can expect to spend 10-20 hours in interviews, reading drafts and facilitating case writer visits, spread over the entire case writing period (usually 1-2 months). Other individuals involved in the case (5-15 is the normal number) would normally expect to spend much less time, perhaps 1-2 hours apiece, at most, spent mainly in interviews with the case writer.

4.   How does the case writing process work?

The case writing process normally proceeds through a series of stages:

a)   *Discovery:* During the first phase, the case writer needs to "discover" two things: 1) the decision that will become the focus of the case and 2) the identity of the authorizing executive who will *release* the case (i.e., authorize for publication). Once the decision has been identified, and the authorizing executive has indicated a willingness to participate in the case-writing process, data gathering for the actual case can proceed.

b) *Data Gathering:* The data gathering phase usually begins with an extended (2-4 hour) interview with the decision-maker who is central to the case (a.k.a. the protagonist). After these interviews, the case writer and protagonist generally decide who should be interviewed and what background material needs to be gathered. As a practical matter, the scheduling of supporting interviews and copying of relevant documents is typically handled by the company.

c) *First Draft:* After the initial and supporting interviews, the case writer usually disappears for a few weeks to write the first draft of the case. Normally, in writing the first draft, the case writer identifies a) additional information that would be useful for the purposes of the case, and b) quotes that need to be authorized by individuals that have been interviewed. Requests for the former are normally forwarded to the protagonist, who determines if the information is readily available. The latter authorizations, in contrast, are normally handled by the case writer directly. Once all additional materials have been acquired and quotes have been authorized, the completed first draft of the case is delivered to the protagonist for initial comments.

d) *Rewriting:* As a first step, the comments of the protagonist are incorporated into any revisions. After that, the case is forwarded to the authorizing executive and/or any staff (e.g., legal, public relations) who wish to verify case content. Any requests for changes are then provided to the case writer.

e) *Release:* Upon receipt of an acceptable version of the case, the authorizing executive will be given a release form to sign, which states that the case writer has been granted the right to use and publish the case in its approved form. In the event a case is not released, it is viewed as sensitive company data and cannot be used in class or be published.

5. What if I decide I don't like the case after it has been written?

If it has not been released, you are within your rights to tell the case writer to destroy it. If it has been released, and you have simply changed your mind, most case writers will destroy it if it is within their power to do so. If the case has already been published, however, there may be little the case writer can do. Under such unusual circumstances, however, it may be possible to rewrite or disguise the case in such a manner that it becomes satisfactory to the company.

6. What type of access to company data will I have to give the case writer?

In general, the case writing process goes most smoothly if you give the case writer the same type of access that you would give to any trusted outsider, such as a consultant. Always remember, as well, that just because you give the case writer a piece of sensitive information--such as a financial statement or business plan--does not mean it will necessarily appear in the case. In most instances, it is useful mainly to help the case writer understand the company situation. And, of course, should it appear in the case you can always ask to have it removed at any time before the case is released.

7. Can I ask the case writer for his or her insights as they relate to the decision that is the subject of the case?

Absolutely. Unlike research cases, teaching cases do not require that the writer exhibit passionless objectivity with respect to the situation being studied. For this reason, most case writers will be happy to give you their opinions on a given case situation (or on any other situation you ask them about, for that matter). Some case writers will even do what amounts to free consulting if they feel it will help them get the case released. In general, however, it is better not to mix consulting and case writing relationships while a case is in progress. At institutions like Harvard Business School, the case writing relationship in often a precursor to a consulting relationship. They generally take care, however, not to confuse the two by doing both at the same time.

8. Who will use the case study after it has been published?

To a great extent, this depends on how good it is and on who publishes the case study. Case studies published by places like Harvard Business School and Prentice Hall have worldwide distribution and are frequently used at 10-20 business schools. Some cases are also adopted for use in executive training sessions. Unfortunately, even experts have trouble predicting the success of a case study before it has been written and used in classes several times.

9. Can I use the case internally, or for external relations (such as looking for investors)?

Although case studies are normally copyrighted by the author or publisher, the case release form typically gives the company the right to make unlimited copies for its own purposes. Many companies use such cases as a convenient way to give new employees or financial partners some background on the company and its industry.

10. Given the amount of company time and effort that goes into writing a case study, what are the benefits?

There is no getting around it, participating in a case study will require a lot of work. There are, however, some benefits--mainly intangible--that often seem to accompany the case writing process. Among these:

- *By allowing a case to be written about your company, you become an active participant in the educational process.* While most executives complain that business schools are too divorced from the real world, those who participate in a case study can take pride in the fact that they are doing something about the problem.
- *A case study can establish or reinforce relationships with the case writer and the case writer's institution.* By the time a case is completed, you will have developed strong, and often enduring, relationships with the individuals who wrote the case. These relationships can prove very helpful when you find yourself looking to hire talented students or need advice on some problem that involves research.
- *A case study gives you a window on how you are perceived by the outside world.* Because the case writer needs to set the stage by describing the industry and the company, the case study necessarily paints a picture of your company as outsiders perceive it. In addition, should you choose to attend classes where the case is used--and you can count on being encouraged to do so!--you can often gain further insights from the way students react to your company based on the case.
- *Participating in a case often helps clarify the issues associated with a particular decision.* Because a case writer's main objective is to gather information relating to a particular decision, the process of deciding what factors are relevant to a decision is often more systematic

than it would have been under normal circumstances. In addition, any insights, information or expertise that the case writer possesses with respect to the decision are always available to the company.

Having said all these things, this case writer's experience has been that most companies that participate in one case are eager to "come back for more". When asked why, the reason they invariably gave was that they found the case writing process to be both stimulating and enjoyable.

Appendix D

Sample Case Release Document

The template I use for teaching cases. Often, it is a good idea to present this, or a similar document, to the key participant early in the process, so his or her sense of control over the process is reinforced.

Case Study Release Agreement between {Case Writer} and {Organization}

{Case Writer}, {Position}, {Institution} and {Contact}, acting as authorized representative for {Organization} in {his/her} capacity as {Position}, having cooperated in the development of the attached case, entitled "{Case name}", agree to the following:

1. {Organization} releases the case to {Case Writer}, giving him and his employer the specific rights to use the case for teaching purposes, to make the case available to other universities and institutions for teaching purposes, and to include the case in academic or professional publications.

2. Such release of the case by {Organization} is specifically not to be construed as an authorization to disclose information acquired in the case-writing process which was not contained in the case itself, and any existing non-disclosure agreements remain in force.

3. {Case Writer}, as the copyright holder, grants {Organization} the right to make unlimited copies of the case for its own purposes.

4. {Case Writer} agrees not to modify the attached case, except for the express purpose of eliminating typographical errors or grammatical inconsistencies, without permission from {Organization}.

5. All parties involved agree to hold each other harmless in the event that release of the case leads to unanticipated consequential damages.

In the event that any legal disputes should arise from this agreement, both sides agree to attempt to resolve such problems though amicable discussions or, that failing, through binding arbitration.

Agreed to by:

_____   Date: _____

{Case Writer}

_____   Date: _____

{Contact}

T. Grandon Gill
Informing with the Case Method
Santa Rosa, California: Informing Science Press.

Appendix E

A Tale of Three Classes

This case is presented as an example of a multi-case research design that employs both cross sectional and longitudinal strategies. The choice of this particular case was motivated by two key factors. First, not only does it demonstrate an unusual design, it also served to reinforce the role played by complexity in determining fitness. Second, because it was published by the *Journal of IT Education*, a member of the *Informing Science Institute* family of journals, it could be included without copyright or royalty concerns. To avoid confusion, appendices to the original article have been relabeled "exhibits" and references have been combined with the book's reference list.

A Tale of Three Classes: Case Studies in Course Complexity

T. Grandon Gill
Joni Jones
University of South Florida
Tampa, FL USA

ggill@coba.usf.edu jjones@coba.usf.edu

Executive Summary

The paper examines the question of decomposability versus complexity of teaching situations by presenting three case studies of MIS courses. Because all three courses were highly successful in their observed outcomes, the paper hypothesizes that if the attributes of effective course design are decomposable, one would expect to see a large number of common attributes emerge in the characteristics of all three courses. Instead, radical differences in course design and delivery are observed across all three courses.

To explain how such different approaches can lead to successful outcomes, the paper draws upon the concept of a rugged fitness landscape (Kauffman, 1993), first introduced in evolutionary biology and later applied in informing science (Gill, 2008), wherein high levels of interactions between entity attributes necessarily lead to multiple fitness peaks. To support the proposition that the courses described exist on such a landscape, the courses (and the evolution of their designs) are examined for qualitative evidence of interactions between characteristics. Looking at four general areas—the instructor, the course content, the design/delivery method and the students—evidence for the presence of interactions is observed. Thus, the three courses appear to confirm the hypothesis that the fitness of a particular course exists on a rugged landscape.

The paper considers how landscape ruggedness may impact research in the area of course design. Informing science research has demonstrated, for example, that when entities on such a landscape individually attempt to maximize fitness, they tend to cluster on peaks. As a consequence, statistical approaches to explaining entity fitness, such as multiple regression analysis and structural equation modeling, may vastly exaggerate the significance of observed relationships (Gill and Sincich, 2008). The huge number of potential interactions between characteristics in even small models may also require huge numbers of observations to perform such tests (as is commonly the case in medicine). Thus, qualitative approaches to understanding the course fitness may become the only rigorous tools that can be applied. Arguably such research is likely to take a very different form—both in terms of length and descriptive content—than much of the past research published in the area of course design.

Keywords: complexity, programming, decomposability, case method, research methods.

Introduction

Pedagogical research is unusual within academic research in that nearly all the researchers in the area are also practitioners, which is to say they teach as well as research teaching. For this reason, interest in the answers to the research questions is personal as well as professional. Will distance learning teaching be as effective as face-to-face techniques? Is the case method really more effective than lecture? Should laptops be allowed in the classroom? The number of questions that might be posed is essentially unbounded.

No one would dispute that research on teaching and learning can be challenging. After all, there are many variables that must be considered. Who could plausibly argue, for example, that factors such as the experience of the instructor, the characteristics of the students, the form of content being presented, the method of delivery and the setting of the class are irrelevant to learning? Nonetheless, often for causal relationships that involve many variables, the individual effects of specific factors can be teased out using techniques such as regression or structural equation modeling (SEM). In such cases, the underlying process can be described as nearly decomposable (Simon, 1981). Additionally, sometimes the interrelationship between variables is so great that such decomposition is impossible. In such cases, the relationship is complex. Where such complexity exists, the research strategy needs to be reevaluated, since an individual variable's impact on overall effectiveness can be highly dependent upon the values of other variables.

A particularly significant implication of complexity relates to the value of quantitative analytical techniques, such as those just mentioned. Recent research has demonstrated that, under the reasonable assumption that individuals continuously attempt to improve fitness, complex underlying relationships can produce statistically significant yet entirely misleading results (Gill and Sincich, 2008). Thus, the assumption of decomposability needs to be carefully tested prior to applying these techniques. At the present time, such tests require qualitative analysis of the process; quantitative tests for this form of complexity have yet to be devised (Gill, 2008).

The present paper considers the question of the decomposability of teaching situations by presenting a qualitative analysis of three case studies of MIS courses. The cases themselves are intrinsically interesting—all three illustrate innovative teaching techniques, 2 of the 3 were winners of the Decision Science Institute's (DSI) Innovative Curriculum Competition, and all demonstrated substantial evidence of learning and student satisfaction. The research also finds that by comparing the three cases side-by-side considerable insight is gained into the complexity of the relationship between teaching approach, course setting and outcome.

The paper begins by introducing the concept of a rugged fitness landscape, taken directly from a model proposed in evolutionary biology (Kauffman, 1993). Then the research design is presented, which involves a qualitative search for interactions across four key areas of the course context: instructor characteristics, content characteristics, design/delivery characteristics, and student characteristics. Each class is presented, with details provided in two appendices, and the key interactions that were observed are identified. Because the first of these courses—referred to as Ism3232.A—evolved dramatically over time, it is presented in both longitudinal and cross sectional terms. The remaining two courses—Ism3232.B and Ism6155.A—experienced relatively few design changes from the time they were first offered. Both are therefore presented only in cross sectional terms. By comparing time slices and cross sectional observations, observational evidence of high levels of interaction between areas is acquired. The paper concludes by considering how this evidence might change the conduct of future research into IT education.

Rugged Fitness Landscapes

The underlying model used in this study is the rugged fitness landscape, as popularized in evolutionary biology by Stuart Kauffman (1993). The concept of a fitness landscape is relatively simple, and its basic form—that some desirable dependent variable is a function of one or more independent variables—should be familiar to nearly any researcher in the social sciences. It begins with some value to optimize or improve—often presented as the dependent variable in a mathematical or statistical model—that is referred to as the "fitness" value. The remainder of the model consists of variables that can be controlled or observed which may contribute to fitness. For example, a linear equation, such as:

$$Y = c_0 + b_1x_1 + b_2x_2 + \ldots b_Nx_N$$

can be viewed as a very simple form of fitness landscape, where each of the N variables contribute independently to fitness. What makes a contribution x_i independent in the above equation is that the value of b_i does not depend on the values of the other variables (i.e., $x_1 \ldots x_{i-1}$, $x_{i+1} \ldots x_N$).

Interactions between characteristics are said to occur when the impact of a particular variable, x_i, on fitness cannot be determined without knowing the values of certain other variables. Where a very limited number of such interactions between variables occur, there are statistical techniques (e.g., using the product of the interacting variables as an additional variable) for accommodating the effect. As the number of variable interactions grows, however, these techniques become impractical. For example, if a model consisted of 30 dummy variables (i.e., binary variables that can only have 0 and 1 values) and they all interacted with each other, you would need to determine 2^{30} (over a billion) coefficients in order to capture every interaction.

In order to capture the degree of interaction in a particular fitness space, Kauffman (1993) uses N,K notation, where N is the number of variables that determine fitness and K is the number of other variables each variable interacts with. Thus, the two extremes become:

N,N-1: Every variable interacts with every other variable. This is sometimes referred to as the *chaotic* case.

N,0: Every variable exerts an influence on fitness that is independent of every other variable. Referred to as the *fully decomposable* landscape in this research.

The term *rugged* is used to describe landscapes that are not fully decomposable or *nearly decomposable* (where interactions can be captured with a few specified interaction terms). The reason that such a term is apt is that such landscapes will nearly always exhibit local fitness peaks—which is to say combinations of values where any change to a single variable value results in a decline in fitness. These peaks present a formidable obstacle to maximizing fitness since moving from one fitness peak to another (higher) fitness peak one variable at a time necessarily involves a reduction in fitness during the period of transition. Conceptually, navigating such a fitness space is like traversing a mountain range. By taking a path that always travels upwards, you are guaranteed to reach a peak. There is no guarantee, however, that you will reach the highest summit. Instead, you may find yourself at the top of a foothill.

A rugged landscape also presents a significant challenge to researchers seeking to apply statistical methods, such as regression and structural equation modeling, for purposes of hypothesis testing. In particular, unless one assumes that entities on the landscape are *not* trying to increase their fitness (e.g., instructors do not try to make changes to their courses in order to improve their effectiveness), entities on rugged landscapes will tend to migrate to peaks. This migration can, in turn, produce serious errors in statistical models that assume the landscape is decomposable (Gill and Sincich, 2008). Thus, before observational data from a particular landscape is analyzed using such techniques, it is critical that the assumption of full or near decomposability be verified. Unfortunately, little (if any) existing research into course design undertakes such an investigation.

There are a variety of types of evidence that could support the hypothesis that a particular landscape is rugged. These criteria include:

1. Highly dissimilar examples of high fitness can be identified; this would suggest the presence of multiple local fitness peaks across the landscape.

2. Incremental changes to fitness—resulting from manipulating the same variable in the same manner—are observed that differ significantly in different situations; this suggests that the variable's effect cannot be established independent of the val-

ues of other variables. It is also possible to observe large changes to fitness resulting from of individual variable changes, since interactions can effectively magnify the impact of such changes. For example, omitting the baking powder from a cake recipe may drastically reduce the fitness of the resulting cake, even though the quantity of the ingredient is small and its impact upon taste negligible. This differs from decomposable landscapes, where the impact of a particular variable is always the same and if many variables participate in determining fitness, the average incremental impact of each will be relatively small.

3. Fitness behavior in a particular setting that varies significantly from findings well supported by previous research; like the second, this suggests a situation-dependence that implies interactions between variables. (Throughout this paper, our use of the term setting is equivalent to "context" or "situation").

4. Sensitivity to small changes in variables. When a landscape is decomposable, changes in most variables exert a predictable (and usually small) impact on fitness. Where the underlying landscape is complex, variable changes can act through interaction and a small change (e.g., omitting half a teaspoon of baking powder from a cake recipe) can dramatically change fitness.

5. The researcher's interpretation of the fitness landscape, based on observation or experience, may supply a logical basis for arguing that such interactions are to be expected.

The last of these, combining perception-based logical arguments with observed data may be somewhat unsettling from an empirical research perspective. Traditionally, the assumption is that the needs of objectivity are best served when the characteristics of the observer appear to exert minimal impact on the observational data that are employed for hypothesis testing—an assumption justifying author anonymity and double blind peer review processes. Unfortunately, as previously noted, a high level of interactions between variables dramatically increases the coefficients that must be determined when standard statistical methods are employed. More coefficients, in turn, can easily raise the number of observations required to determine their values to levels that are impractical (e.g., tens of billions of observations in the case of 30 highly interacting variables). Thus, further progress is likely using techniques that allow for deep study of fewer situations, such as case-based research. In such methods, the use of many sources of data, mixed with a liberal amount of interpretation by observers whose expertise must be demonstrated, is encouraged as part of a process referred to as triangulation (Yin, 1994). Indeed, some of the most influential case research has relied heavily on researcher-interpreted analysis (e.g., Allison, 1971).

Research Design

The central research question being investigated is the degree to which the fitness landscape for course effectiveness can be characterized as rugged. As noted in the introduction, qualitative methods appear to be the only approach suitable for addressing this question at the present time. For this reason, a multi-case design—incorporating in-depth process observations—was employed.

Unfortunately, the five criteria for demonstrating ruggedness in the fitness landscape present a formidable research design challenge—since evidence needs to be gathered from nearly opposite sources. For example:

- Criterion 1 (existence of widely separated high-fitness peaks) is best served by observations that *differ from each other in a many ways as possible.*

- Criteria 2, 3 and 4 (variables that behave differently in different situations or which differ from widely observed behaviors) are best served by controlled experiments where *manipulations limited to a single (ideally) or very small number of variables are observed.*

- Criterion 5 (investigator interpretation) is best supported by archival data gathered prior to searching for ruggedness, thereby reducing the impact of investigator bias.

As it turns out, the cases investigated in the present paper simultaneously meet these criteria to a reasonable extent. The research described in the present paper involves three classes (representing two distinct courses) and two different instructors. Details on the instructors and classes are provided in Exhibit A and Exhibit B. The classes can be summarized as follows:

- **Ism3232.A**: A section of an undergraduate introductory programming course taught by Instructor A. Including the instructor's time at a previous institution (where the course had the same number and description), the course had been taught for over a decade. During the period from 2003 to 2008, extensive data had been collected through surveys and other means each semester, providing a continuous series of data points that could be used to assess the effectiveness of the course.

- **Ism3232.B**: A section of the same undergraduate programming course taught by Instructor B for the first time in the fall semester of 2007.

- **Ism6155.A**: A graduate capstone class for the university's MS-MIS degree program taught by Instructor A. This objective of this course was to help students in the MS-MIS program develop a greater appreciation of how business functions and MIS work together to determine organizational effectiveness.

The data that was accumulated from these courses was not the result of a research project. Rather, the research endeavor stemmed from the interesting—and sometimes seemingly inexplicable—results we encountered as the courses were taught over time. Naturally, the qualitative character of the findings presented was a result of process by which evidence accumulated. As Hambrick (2007) points out, however, detection and reporting of anomalies in existing data can lead to important additions to our knowledge even where the findings are not the product of theory-driven design. Thus, our goal is to explain the results that had already been accumulated, particularly where anomalies inconsistent with existing theory and practice were detected.

In looking for evidence of ruggedness, attributes expected to impact fitness were classified into four categories: instructor characteristics, course content, course design/delivery, and student characteristics. These categories were chosen because they map, respectively, to the *sender, message, delivery system* and *client* components of Cohen's (1999) original conceptual model used to define informing science. Here, the sender maps to the instructor, the student maps to the client, the delivery system (also referred to as the *channel*) maps to the instructional design/delivery, and the message maps to the course content.

Viewed from an overall design perspective, the three classes investigated varied by instructor and content as shown in Figure 1. The columns in the figure represent the instructor. Key elements of the background of the two instructors relative to their experience teaching the courses are presented in Exhibit A. The rows represent content. The two courses investigated, an introductory programming course taught to undergraduates and the capstone course of the university's MS-MIS program, were very different in their learning objectives. This fact, combined with substantial differences in the backgrounds of Instructors A and B, provided a diversity of settings suitable for testing criterion 1.

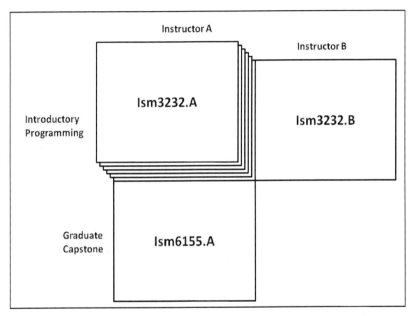

Figure 1: General Research Design. Instructor is held constant for two forms of content. Content is held constant for two instructors. A series of longitudinal observations hold instructor and content constant, while delivery technique varies.

The multiple boxes in the Ism3232.A cell indicate the presence of longitudinal observations. As previously noted, this particular class had evolved over time through a series of incremental changes that had been tracked with a comprehensive survey instrument. The evolution of the course and its outcomes had also been documented extensively in previous research (e.g., Gill, 2005a; Gill, 2006a, Gill and Holton, 2006). Taken together, these offered a plausible basis for testing criteria 2, 3, 4 & 5. Many of the major elements of the context of these courses were outside of the investigators' control. Notably, in the case of the longitudinal study, none of the variables observed could be controlled for experimental purpose, so we were constrained to using a natural experiment.

Probably the greatest challenge in this research was coming up with a measure for course "fitness". Particularly when comparing courses with highly different content, such as Ism3232 and Ism6155, there is no obvious way to compare the amount of learning that has taken place on any objective scale. For this reason, once again, triangulation from a variety of sources was employed:

1. *Instructor evaluations.* Although frequently disparaged as an indicator of student learning, these measures often correlate with other indicators of student learning (McKeachie, 1990). They also provided two other advantages: they were the only comparable measure available across courses/instructors, and—from the instructors' perspective—they were a particularly impactful measure of fitness, inasmuch as annual evaluations used for pay and promotion relied almost exclusively on these measures for the assessment of faculty member teaching performance.

2. *Course attrition:* For programming courses in particular, high attrition rates are often encountered. Ism3232 was graded on a letter scale, going from A to F. Grades of A, B and C were sufficient to allow students to proceed with the program. Thus, the percentage of students receiving D, W (withdrew from course) or F (failed the course) grades is a reasonable indicator of course fitness for such courses. In the graduate course studied, attrition was almost non-existent and almost no C grades were awarded, so the measure was not particularly useful in this context.

3. *Course performance:* For Ism3232.A, a fixed curve and fixed set of materials was employed for a sustained period of time (from late 2004 to early 2006). As a consequence, student grades and GPA data were directly comparable during this period and could be used as an estimate of relative learning across sections. When Ism3232.A changed format in Fall 2006, this comparability was broken, however. Similarly, direct comparisons between Ism3232.A and Ism3232.B could not be made, owing to different grading and testing strategies.

4. *Peer review assessment:* Reviews of course fitness by other faculty members. In this context, outcomes of two of the classes (Ism3232.A and Ism6155.A) were both reviewed extensively as part of the *Decision Science Institute's* (DSI) Instructional Innovation Competition. Less formally, Ism3232.B was evaluated by Instructor A during the semester when it was first offered.

While none of these measures individually can be viewed as a truly reliable indicator of course fitness, when they converge a strong case for fitness can be made. Yin (1994) advocates the use of such an approach as part of data collection.

Results

For the sake of compactness, results are presented in the form of a series of tables, subsequently analyzed in the discussion section. In parallel with this, narratives that describe the classes more fully are presented in Exhibit B. These should serve to further clarify the results tables and should also be of interest to the reader seeking to better understand the teaching approaches employed in the three classes, perhaps as a basis for adapting them for his or her own teaching use.

Fitness of the Three Classes

In order to demonstrate ruggedness according to criterion 1 of the previous section, it is necessary to identify multiple fitness peaks within the domain being studied. Proving a particular class represents an actual peak (i.e., the combination of attributes is locally "optimal") is likely to be impossible given the subjective nature of many of the criteria used to assess fitness, yet the three classes all demonstrated very high fitness and informally the term peak is used to describe any position in the region of high fitness close to the formal peak. Using the triangulation measures of fitness specified in the research design section of this paper, evidence of the fitness of three courses (using their December 2007 offering, the semester during which all three classes were offered) is presented in Table 1.

On all four dimensions of fitness, each of the three classes performed very well. As noted in Exhibit B, the student evaluations of the instructors for Ism3232.A and Ism3232.B represented the highest and second highest scores in the history of the course. The Ism6155.A evaluations continued a long trend of high scores for the course. In all three courses, student comments were highly positive. The DWF rate for both Ism3232 sections was under historical averages of 30-50% (see Table B.1 in Exhibit B). (The 0% DWF rate for Ism6155.A was fairly typical for MS-MIS classes, and was therefore less noteworthy.)

Table 1: Measures of course fitness

	Ism3232.A	Ism3232.B	Ism6155.A
Instructor Evaluations	• Extremely High (4.89/5.0) • Highly positive student comments	• Extremely High (4.79/5.0) • Highly positive student comments	• Very High (4.64/5.0) • Highly positive student comments • Most positive mentions in program exit interviews
DWF	< 3%	21%	0%
Student course performance	• Large body of content covered • High self-reported work load	• Large body of content covered • Strong exam performance	• High level of student interaction
Peer review	• DSI competition winner in 2007 • University teaching award in 2007	• Reviewed by Instructor A	• DSI competition winner in 2007

Student course performance was more difficult to assess across sections and courses, since the material being conveyed and instructional techniques employed were so dissimilar. Nonetheless, as pointed out in Exhibit B, the amount of content being conveyed in both of the Ism3232 sections was unusually large for an introductory programming course (e.g., at Instructor A's previous institution, the decision had been made to spread the same content over two courses) and the self-reported workload of Ism3232.A students was roughly twice that reported for other undergraduate courses in the MIS major. For

Ism6155.A, performance assessment was subjective, and was based largely on instructor observations related to the quality of work and level of class participation.

With respect to peer review, both the Ism6155.A and Ism3232.A had been reviewed as part of the DSI's Innovative Instruction Competition. The initial entry consisted of a 30 page report documenting course effectiveness. Three finalists each year gave a live 30 minute presentation before judges at the DSI annual meeting. Both of the classes won the competition, in 2005 and 2007 respectively. A document detailing Ism3232.A's effectiveness was also submitted as the basis for Instructor A's university award for excellence in undergraduate instruction, received in 2007. Although Ism3232.B did not undergo formal peer evaluation of this type, Instructor A—in his role as course coordinator for all Ism3232 sections offered by the university—did perform a thorough inspection of the course and, after previewing the course examinations, predicted average test scores far lower than those actually achieved by Instructor B's students. Given Instructor A's decades of experience in teaching the same course, the surprisingly strong performance of these students can be characterized as objective evidence of student achievement.

Collectively, then, it is reasonable to conclude that all three classes were high fitness offerings. In order to support the contention that they resided on separate peaks, the characteristics of the three offerings are now compared.

Characteristics of the Three Classes

The strength of the assertion that the high fitness classes occupy on separate fitness peaks will be determined by the degree to which the classes differ in characteristics (independent variable values, in the terminology of multiple regression analysis). To assess this separation, key attributes of the class offering are presented in Table 2. From this table, the following conclusions can be drawn:

- If an attribute has strongly different values across the three classes AND its effect is decomposable, then it does not materially contribute to fitness. This follows because, in the previous section, it was argued that all three classes seemed to be close to fitness peaks.

Table 2: Cross-Course Comparison, based upon Fall 2007 semester. With all three courses existing at high fitness levels, the fact that no attribute values are consistent across all three classes implies that the attributes are either of minor importance (decomposable assumption) or that their impact on fitness is through interactions with other variables (complex assumption)

Category	Attribute	Ism3232. A	Ism3232. B	Ism6155. A
Design/Delivery	Classroom Lectures	No	Yes	Minimal
Design/Delivery	Multimedia Lectures	Yes	No	No
Design/Delivery	Moderated Classroom Discussions	Optional	No	Yes
Design/Delivery	Paired Student Problem-solving	No	Yes	No
Design/Delivery	Student Presentations	No	No	Yes
Design/Delivery	Deadline Flexibility	Yes	No	No
Design/Delivery	Mandatory Attendance	No	Yes	Yes
Design/Delivery	Examinations	No	Yes	No
Design/Delivery	Outside Class Projects	Yes	No	Yes
Design/Delivery	Level of Performance Feedback	High	High	Low
Design/Delivery	Grade Subjectivity	Low	Low	High
Design/Delivery	Source of course organization	Evolved	Designed	Designed
Student	Student Level	Undergraduate	Undergraduate	Graduate
Content	Topic	Programming	Programming	Capstone
Instructor	Instructor	Instructor A	Instructor B	Instructor A
Instructor	Instructor Experience with Course Subject Matter	High	Low	High

- Since all of the attributes in Table 2 have different values, it follows EITHER that none of them has a material impact on course fitness (assuming that their effect is decomposable) OR that many or all of their effects involve interactions with other characteristics.

- If interactions with other characteristics are an important contributor to fitness, then the three classes do, indeed, occupy separate fitness peaks.

Given the number of the attributes presented—including many aspects of course design/delivery as well as instructor and content characteristics—it seems unlikely that most are not material contributors to fitness. As a consequence, the diversity of values in Tables 1 and 2 provide strong support for the presence of ruggedness, based upon the likely existence of multiple peaks (criterion 1).

The cross course comparison is most compelling with respect to peaks existing in the Design/Delivery areas. Evidence for interactions involving student characteristics, instructor characteristics and content characteristics are somewhat less compelling, since it is harder to identify specific attributes for classifying students, content and instructors. There are, however, some observations that can be interpreted as evidence for interactions across areas. For example:

1. The fitness of Ism3232.A and Ism3232.B in Fall 2007 appeared to surpass all previous fitness levels for the Ism3232 course (even prior instances of Ism3232.A). Both Instructor A and Instructor B attributed part of this to the fact that during the first week of class, each urged students to consider carefully the different designs of the two sections and to switch if they wanted a more self-paced (Ism3232.A) or structured (Ism3232.B) experience. Some switching (4 or 5 students) did appear to take place and, perhaps as a consequence, the small number of negative comments on the Ism3232.A organization—the only section for which comparative data was available—that were routinely encountered in prior semesters of Ism3232.A were absent. Such strong negative reactions can have a significant impact on overall evaluation averages (explaining the improvement) but would also indicate a significant interaction between student and design/delivery.

2. Instructor B's comments regarding her discomfort with the pure self-paced structure of Ism3232.A suggests a significant

interaction between instructor and design/delivery characteristics.

3. A number of students took both Ism3232.A and Ism6155.A, since students who needed to take a programming course as a prerequisite sometimes were admitted into the MS-MIS program. In their comments to Instructor A, they reported a very different reaction to the two courses—some preferring the former and some the latter. Since the instructor was the same in both courses, this suggests the presence of a two or three way interaction between student, content, design and delivery.

Longitudinal Analysis

As more fully described in Exhibit B, the evolution of Ism3232.A between Fall 2001 and Summer 2006 provides an interesting source of insights on ruggedness because, during that period, both instructor (Instructor A) and course content remained virtually unchanged (e.g., with the exception of adding a major assignment in Spring 2002, the same assignments and grading scale were used). Thus, variability in course fitness was necessarily attributable to changes in design/delivery, students and the interaction between the two.

As suggested by the variability of course evaluations during the period (e.g., see example student comments in Exhibit B, Period 1), the student population cannot be viewed as homogeneous. Rather, such variation seems to point to both student-instructor and student-design/delivery interactions. Equally interesting, and as noted in a previous study (Gill and Holton, 2006), some effects that have been widely observed in the literature—those between programming course performance and both gender and prior programming experience (e.g., Goold & Rimmer, 2000; Hagan & Markam, 2000; Holden & Weeden, 2003; Roberts, 2000)—were entirely undetectable in Ism3232.A. This falls under evidence criterion 3—behavior substantially different from widely reported findings in the literature.

Even more compelling evidence for interactions can be found when the evolutionary narrative (see Exhibit B) is summarized, as shown in Table 3. Over the 6 year period (from before 2001 to summer 2006), there were roughly three periods where a strong case could be made that the class had achieved high fitness (identified using the point numbers specified in Exhibit B). In comparing Period 0 with Period 2 and Period 6, only one attribute (online support through asynchronous discussion groups) remains consistent. (Moreover, by the time Point 6 had been reached, the degree to which these discussions were actually used had dropped precipitously from earlier sections, where several hundred postings per assignment were not unusual.) Thus, the choice is either to conclude that none of the conflicting attributes are material to course fitness or to conclude that they interact.

Table 3: Longitudinal Comparison of Ism3232.A sections

Attribute	Period 0	Period 1	Period 2	Period 3	Period 4	Period 5	Period 6
Classroom Lectures	**Yes**	Yes	**Yes**	Yes	No	No	**No**
Multimedia Lectures	**No**	No	**No**	Yes	Yes	Yes	**Yes**
Multimedia Walkthroughs	**No**	Yes	**Yes**	Yes	Yes	Yes	**Yes**
Asynchronous Discussions	**Yes**	No	**Yes**	Yes	Yes	Yes	**Yes**
Self-Paced	**No**	No	**No**	No	No	Yes	**Yes**
Progress Monitoring	**No**	No	**No**	No	No	No	**Yes**
TA support	**Yes**	No	**No**	Yes	Yes	Yes	**Yes**
Examinations	**Yes**	Yes	**Yes**	Optional	No	Yes	**No**
Fitness	**High**	Low	**High**	Medium	Medium	Medium	**High**

The adaptations that took place as the course evolved provided many further examples supporting the assertion that interactions between characteristics were material to fitness. For example:

1. Instructor A had the strong belief that student's should not be forced to come to class once they reached the college level. Attendance was never a problem in Period 0, however, since it was

nearly impossible for students to complete course projects without attending class, so they came. This is an interaction between the instructor and design/delivery.

2. When multimedia assignment walkthroughs were introduced in Period 1, completing assignments without lectures became much more feasible. Attendance fell dramatically, yet outside support from other sources (such as an online discussion groups or teaching assistants) was very limited. Thus, students who decided to take full advantage of the additional materials often found themselves isolated from the class when they were confused. This would be an example of a criterion 2 effect: adding multimedia walkthroughs would be expected to positively impact course fitness (or at least not hurt it) yet when interacting with the absence of a mandatory attendance policy—preferred by Instructor A but not by all instructors—it actually appeared to exert a disproportionately large negative impact. Not all students were thus affected, however, suggesting a further interaction between student characteristics and design/delivery.

3. When additional structure was added to the course, through a change to content (flow charting assignment), earlier oral exams and the incorporation of online asynchronous support, the degree of disconnect between some students and the course was reduced. The course then returned to higher fitness, confirming the previous interaction.

4. As more and more material became available through taped classes and, later, web-based lectures, the potential disconnect between students and the class again grew. With virtually no students attending classes, the decision to eliminate live lectures was made. This led to an interaction between students and assignment due dates. Students who were comfortable with the format handed in assignments on time and therefore received full credit. Students who had trouble adapting to the format tended to procrastinate and therefore had late points deducted from their assignments. This led to a paradoxical situation where the students having the greatest problems ended up having to do more work to get the same grade as students having an easier time. Realization of this led to Instructor A's decision to go entirely self-paced. Here, student characteristics again interacted with course design/delivery and instructor characteristics.

5. Although the self-paced format seemed to improve fitness with respect to retention (see Table B.2 of Exhibit B), it made it virtually impossible for Instructor A to ascertain the overall progress of the class. To rectify this, a progress monitoring system was implemented (a tool made necessary solely as a result of the course's self-paced structure). Providing an additional source of communication with students, class fitness returned to high levels. Once again, a three-way interaction (student-design/delivery-instructor) seems evident.

The structure of Period 6 was largely adopted for the cross-sectional version of Ism3232.A (Fall 2007). The principal difference was that a new department chair preferred that the multiple sections of the course have different instructors, so that TA support for the course would no longer be necessary. Instructor A therefore replaced oral exams to validate assignments with random block multiple choice exams administered through Blackboard—an interaction between administrative requirements and course design/delivery—and used the SCORM facility on Blackboard (which allowed student access to online lectures and readings to be tracked) to enhance the progress monitoring system. This represents an interaction between technology and design/delivery.

Discussion

Beyond the specific sections discussed, the patterns described in this paper are consistent with our observations for 12 sections of Ism6155 (from 2003-2009), 8 sections of Ism3232.A in its post-longitudinal form (from 2006-2009) and 6 sections of Ism3232.B (from 2007 to 2009). In assessing our findings, it might first appear that great deal of effort was made to justify a point that most experienced instructors would instantly concede: that many good ways to teach a particular body of material exist and choosing the "best" in a given situation is likely to depend on the characteristics of the instructor, students, content to be conveyed and tools available for teaching. Thus, the reader might well ask "what is all the fuss about?"

In fact these findings are more profound than they may, at first glance, appear to be. For example, if statistical analysis of observations from a rugged fitness landscape is to be performed, it is critical that material interactions between variables be included as terms (Gill and Sincich, 2008). In the examples presented, however, over a dozen different variables were used to describe design/delivery alone (and these variables would be far from sufficient for describing *all* design/delivery options). No attempt was made to postulate the variables necessary to adequately capture the attributes of instructors, content, instructional technologies or students. To imagine the entire course setting could be adequately described with even hundreds of variables is highly optimistic (e.g., over 30 characteristics have been proposed to describe student learning style alone; Gill, 2008). With so many variables, however, the number of possible N-way interaction terms (roughly 2^N for N binary independent variables) rapidly exceeds the number of atoms in the universe. Thus, these statistical tools become useful only where you can adequately predict all the interactions in advance. Here the ups and downs of Instructor A's Ism3232 in periods 0 through 6 are instructive. Even a highly experienced instructor, teaching a course that he had taught for a decade, was unable to anticipate many of the interactions that occurred as new technologies and students were encountered. Thus, in the absence of near decomposability, it is doubtful that useful models of effective instruction can be developed that are sufficiently robust to handle even modestly novel instructional situations.

Research Design Issues

The research challenges presented by rugged fitness landscapes have been previously outlined (Gill, 2008). These include:

- When a set of observations are drawn from the portion of the landscape associated with a particular peak, any findings only apply to that peak. Or, stated in concrete terms, what works to improve fitness in a particular course setting (e.g., Ism3232.A) will not necessarily work in a course setting that is significantly different in its characteristics (e.g., Ism3232.B).

- When observations are drawn from multiple peaks—and interaction terms are not explicitly included—the results will often vastly overstate the statistical significance of terms when tools such as multiple regression and SEM are employed (Gill and Sincich, 2008).

- The nature of the theory that can be generated from such landscapes can be characterized as "ugly", which is to say it will not be compact, it will not generalize well outside of the observations used to develop it, and it will tend to grow in size as new observations are incorporated into it.

For these reasons, different research strategies are likely to be necessary to effectively research such landscapes. A number of these strategies are evident in the present paper:

1. *In researching a rugged fitness landscape, it is generally better to focus on identifying and studying peaks rather than on acquiring many observations.* As previously noted, the compact and rigorous theory that results from analyzing many observations drawn from a decomposable landscape simply cannot emerge from a truly rugged fitness landscape. Instead, gathering many observations without an understanding of the landscape structure can easily lead the investigator to fall prey to statistical illusions (Gill and Sincich, 2008). Identifying combinations of attributes that produce peaks, on the other hand, can provide useful guidance to other entities existing on the same fitness landscape.

2. *Understanding the history of an entity can provide important insights into the structure of a rugged fitness landscape.* Entities on a rugged fitness landscape will tend to adapt in a manner that continually seeks to increase fitness. This may either occur as a generational phenomenon (e.g., survival of the fittest) or through a process of intelligent adaptation. As a consequence, studying the changes leading up to a particular state will often provide useful information regarding whether or not a peak has been achieved and what types of interactions are being encountered.

3. *Transformational, rather than incremental, changes may be required to increase the fitness of an entity.* The challenge for entities operating on a rugged fitness space is local peaks. Once a local peak has been reached, any incremental change—no matter how well intentioned—leads to reduced fitness. To move to a higher fitness peak, it may be necessary to transform a whole collection of characteristics at once. To motivate that change, a clear understanding of the target peak (see item 1) is likely to be required. What this implies is that research describing *how* to get to a particular peak (i.e., implementation descriptions) may well be more valuable than any theory that helps to identify what peaks may exist. This further reinforces the value of historical data that describes the process by which other entities reached the desired peak (see item 2).

4. *Desirability of replications.* Where a fitness landscape is decomposable, the best research questions tend to be original; replications of this research, in different domains, are expected to yield roughly the same answer as the (properly conducted) original research, meaning their contribution to knowledge is limited. Holes in the literature therefore provide the most fertile ground for new discoveries and many prestigious journals specifically refuse to publish replications of prior research. In a rugged fitness landscape, on the other hand, important questions need to be asked over and over again since different regions of the fitness landscape can yield very different results. As was shown clearly in the case of Ism3232, where five quite different high fitness combinations were observed—three of which had a common instructor and nearly identical content (Period 0, Period 2 and Period 6).

A rather dramatic illustration of how the assumption of landscape ruggedness can impact the amount of data and replications needed to validate empirical findings can be found in the case of clinical surveys in medicine—a domain where interactions between independent variables are expected and routinely encountered (e.g., the warnings on broadcast advertisements for pharmaceuticals). Consider, for example, the (seemingly) simple question "Is coffee good for you?" The question has been considered in roughly 19,000 different studies (some of which had over 100,000 participants observed over a period of decades) and has yielded a number of results of high statistical and clinical significance—such as a huge drop in the incidence of Type II diabetes among males who drink 6 or more cups a day. Nonetheless, the only uncontested conclusion of that research seems to be that more research is needed (Gill, 2008, citing Kirchheimer, 2004).

The form in which research is presented is also likely to be impacted when domain that is being researched is a rugged fitness landscape. As a consequence of favoring peak research over observation gathering and in light of the value of exploring the history of the observation, an in-depth case study is likely to be more useful than either empirical analysis of many observations or theory building involving the presentation of compact models. An unfortunate result may be an increase in length associated with such research, a common criticism leveled against case research (Yin, 1994).

Rugged Landscape Researchers

A further implication of the different approach to research necessitated by rugged fitness landscapes is increasing dependence on the observational expertise of the researcher. Typically, such landscapes involve hundreds of possible variables, some of which will have influence in a particular region and some that will not. In the classes discussed, for example, Blackboard discussion groups appeared to play a pivotal role in some sections (e.g., Period 2) and yet were almost entirely ignored in others (e.g., Period 6)—despite the fact that the topics, tools and protocols were identical in both cases. Only a skilled observer will be able to distinguish the relevant from the irrelevant. Statistical analysis is likely to be of limited use in such cases; frequently, new variables will need to be invented to capture new situations and the reliability of such measures will always be subject to question. Rather, they become highly dependent on the investigator's judgment as a source of rigor.

This dependence upon the researcher's expertise can become particularly problematic when studying areas related to learning. The demands of the research in these cases threaten both objectivity and anonymity. In virtually any educational setting, the characteristics and background of the instructors involved are likely to be important contributors to fitness. In higher education settings, however, there is a very high likelihood that any instructor involved is also a participant in the research and is therefore a co-author of any manuscript produced. Even in those rare instances where this is not the case, the reviewer is likely to assume that it is. Thus, researchers are faced with a choice: a) provide all relevant details regarding the instructors involved in a particular educational setting and risk the wrath of reviewers, or b) omit relevant details relating to the instructors and thereby potentially undermine the rigor of the analysis. This is not an easy choice to make, but it is an inevitable one if, as the present paper concludes, the domain of IT education is highly rugged.

Generalizability, Diversity and Adaptability

An obvious argument against the broader conclusions that have been presented is the appearance of doing the same thing was cautioned against: using research conducted in a relatively small domain (i.e., two types of courses and two instructors) to generalize it to a much larger domain. It is conceivable, since only a tiny fraction of the course fitness landscape has been explored, that this research just happened upon the one particularly rugged portion of the landscape, and that the remaining area not examined can actually be described as a smooth, decomposable landscape with a single peak that responds well to conventional research approaches (and attitudes towards research).

Actually, it is likely that the course fitness landscape was once far more decomposable than it is today. Fifty years ago, for example, it would not be much of an exaggeration to characterize U.S. business education as a group of young white males, largely drawn from the privileged class, being taught by older white males, of similar background, employing classroom technologies that consisted of chalk and, perhaps, a slide projector. Under such circumstances, one might well find that only a few course-fitness peaks were accessible—perhaps one for lecture-oriented delivery and one for case discussions. With so few peaks, research conducted in each domain might generalize well from one instructional setting to another.

Today, obviously, the educational context is very different. There are a blend of genders and a mix of students drawn from many backgrounds and nations. A similar transformation in the characteristics of instructors is taking place, albeit lagging the change in students. The range of technologies available for instructional use in the classroom has exploded, as has the range of tools available for use outside the classroom, such as computers and the Internet. A similar transformation has occurred in the number of topics that can be incorporated into business and communications curricula. The work of Kauffman (1993) is based on the mathematically derived premise that landscape ruggedness results from the number of elements in the system (N) and their degree of interaction (K). The changes of the last 50 years have contributed to vast increases in both. Thus, the landscape should be *expected* to be rugged and to grow increasingly so.

Although growing diversity may force a change in how research is conducted, such growth should not be viewed as undesirable. To the contrary, fitness landscapes involving living systems are generally not static. Rather, the location of peaks and valleys tend to be influenced by co-evolving systems (Kauffman, 1993). In IT education, these systems involve both business and technology. Many of the same forces that transform the teaching landscape—such as technological innovation and globalization—are increasing the ruggedness of these co-evolving systems as well. The problem with single-peak, decomposable, fitness landscapes is that they tend to lack the adaptability to survive major changes in how fitness is achieved (Kauffman, 1993). Thus, ensuring that collective teaching activities are widely distributed across multiple peaks may be the best way of ensuring continuing effectiveness. The need for research that explores these peaks in an impactful manner—e.g., one that encourages readers to consider adopting course design combinations that they had never previously thought of—has never been greater.

Conclusions

Whenever you teach a course, you are on a fitness landscape. Assuming you are motivated to improve your course—and nearly all of us who read this journal are—then you will welcome the insights that research can provide. If that landscape is decomposable, those insights can be in the form of a check list. Independently set each characteristic to its most desirable value and you maximize fitness. If the landscape is rugged, on the other hand, your needs are very different. To navigate a rugged landscape what you most need is a map that tells you where you are, identifies places that you may want to go, and provides some direction on how to move from one place to another in the least painful manner. The three cases that have been presented suggest a straightforward conclusion: that the fitness of a particular class is described by a rugged fitness landscape. The arguments supporting this include: 1) the existence of several high fitness classes with very different characteristics (e.g., classes reside on multiple peaks that were very different), 2) the presence of variables that appear to exert different impacts on fitness in different settings (e.g., the added availability of multimedia walkthroughs actually cause class fitness to decline in one setting), 3) the presence of fitness behaviors differing from those widely reported in the literature (e.g., lack of experience and gender sensitivity in one of the programming courses considered), 4) observed sensitivity to small changes, and 5) through qualitative interpretations of knowledgeable observers.

Given the small number of cases considered, it is reasonable to question the generalizability of these findings. Viewed in statistical terms, an N of 3+ is far from compelling. Yin (1994) argues, however, that it is often more appropriate to treat case studies as individual experiments, rather than as individual observations. How many balls, for example, would you insist that Galileo drop from his tower before you were ready to concede that large and small balls fall at the same speed?

Viewed in this context, these findings clearly support the conclusion that the landscape being studied is rugged. Assuming this finding can be replicated—just as you would probably want to drop balls from another tower, just to be sure—then you are faced with two possibilities. Either you happened to come across an unusually rugged patch in a broader domain that is otherwise decomposable or the domain is generally rugged. The latter is a more reasonable initial hypothesis. Only additional research can lead to conclusive evidence.

Were we to accept the conclusion that the IT education research domain is a rugged fitness landscape, existing research priorities would need to be carefully re-examined. Much of the research that is published today seems far better suited to a decomposable world. Empirical statistical analysis and conceptual frameworks are of greatest value when the findings are likely to generalize well to settings outside of the narrow domain observed. If the landscape is unlikely to permit such generalizations, research should focus on enriching descriptions of the processes encountered and the variables found to be relevant. If a variable's impact is not expected to generalize, it really doesn't matter that its impact on local fitness is statistically significant unless that same impact is also substantial—in which case computing the precise significance is largely a statistical exercise, since impacts that are truly substantial are nearly always significant in the statistical sense. Indeed, in the unlikely event there is *any* doubt with respect to the statistical significance of a *substantial* impact, it would be much better to investigate that impact further (using whatever qualitative methods are available) as opposed to ignoring it because it failed to pass the test.

In a rugged fitness landscape, it also makes sense to spend far more energy on understanding implementation processes since the decision to transition from one peak to another is likely to depend heavily on how much it costs to travel the path between them. It is remarked that much of the research in IT education has little impact—a comment that applies equally to disciplinary research (Gill and Bhattacherjee, 2007) into the co-evolving systems that determine what needs to be taught. Until research is conducted in a manner that is harmonious with the properties of the fitness landscape that is being researched, this deplorable state will continue.

Exhibit A: The Instructors

In this exhibit, key elements of instructor background are summarized.

Instructor A

Instructor A, who designed and implemented the Ism3232.A and Ism6155 courses, was a tenured faculty member at the time of the case. He had entered academia, after 10 years in business and the military. With respect to Ism3232.A, his programming expertise was largely self-taught. His first commercial programming experience came between his first and second year studies for an MBA at a well known case method-oriented business school. Subsequent to graduation, he developed a thriving computer modeling consulting practice until, eventually, he returned to the same business school to get a DBA in Information Systems. While getting his DBA and during subsequent academic postings he continued to program commercially while, at the same time, developing an extensive library of self-authored case studies. He also authored a programming textbook, published by Wiley (Gill, 2005b). That textbook incorporated many of the innovations used in Ism3232.A.

With respect to Ism6155, the case-method approach that was central to the design of the course was highly familiar to him. He had completed his MBA at a well known university that relied entirely upon the case method for that program. Prior to and in the course of completing his DBA at the same university, he authored numerous case studies and employed the case method in his graduate teaching.

Instructor B

Instructor B was an untenured assistant professor with a strong research record who had joined the department in 2003. Although she had a substantial breadth of experience in teaching MIS-related classes, both at the university and prior to receiving her doctorate, Ism3232.B was her first programming teaching assignment. In addition, unlike Instructor A, she had never programmed commercially, although she had created a large application using the C++ programming language as part of her dissertation. To help her prepare for the course, she chose to sit in on Ism3232.A during the Spring 2007 semester. Although Instructor A encouraged her to use all the materials that he had created for her own course development (lectures, assignments, draft text-book), she felt uncomfortable doing so. In an email to Instructor A, she stated:

> The current design of the course is very self-paced and deliv-ered primarily online. Remedial face-to- face lecture was pro-vided to assist those who need personalized help with various topics. I discovered that the current structure was not in line with my teaching style and philosophy.
>
> My teaching style is active and interactive. Although, the cur-rent course [Ism3232.A] was active, I needed a more structured set of interactions with the students.

As a consequence of these feelings, she decided that she would rede-sign her section of the course to fit her own personal style.

Exhibit B: Course Designs

Qualitative descriptions of the three courses are now presented. In the case of Ism3232.A, this description includes details on its evolution from a more traditional programming course, using the C and later C++ programming language, to its final form as a C# course.

Evolution of Ism3232.A

Unlike the other two cases to be discussed, Ism3232.A evolved into its unusual structure gradually, through a series of tentative introductions of elements. These are identified as a series of periods, each of which has represents either distinct characteristics or outcomes, summarized in Table 3 of the paper itself.

Period 0: Ism3232 at prior institution

The original course design, developed in the early 1990s was a traditional lecture course with exams and programming exercises. The first major modification to the course came in 1994 when a student—who had been receiving near perfect assignment scores and single digit exam scores—contended that his exam scores were not reflective of his knowledge. Although understandably suspicious Instructor A orally quizzed him on the material The unexpected result was that the student's overall course grade was immediately changed from a D to an A and the oral exam was made available for all other students as a means of compensating for poor performance on written tests.

By the late 1990s, Instructor A had made oral examinations an option for the last two project assignments in the course and allowed those project grades—if validated by oral exam—to be substituted for a final exam. By that time, nearly all the students in the course began taking the oral exam option—for those who did not, it was usually a consequence of not having completed the assignments. When individuals did not pass the oral exam, they received no credit for the assignments. They were, however, given the opportunity to take a second oral exam with the instructor.

Throughout period 0 Instructor A's course evaluations were considered excellent by the standards of programming courses, winning him the university's undergraduate teaching award in 1996. Retention rates were comparable to other MIS courses. At no time throughout the period were any doubts expressed regarding the effectiveness of the course. Thus, course fitness can be characterized as high during this period.

Period 1: Fall 2001

In Fall 2001, Instructor A joined another institution.. Upon arriving, he transferred over the complete course design from his previous institution, which was quite similar in demographics and a member of the same state university system. To that design, he added one major improvement: narrated multimedia animated screen captures that were supplied to students on CDs. These segments demonstrated the use of Microsoft's Visual Studio programming tool and walked students through some the course exercises. In a teaching case study describing the course (Gill, 2006a, p. 7), the results of the class were described as follows:

> [Instructor A]'s first... classes were among the quietest he had ever encountered. Students virtually never initiated questions and seemed reluctant to respond to the numerous questions... posed to them during lectures. Nonetheless, their median score on the midterm was in the high 50s, slightly above what he was used to seeing at [his prior institution]. Student course evaluation forms were handed out very early, in mid-November. The reason for this was that the last three class meetings covered topics not related to assignments—so designed to give students time to complete their last two projects—and [Instructor A] knew they would be sparsely attended. Starting right before Thanksgiving, and continuing through the end of the semester in mid-December, [Instructor A] administered well over a hundred oral exams on the last two assignments. The general atmosphere of these exams seemed to be quite upbeat, with relatively few retakes being required. It seemed to [Instructor A] that the students had finally gotten their act together— although he naturally wished that they had started earlier.

> When student evaluations came back in January, [Instructor A] was in a state of shock. His overall instructor rating average of 2.63 (on a 1 to 5 scale, with 5 being best) was so far below anything that he had ever received in the past that he initially thought he was reading the scale backwards.

Another remarkable feature of the course was an extraordinary variability of student reactions to the course and instructor. These ranged from (Gill, 2006a, p. 19):

> I thought the course was wonderful. [Instructor A] made information for the class accessible in many, many ways. The CD for the class is the greatest thing. I wish I had other classes like this one. My overall evaluation of [Instructor A] is perfect. I have not had a better teacher at USF.

to:

> Up to this point I am still wondering why this monster became a professor. He is a self-righteous person. He needs to go back where he came from.

Retention was comparable to other sections of the course. Some argument might be made that the amount of material covered should count positively in assessing class fitness. In addition, based upon his observations and many face-to-face contacts with students during the oral exam period, Instructor A believed that the low evaluations were largely a result of the evaluation forms being distributed more than a month prior to end of the semester—before the oral exam process began—and therefore may have been strongly influenced by student grade anxiety. Nonetheless, the low teaching evaluations seemed to call for an overall course fitness assessment of low, particularly when contrasted with other semesters of the same course.

Period 2: Spring 2002

Gambling on his belief that the course was fundamentally better than its instructor evaluations suggested, in Spring 2002, Instructor A modified the course in relatively minor ways diametrically opposed to the many student comments indicating that the course workload was too high. He added another project with a required oral exam to the course due just prior to the course midterm. He also set up a discussion board on the university's Blackboard course management system to answer student questions. The result of these efforts—which did not fundamentally alter course content or design—was an extraordinary rise in student evaluations between Fall 2001 and Spring 2002, from 2.63 to 4.47 on a 1 to 5 scale (Gill, 2006a). With comparable retention to other sections of the course and strong student demand for Instructor A's subsequent sections of the class, the fitness of the Spring 2002 class could be reasonably characterized as high.

Period 3: Fall 2002 though Fall 2003

During the period from Fall 2002 to Summer 2006, Ism3232.A continuously evolved while, at the same time, being buffeted by changes in MIS enrollments that echoed national trends. At the time when Instructor A had joined his university, in Fall 2001, the principal concern had been on how to deal with the explosive growth in MIS majors, whose numbers had swelled from the mid-200s in the mid-1990s to over 1100 in 2001, making it the largest major in the university's College of Business. This growth had two practical consequences. First, high retention was not necessarily viewed as an important contributor to course fitness; some faculty instead argued that Ism3232 should be viewed as a gatekeeper course, screening out individuals not suited for the major. The second consequence was that Instructor A's department chair had encouraged the development of a more efficient delivery system. In Fall 2002, Instructor A began holding lectures for his three Ism3232.A sections (with combined enrollments of nearly 120) in a TV studio for one section, with undergraduate teaching assistants replaying the tapes in classrooms for the other 2 sections.

During this period, course evaluations dropped into the 3.5 to 3.9 range out of 5 (a drop also experienced by sections of the programming taught by other instructors). DWF rates of nearly 50% were also comparable to other sections not taught by Instructor A. In addition, what roughly constituted a peer review of the course took place in the Fall 2002-2003 period, when a major publishing house agreed to use the course content as the basis for a programming textbook (Gill, 2005). As a consequence course fitness during this period could be characterized as medium.

Period 4: Spring 2004

By Spring 2004, drops in MIS enrollments had become highly noticeable and Instructor A became the sole instructor. During that semester, for the first time, Instructor A placed alternative multimedia versions of his lectures, as well as tutorial materials, on Blackboard. One immediate side effect of that action was described as follows:

…median attendance at the live lecture section had dropped to 2 students (out of 35) and TAs reported that taped lecture replays were faring little better. At that time, the decision was made to eliminate traditional lectures altogether (Gill, 2006a, p. 6).

In addition, because nearly all students were validating assignments through oral exams in preference to taking written exams, the decision was made to eliminate written exams altogether. Because of the large number of changes being implemented, and overall course ratings continued their gradual decline to the 3.2 to 3.8 range (on a 1 to 5 scale), Instructor A also developed and began to administer an extensive (250+ question) survey of student perceptions of the class, provided in parallel with the university's 8 question survey. To provide incentive for survey participation, a flat grading scale (i.e., no plusses or minuses) was adopted, with individuals filling in the survey (submitted to a departmental secretary, so as to avoid any possible impact on grading) getting a + appended to their grade. This survey, derived from 3 separate instruments developed under the auspices of the National Science Foundation, allowed a clearer picture of the course's strengths and weaknesses to be developed. On the strength side, students reported:

- Satisfaction with the course's flexibility
- Enthusiasm for the degree of group work allowed
- Great enthusiasm for the availability of online content and support

In addition, course performance appeared to be entirely independent of student gender and prior programming experience (the latter being highly diverse, with roughly 50% of the class never having taken programming before, 25% having taken one course and 25% having taken 2 or more courses). Both these results were highly unusual and desirable, since gender and experience-based performance differences were widely reported in the computer science educational literature (e.g., Goold & Rimmer, 2000; Hagan & Markam, 2000; Holden & Weeden, 2003; Roberts, 2000). The former, in particular, was also a source of great concern in the field (Sackrowitz & Parelius, 1996).

Less positive aspects of the survey included the fact that only about 15% of students anticipated that they would be programming at some point in their career, a general distaste for programming-related activities was indicated and the self-reported weekly work load of the course was extreme (typically ranging from 15-20 hours/week). While Instructor A was highly suspicious of the precise self-estimates, there was a consistency in ratios across surveys. Specifically, students reported working twice as long on the course as they did on other MIS courses and three times as long as they did on other business courses (Gill and Holton, 2006).

Table B.1: Retention by semester [1] (from Gill and Holton, 2006)

Value	Spring '05	Fall '04	Summer '04	Spring '04	Fall '03
Enrollment	71 [2]	79	34	93	116
Passing	65%	63%	68%	54%	50%
D & F	13%	20%	11%	24%	19%
WD	19%	18%	22%	22%	31%
DWF	35%	37%	32%	46%	50%
Completing class (count)	57	66	29	72	80
A grades	38%	33%	0%	17%	26%
B grades	22%	23%	21%	17%	25%
C grades	24%	20%	66%	36%	21%
Passing %	84%	77%	86%	69%	72%
D & F	16%	23%	14%	31%	28%

[1]: A chi square test confirms that the pattern of passing and not passing students observed across semesters is different from what would be expected by chance ($p \leq .05$). These differences are notable in light of similarities in the student body across semesters: MANOVA detects no significant between group differences in age, pre-university programming course work, MIS and software development work experience, or MIS and software development work aspirations.

[2]: For the purpose of the analysis, excused incomplete ("I") grades were omitted from the enrolment figures

Balancing the decline in evaluation scores was a gradual improvement in retention that began to appear in Spring 2004 (see Table B.1). In part, this was due to increased priority being placed on retention—since the department's principal challenge had rapidly changed from having too many majors to having too few majors. Making materials available to students in many different forms was part of this. Taken together, then, the overall fitness of the class could be characterized as medium.

Period 5: Summer 2004

In Summer 2004, Instructor A instituted two new course policies. First, he required a personal individual meeting with each student so as to ensure each student understood the course's policies. Second, Ism3232.A became entirely self-paced, with all late penalties being eliminated. Prior to that time, each assignment had a specified due date, with late submissions resulting in a 10%/week late penalty. The logical problem with this arrangement was it meant that a chronically late C student needed, by the end of the semester, to earn enough points for a B in order to get a C grade. Given that there were no set test dates— oral exams were given on demand—there was no logistical justification for exacting such a penalty. Moreover, with the drops in MIS major enrollments, there was a strong incentive to provide positive experiences for students and not lose those students by virtue of their either not fulfilling the requirements of the major (C grade or better), withdrawing, or failing—collectively referred to as DWF—in situations where they could ethically be passed.

The transition to a pure self-paced organization was not without excitement. During Summer 2004, with less than 10 days left in the abbreviated 10-week semester, only 2 of the 34 registered students had accumulated enough points for a C grade (Gill, 2006a). Instructor A's teaching assistants had begun to notice this phenomenon in early June (three weeks into the course) and, despite numerous emails requesting an explanation from the students, were at a loss to explain it. The bloodbath Instructor A had feared did not materialize, however. Instead, during the final 10 days of the course, the students submitted and validated sufficient assignments to pass. In fact, the 14% DWF rate for that summer was the lowest the course had ever experienced and the 3.9 instructor evaluation was the highest than had been received for more than a year. Moreover, these results were achieved without a single A grade being awarded that semester.

With improved evaluations and retention, the fitness of this section could be characterized as medium/high. Working against it was the weak overall student performance. This can be verified by the grade distribution not having any A grades, since the structure of the course's grading curve placed a much higher weight on the number of modules completed and validated than it did on individual project grades (which tended to be close to 100% for most projects). Thus, overall fitness might be described as a high medium.

Period 6: Fall 2004 – Summer 2006

Buoyed by the dramatic improvement in retention and the slight improvement in instructor evaluations, Instructor A decided to keep the self-paced design. Not wishing to repeat the uncomfortable feeling of imminent disaster that he had experienced towards the end of the summer, however, he developed a novel progress monitoring system for the course. Under that system, each week students could acquire 5 points (out of 1000 for the entire course) by either filling in a web-based form (at a link Instructor A provided) or by making an entry to a personal journal hosted on the LiveJournal web site—where students could sign up for free accounts. Instructor A also developed software that allowed him to consolidate Blackboard grades, weekly check-in forms and RSS feeds from LiveJournal automatically into personal progress summaries for each student. These progress summary reports were then inspected by Instructor A and emailed to each student weekly. After these changes, the retention gains persisted (see Tables B.1 & B.2) and, significantly, the amount of material completed the typical student grew. Instructor evaluations improved to the 4.0-4.3 range, comparable to other undergraduate courses in the major. Thus, fitness during this period could be characterized as high.

Table B.2: DWF versus passing grades, counts of students (from Gill and Holton, 2006)

	Self-paced	Not self-paced
Pass	119	108
DWF	65	101

$p < 0.01$ likelihood that self-paced and not self-paced came from same distribution, using chi-square test.

Ism3232.A: Final Version

By mid-2006, there were a considerable number of forces that favored making changes to the Ism3232.A design. Among these:

- The department's MIS enrollments continued to plummet (from 1100 MIS majors in 2001 to around 200 in 2006). With programming being a relatively unpopular element of the major, Instructor A had spearheaded an effort to remove a second, more advanced, required programming course from the major. That had, in turn, made introducing object-oriented programming in Ism3232.A important, since students might not encounter programming again in their studies.

- The 2005 version of the Microsoft Visual Studio tool used in the course had been released, meaning that online lecture and assignment content needed to be redeveloped.

Based on these factors, Instructor A decided to change the language taught in Ism3232.A from C++ to C#, the latter being inherently object-oriented, easier to explain and more supportive of MS-Windows programming. The last of these was particularly attractive to Instructor A, since it would allow students to create programs that seemed more "real world" than the text-based programming exercises that he had required of his C++ students.

Based upon his student survey findings—where a strong minority had always expressed an interest in learning how to program video games— Instructor A completely redesigned the course around a game-based metaphor. In addition, during the transition period (Fall 2006), he realized that he was likely to have little or no teaching assistant (TA) support, primarily because he wouldn't have any past students who knew the C# language or who had completed the newly designed exercises. For this reason, he developed a new assignment validation system which employed proctored multiple choice exams, delivered on Blackboard, as a substitute for oral exams (although the latter remained available upon request).

Another important change that occurred in Fall 2006 was a fundamental shift in how class time was employed. Prior to the new design, class time had revolved around a TA playing a recorded lecture (also available online) and answering questions. A fundamental weakness of this approach in a self-paced course was the wide range in student progress that emerged as the semester progressed. How interested would a typical student be in a lecture that related to an assignment that he or she would not be starting for another month? Perhaps even more significantly, how interested would a student be in coming in to watch a lecture that he or she could view from home? To address these, Instructor A eliminated in-class lecture session altogether, replacing them each week with:

- 75 minute interactive problem solving sessions, where the instructor posed problems to students who then attempted to solve them (using Tablet PCs provided to Instructor A through a Hewlett Packard teaching grant), after which the efforts were discussed.

- 75 minute help sessions, conducted in a computer lab, where students could take proctored validation exams or get help from the instructor in completing their assignments.

These sessions were optional, with attendance typically ranging from 15-25% of the entire class. An example of the software used in problem solving session, taken from an actual class, is presented in Figure B.1 showing student submissions to an assigned task.

The content for the course was selected to meet three key goals: A) to motivate students by presenting them tasks that they actually wanted to accomplish, B) to emphasize topics that would be of use in subsequent courses, including non-programming courses (e.g., databases), and C) to engage them in activities that would resemble the type of activities they might be expected to perform in an IT work environment. To meet goal (A), programming activities were designed around a game theme, with the three major course projects involving: 1) building a simulation of the institution's MIS major (designed around a fantasy game theme), 2) creating a Bingo player/caller application, and 3) creating an aquarium simulation, where the player needed to click on fish to keep them in a simulated aquarium. To meet goal (B), numerous topics from other courses were embedded into the projects. For example, the Bingo server incorporated programmatic links to an external database (highly relevant to the database required course). The MIS major simulation incorporated code to manage an embedded web browser (relevant to data communications) and media player (relevant to the multimedia design elective). Finally, to achieve goal (C), the course focus was on understanding and modifying large bodies of code (supplied by the instructor), as opposed to creating code from scratch. Such activities would be far more reflective of the types of tasks that an entry level IS employee would be assigned than would be creating complete, but very simple programs.

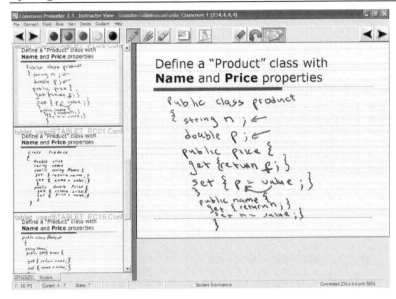

Figure B.1: Classroom Presenter allowed students to answer questions by writing on their Tablet PCs. Students submitted electronically to the instructor (see left column), who could then decide what answers to project and discuss (see right column, with instructor annotations [arrows], which is projected on the overhead without the left column being visible).

The results of the Fall 2006 were highly positive, as summarized in Table 3. In addition to the items summarized, student evaluations scores showed dramatic improvement on all 8 items. These positive changes persisted over the next 3 semesters. In Summer 2007, for example, the class experienced a DWF rate of 0%, for the first time in its history. In Fall 2007, the overall evaluation of the instructor climbed to 4.89 out of 5, the highest in the history of the course (and also the highest that Instructor A had ever received for a programming course) with a 2.5% DWF (1 F, in a class of 40 students). But in Fall 2007, another change occurred as well. A second version of the same class was offered, taught by Instructor B.

Table B.3: Results of Fall 2006 change to Ism3232.A

	Fall 2006	Spring 2006	Fall 2005	Spring 2005	Fall 2004	Spring 2004
Overall Evaluation (1=Poor, 5=Excellent)	**4.53**	3.94	4.13	3.38	3.88	4.00
Students Enrolled	**71**	70	77	86	82	91
Students Surveyed	**41**	28	34	39	36	34
Retention (% of A, B and C grades for combined sections)	**72%**	63%	61%	52%	61%	56%
Missing student % – Percent of students accumulating no points	**1%**	11%	13%	9%	10%	11%
Average grades of retained students (not DWF)	**3.27**	3.32	2.90	3.06	3.14	2.50
Average points accumulated (out of 1000) of students surveyed	**703**	725	640	713	681	585
Satisfaction with type of assignments (1=very dissatisfied, 5=very satisfied)	**4.00**	3.85	3.50	3.38	3.30	3.37
Satisfaction with multimedia content (1=very dissatisfied, 5=very satisfied)	**4.63**	4.25	3.78	3.75	3.75	3.66
Self-paced format (1=not helpful at all, 3=moderate help, 5=extremely helpful)	**3.78**	N/A (survey inst. error)	3.20	2.53	3.00	2.80

Ism3232.B

As Ism3232.A evolved and MIS enrollments plummeted, Instructor A had become the only faculty member teaching the course. By Fall 2006, a high priority of the incoming department chair was to ensure faculty redundancy for all required classes. Thus, he had requested that Instructor B teach a section of Ism3232, starting in Fall 2007. The experience of the section (termed Ism3232.B) is the second case to be discussed.

In developing her own version of Ism3232, Instructor B incorporated a mixture of elements, some quite traditional, some quite innovative. On the traditional side, she chose to use an established textbook (Deitel *el al.*, 2007), administer both midterm and final examinations (accounting for 40% of each student's grade), and enforce a strict set of deadlines for student work. In explaining her choice of textbook, she stated:

> …programming skills cannot be learned without spending a great deal of time experimenting with and writing code. I selected a textbook that taught the concepts by providing the students numerous examples and working applications that the students develop interactively using the various constructs. Each module contains fairly simple exercises as well as challenging tasks. I routinely choose a combination of these exercises as the basis of the labs. Depending on the students' confidence level I incorporate easier exercises to build self-assurance or more difficult exercises to challenge and extend their skills.

On the innovative side, nearly all instruction was conducted in a lab setting. Lab sessions would begin with a short lecture, followed by a programming activity. During the programming activity phase, students would individually complete problems provided at the end of each chapter of the textbook. Although the students knew in advance what chapter would be discussed, they did not know what problems would be assigned. Moreover, by about the third week of class—according to Instructor B—students determined that they needed to study the assigned chapter in advance of coming to class if they were to have any chance of completing the activity. Each lab was graded and the student's top 10 grades from the 12 sessions represented 60% of their final grade.

In explaining the philosophy that guided her course design, Instructor B made the following comments:

I believe that true learning occurs through exposure to, experience with, and reinforcement of concepts. It is essential that all three steps are present to ensure ownership of the knowledge being transferred. I emphasize the latter steps as they support active learning. Students are more engaged when they are actively, rather than passively, involved in learning. I therefore I chose to incorporate weekly in-class labs as a primary learning tool. I felt the labs would accomplish a number of goals:

Allow the students to practice the skills demonstrated in the text and during lecture.

Require students to stay on pace with the planned syllabus of topics. During my observation of the current course I found myself procrastinating and struggling to finish the projects at the end of the semester. Because of this I did not assimilate and retain the material as well as I could or should have. I was not incentivized with a grade for the class but feel that if I had fallen victim to procrastination some of the students would have as well.

Gain confidence and a sense of accomplishment by completing a functioning application with the instructor available to assist with problems. The labs were designed to be complex enough to be challenging yet be completed within the time allotted in class. The decision to stage the labs in class rather than as homework was motivated by a desire to prevent or reduce the frustration induced by hours spent trying to overcome a simple syntax error. By observing the students efforts in lab I would be able to provide guidance to possibly decrease the time spent struggling with a problem that a hint might resolve.

Prevent cheating. In-class labs avoid the opportunity for students to inappropriately collaborate or cheat on the homework. It is unfortunate that we must account for this possibility but the reality is that cheating is prevalent, especially at the undergraduate level.

For purposes of comparison, the lab exercises in Ism3232.B were very different from the programming projects employed in Ism3232.A.

Whereas a typical Ism3232.A project could take 3-6 weeks for a student to complete and involve the student writing several hundred lines of code (in addition to the hundreds or, in one case, thousands of lines provided by Instructor A), a typical Ism3232.B lab assignment—which normally needed to be completed in under 2 hours—would rarely exceed a hundred lines of student-authored code. Similar to Ism3232.A, many of the labs consisted of extending fairly complex applications for which some of the code was previously written. While Ism3232.A focused on completing 3-4 projects the Ism3232.B labs required students to complete 19 applications during the course of the semester. The core objectives of the two courses also differed slightly. Since this was an introductory programming course Instructor B's primary objective was to teach the core constructs of object-oriented programming. Namely, variables, memory concepts, algorithms, various visual controls, event handling, repetition constructs, choice constructs, collections and arrays, methods, and class concepts. Similar to Ism3232.A, the Ism3232.B labs reflected applications that could be encountered in a business environment, albeit on a smaller scale.

In assessing the outcomes of Ism3232.B, there is only a single data point—the Fall 2007 semester—where both instructors taught the course at the same time. Based on those results, however, the course design would have to be characterized as a spectacular success. Among the indicators considered:

Instructor B's course evaluation of 4.79 was the second highest in the history of the course (with Instructor A's evaluation during the same semester being the highest). The numerical result was supported by highly positive student comments. It was also above Instructor B's average for other courses, although that was also very high.

The DWF rate of 21% (4W, 1F out of 24) was well below the historical course average.

Student performance on examinations indicated a high level of comprehension.

The last of these assertions is supported by Instructor A's own observations of the Ism3232.B exams. Prior to the administration of the Ism3232.B Fall 2007 midterm, he inspected the test that Instructor B had developed. Based upon the difficulty of the test and his extensive experience with undergraduate programming students, he confidently predicted a median of around 40% with somewhere around 20% of the class scoring at the level of random guessing. The actual exam results forced him to eat his words. With a median of nearly 80%, he conceded that Instructor B's students had scored substantially higher than his own students would have.

Ism6155.A

The final case to be considered is that of Ism6155.A, Enterprise Information Systems, the capstone course for the department's MS-MIS program. The course was introduced in Fall 2002 and its basic design remains unchanged to the present day. Combining many innovative aspects, in 2005 it won the DSI Innovative Curriculum Competition. Because the class was taught by Instructor A, including it in the analysis allows us to explore the relationship between instructor and course design.

Ism6155.A was organized around three activity streams: case discussions, debates, and a multi-semester research project. Although use of the case method in business education could hardly be described as ground breaking, the course introduced a number of new variations. These include: a) an instructor-developed case detailing a classroom uprising to introduce the case method to students, b) incorporating a classroom response system into case discussions, and c) experimenting with three different modes of discussion: classroom, asynchronous online, and synchronous online.

The debate pedagogy, nearly absent from the business education literature, facilitated focused discussions on topics of current interest. Topics were loosely synchronized with the cases being discussed, and each week about one third of the class was assigned to the panel—presenting the pro and con sides prior to opening the debate to general class discussion. Although students were given some choice regarding what topics they would prefer to present as panelists, they are given no choice of side—often forcing them to look at issues from new perspectives. A research project required each student to trace the evolution of two strategic information systems, chosen from an instructor-developed list, that were introduced somewhere between the late 1970s and early 1990s.

The project activity was intended to build research skills and foster an appreciation for how MIS has evolved. Over a scheduled three year period, each system was researched at least three times (using a data gathering instrument designed by the instructor). The ultimate goal of the project was to establish system histories sufficiently rigorous so as to be useful to the MIS community. A more complete description of the course can be found in Gill (2006b).

The case for the effectiveness of Ism6155.A was presented in the 2005 DSI competition entry, which stated identified the following indicators of effectiveness:

- *Student evaluations* of the course and instructor are far above college averages. The most recent set of evaluations [Fall 2004], with a 74% response rate, awarded both the course and the instructor perfect (5/5) scores—an event so noteworthy the department chair circulated a memo to the faculty.

- *High quality of student-prepared work*, with both debate preparation and research papers far exceeding the instructor's original expectations. Anecdotally, it is a rare debate where the instructor does not learn something material about the topic. Also, one manuscript—written by a doctoral student and inspired by observations made in project reports—is already under review.

- *High levels of effort*, with students reporting spending more time on the course than on their average MS course. By way of supporting evidence, the Fall 2004 consolidated research logs of 18 students came to 309 single-spaced pages (when imported into MS-Word).

- *End-of-semester survey items relating to course design* not only show students are satisfied with each course activity, but also show complete lack of consensus regarding any alternative design direction.

- *Enthusiastic participation in course activities*, such as the online class day—offered up by the instructor as a possible voluntary activity in late January 2005. (Amazingly, 17 of 19 students surveyed anonymously afterwards opted for a second online day, despite the extra effort required).

Appendix F

DSI 2005 Competition Entry

To illustrate how case studies can be blended with other content elements in a course design, I have included the summary section of my entry to the *Decision Science Institute's* **Innovative Instruction** competition in 2005. The course was selected as one of three finalists that year, and went on to win the competition.

Ism6155 Design: Summary Section

a. Topic or Problem

The approach being presented involves the redesign of ISM-6155 (Enterprise Information Systems Management), the capstone course in a fairly technical Master's of MIS program offered at a large, public, U.S. university. The intended role of the redesigned course was to help students tie together the knowledge acquired in previous, more specialized, courses in the program. It was also hoped that such a course might stimulate interest in further (doctoral-level) study for some of the strongest students.

Over the years prior to the redesign, two fundamentally different approaches to the course had been tried. The first, to which the course owes its name, took a technical perspective—with the stated course focus being enterprise requirements planning (ERP) systems. That perspective led to course content that was highly specialized in nature (as opposed to serving to tie together diverse strands from previous courses) and it proved to be extremely difficult to staff with terminally-qualified faculty once the original designer left. The subsequent design was a lecture-based survey course. While offering an appropriate degree of breadth, course content and delivery closely paralleled that of the introductory MIS course—leading to student questions regarding its incremental benefits. Thus, at the time of the redesign presented here (Fall 2003), the possibility of dropping the capstone requirement altogether was being considered.

b. Level of Students

Students are typically MS-MIS candidates in the final semester of the program, which is offered by a large, public, Research I, university in the U.S. Over 50% work full time, and roughly 50% are international students. Student ages range from late-20s to early-60s, with commensurate diversity in work experience.

c. Number of Students

The course is offered during the spring and fall semesters. Currently, 72 students have taken the redesigned course (21-Fall 2003, 32-Spring 2004, 19-Fall 2004), with another 26 currently enrolled.

d. Major Educational Objectives

As stated in the syllabus, the course objectives are as follows:

To ensure students leave the MsMIS program with:
1. An appreciation of the complex interaction between individual/organizational forces and technological issues in the development, deployment and use of information systems, with a particular focus on organizational strategy
2. An understanding of how events in the evolution of MIS have impacted its current form in organizations
3. The ability to articulate convincing positions with respect to some of the most critical debates in the field of IT today
4. Familiarity with some of the types of activities that constitute MIS research

---

Superimposed upon these specific objectives are a series of more general, pedagogical goals. Foremost among these is enhancing each student's communications skills—in discussion, in presentation and written. Additionally, the course attempts to introduce students to a constructivist, active-learning approach to teaching—ubiquitous in some programs (e.g., case-method business schools) but uncommon in the relatively technical MS program. In addition, it familiarizes students with a number of technological tools for learning (e.g., infrared response systems, library data bases, synchronous online discussions), all having substantial industry, as well as academic, applicability.

e. Innovative Features

The course is organized into three activity streams (case discussions, debates, and strategic system research) which, collectively, represent 100% of the student's grade. Each stream has a number of innovative elements.

Case discussions: The case discussion pedagogy is widely used in business schools. For the purposes of the course, however, a number of innovations have been introduced. First, because the students—for the most part—have never engaged in the case method, the first discussion case used in the course is not an MIS case, but rather a case—written by the instructor—about a case method Executive MBA class that went into open rebellion shortly after its first session. Discussion of the case introduces students to case method protocols and clarifies the expectations of the instructor, without resorting to the self-defeating expedient of lecturing students about what a case discussion is like. Another innovation, introduced in Spring 2004, is the use of a classroom response system (CRS) that allows students to register responses using infrared remotes. Each case begins with a 5 or 6 question multiple-choice quiz on the case facts, with the top scorer being announced to the class and sometimes (based on a coin toss) being given the choice of whether or not to open the case. A final innovation, introduced in Spring 2005, is the "online class week". During that week, three case discussions are conducted, each using a different protocol: 1) an in-class discussion, 2) an asynchronous online discussion (using Blackboard) and 3) a synchronous online discussion. The last of these is conducted using Elluminate, a tool providing a diverse set of useful capabilities that includes text and voice chat, shared whiteboard (for drawings or slides), online testing and private breakout rooms—all of which are used during the discussion.

Debates: Despite the lack of examples of debating being used as a teaching tool in business education, the instructor was attracted to the technique for three reasons: 1) prior experience had convinced him that conducting more than one case discussion during a 3-hour night class session resulted in a considerable decline in discussion intensity, 2) the analytical skills involved in debating seemed similar to those associated with case discussions, and 3) although debates offered the opportunity for students to make presentations, they were also an activity that could involve the entire class.

The instructor's protocol begins with creating a list of 9 or 10 topics each semester. A topic is generally expressed as a short statement, such as:

> **Resolved:** *Within 50 years, we can expect to see information technologies capable of the same type of flexible, common sense reasoning that humans alone are capable of today.*

Each student is required to sign up for 3 topics. Once groups have been formed for each topic, members are assigned—at random—to the Pro and Con sides, with one student also being assigned to the moderator role. No allowance for student preferences is considered when making these assignments. Indeed, students frequently find themselves arguing against a position they strongly favor. At least a week before each debate, the moderator posts a 1 to 3 page briefing paper to a forum on Blackboard that defines specific questions to be addressed. From that point until the day of the debate, the pro and con teams post the references they intend to use on Blackboard, for everyone in the class to see (including the opposing side).

In class, each debate begins with a survey of opinions on the debate, conducted using the CRS with summary results displayed to all students. An instructor-developed five question multiple-choice test on the contents of the moderator's briefing paper is then administered to the entire class—not just panelists. The moderator then gives a short (~5 minute) introduction to the topic, followed by short presentations by the pro and con sides, after which the moderator (assisted, when needed, by the instructor) leads a discussion between panelists and the class as a whole. At the conclusion of the debate, the opinion survey (conducted at the beginning of the session) is repeated. No attempt to announce a "winning team" is made. The reasoning here is to avoid creating incentives that could lead to "gaming" the system (e.g., withholding key references from the opposing team until minutes before class begins).

During online class day, a synchronous online debate is also conducted—run by a student moderator trained to use Elluminate by the instructor.

Strategic Systems Research Project: The strategic systems research project is another technique developed specifically for the course. The project revolves around fostering a deeper understanding of the nature of "strategic information systems"—not just for the students in the class, but for the MIS community at large.

The role played by each individual student in the project is to choose two such systems (drawn from a list of over a hundred systems compiled by the instructor and a doctoral student) then to:

a) classify them according to schemes developed in references provided by the instructor, and

b) trace their impact to the present day.

The project differs from a traditional masters-level class paper in a number of ways. First, each paper is intended to be part of a larger research project that will ultimately become an online database made available to the MIS research community, as well as being the principal source for a number of research papers detailing the project's findings. Second, to ensure rigor, the research is being carried on across multiple semesters. In Spring 2005, for example, each student is required to research two systems. The first is researched from scratch (usually replicating a student project from a previous semester). For the second system, the student compiles (and reconciles, if necessary) the two reports already written in previous semesters. Third, the principal grading activity on these reports occurs more than a month before the final drafts are due. The objective here is to get students to respond to comments (a doctoral student and the instructor both review and comment each submission), much the way an author responds to reviewer comments during the manuscript submission process. Finally, rather than having students write a free form paper, they are given a structured questionnaire to fill out and they are required to keep an online journal of their findings, checked weekly by the instructor during peak project activity periods.

f. Content

In addition to the three streams previously presented in topic (e), some traditional course content (e.g., lectures) is also used in support of course objectives. Specifically, lectures intended to help students better understand the nature of strategic systems are presented early in the semester. In addition, each semester the instructor arranges to have students attend a 90 minute session—conducted by a research librarian and tailored to the strategic systems project—that identifies the location of the most relevant information sources (print and online) and highlights some of the challenges associated with researching historical systems.

Towards the end of the semester, the instructor gives a lecture attempting to tie together some of the lessons learned from the cases. Finally, students are invited to an optional session that discusses the ongoing findings of the strategic systems project that is held during the class's (unused) final exam time slot.

g. Organization

The typical semester of ISM-6155 consists of 15, 3-hour class blocks. These blocks are broken into two 75 minute segments. Normally the first segment consists of a case discussion, while the second consists of a debate. As shown in Figure F.1, cases relating to similar topics are grouped together, and debate topics relating to similar issues are normally scheduled for a week or two after the corresponding case. Lectures, shown in white, take place at the beginning and end of the course. A 90 minute period is also set aside specifically for filling in class-related forms, which include the university's course evaluation, the department's exit survey for MS-MIS students, and the instructor's own data gathering instrument. Finally, content with strong ethical considerations and global management implications is spread uniformly throughout the semester.

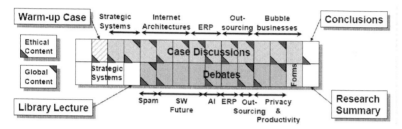

FigureF.1: Sequence of course topics

h. Presentation

The DSI competition's description for this topic begins: "Discuss how you designed the explanation and illustration of the material or content..." The most direct response to this would be "not applicable". The design of the course, built around the principles of constructivist, participant-centered learning, ensures that little material or illustrative content is actually "designed". Instead, what has been designed is the process for fostering learning activities—principally through the innovations discussed in topic (e). To make a musical analogy, the instructor's role is in the course is best viewed as being that of conductor, rather than performer or composer.

i. Effectiveness

The redesigned course has not been running long enough to provide definitive evidence of its effectiveness (e.g., reports from former students on the relevance of the material), nor is subsequent course performance available for a capstone course. Nonetheless, evidence from a variety of sources suggests high effectiveness. Among these:

- *Student evaluations* of the course and instructor are far above college averages. The most recent set of evaluations, with a 74% response rate, awarded both the course and the instructor perfect (5/5) scores—an event so noteworthy the department chair circulated a memo to the faculty.

- *High quality of student-prepared work*, with both debate preparation and research papers far exceeding the instructor's original expectations. Anecdotally, it is a rare debate where the instructor does not learn something material about the topic. Also, one manuscript—written by a doctoral student and inspired by observations made in project reports—is already under review.

- *High levels of effort*, with students reporting spending more time on the course than on their average MS course. By way of supporting evidence, the Fall 2004 consolidated research logs of 18 students came to 309 single-spaced pages (when imported into MS-Word).

- *End-of-semester survey items relating to course design* not only show students are satisfied with each course activity, but also show complete lack of consensus regarding any alternative design direction.

- *Enthusiastic participation in course activities*, such as the online class day—offered up by the instructor as a possible voluntary activity in late January 2005. (Amazingly, 17 of 19 students surveyed anonymously afterwards opted for a second online day, despite the extra effort required).

j. Transferability

The protocols developed for the current course appear to be highly transferable along two dimensions. First, there is nothing in the protocols devised for the course that is MIS dependent. Thus, any discipline where the case method can be used effectively would seem to be a reasonable candidate. Suitable debate or research topics, specific to the field, can be chosen by the instructor or—even better—identified based upon student input (in the constructivist tradition).

The second dimension of transferability is to distance learning. The instructor's experience with the online class day (admittedly, a regrettably small sample) suggests that case discussions and debates can move online relatively seamlessly—given the proper IT tools. In addition, resources required for research projects are increasingly available online at universities supporting strong research libraries. The implication, then, is that such a design can be moved online with only modest modifications.

Appendix G

EMBA 2002 Case Series

I lead off most case method courses that I teach with the EMBA (A) case so as to provide students with an introduction to the case method that does not involve me lecturing them.

EMBA 2002 (A)[1]

Dr. Grandon Gill, Associate Professor of Information Systems & Decision Sciences at the University of South Florida, was very concerned. Within three days of his first class meeting in a course being given to the university's Executive MBA program, the director of the program had forwarded to him two email messages from students that complained about virtually every aspect of the course (see Exhibit 1). In addition, he had become involved in an e-mail exchange with another student that appeared to suggest similar dissatisfaction (see Exhibit 2). Since the class consisted of only 20 students, even three e-mail messages represented a significant percentage of the class. Furthermore, Dr. Gill felt it was unlikely that these individuals had acted alone. Thus, in single morning of lectures, it appeared that he had angered a large minority, if not the majority, of the class.

Gill felt he had a number of options available to him for dealing with the situation. First, of course, was to act as if nothing had happened. The most likely result of doing so would be poor course evaluations at the end of the semester. Since Gill was tenured, however, the main practical import of such evaluations would likely be that he would not be invited back to teach the EMBA again—which hardly seemed like a "worst case" scenario, given the present happenings. At the other extreme, he could completely redesign the course: relying on more in-class case studies, drastically reducing the outside workload, and changing the curve to reflect the "norm" of EMBA grading practices, which appeared to be giving mainly, if not entirely, A grades. Gill felt sure that this would mollify the students and, given his extensive past experience using the case method, might even lead to a high level of group satisfaction.

Two important factors complicated the decision. First, the course being taught consisted of only seven 4-hour sessions that met weekly. That

---

meant that any delay in deciding could lead to nearly a third of the course being completed prior to its redesign being finalized. Second, the primary pedagogical tool being used in the course was the case method. For such a method to be successful, considerable "buy in" among participants was required. Without such "buy in", what was supposed to be active learning degenerated into "lecturing via the case method"—negating nearly all the benefits the method was presumed to offer.

As he stared into his computer screen at the two e-mail messages, Gill muttered: "Why did they ask me to teach in this program, anyway?"

Grandon Gill

Grandon Gill had a varied background that strongly impacted his teaching styles and pedagogy. He had completed the requirements for his undergraduate degree from Harvard College at the age of 19 in Applied Mathematics and Economics in 1975. He then joined the U.S. Navy, where he served as a nuclear trained submarine officer. With the eighteen hour days and two-and-a-half month patrols, he unequivocally stated that the experience was, by far, the toughest job he ever had. He also conceded that he was, at best, mediocre in that particular career. The nature of the job, emphasizing strict adherence to complex procedures—creativity is bad when you're trying to keep a nuclear reactor running (and safe)—simply did not suit his temperament.

When he enrolled at Harvard Business School's (HBS) MBA program in 1980, Gill was determined to have a bit of fun, to make up for the previous five years. As a result, he set modest academic goals for himself, targeting the middle of his class—roughly the same as his standing as an undergraduate. This was a decided contrast to nearly all his classmates, who were either worried about passing or were envisioning themselves at the top of the class, in about a 50-50 split.

During his first week of the program, Gill quickly discovered that he had a special kinship with the case method, as employed at HBS. The first day of class, each student was assigned to one of ten 80-person cohorts, referred to as a section. For the remainder of the first year, each student took all of his or her classes with that section. Whereas many of his classmates dreaded the need to speak up in front of the section, Gill found he relished the opportunity. Indeed, by the end of the first week, all concerns about whether he could make pass the program had vanished. Instead, he felt completely comfortable tossing in irreverent comments, taking sides of arguments that were diametrically opposed to his actual views, and, generally having the time of his life with the process.

Largely as a consequence his total lack of anxiety about anything he said in class, Gill's performance in the MBA program that far exceeded his goals. The HBS program was graded on a very strict curve, with 10-15% getting E (excellent), 70-80% getting S (satisfactory), and 10-15% getting LP (low pass). Variations from this curve for an individual first year course were not allowed, except through a vote of the full faculty. Naturally, this meant that such variations never happened. By the end of his two years in the program, Gill had amassed 21 credits of E and 6 credits of S, placing him within the top 2% of his class and leading him to be named a "Baker Scholar", after the individual who provided the donation that founded the school.

Upon leaving the school, Gill pursued a number of entrepreneurial ambitions and also served as the senior vice president of an agribusiness consulting firm that had been founded by one of his professors. While in this capacity, between (and during) his consulting assignments, he was asked by that professor to write some cases for use at HBS. Gill enjoyed the case-writing process and found his cases to be well received. In fact, one of his first cases (Cape Cod Potato Chips) was used as the lead-off case for the Agribusiness courses offered at HBS and at Harvard's Kennedy School of Government for nearly 20 years. Despite his success in the consulting arena, and a strong entrepreneurial bent, Gill found that he missed the type of interaction he had experienced back in the MBA program. He also found that he had a growing interest in computer modeling, but lacked even rudimentary programming skills. As a consequence, he decided to change directions in his career, and entered the HBS doctoral program in information systems.

While working on his doctorate, Gill soon realized that business research was entirely different from case-writing and, even at HBS, such activities were not viewed as serious research. Indeed, much of the case writing at HBS was left to doctoral students—which turned out to be the part of the program he most enjoyed. Moreover, even those schools that did reward case writing, such as HBS, were starting to de-emphasize it, perhaps in order to achieve the more mainstream academic recognition that came with refereed journal articles. Thus, when it came time for him to decide where he was to go, he ignored strongly stated counsel of his advisor that he join a research-focused institution and, instead, considered only those schools that met three main criteria: a balance in assignments that favored teaching over research, the opportunity to teach both technical (e.g., programming) and managerial (e.g., case study) courses, and a location that his family could be happy with. Using those criteria, in 1991 he selected Florida Atlantic University, in Boca Raton, as his first academic posting.

The Case Method: "HBS Style"

The case method, as a pedagogical device, made its debut in the early twentieth century. HBS was almost entirely responsible for tailoring it to the purpose of educating managers and, as practiced there, remains a mixture of formula and art. The typical HBS teaching case has a body of 7-15 pages of single-spaced, 11 point text. It will also have a number of exhibits, on separate pages, at the end of the case. It is normally organized into sections, the first being an introductory section outlining the problem to be addressed, followed by a series of sections providing necessary background (e.g., industry, product, company) and, finally, concludes with a section that explores the problem to be addressed in greater detail. Although not every case follows this formula, the best tend to—because the purpose of a teaching case is to stimulate active discussion, not to serve as a vehicle for lecturing about some particular organization's achievement or failure. Indeed, the front page of nearly every HBS case includes a footnote stating: "[this case was prepared] as the basis for class discussion rather than to illustrate the effective or ineffective handling of an administrative situation".

A case discussion, performed according to the HBS protocol, typically proceeds in 4 stages:

1. Preparation: Students preparing a case for discussion typically spend 2-3 hours in the process of analyzing and dissecting the key elements of the case. The active process of preparing a case is very different from reading a case. One of the advantages of HBS cases is that their length allows many extraneous facts to be included with those most relevant to the situation, which is much more realistic than the paragraph-long cases that often appear in management texts. The distinction between relevant and irrelevant is nearly always lost in a casual reading. Only through detailed study of the text, analysis of the exhibits (including "running the numbers") and careful thought can a case be truly understood. Some professors provide study questions to guide the students in this analysis, while others don't. Normally, a student's goal in preparing the case is to come up with a plan of action and an outline organizing their thoughts in the event they are called a upon to give the "dreaded" opening. Frequently, after individual preparation, students get together in small study groups to share their observations and analysis.

2. Opening: In a normal HBS class, e.g., in the MBA or in a graded executive program, the classroom case discussion begins with a "cold call", whereby a student is asked—without prior notice—to present his or her analysis of the case. During this presentation, the instructor stands at the chalk board and writes down key points, attempting to keep them organized.

The length and content of student openings vary considerably, as does the instructor's reaction to them. Some students attempt to present every case fact—relevant or irrelevant—as part of the opening. Seeing this, instructors will often cross-examine students to see if there is "a point". Alternatively, some students will simply make recommendations without supporting them. In such situations, the instructor may prod the student for more details, effectively administering a public oral examination on the case. Occasionally, a student is called upon who is totally unprepared to open. Such students may choose to "pass", typically earning them a sharp glance from the instructor, who will then move on, or the student may attempt to open anyway. Upon encountering a student trying to open without preparation, the instructor may choose to call for volunteers to "help him/her out" or may choose to grill the student without apparent mercy. The choice tends to depend on both the instructor and on the student involved. For example, most instructors tend to reserve the "grilling" approach for their best students (who, experience tells us, are every bit as likely to come in unprepared as weaker students), which accomplishes the primary goal of such intimidation (ensuring everybody comes to subsequent classes well prepared) without producing lasting anxiety in the hapless "victim".

3. Discussion: Once the opening is complete, the class continues to discuss the case, normally for about an hour. During this period, the instructor may either allow the class to follow its own path or may direct the discussion to specific topics. The best case instructors appear to do both, letting the class do nearly all of the talking, yet making sure that the most interesting aspects of the case are covered. Inexperienced instructors will sometimes take complete control of the discussion, calling on students one-by-one to answer specific questions about the case. Such an approach is disdainfully referred to as "lecturing via the case method" by case aficionados—who liken it to the way that case "discussions" are conducted a law schools, a serious insult indeed for the typical manager.

From the instructor's point of view, there are a number of challenges associated with teaching HBS-style courses. First, it is nearly impossible to surface all the issues associated with a given class during a single class period. Instructors feeling obligated to do so tend to begin lecturing early in the class, at which point active discussion quickly transforms to passive learning. Second, if the majority of the students in the class have not seriously prepared" the case—contrasted with merely reading it—discussion quickly fades into a series of "I agree with.." statements that add little to anyone's understanding. Finally, the instructor has to orchestrate the discussion while keeping mental note of who says what for the purposes of grading (inasmuch as jotting down notes while students are talking tends to make them very nervous).

4. Summary: At the end of each case discussion, the instructor typically takes 5-10 minutes to summarize the highlights of the case, reinforcing the lessons learned.

It is nearly impossible for an instructor to conduct a good case discussion without a detailed plan. Such a plan would typically include "must cover" points, "nice to see" points and "move on" points (e.g., topics that are likely to lead to nowhere). The plan also normally includes an expected discussion flow and, in some cases, an expected organization for the writings on the board. At HBS, instructors teaching the same course typically meet for 2-3 hours to discuss the case they are about to teach, in order to come up with a uniform plan across all sections.

Every instructor teaching a case class adopts, either implicitly or explicitly, a persona that they will use for the class. The persona reflects the "personality" that is to be used by the instructor in conducting the case. How he or she will make assertions about the case, question students, deal with bad openings, and so forth. Establishing such a persona makes it easier for students to decide how to react to instructor comments, when it makes sense to challenge the instructor, and determine what is important. Although many instructors adopt a persona similar to their natural personality, others may behave quite differently in a case class than in other situations.

Gill affectionately referred to his particularly theatrical persona for conducting case discussions as the "blowhard", modeled after that used by some of his favorite instructors at HBS. At first contact with his class he would assert his mastery of the case method, act as if he was the final word in academia, and threaten extraordinarily dire consequences for anyone who came in unprepared to open. During the conduct of each class, he would rush around the room, rant and rave when statements were not to his liking (and, as often as not, when they were to his liking, as well), and generally appear as if he was about to go over the edge.

Among the advantages Gill found in adopting this persona were: 1) virtually every case he could remember from his own MBA program had been discussed in a class where some version of that persona was used, 2) it ensured high levels of preparation in the critical early classes, where class norms were being established, and 3) over time, the class usually discovered that the best way to deal with a blowhard is to challenge him (when successfully challenged, Gill would quickly start to cringe and appear to become entirely deflated). Towards the end of a semester taught in blowhard fashion, there were few things that he could say that weren't subject to immediate scrutiny by the class. To Gill's way of thinking, this represented the essence of active learning.

Although it had proved relatively successful for Gill, earning him two "Most Outstanding Professor of the Program" awards in FAU's EMBA program, employing the "blowhard" persona was not entirely without risks. If students came to believe that it was his actual personality, as opposed to being in a constant state of guessing regarding how much of it was an act, some of the behaviors exhibited while acting in the persona could be viewed as highly non-professional. Gill always tried to offer humorous hints that all might not be as it seemed. But, sometimes, one or more students did not pick up on these. Gill suspected that this might be part of the problem in his current situation.

Executive MBA Programs

The goal of the Master of Business Administration (MBA) degree was to teach students the fundamentals of managing a business through a series of courses normally divided into business functions (e.g., finance, management, marketing, information systems) and special topic areas (e.g., international business, e-commerce). The requirements of the degree varied dramatically between graduate schools, from 2-year full time programs at institutions such as Harvard, Stanford and MIT to unaccredited degrees offered over the Internet. In most universities, an MBA consisted of a program requiring between 30 and 40 credits of coursework, once prerequisites had been met. Since many MBA students also worked, most regular MBA programs tended to be non-resident, with many courses offered at night.

Executive MBA programs differed from traditional Master of Business Administration (MBA) programs in a number of ways. First, they tended to be much more selective, particularly with respect to work experience, so that students who were enrolled came in with much more business experience with their regular counterparts. Second, they tended to be organized so that students went through the entire program as a group, typically over a 15-18 month period with classes on weekends, and had a designated program director who tried to isolate them from the administrative aspects of being a student (e.g., registering for classes) as much as possible. Third, nearly everyone in an executive program tended to be employed full time.

The combination of the three factors tended to make teaching EMBA programs both more challenging and, potentially, more rewarding than regular courses. As a result of the selectivity, it was not uncommon for EMBA students to feel that they were entering the program with more business knowledge than many regular MBA students possessed upon graduation—a feeling that was often justified. Similarly, between work and family, the outside demands on their time were sufficiently great that the students resented any assignments or coursework that they did not feel offered immediate value. Also, because they became quite organized over the duration of their program, they tended to be quite comfortable voicing their complaints to the director of the program when they felt something did not suit them.

Gill's previous experience teaching EMBA programs had been extensive, and generally quite positive. He began teaching during the second year of FAU's newly created EMBA program. The professor who had taught the previous class, using a curriculum very similar to the one he had used for his undergraduate business students, had been so thoroughly roasted by the class that he had vowed never again to teach in the program. Gill's case method approach, however, seemed to resonate with the class, and the following year the class gave him the "Most Outstanding Professor of the Program" award at their graduation dinner. The class that followed give him a similar award, "The Most Memorable Professor of the Program Award"—remembered particularly affectionately by Gill because the student who handed him the award (the top in the class) had been given the pounding of his life (by Gill) upon trying to open a case unprepared. A fact the student ruefully—and appreciatively—noted as he presented Gill with the award.

Although subsequent classes stopped singling out a single professor for an award, his rapport with the EMBAs continued. While he was teaching his third group, he launched an FAU case series and developed three case studies on local companies, all of which were then picked up for publication by Prentice Hall. Eventually, he either developed or supervised the development of ten such cases.

Gill's experience with his fourth EMBA class proved to be very different from the first three. The class itself differed from his previous classes in a number of respects. First, as a result of an accreditation requirement (brought to the attention of the accrediting agency by the director of a competing EMBA program in FAU's service area), they had been required to do more coursework than previous classes—a fact discovered while they were in the middle of their program. Citing the unfairness of this change, the students had been able to negotiate reduced workload from most of their other professors. Second, they were nearing the end of their two-year program, whereas all of Gill's previous courses had occurred early in the program, before students became quite as vocal and organized.

On the first day of the class in question, the leader of the EMBA section had raised her hand and stated:

"We've seen the requirements in the syllabus. Now what are the real course requirements?"

Not being aware that other instructors had been making concessions, and honestly believing it to be a joke. Gill had replied:

"They are what they are. Is there something I don't understand?"

What followed was ten-minute discussion of work requirements that Gill had finally cut off, abruptly. Given that he had already pared down the work considerably from what he required in his regular MBA class, he felt the discussion was becoming wasteful of class time.

The class had proceeded uneventfully for the next five weeks, albeit with an undercurrent Gill did not entirely understand, until a Saturday class day when he called on a particular student (a PhD in psychology) who was completely unprepared to open. Because, based on Gill's earlier experience, the individual was not one who would react well to a "roasting", he simply said "let's try someone else", and called on another individual, who did a decent job finishing up.

The following Monday, Gill had received a call from his department chair that the EMBA was up in arms, and some had appointed themselves to visit the director and demand that something "be done" about him. (Threats of a lawsuit to compensate for the embarrassment experienced by the unprepared student were also mentioned.) Given his past reputation in the program, the Director left the matter totally in Gill's hands.

The solution that Gill proposed, which was based on intuition rather than common sense, was to offer each student the following choice:

They could "opt out" of the remainder of the course participation requirement and be given an "average" participation grade. They would also be exempted from doing the remaining outside programming assignments, meaning their final grade would be determined by a final project or written case analysis.

They could "opt in" to the participation requirement, be required to do all programming assignments, get no extra credit and, as he put it, in his best blowhard form, "face the prospect of being harassed unmercifully by me during case discussions if you come in unprepared"

Both the program director and the department chair had advised the strategy was too high risk to pursue—since students who chose to "opt out" would have a workload substantially lower than that for those choosing to "opt in". But Gill felt he needed "buy in" if the case class was to be effective. The results were that 2 students (the PhD and the section leader) chose the "opt out" option, while the remaining two dozen in the class chose to "opt in", much to the pleasure of Gill (and to the surprise of his superiors). The remainder of the course went smoothly and Gill's anonymous course evaluations were very good—even though weighted down by 2 unknown students who marked him in the lowest category.

After his experience with the last EMBA section he taught, Gill chose not to do any more teaching in the university's standard EMBA program. Instead, he chose to focus on the university's newly created Environmental MBA program, also an executive program, where distance learning was featured. In deciding to leave the EMBA program, he joined a large group of other senior faculty members—the original advocates of the program—who felt that they were being forced to compromise their standards in order to meet the demands of the students. Pressure to reduce workload to levels far below the normal requirements for regular MBAs, and to offer a grading curve far higher than that typically given to regular MBA students were the most common complaints. The time taken up responding to complaints was also sometimes cited, in their private conversations with Gill (who was the head of the college's Executive Education council). As a result, the FAU program was already starting to see a trend where, in many disciplines, junior faculty and instructors were being brought in as a substitute for senior faculty to teach the executive courses.

USF EMBA 2002: The First Week

In the summer of 2001, right before he joined the faculty at USF, Gill's department chair had called him to ask if he was willing to teach in the EMBA (instead of in the Master's in MIS program, where he had been originally slotted). The department chair gave three reasons for believing it was a good opportunity:

- Highly motivated students
- 7 class meetings instead of the usual 15
- A modest stipend added to his regular salary

Given his past experience teaching EMBA classes, Gill had jumped at the chance, although he did wonder why he was getting such a plum assignment, given that he hadn't thought to ask for it as part of the job negotiations.

Gill had jumped into preparing the course with considerable relish. Because of the limited number of class meetings, it seemed unrealistic to offer a pure case course; Gill had found that one MIS case per day was sufficient to drain the energy reserves of most classes. He therefore decided to offer a hybrid course, with online case discussions (using a protocol he had originally developed for the FAU Environmental MBA program) supplementing the in-class discussions.

He also envisioned creating a business plan exercise, in which the entire class created a business plan for a technology-related IT product—and was held accountable for results (through adjustments to the grading curve). The notion was that he would supply the class with a technology product, in its infancy, and get them to figure out how to make a business out of it. As he was trying to figure out how to make this happen, Gill also became involved in a software testing research program. It occurred to him that he could create an application, a GIS (geographic information system), that could serve double duty. First, it could become a test bed for software research (with the ability to inject errors at will), so the way in which individual characteristics impacted the software testing process could be studied. Second, it could serve as the "prototype" version of the application for which the EMBA students would create a business plan for, since the GIS market was ripe with opportunities.

To complete his course design, Gill also developed six hours of entirely new classroom lecture content, dealing with architectures, software development and the make-or-buy decision that he hoped would help thing think about their plan. He also decided to include a database assignment that he had used for years (in both executive and regular MBA programs) that had always been well received and would provide them with insights on how GIS technology could be enhanced. The previous summer, he had developed a series of narrated video clips that could be played on the computer for FAU's Virtual MBA program, conducted entirely on-line. That meant that the normal 4-5 hours of classroom lectures on database topics could be shifted out of the classroom, and the executives could do the assignment at their own pace.

In designing the course, Gill chose what he believed to be an appropriate workload, targeting in the range of 8 to 10 hours per week. Since the last day of class was eight weeks after the first, this meant that he needed to keep the total outside workload less than 80 hours. Based on his estimates (See Exhibit 3), he computed the outside course load as roughly 60 outside hours, or 7.5 hours per week, using the minimums for each assignment.

Prior to finalizing the syllabus, he ran it by the director of the program, who returned an email saying "lovely". Gill knew he was ready to go.

Saturday: The First Class

Gill arrived early to his first class, on Saturday 9 February, in order to get all his equipment set up. He began his first lecture, an overview of the course, in his finest "blowhard" style—setting up the class for the next week's first in-class case study. The class was extremely lively, and seemed to be going well. Indeed, a proctor from the LSAT exam, being administered in the room below, had to come up to ask Gill to quiet down—much to the class's amusement. As he went over the course requirements, a few eyes seemed to widen but he considered that hardly surprising. He joked how his main goal was to steal time away from the "Business Problem Solving" professor—who was teaching the class that ran in parallel with Gill's—and the expected laugh came, although a little weaker than he had anticipated. Also, he observed that quite a few private conversations started when he mentioned his typical EMBA grade distribution (50% A, 50% B) and added that the curve would be adjusted based on the entire class's performance on the business plan assignment. He assumed that the conversations resulted from the fact that the assignment was: a) a novel concept, and b) a really sweet deal—provided the class pulled together.

After the first break, when he began lecturing on actual course content, the class seemed a bit more subdued. But, since he didn't really consider lecturing his forte, once again he was not too concerned.

During the second break, two things that struck him as a bit odd occurred. First, when one of the students was kind enough to show him the way to the program office in the maze that was the USF College of Business, she kept emphasizing she wasn't doing it to "brown nose" him. On the one hand, it was amusing. On the other, he asked himself, why would an EMBA even feel the slightest need to worry that common courtesy could be construed as an attempt to curry the instructor's favor? On the way back, a couple of students approached him and, more or less, directly stated that the 18 hour/week requirement of the course was way over the top. They also explained to him—as if he had never taught an executive program before—that they all had professional lives that needed to be maintained. Since Gill had already had an unpleasant experience in an EMBA relating to workload issues, he responded cautiously—pointing out that the length of the program (7 weeks) would require a correspondingly higher workload than a typical 14 week course. But, in his mind, he vowed he'd check his syllabus as soon as he got home. He had no idea where the 18 hour figure came from.

Finally, he found himself feeling a bit uncomfortable when joining the group for lunch—which he had been strongly urged to do by the program director. Despite the fact that he was their "guest", he found himself awkwardly inviting himself to sit at a table with some students. Nor was he absolutely certain they were that eager for his presence. But he also noted that the two other faculty members in the room were more or less sitting alone. Perhaps that was the norm.

Monday

By Monday morning, 11 February 2002, Gill was becoming genuinely alarmed. Although he had not received any communications indicating that there was a problem, he had noticed an extraordinary sluggishness in his online discussion of the class's first case: *HE Butt Grocery Company: The New Digital Strategy*. Indeed, only a couple of postings from students discussing the case had appeared. This was totally inconsistent with his experience in prior courses, where postings had appeared almost immediately. The hairs on the back of his neck started to give him the same sensation he'd had with his last EMBA group, back at FAU.

He went into the office early that morning, and called the director of the program—indicating his concern that something was very wrong. The director reassured him, and they traded war stories about experiences in the programs. Gill also mentioned his grading curve, figuring it was pretty standard for the program. Here, the director paused, and emphasized that it was really up to the discretion of the instructor. Some chose to give all A's, while others chose to award a mixture of grades.

By 7 PM on Monday night, three out of the four openings that had been assigned for the HE Butt online case had appeared. The fourth was missing. Gill was quite surprised to have a missed opening, something he had *never* seen in any of the six courses he had taught using his online discussion protocol. Then he received an e-mail from the student who had missed the deadline (see Exhibit 2 for entire e-mail exchange). Although the student's reason seemed justified, Gill recalled that he had sent out the message to the student assigning the opening on Saturday. Gill felt that the student—anticipating such an important deal—could have, at least, informed him, so he could have reassigned the opening. Rescheduling, in an orderly fashion, didn't bother Gill. In fact, he had already moved the owner of a chain of flower shops out of the opening slot, unbeknownst to anyone, because of the proximity of Valentine's Day.

These factors, combined with the fact that the online discussion continued to proceed very slowly (exacerbated by the fact that one of the openings was missing) led Gill to take a hard line, responding with his own message. A few hours later, the student came back with one last message, complaining about the course, this time directed to the program director rather than Gill (who was copied). Gill, in a mixture of exasperation and amusement, sent back one more message, calling into question some of the mathematics involved.

Tuesday

On Tuesday morning, Gill called the director of the program again to talk about his interchange. The director opened the conversation with words to the effect of "well, you've certainly got their attention". But he didn't seem quite as buoyant as he had the day before. Later, Gill understood why. The first of the two e-mails contained in Exhibit 1 had already been received.

Later that day, Gill received an e-mail from the director containing both the first and second emails he had received from students that called the design of the course, as well as Gill's qualifications, into question.

The Dilemma

Gill now felt he was facing a very serious dilemma. In a class like this, always together as a group, three dissatisfied emails probably indicated at least ten dissatisfied students. At least half the class, he guessed. This was not good. This was not what he got into teaching for.

Furthermore, none of his alternatives seemed very palatable. On the one hand, he could truly adopt the "blowhard" persona, this time for real, and choose the "make the bastards pay" approach. No changes. No concessions. Make the course a punishment (for both the class and for himself). And, of course, never teach in the EMBA program again.

On the other hand, he could very easily comply with all the requests in the email. Toss in a few lectures that addressed the requests in the e-mail, so as to would appear responsive. Get rid of the database assignment. Throw out the online cases. Kill the business plan assignment. Knock down the outside hours to 2 hours a week, explaining he hadn't realized how demanding their jobs were (an untruth, to be sure, but one he suspected that they might be ready to accept). Maybe even hint, along the way, that all A's would be forthcoming, in recognition of their brilliant discussion—an outcome that would also make the course much easier for Gill, who wouldn't have to pay attention to a single thing that his students said or wrote if he already knew what their grade was going to be. And, of course, never teach in the EMBA program again.

The problem was, Gill liked the challenge that teaching EMBA students brought to the table. Since both the options on the table ensured that he would never teach in the program again, there had to be better alternatives. But what were they?

"Why *did* they ask me to teach in this program, anyway?", he asked aloud, to no one in particular.

Exhibit 1: Email Sent to the Director

On Tuesday, 2/12/02, the Director of the Program forwarded the following e-mail excerpts to Dr. Gill, identifying the authors only as "excellent students"

E-mail #1:

...Although Dr. Gill does seem to have a much better grasp of information technology basics than did [a previous professor], his approach to ensuring that we capture the content of the course is not conducive to our executive schedules and other course expectations in the final weeks of the program.

It is clear to me that this is Dr. Gill's first experience teaching an executive program at USF. Unfortunately, instead of showing the same professional flexibility we have come to expect of the EMBA program, Dr. Gill appears to be myopically focused on teaching this course as he did at other universities' regular MBA programs.

Additionally, Dr. Gill is unusually concerned with performing some of our assignments on-line as he did with one of his courses that was conducted in its entirety over the Internet. Although one would imagine that this would provide the exact type of flexibility we yearn for in a course, it in fact has proven to do the exact opposite. For example, if a student does not post an opening to an on-line case discussion by a certain due date and time, Dr. Gill will purportedly deduct points from that individual's grade. As well, Dr. Gill's expectation for time spent on this single task is 4-5 hours per week (keep in mind that this is just one of the tasks that must be completed for his course.)

Further, Dr. Gill has focused one section of the course (and our grade) on a database project. I cannot agree more that database skills are very important for the modern executive to master - however - Dr. Gill is requiring that students learn Microsoft Access to complete this section of the course. This requirement is not fulfilled by Dr. Gill reviewing the program with us, but instead by requiring that students watch an exhaustive 5+ hours of self-made (Gill Software Inc. ??) computer based training with a voice-over by Dr. Gill himself. I can tell you that this is not the way to teach a computer application. Even the best professionally made computer based training programs (that use real multimedia including video, application simulation, and feedback) require some classroom instruction to be 100% effective. As well, the professionals in the EMBA program are at a point in their careers where they should be more interested in knowing the skill sets to look for when hiring a database professional than learning how to create complex queries on their own.

In closing, I am sure that Dr. Gill earnestly wants to teach an effective MIS course. Within this, most of Dr. Gill's course objectives are relevant, however, the manner by which he is expecting to provide us with MIS enlightenment is off target:

1. The case studies are a great tool. I've already read ahead on quite a few of them. Our class is a mature group of executives and will conduct meaningful discussions on the subjects at hand without having Dr. Gill "surprise" one of us by having to present a 10 minute opening on the case "Harvard style."

2. The on-line case studies are a nice idea, however imposing time requirements and stringent due dates and times for posted openings (again by "surprising" one of us with this task) is not conducive to our schedules.

3. Studying databases is on target - but it's what we study about them that matters. How to create a query will be forgotten before you hand us our diplomas. What the capabilities of a database are, and how to hire a database professional would be useful to the members of the class. As well, as I've mentioned before some content on ERP and CRM is sorely needed in the program - this is where the IT focus is for the modern executive!

4. Dr. Gill's final project of creating a business plan for his software program sounds interesting, but he could easily scale this project down (or give us all an equity stake in his software company). We have already completed almost identical coursework in our Marketing and International Business course.

Email #2

I don't think I've ever felt the need to send you a note regarding any of our classes, but feel compelled to do so regarding Dr. Gill's class.

While I think the case approach to teaching that Dr. Gill is using is quite educational, he seems driven by, and even stated, the fact that he wanted us to have so much work to do for him that our other concurrent professor would complain. This seems immature to me. As you are well aware, we are executives who know how to manage time. Dr. Gill is giving us assignments due between class meetings, which must be accomplished by specific times (assignments given on Saturday night due Monday night and given Wednesday night due Thursday night) in addition to our preparation for class (when he will 'surprise' us with assignments). This seems arbitrary and burdensome. Furthermore, he seems inflexible to any deviation from his process, and will deduct points even for justified delays.

I could, however, accept this if it was the entirety of his expectations for us. What I find unacceptable is that he's given us this work, along with 2 projects (1 database, another Capstone). The Capstone project he's assigning seems to serve only a personal objective for him – to get free MBA labor on a project he's working on for himself. I believe we've already met the requirements for writing business plans in our Marketing, International Business, and Business Problems Analysis classes.

While we may in fact get something out of it, we're not going to have much time to a good job at anything he's assigned, due to the sheer volume of work in this class (not to mention that we're also preparing weekly presentations for [Business Problem Solving professor's name] course). As an aside, I also believe his style is somewhat offensive to myself and others, and would not foresee him getting good marks on the "respect for students" category. He's put himself on a pedestal, which does not add to an educational experience for Executives.

I understand that Dr. Gill hasn't taught in the EMBA program before. If there's any way you could express to him that this sounds like overkill, and he should pare back the assignments, I'd certainly appreciate that. I've really enjoyed my EMBA experience, and don't want to leave with this bad taste in my mouth. (nor do I want to blow my GPA by not meeting unreasonable expectations).

Exhibit 2: Email Exchange with Student

Received by Grandon, Monday 2/11/02, 6:58 PM

Grandon,

I will work on the Butt Grocery Company case tonight, I just arrived home from work and it is 6:54 PM so needless to say I do not have the time to get it done by 7:00 PM. I was out of town yesterday and only received your e-mail this morning before going to work.

Sorry, but I am a Business Development Director so demands at work keep me extremely busy. I had a 5:30 conference call on a $2 million acquisition I am doing in North Florida.

(Kind of like Graduate School in real life!)

Thanks,

[Name omitted]

Grandon replies, Monday 2/11/02, 7:36 PM

[Student First Name]:

I am sure that were I in your position I would have made the same decision: to put off course responsibilities in order to meet job responsibilities. For you to do otherwise would be a failure to meet your obligations as a manager.

I am equally sure that you understand that the late points that are deducted any time an assignment is late must be deducted consistently-- whether or not the reason was a $2 million deal, or the desire to attend a child's soccer practice. For me to do otherwise would be a failure to meet my obligations as an instructor.

Regards,

Grandon

Received by Grandon, Monday 2/11/02, 8:23 PM, as a copy on an e-mail to the director of the program

[Director of the Program's First Name],

I believe I will have a problem with this class's requirement on my time. Looking at Grandon's syllabus, I compute an 18 hour per week studying requirement, never mind the CD learning, and class time required. I spoke to Grandon about this issue and his response was to the effect that this is equivalent to a regular MBA class if it were condensed into a 16 week timeframe. This is obviously not geared toward the E's in the EMBA program.

DR Gill needs to do what he needs to do but I will tell you right now; this is too much work for the EMBA curriculum. Unless of course you wish to joint venture with Harvard, in which case you need to change my diploma to read as such.

There is not enough time in a week to reach DR Gill's expectations. Can we address this? Although I did not broadcast this to my classmates, I know they feel like I do, feel free to poll them to validate or invalidate their positions.

Thanks,

[Student Full Name]

DR Gill,

Deduct the points on my opening as you see fit. Although I understand your position, I fail to agree with it. I also did not understand, nor was your presentation clear (from what I heard) that openings were time sensitive. I understood closings to be limited to 250 words and due on a timeframe.

Sent by Grandon, Monday 2/11/02, 9:04 PM, with a copy to the director of the program

[Student First Name]:

A couple of things:

1st, the "18 hour" computation was so self-serving I assumed it was purely done as a matter of negotiation. It never occurred to me that anyone would actually believe it. First, it required taking the maximum number of hours for each activity (totaling 105), second, it required double counting the class time allocated to working on assignments (10 hours), third, it involved dividing by 6 weeks for a 7 session class--leading to 17.5. I would argue, since my numbers were based on my experience with typical--rather than executive--MBAs, a fairer calculation would have been to:

a) total the minimums in each range, given that--as executives--you should be more efficient (70 hours)

b) subtract off the 10 hours associated with the final project that are in-class hours (as clearly noted on the syllabus), and

c) divide the resultant 60 hours by the 8 weeks over which they will take place--since two weeks have no class (and, by the way, I didn't make you come into the first class having done an assignment).

The resultant value is around 7.5 hours per week. Naturally, the CD learning was included in the time allocated for the database assignment.

2nd, with respect to your comment "I also did not understand, nor was your presentation clear (from what I heard) that openings were time sensitive.", all I can do is quote from the e-mail message that I sent to you personally on Saturday, which stated:

"By Monday, 2/11/02 at 7PM I'd like each of you to post an opening to the H.E. Butt discussion group, opening a new thread."

My question is this: what could I have possibly said that would have made it more clear that I expected the openings by 7PM on Monday? Indeed, to quote from the e-mail you sent me at 6:58 PM, on Monday, which stated "I will work on the Butt Grocery Company case tonight, I just arrived home from work and it is 6:54 PM so needless to say I do not have the time to get it done by 7:00 PM.", I more-or-less assumed you had acknowledged your posting would be late. Was I incorrect in this assumption?

You will also be relieved to know, I am sure, that I was quite concerned when I heard rumblings about the class workload on Saturday. For that reason, I contacted [EMBA Director] early Monday morning to discuss the situation. As a result, your e-mail to him should come as no surprise.

If you feel that I have been unreasonable in my analysis of the above, I hope you will feel free to broadcast this message to your classmates, in its entirely.

Regards,

Grandon

Exhibit 3: Excerpts from Course Syllabus

Objectives:

1. To acquaint students with different ways in which IT can be employed in business, considered across a wide variety of functions
2. To develop insights into how use of IT can impact the organization in which it is deployed
3. To identify situations where the interpersonal, cultural (e.g., international) and ethical climate within the organization can affect IT and its usage

Course Requirements:

Assignment Type	Description:	Time to Prepare:	Total Weight:
In-Class Case Studies	Grade based upon class participation in 5 in-class case studies	2-4 hours per case	25%
Online Case Studies	Grade based upon participation in 5 on-line case studies.	4-5 Hours per case	25%
Database Proficiency	Assignment in performing database queries	10-20 Hours	20%
IT Project Proposal	Grade based upon presentations created for Mapper class project	30-40 Hours (~10 in class)	30%

EMBA 2002 (B)[2]

The most frightening button on the computer is the e-mail "Send" button, thought Dr. Grandon Gill, Associate Professor of Information Systems & Decision Sciences at the University of South Florida, as he debated with himself whether or not to press it.

He had just composed a lengthy response to a series of complaints from students regarding his EMBA class in information systems, included as Exhibits 1 & 2. Within the attachment to the e-mail (Exhibit 2) he had attempted to do two things:

- Clarify certain factual issues that had surfaced in the e-mail messages that the director had received, and
- Present the class with a series of alternatives for the design of the remainder of the course, ranging from maintaining the original design unaltered (alternative 1) to completely changing the structure of the course (alternative 4).

As the message and its attachment sat staring him in the face, Gill wondered if he should wait. Was his radical response an overreaction? He had already learned that the student who had sent one of the original messages (see Exhibit 2 in *EMBA 2002 (A)* case) was going through a difficult divorce which (according to that same student) had contributed to the forcefulness of his e-mails. He had later sent an e-mail to apologizing to Gill for the manner in which he had expressed his original complaints. Subsequently, he and Gill had entered into a rather humorous exchange of e-mails, in which both sides had strongly conveyed the message "no hard feelings".

Maybe the whole situation would solve itself if left alone. Or perhaps it would be better if he waited until the next class to confer with students before making the decision. On the other hand, the time pressure he felt was intense. Did he really want almost a third of all his class time to have elapsed before knowing what his course design was going to be?

He took a breath and counted to ten. The situation had not become any clearer.

He pressed the "Send" button.

Now we wait, he thought, as he saw the "message sent" prompt appear on his status bar.

Exhibit 1: Email to EMBA 2002 Class

EMBA Class:

[Director of the Program] shared a couple of e-mails with me that are cause for concern, since any case method course is critically dependent on participants "buying in".

I have proposed some alternative ways in which the situation could be addressed, and am hoping that you will chose between them as quickly as you can, since time remaining in the semester is very short.

Thanks for your assistance in this matter.

Regards,

Grandon

<< Attachment MBAOptions.doc >>

Exhibit 2: Attachment to Exhibit 1

[Copy of e-mail messages #1 and #2 from EMBA 2002 (A), Exhibit 1]

Well, it's certainly nice to know that I've made such a strong first impression. Before I make a series of proposals, there are a few things I'd like to do.

First, I would like to clear up some minor misconceptions that I apparently left you with on Saturday:

1) *That this is my first executive MBA program.* It is quite correct that this is my first USF EMBA. It is, however, my seventh EMBA—the remaining six having been taught at Florida Atlantic University. They offer a program quite similar to USF's, with roughly comparable student demographics.

2) *That I, in some way, stand to profit either from the software associated with the business plan exercise or the various pieces of courseware I supplied.* Definitely not the case. When I decided to put together a business plan exercise, I felt it would be more compelling if you could be given a hand-on of an early version of the "product". To justify the significant expenditure of effort, I decided to join it with a software testing project I was planning to work on. However, you can be sure that you would have had the opportunity to "opt out" of participating in the research, and that all data collected would have been done anonymously. Similarly, the 4 hours of .avi files that accompany the database exercise are not a money making operation. Rather, I have found the media to be an extremely efficient way of teaching software-related topics. You can pause it, run in parallel with it, and rewind to see how something is done. I incorporate this technology into any class I teach where it seems to be relevant.

3) *That I really want to steal time away from your other professor.* I apologize to anyone who though that comment was anything more that an attempt at humor. What I was trying to convey was that I know your time is in limited supply, and I hoped that the work I was asking you to do would prove sufficiently engaging so that you would choose to do more of it than was required.

Second, I'd like to talk a bit about the underlying rationale for the particular course design I chose, since there appear to be some concerns along those lines:

1) In Class Case method: The only way the case method can be effective is if the vast majority of the class is actively engaged in the discussion, which means that they have been well prepared. The time-honored technique for that, even in degree granting executive programs, is the "cold call", the technical name for what was called the surprise opening. EMBAs are not unique in having many demands on their time and human nature being what it is—no matter how well intentioned—will result in many students, in *any* program, coming in having merely "read" the case, which is an entirely different state of mind from having prepared it. What some professors do to avoid this is to require students to submit a write up for each case they prepare. This, in my opinion wastes a lot of time, since such write ups are rarely read and virtually never analyzed in depth. I believe that the cold call is a much better way of handling this. And, if everyone is prepared, should be viewed as an opportunity for the student rather than a burden.

2) Database assignment: I believe that the only way one can get a handle on database technology, probably the foundation technology of MIS, is to "get down and dirty" with databases. I have also found that in a typical EMBA class, perhaps 25% of the class already have such familiarity (and therefore accrue relatively minor benefits from doing such an assignment) while 75% learn to think about data in a different way after doing the assignment. The assignment was never about doing Access queries, per se (otherwise, I'd never have agreed to let people submit their queries in SQL). Rather, I believe, it serves as a concrete lesson on how data is organized and what you can do with it. These lessons, I believe, stick with the student long after they get their degree. I also believe they will be far more long-lived than lectures on advanced database technologies to students who don't really have a feel for data.

3) Business plan assignment: The business plan assignment is intended to be a comprehensive, conceptually demanding assignment of the type that I could only give to executives. In fact, I tried a similar assignment a few years back with some regular MBA and it was a bit of a flop— which proved quite embarrassing because that time I had a real CEO who had volunteered to be a guinea pig. I was, and am, rather proud of the innovative aspects of the design for this particular project, which include, a) giving you a partially finished product to make the whole exercise more concrete, b) forcing you to tie all your business knowledge together, and to rely on each other, and c) giving you a grading scheme that awards cooperation far over competition. I did not think whether or not you had "done" business plans was a relevant question (I presumed you had). Personally, I've "done" about 10-15, some funded, some not, and I find I learn something new doing each one.

Now, to the proposals…

One thing about the case method is that it cannot function effectively in an atmosphere where the participants have not "bought in". Had it been I, I might have waited to see how the first case went before launching into quite such intense criticisms as the above, but—as the saying goes—the die is cast. Since I am far more dependent on you than you are on me to make this work, we therefore need to come to some workable solution immediately. Furthermore, that solution needs to be "doable" in the time remaining to us, given the skill set that I bring to the table.

Here are the alternatives that I propose:

Alternative 1: Current Design

We continue to give the current design a try. The one minor modification I would make is that I would post a schedule of the remaining online openers as to what case each would be opening. The only reason that this was not part of the original plan was that I knew that four of you, the first four, would not have such notice so, for the sake of fairness, I did not plan to tell anyone. But, since so many concerns were expressed on this matter, and it makes not one iota of difference in terms of academic value, I am more than happy to give advance notice. Curve before project adjustment: roughly 50-50, A-B, (Cs only for performance far below EMBA expectations). Estimated outside hours per week: 8.

Alternative 2: Modified Current Design

The current design above except that the database project would become an individual (rather than group) extra credit assignment and the class curve (without the extra credit) would be more heavily weighted towards Bs (80-20 B-A, before extra credit projects are handed in and before the business plan project is handed in, Cs only for performance far below EMBA expectations). Estimated outside hours per week: 6, excluding extra credit.

Alternative 3: Major Redesign

The class would design its own comprehensive project to substitute for the Mapper project. In class case studies would include "cold calls". The database project would be an individual assignment for extra credit. Participation in the online forums would be extra credit. The curve, before extra credit and before adjustment for the project would be 80-20 B-A (Cs only for performance far below EMBA expectations). Estimated outside hours per week: 4-5 five, excluding extra credit.

Alternative 4: Complete Redesign

We go to a complete case-study format, with no "cold calls". We will add 6 new cases to the curriculum and one case write up, per week, will be required from each student. Participation in the online forums will be for extra credit, as will the database assignment. The curve will be roughly 15-70-15 A-B-C (the required HBS curve), before extra credit. Estimated outside hours per week: 4, excluding extra credit.

What I need is for you to organize yourselves, in some fashion, and come to a consensus on which of the options you would like to pursue. Realistically, I also need to know by Thursday morning, so that I can come to class on Friday prepared.

Although, personally, I like (1) or (2) best, I believe all of these represent academically reasonable options. Whichever you choose, I will do my best to deliver you value for your money (or your company's money).

I eagerly await a decision from whomever you select to be your designated representative.

Thanks!

Grandon

EMBA 2002 (C)[3]

When Dr. Grandon Gill, Associate Professor of Information Systems & Decision Sciences at the University of South Florida, opened his e-mail the morning of Thursday, 13 February 2002, he read the following message:

Grandon,

The majority of the class (so far all) would like to go ahead with Option #1. We do reserve the right to complain, nag and generally make a complete ruckus in the future if, and/or when, my other classmates join me in divorce court. (save and except [names of various single students in the class]) Please remain sensitive to our time constraints as we proceed into this venture we call ISM6305.

There was one request from a student which read "The only amendment I would make to option #1 is to make sure that we know who is going to open and who is going to close the on-line cases. This way we can plan our schedules and it still makes everyone have to participate." Which seems reasonable.

So until we meet again on Friday, proceed under option #1. We will try to refrain from launching spitwads unless otherwise forced to.   :)

Thanks,

EMBA Class of 2002 as represented by

[Name of Student]

Gill found the message surprising for two reasons:

---

1. He had felt it very unlikely that the class was going to be able to reach a consensus in such a short period of time—that they had managed to do so was quite impressive, and

2. The student who had been designated the class representative was the same student who had initiated the e-mail exchange that had precipitated the crisis (see Exhibit 2 in *EMBA 2002 (A)* case)

It is going to be an interesting semester, he thought to himself. And, for the first time, that did not seem like a Chinese curse.

T. Grandon Gill
Informing with the Case Method
Santa Rosa, California: Informing Science Press.

Appendix H

Student Guide to Preparing a Case

Since most of my students have never done a case analysis before, I have started handing out a "lifeline" that they can use when first encountering a case. Generally speaking, it is quickly abandoned after a case or two.

Case Preparation Worksheet

Caution: This worksheet is intended to act as a general purpose guide to preparing discussion cases. It is important to recognize, however, that every case study is unique. As a result, it is okay—even inevitable—that some steps will be skipped. Use it as a checklist for things you might want to look at.

Step 0. *Do an initial reading of the case*

Before any detailed analysis can be performed, it is critical that an overall sense of the case is acquired.

Step 1. *Determine the goal of your analysis*

_____ Recommend a decision and/or action plan

_____ Understand and/or critique decisions that have already been made

_____ Learn an approach to dealing with a particular situation

_____ Other: _____

Important: Your analysis should always be focused on achieving this goal. For discussion cases, the vast majority will be the first.

Step 2: *Determine your units of analysis*

Most case studies will have units of analysis that fall into two categories: *environments* that determine the context of the case and *stakeholders*, the individuals or collections of individuals directly impacted by decisions made, or to be made, in the case.

Environment units can frequently be defined as systems or subsystems of one another. For example:
- Global economy → Industry → Company → Relevant Business Unit
- State Education System → School District → School → Grade

- National Policy → State Policy → Local Policy → Organizational Policy

Analysis of environment units usually revolves around determining *current context* and *expected trends*. Frequently, understanding both will be facilitated by looking at how the current context evolved.

Stakeholder analysis involves understanding who a particular decision might impact. Stakeholders are the "actors" in the case, and may include both individuals and organizations. (In scientific cases, they might even extend to other non-human "actors", such as a species endangered by a particular production byproduct.) The nature of key stakeholders depends heavily on the nature of the case. For example:

- *Business*: e.g., Employees, executives, shareholders, competitors, customers, suppliers, unions, co-workers, general public
- *Education*: e.g., Teachers, administrators, students, parents, school boards
- *Public policy*: e.g., Elected officials, public employees, voters, underrepresented minorities, businesses, lawyers

With stakeholders, what is often crucial is to understand *whether a particular decision exerts a positive or negative impact* and *likely reactions to a decision*.

It is usually feasible to organize a case analysis around the most relevant units of analysis.

Unit 1: _____ Type: _____

Unit 2: _____ Type: _____

Unit 3: _____ Type: _____

Unit 4: _____ Type: _____

Unit 5: _____ Type: _____

Step 3: Assemble and organize facts

For each unit of analysis assemble facts from the case. One way to do this is to create a table, such as the following, on a separate page for each unit:

Important	Might be Important	Probably Irrelevant

Write down each fact in the appropriate column. Expect these classifications to change as you conduct your analysis.

In general, the most relevant facts for system units will be those that define the current state or that suggest possible trends. For stakeholder units, they will be facts that help us understand whether actions to be considered will be viewed in a positive or negative light, and facts that telegraph how they might react to such actions.

Step 4: *Analyze how the protagonist is likely to fare in the present and future*

Typically, a case study will revolve around a central decision making figure or entity, referred to as the *protagonist*. It can be helpful to specifically look at the context facing that decision-maker. While no tool for doing this can be applied universally, SWOT (strength, weakness, opportunity, threat) analysis is an old standby if some other framework has not been supplied. SWOT can be organized in a grid along the following lines:

	The Present	The Future
Positive	Strengths:	Opportunities:
Negative	Weaknesses:	Threats:

General Comments:

- Particularly where a case study involves analyzing or understanding decisions that have already been made, it may be useful to look at how the SWOT snapshot has changed over time.
- Quantitative analysis will often be necessary to fill in these grids, particularly where financial factors play a significant role in a case
- Where the protagonist's actions are expected to provoke strong reactions from other stakeholders (e.g., a competitor in a business setting), it may make sense to conduct a similar analysis for that stakeholder as well.

Step 5: *Identify possible alternatives*

Frequently, a decision-focused case will supply a set of alternatives. Sometimes, however, alternatives (and/or an action plan) must be created by the participant. Where a case involves understanding a decision that has been made, it will nearly always be valuable to consider alternatives that *could* have been considered. Ideally, the result of this should be a list of two or more alternatives that could be/could have been chosen by the protagonist.

Alternative 1: _____

Alternative 2: _____

Alternative 3: _____

Alternative 4: _____

Typically, the Step 4 analysis will suggest one (or more) of these as being the best fit with the case.

Step 6: *Broaden the analysis to include all stakeholders*

It is easy to conclude analysis once the protagonist's reaction to alternatives has been established. For each alternative, however, it is important to consider the impact of a decision on all stakeholders. Where there is conflict, there is often a strong potential for ethical issues and potential for reprisal to arise.

A grid such as the following may be prepared for each alternative, breaking each alternative into elements as necessary, since some decisions will have both pros and cons for a stakeholder. The final column captures the likely or possible responses the stakeholder might make in light of a particular decision.

	Positive Impact	Negative Impact	Likely Response
Stakeholder 1			
Stakeholder 2			
Stakeholder 3			
Stakeholder 4			

Collectively, this analysis provides the basis for a *balanced scorecard* approach to analyzing the case. The idea is to avoid focusing too heavily on a particular metric (e.g., share price) or individual player (e.g., the CEO). In some cases, this might alter the recommendation. Almost always, however, it will surface issues that are worth considering.

Step 7: *Develop a concise "solution" that addresses the goals of the case*

Depending on the goal (see step 1), this might involve:

- A decision choice

- An action plan

- An explanation of where a protagonist went wrong or did the right thing

- A list of important lessons that can be discerned from the case

Step 8: *Develop an opening outline*

The final step that is usually desirable in analyzing a case study for discussion is preparing an opening outline. This is particularly relevant in situations where opening is determined by a "cold call". It is very unlikely that a general framework exists that is best—or even adequate—for all case studies. One that seems to work reasonably well for many cases is organized as follows:

I.   *Introduce the goal of the case (Step 1) and provide a concise summary of your solution (Step 7).* Some participants like to build suspense in their openings by not leading with their "solution" of the case. Generally, the effect of doing so is to create the sense that the opener does not know where his or her arguments are leading.

II.   *Summarize the most relevant facts from the case for each unit of analysis (Step 2 & 3).* Only those facts that made the "important" column should be included in an opening.

    a.   A common mistake made by novice participants is attempting to provide a synopsis of the entire case, organized in the same order that the case is organized. This almost never results in a good opening, although it assuredly leads to a long one.

    b.   Drilling down from broad systems (e.g., the global economy) towards problem-specific systems (e.g., the relevant organizational unit) often proves to be a sensible ordering.

      c.   Key stakeholder units can be discussed in conjunction with the systems in which they participate.

III.   *Offer analysis of the specific decision or problem that is the focus of the case.* The types of analysis performed in Steps 4 through 6 can be presented here.

IV.   *Weigh any concerns relating to the recommendation (Step 7) and present a final argument to justify the choice that has been made.*

T. Grandon Gill
Informing with the Case Method
Santa Rosa, California: Informing Science Press.

Appendix I

Evaluation Plan for NSF Proposal

I cannot lay claim to have any magic formula for gaining approval from an Institutional Review Board (IRB) for case study development. The best I can offer is the evaluation plan that I provided to the USF IRB describing the steps we planned to take for an NSF grant that involved both developing discussion cases and evaluating their impact. The outcome of this submission was a full exemption, which was more that we had asked for.

Incorporating Complex Open Authentic Case Studies into a Capstone Course

Introduction

The project associated with the proposal involves developing an undergraduate capstone course for undergraduate MIS majors built around real world case studies. The key research question being addressed is:

> Can the use of real world cases at the undergraduate level improve the problem solving skills of our students?

A central aspect of the project is the development of tools and instruments to measure the student learning that results from this course. The purpose of this evaluation plan is to outline the alternative methods of evaluation that are currently planned to assess learning, recognizing that further development of these tools will take place during a faculty workshop that will be conducted prior to the course development. Of particular relevance in achieving this purpose are two important issues:

1. Identifying what evaluation approaches are already in place
2. Identifying what components of the proposed project are likely to be exempt from review by the Institutional Review Board (IRB) and which components must be approved prior to funding.

For the most part, the current evaluation plan consists of techniques for formative and summative assessment of student learning outcomes. As such, we anticipate them to be exempt from formal IRB review under 45 CFR 46.101 b, which states:

(b) Unless otherwise required by department or agency heads, research activities in which the only involvement of human subjects will be in one or more of the following categories are exempt from this policy:

> *(1) Research conducted in established or commonly accepted educational settings, involving normal educational practices, such as (i) research on regular and special education instructional strategies, or (ii) research on the ef-*

fectiveness of or the comparison among instructional techniques, curricula, or classroom management methods.

(2) Research involving the use of educational tests (cognitive, diagnostic, aptitude, achievement), survey procedures, interview procedures or observation of public behavior, unless:

(i) information obtained is recorded in such a manner that human subjects can be identified, directly or through identifiers linked to the subjects; and (ii) any disclosure of the human subjects' responses outside the research could reasonably place the subjects at risk of criminal or civil liability or be damaging to the subjects' financial standing, employability, or reputation.

Where our investigation may extend beyond this, we seek IRB approval. In addition, some of our activities—most notably the development of teaching cases—seem unlikely to qualify as "research" under the prevailing definitions used by the IRB. For these, our intention is to show that we are following the same stringent guidelines for protecting the individuals involved in the development of cases that would be required for activities defined as research.

Project Activities Involving Interactions with External Individuals

The project being undertaken will involve a number of different interactions between investigators and individuals outside the project—both students and business practitioners. From a human subjects point of view, we focus on those that involve gathering data for subsequent analysis or publication beyond what would normally be done for a class. These activities are as follows:

A. Development of real world case studies by project investigators
B. Use of a pre-test/post-test instrument intended to assess learning over the period of an entire semester.
C. Use of a pre-test/post-test instrument to assess learning taking place as a consequence of a specific case discussion
D. Use of a post course case matching instrument to assess student grasp of key concepts
E. Interviews with selected student participants

F. Use of demographic and personal data instrument with the specific goal of identifying the impact of the course on segments of the population that are under-represented in STEM fields

These activities fall into three broad categories:

1. Activities that would not normally fall under the heading of research as classified by the IRB (Activity A). For this, our objective is to show that we are nevertheless following strict procedures to ensure that participants are protected.
2. Formative and summative evaluation activities that would normally be exempt because they represent research on effectiveness of instructional techniques, as per 45 CFR 46 101b(1). For these activities (B through E), we seek confirmation of the exemption so that we can feel free to make those modifications we deem necessary as the project progresses.
3. Activities for which we anticipate IRB approval may be necessary (F). Here we intend to show that the protocol we employ id designed to protect participating human subjects from any conceivable adverse effect, while offering potential long term benefits to the population as a whole.

Each of these three categories is now discussed.

Activity Type 1: Case Study Development

The development of case studies is a long-established practice in business education. These would normally be exempt from IRB approval for two reasons:

- Their design intent is not necessarily the same as what research is defined to be, namely:

> "Research means a systematic investigation, including research development, testing, and evaluation, designed to develop or contribute to generalizable knowledge." - 45 CFR 46.102 (d)

Rather, their objective is to provide a basis for class discussion.

- Frequently, it is difficult to identify who the "subject" is, since the practitioner protagonist of a case study is frequently listed as a co-author of the subject

Despite the fact that business discussion case development would be classified exempt from IRB approval in all but the most unique circumstances, the underlying principles of respect for persons and beneficence are strongly followed in case development. This is illustrated in Exhibit A (a series of FAQs that the PI has developed for case study participants) and in Exhibit B (a release document that must be signed by the organization before a case study can be used).

These documents serve to:

- Clearly inform the participant of the costs and benefits associated with participating in case development
- Provide the participant with the ability to "opt out" at any time up to the final publication of the case
- Provide the participant with ability to suggest or require modifications to the case throughout the process.

Activity Type 2: Formative and Summative Evaluations

A central goal of the project is to assess student learning that occurs as a result of employing the case method in the course. Learning assessment of this type is normally exempt from IRB approval, as per 45 CFR 46 101b(1), but the number of different evaluation approaches to be employed is sufficiently unusual that it warrants explanation.

The justification for employing all these evaluation approaches is twofold. First, it provides a method of triangulating outcomes. As noted in the original proposal, it is widely acknowledged that there is no universally accepted measure of case method learning. Having a variety of approaches should provide greater confidence in outcomes than could be achieved with a single measure. Second, it will allow us to perform statistical analysis of the relationship between different outcomes. This will be valuable for future instructors, as it may allow some approaches to be discarded in the grading process should they prove to be highly correlated with other measures.

The specific evaluation approaches discussed in the grant proposal are now summarized.

Case analysis evaluation

The first approach to be taken is a pre- and post-course evaluation where students are given a small constructed case and are asked to analyze it. An example of what such a case would look like is presented in Exhibit C. This is just an example, as further development of these exercises will be an agenda item for the first workshop.

The method that will be applied to evaluating student responses will be designed to maximize the reliability of the process. In brief:

- Two exercises of roughly equivalent difficulty will be developed

- Students will be randomly assigned to treatment group A and B (equal numbers in each group).

- Group A will get exercise 1 at the start of the course and exercise 2 at the end; Group B will get exercise 2 at the start of the course and exercise 1 at the end.

- Two graders (not the course instructor) will grade all the student responses on a 1 to 5 scale according to a rubric developed in the workshop. Both student identity and whether the response is pre- or post-course will be unknown to the grader.

- Comparison of the two grades for each student-exercise pair will be used to assess the reliability of the grading process

- Comparison of pre- and post-course aggregate scores will be used to assess the learning associated with course

- A similar comparison will be done on the difference of pre- and post-course responses for each student will be used to assess the variability of improvement between students

Individual case learning evaluation

Using a protocol that is already used by the PI for the graduate case method course, individual student learning outcomes for each individual case study will be assessed with pre- and post-case instruments.

- *Pre-case*: The instructor will pose a question at the beginning of the class and give students 15 minutes to response and post their answer tor Blackboard. This is intended to assess student preparation prior to each discussion.

- *Post-case*: The instructor will ask students to identify and reflect upon their key learning outcomes as a consequence of reading and discussing the case.

Samples of the forms currently being used by the PI in the graduate course, adapted to the undergraduate project, are presented as Exhibit D and E. Each week, the course instructor assigns grades to each student for each instrument on a Weak-Satisfactory-Excellent scale.

Case matching evaluation

At the end of the class, each student's grasp of overall course concepts resulting from the case discussions will be assessed using a technique developed by the PI and described in:

> Harold Webb, T. Grandon Gill and Gary Poe, "Teaching with the Case Method Online: Pure vs. Hybrid Approaches", *Decision Sciences Journal of Innovative Education*, 2005, 3(2), 223-250.

The assessment tool—which cannot be fully developed prior to knowing the specific portfolio of cases to be used—uses matching to assess whether student's grasped the big picture with respect to the cases. Exhibit F provides an example of the instrument, used in the referenced research. For this instrument, scoring is done relative to the instructor's benchmark.

Interviews

Selected students will be interviewed by investigators other than the instructor) subsequent to the course. Such interviews are generally unstructured and are routinely used as part of the department's program and learning assessment activities.

Activity Type 3: Acquisition of Demographic and Personal Data

A particularly pressing problem in the STEM fields is ensuring representative participation of underrepresented groups, particularly women and minorities. As part of the project, we intend to investigate whether or not the characteristics of the protagonist in a particular case appears to exert a particularly strong influence on students sharing some or all of those characteristics. Given the large literature that documents the strong positive impact of homophily on informing (i.e., sender and recipient sharing many similar characteristics) it makes sense to anticipate such a result. Nevertheless, to the best of our knowledge, the assumption has never been tested empirically.

Much of the data that would be required in order to test for such an effect would already be available from the results of the Activity 2 acquisition (most notably, the individual case learning evaluations). What would be needed beyond this are two things:

1. Characteristic data on case protagonists. Such information would nearly always be acquired as part of the case writing process, as issues such as the protagonist's gender and background are nearly always material to the case.
2. Data relating to individual students.

It is data of the second type for which we anticipate that IRB approval would likely be necessary, or at least desirable.

Our plan is to give students a form—along the lines of Exhibit G (modified from another course, where it is used for assessment not research)—as part of the final class.. Questions regarding background and experience are also asked, to help avoid confounding variables and to prevent the survey from being viewed as overly focused on gender/minority membership.

For the demographic analysis, only data from those students who opt-in by signing the an informed consent form (Exhibit H) will be used. These forms (Exhibit G and H) will be handed out with course evaluations—as departmental supplements often are—and collected by a student. The instructor will not have any access them until after grades have been submitted, precisely the same process used for course evaluations.

Prior to data entry of the paper forms, the Part 1: Student Background Information section of each submitted form (Exhibit G) will be marked "unusable" for any student for whom a signed informed con sent form has not be received. Within the database, these data elements for the student will be entered as "missing".

Conclusions

The process described in this document represents, to the best of the PI's knowledge, a more systematic attempt to assess case method learning outcomes than any previously reported in the literature. Because it involves a number of pioneering approaches, we anticipate—indeed, we hope—that sensible modifications will be made as part of the initial design workshop and subsequent to the first offering of the course in Fall 2011. For this reason, this document needs to be viewed as a starting point, not a final description of what is to take place.

Exhibit A: 10 Frequently Asked Questions

(See Appendix B of this book.)

Exhibit B: Sample Case Release Document

(See Appendix B of this book.)

Exhibit C: Sample Exercise Case

Turnaround LLC

Janet Washington was frustrated. In her role of CIO of Turnaround LLC, a medium-sized real estate company that specialized in turning around foreclosed properties, she had promised her boss Ellen—the company's CEO—that she would have a new application to manage the rapidly growing business in place by April. It was now June and, according to the project's lead developer, Fred, completion was still two weeks away. The problem was this: completion had been "two weeks" away for the last three months! What was she going to do?

The Company

Turnaround was a participant in the residential real estate industry. Its original principals were three real estate agents whose brokerage firms had gone out of business during the collapse in real estate that occurred within Florida starting in 2008. Rather than leave the business entirely, as many of the unemployed agents within the state had done, the trio had decided to get into the business of taking properties under the imminent threat of foreclosure and packaging them for rapid sales. Their business model was to work collaboratively with both owners and lenders to achieve a compromise that was beneficial to both and then to aggressively market the properties to buyers. The major source of the company's buyers was international investors and individuals seeking vacation properties. Boosted by a combination of rapidly dropping property values, low interest rates and a declining U.S. dollar, it was often possible for these customers to acquire properties at a 60% discount from what they would have paid in 2007, at the peak of the Florida real estate bubble.

In the two years since the company's inception, it had grown from the three founders to over 100 employees. The key to success in the foreclosure industry was information. To put together a deal, Turnaround needed to be first to identify attractive properties that were likely to enter foreclosure. It then needed to contact the owners of the property to determine if they were amenable to working with Turnaround and also contact the lenders to determine if they would consider a short sale (i.e., a sale where the price paid for the property was less than the amount owed on the mortgage, meaning that the bank would need to write down its loan). Finally, the company had to determine whether or not the property was a match for any of the potential clients who had signed up for the service. When all three conditions were right, a deal could be structured. Typically, Turnaround received a 6% commission on any deal that closed, 2% paid by the seller, 2% by the purchaser and 2% by the lender. Such a commission structure was unusual in the industry—where the seller was usually responsible for the entire commission—but it was attractive for all three parties in the event of the challenging type of sale that Turnaround usually put together.

By early 2011, the time of the case, Turnaround was brokering roughly 1400 properties a year, averaging $8000 in commission from each transaction. The company had worked successfully with 11 different lenders and in six different Florida counties—a significant factor since rules for closing properties and responsibility for closing fees varied by county. To assist in the transaction volume, the company had acquired a title company in 2009 to help perform the closings. Generally speaking, Florida law, however, mandated that the purchaser have the right to choose its own title company to close a purchase sale. About 90% of purchasers chose to use the Turnaround affiliate title company. Those who chose to pick their own closing agent were required to pay a $500 consulting fee to Turnaround. The purpose of this fee was to verify the quality of the closing documents, since errors in a near-foreclosure situation could be very costly.

The MIS Department

Within a year of Turnaround's founding, the company was swamped in paperwork. Since none of its founders had an MIS background, all their processes had been manual. They did use the computer—e.g., to do their bookkeeping, to search county records for liens on properties (often a precursor to foreclosures), to perform credit checks on both buyers and sellers, and to perform online appraisals—but their use was task-driven, with no integrated workflow. In late 2008, the company hired Janet Washington, the MIS supervisor for a local mortgage broker that was cutting staff. She developed a series of spreadsheets to help keep track of business flows, set up a wireless network to handle the multiple workstations that were being added, installed a fax server and developed the company's web site. As the company grew, however, she found that she was spending nearly all her time training new hires on how to operate the various pieces of software used by the company and on keeping the system up and running.

By mid-2010, the company decided it needed a professional developer. Fred Eccles, a recent graduate of a local MS-MIS program, had applied for the job and everyone had been impressed by his "can do" attitude and his easygoing personality. His first month on the job, he successfully installed a Microsoft SharePoint server that was then used as a portal for document tracking and business process management. The installation was major success, allowing individual agents to identify and qualify potential buyers/sellers/properties 27% faster. Average turnaround time on each deal also declined from 11 weeks to 9 weeks. By December 2010, the installation was completed. By that time, Janet had another project in mind for him.

The "Turnaround Central" Project

The "Turnaround Central" project was originally based on something that Fred had read about on the Google site[1]. In November 2011, the company had introduced a product referred to as "Google Bust" that could be used to identify properties likely to enter foreclosure across the country. The product, currently in beta release (as was typical for Google), accessed county online records covering about 94% of the U.S. population (99% of Florida) and used a proprietary algorithm to assess the likelihood that they would enter foreclosure. More importantly, Google provided a free application program interface (API) that developers could embed into their code, making it possible to bring the data into the application, analyze it, then display it on a map (using another Google API for mapping). What Janet immediately perceived when Fred brought the API to her attention was that it could be the core of a new application that could be used to match client requests to suitable properties in real time. Fred further suggested that, using another API from Skype and an open source text-to-voice product, the product could be made to automatically call out to clients when a match appeared likely to determine if they were interested. In addition, he proposed that the system could be used to create and populate with data (e.g., property location, owner information, lender and mortgage facts) all the documents needed to initiate a workflow using SharePoint. This last activity alone, Janet estimated, could save the company up to 4 hours per property.

---

1 Note: The "Google Bust" product described is fictional and is introduced solely for the purposes of the example case.

Fred, who had taken two programming courses as part of his undergraduate degree in MIS had suggested the program be developed using agile methods. Specifically, he planned to create a series of prototype applications with successively increasing functionality until a useful tool had been reached. From that point on, he planned to add features as needed. He was really excited about building the system and worked 12+ hours per day over the holiday period to develop the first prototype, intended to demonstrate the interface. Janet and her boss, Ellen Sanchez, had been so impressed that the two decided to hire another MIS employee so that Fred could complete the development as fast as possible.

In February 2011, Fred had demonstrated the system using test data—a little ahead of the informal schedule. At that time, Ellen had expressed her pleasure with how things were going. She had also suggested a few more features, ones that would be easy to implement (in Fred's opinion). Since bringing in real data seemed to be a largely mechanical activity—Fred had extensive database experience from three classes in his Master's program—he had estimated two weeks to completion. Since that time, however, the project had seemed to advance in fits and spurts. Certain features, such as the generation and loading of documents to SharePoint had been implemented rapidly. Other functionality, such as acquiring data from the Google API had caused problems from the very start—the amount of data was huge and the format in which it arrived seemed to vary from county to county. The potential customer database had been successfully imported from the spreadsheet where it was stored, but it was not clear how the system would be kept up-to-date.

The Current Situation

After hearing Fred's most recent two week estimate, Janet was very concerned. In anticipation of the productivity increases expected from the system, Turnaround had been very conservative in its hiring. As a result of the delays, however, average turnaround on a property had crept up to 12 weeks. This was serious, since part of the incentive for banks to work with Turnaround was to get delinquent properties off their books quickly. Moreover, the bad real estate market was not going to last forever. If they missed opportunities now, they might be gone forever.

Meanwhile, she could see that Fred realized the issue and was working like mad to try to get the project completed. And, to be sure, he was making progress. But was two weeks more work believable? Unfortunately, there was no documentation on the system—Fred ensured her the tools he was using were self-documenting—so she was having a very hard time getting a handle on what remained to be done.

Questions

1. What is your assessment of the "Turnaround Central" project and where it now stands?

2. If you were Janet Washington, what actions would you consider taking at this point and what do you think would be your best choice?

Both explanations should refer to the facts as stated in the case.

Exhibit D: Sample Pre-Case Form

Pre-Case Question

Name:

Case Name: {*type name here*}

Question Posed:

Your response:

Exhibit E: Sample Post-Case Form

In-Class Case Reflection Form

Name:

Case Name: {*type name here*}

Case Study Assessment:

Reflects combined impact of reading the case and participating in the discussion. Place an X in the desired column

Statement	Strongly Disagree	Moderately Disagree	Neutral	Moderately Agree	Strongly Agree
I was strongly engaged by the case itself					
I was strongly engaged by the discussion					
Overall, this case and discussion was a valuable learning experience					

What were the three most important things you learned from the case?

How did the case discussion change your understanding of the

case?

Exhibit F: Sample Case Matching Assessment Form

ID	Name (Note: not all cases will be relevant)
A.	Abbott & Cobb
B.	American Financial Network
C.	AucNet
D.	Etc…

How central was this theme to the course? (Circle a number between 1 and 7) Note: you answer should reflect the theme's importance **to the course**, not necessarily its overall importance to business.	**Course Themes**	Identify up to three cases that you feel are most relevant to this theme (using letters from table above). Leave blank if none are relevant
Not at all 1..2..3..4..5..6..7 Very	1. In a global marketplace, the qualitative characteristics of markets being entered are more important than their size	1.____ 2.____ 3.____
Not at all 1..2..3..4..5..6..7 Very	2. Technologies that allow an organization to interact directly with its customers require a strategic mindset in their design	1.____ 2.____ 3.____
Not at all 1..2..3..4..5..6..7 Very	3. The adoption of an IT can have a major impact on the nature of the work performed by an organization's employees.	1.____ 2.____ 3.____
Not at all 1..2..3..4..5..6..7 Very	4. Support technologies should be viewed as cost centers, while strategic technologies should be treated as profit centers	1.____ 2.____ 3.____

Not at all 1..2..3..4..5..6..7 Very	5. When managing IT divisions or projects, you should never be too accepting of underperformance by your staff.	1.____ 2.____ 3.____
Not at all 1..2..3..4..5..6..7 Very	6. You frequently need to restructure organizational processes to take advantage of the capabilities the technology provides	1.____ 2.____ 3.____
Not at all 1..2..3..4..5..6..7 Very	7. In a changing environment or in the presence of ill-defined objectives, you should not build systems that are inflexible.	1.____ 2.____ 3.____
Not at all 1..2..3..4..5..6..7 Very	8. Outsourcing strategic systems can leave a company extremely vulnerable its vendors in future negotiations	1.____ 2.____ 3.____
Not at all 1..2..3..4..5..6..7 Very	9. Failing to recognize the importance of a strategic system is sufficient to warrant the discharge of an IS manager.	1.____ 2.____ 3.____
Not at all 1..2..3..4..5..6..7 Very	10. IT products have a short lifecycle and must therefore be redesigned continuously or they will cease to be commercial	1.____ 2.____ 3.____

Exhibit G: Student Data Survey

IMPORTANT: Your Blackboard ID: _____

Part One:
Student Background Information

Sex:	[dropdown]
Age (in years)	[text field]

Please indicate which, if any, of the following groups you belong to:
- ☐ African American
- ☐ Hispanic
- ☐ Native American
- ☐ Non-US Citizen

Please specify your major [dropdown]
Pease specify your student status [dropdown]
Please specify your current employment status [dropdown]

Please specify your total experience in each of the following job categories, using a 1 to 6 scale as follows:

1. None
2. Part time
3. Full time (less than 3 months)
4. Full time (3 months to < 1 year)
5. Full time (1 year to 5 years)
6. Full time (> 5 years)

Non-IT entry level positions (e.g., food service, retail, construction) [dropdown]

Non-IT management positions [dropdown]

IT non-development entry level positions (e.g., technical support, network administration, database administrator, technology sales) [dropdown]

IT development entry level positions (e.g., programmer, web developer, systems analyst, database designer) [dropdown]

IT non-development senior position (e.g., network manager, database manager, technology sales manager) [dropdown]

IT development senior positions (e.g., senior programmers, development project manager) [dropdown]

Rate the following occupations based on **how attractive they are to you**, personally, as career areas or professions, using the following 5 point scale

1. Very unattractive
2. Somewhat unattractive
3. Neutral/Have no opinion
4. Somewhat attractive
5. Very attractive

General management ▼
Programming ▼
Database management ▼
Network management ▼
Sales ▼
MIS project management ▼
CPA ▼
Lawyer ▼
Medical Doctor ▼
Computer game developer ▼

How has taking this class **changed the attractiveness** of each of the following career areas or professions?

1. Much less attractive
2. Less attractive
3. Unchanged
4. More attractive
5. Much more attractive

General management ▼
Programming ▼
Database management ▼
Network management ▼
Sales ▼
MIS project management ▼
CPA ▼
Lawyer ▼
Medical Doctor ▼
Computer game developer ▼

How **likely** is it that you will be employeed in each of the following career areas or professions within the next 10 years?

1. Very or extremly unlikely
2. Pretty unlikely
3. Possible or don't know
4. Pretty likely
5. Very or extremly likely

General management ▼
Programming ▼
Database management ▼
Network management ▼
Sales ▼
MIS project management ▼
CPA ▼
Lawyer ▼
Medical Doctor ▼
Computer game developer ▼

How likely is it that you will acquire each of the following **degrees or professional certifications** within the next 10 years?

1. Very or extremly unlikely
2. Pretty unlikely
3. Possible or don't know
4. Pretty likely
5. Very or extremly likely

MBA ▼
Masters degree in Computer Science ▼
PhD in Computer Science ▼
Masters degree in MIS ▼
PhD in MIS ▼
CPA ▼
LLD or JD (Law degree) ▼
MD, DDS or other medical degree ▼
Masters degree in another field ▼
Doctorate in another field ▼

Part Two:
Student Assessment of Learning Gains (SALG)

To what extent did you make gains in any of the following course areas as a result of what you did in this class?

1. Not at all
2. A little
3. Somewhat
4. A lot
5. A great deal
N. N/A

Understanding the main concepts ▼
Understanding the relationships between concepts ▼
Understanding the relevance of the field to real world issues ▼
Appreciating the field ▼
Ability to think through a problem or argument ▼
Confidence in your ability to work in this field ▼
Feeling comfortable with complex ideas ▼
Enthusiasm for the subject ▼

How much of the following do you think you will remember and carry with you into your other classes or aspects of your life

1. Not at all
2. A little
3. Somewhat
4. A lot
5. A great deal
N. N/A

The core concepts of MIS ▼
How to solve problems ▼

Exhibit H: Informed Consent Form

Informed Consent to Participate in Research
Information to Consider Before Taking Part in this Research Study

IRB Study # _____

You are being asked to take part in a research study. Research studies include only people who choose to take part. This document is called an informed consent form. Please read this information carefully and take your time making your decision. Ask the researcher or study staff to discuss this consent form with you, please ask him/her to explain any words or information you do not clearly understand. We encourage you to talk with your family and friends before you decide to take part in this research study

We are asking you to take part in a research study called: **Incorporating Complex Open Authentic Case Studies into a Capstone Course**

The person who is in charge of this research study is **T. Grandon Gill.** This person is called the Principal Investigator. However, other research staff may be involved and can act on behalf of the person in charge.

The research will be conducted in the classroom.

This research is being sponsored by the **National Science Foundation**.

Purpose of the study

The purpose of this study is to:

- Explore how a student's background influences his or her learning from the case method

Study Procedures

If you take part in this study, you will be asked to:

- Allow the principal investigator to use the information you will be providing as part of your end-of-semester survey and link it to other information gathered as part of the course. This will not require any additional work on your part.

Total Number of Participants

About 80 individuals will take part in this study at USF.

Alternatives

You do not have to participate in this research study. If you choose not to, we will not use the information from your survey for the purposes of the research.

Benefits

The potential benefits of participating in this research study consist of helping us better understand how we can write and use case studies in a manner that makes them more effective for future classes.

Risks or Discomfort

This research is considered to be minimal risk. That means that the risks associated with this study are the same as what you face every day. There are no known additional risks to those who take part in this study.

Compensation

You will receive no payment or other compensation for taking part in this study.

Privacy and Confidentiality

We will keep your study records private and confidential. Certain people may need to see your study records. By law, anyone who looks at your records must keep them completely confidential. The only people who will be allowed to see these records are:

- The research team, including the Principal Investigator and all other research staff.
- Certain government and university people who need to know more about the study. For example, individuals who provide oversight on this study may need to look at your records. This is done to make sure that we are doing the study in the right way. They also need to make sure that we are protecting your rights and your safety.

- Any agency of the federal, state, or local government that regulates this research. This includes the Food and Drug Administration (FDA), Florida Department of Health, and the Department of Health and Human Services (DHHS) and the Office for Human Research Protection (OHRP).

- The USF Institutional Review Board (IRB) and its related staff who have oversight responsibilities for this study, staff in the USF Office of Research and Innovation, USF Division of Research Integrity and Compliance, and other USF offices who oversee this research.

We may publish what we learn from this study. If we do, we will not include your name. We will not publish anything that would let people know who you are.

Voluntary Participation / Withdrawal

You should only take part in this study if you want to volunteer. You should not feel that there is any pressure to take part in the study. You are free to participate in this research or withdraw at any time. There will be no penalty or loss of benefits you are entitled to receive if you stop taking part in this study.

New information about the study

During the course of this study, we may find more information that could be important to you. This includes information that, once learned, might cause you to change your mind about being in the study. We will notify you as soon as possible if such information becomes available.

You can get the answers to your questions, concerns, or complaints

If you have questions about your rights as a participant in this study, general questions, or have complaints, concerns or issues you want to discuss with someone outside the research, call the USF IRB at ...

Consent to Take Part in this Research Study

It is up to you to decide whether you want to take part in this study. If you want to take part, please sign the form, if the following statements are true.

I freely give my consent to take part in this study. I understand that by signing this form I am agreeing to take part in research. I have received a copy of this form to take with me.

_____

Signature of Person Taking Part in Study   Date

_____

Printed Name of Person Taking Part in Study

Statement of Person Obtaining Informed Consent

I have carefully explained to the person taking part in the study what he or she can expect from their participation. I hereby certify that when this person signs this form, to the best of my knowledge, he/ she understands:

- What the study is about;
- What procedures/interventions/investigational drugs or devices will be used;
- What the potential benefits might be; and
- What the known risks might be.

I can confirm that this research subject speaks the language that was used to explain this research and is receiving an informed consent form in the appropriate language. Additionally, this subject reads well enough to understand this document or, if not, this person is able to hear and understand when the form is read to him or her. This subject does not have a medical/psychological problem that would compromise comprehension and therefore makes it hard to understand what is being explained and can, therefore, give legally effective informed consent. This subject is not under any type of anesthesia or analgesic that may cloud their judgment or make it hard to understand what is being explained and, therefore, can be considered competent to give informed consent.

Signature of Person Obtaining Informed Consent / Research Authorization

Printed Name of Person Obtaining Informed Consent / Research Authorization

About the Author

T. Grandon Gill is a Professor in the Information Systems and Decision Sciences department at the *University of South Florida*. He holds a doctorate in Management Information Systems from *Harvard Business School*, where he also received his M.B.A. His principal research areas are the impacts of complexity on decision-making and IS education, and he has published many articles describing how technologies and innovative pedagogies can be combined to increase the effectiveness of teaching across a broad range of IS topics. His most recent book, *Informing Business: Research and Education on a Rugged Landscape*, deals with how we might better align business academia with the complexity of business practice. Currently, he is Editor-in-Chief of *Informing Science: The International Journal of an Emerging Transdiscipline* and an Editor of the *Journal of IT Education*.

References

AACSB (2008), Final report of the AACSB International impact of research task force, *AACSB International*, Retrieved from http://www.aacsb.edu/resource_centers/research/Final/Impact_of_Research_Report-FINAL.PDF

Agile Manifesto (2001), Manifesto for agile software development, *Agile Alliance*, Retrieved from: http://agilemanifesto.org/

Allison, G.T. (1971), *Essence of decision: explaining the Cuban missile crisis.* Boston, MA: Little, Brown and Co.

Austin, R.D. (2001), Teaching Note: Tektronix, Inc.: Global ERP implementation, *Harvard Business School Publishing, 5-602-078.*

Austin, R.D., Nolan, R.L., Westerman, G. & Cotteleer, M. (1999), Tektronix, Inc.: Global ERP implementation, *Harvard Business School Publishing, 9-699-043.*

Bak, P. (1996), *How nature works: The science of self-organized criticality.* New York: Copernicus.

Barnes, L.B., Christensen, C.R. & Hansen, A. (1994), *Teaching and the case method*, Boston, MA: Harvard Business School Press.

Barney, J. & Clifford, T. (2010) *What I didn't learn in business school: How strategy works in the real world*, Boston, MA: Harvard Business Review Press.

Benbasat, I. & Zmud, R. (1999). Empirical research in information systems: The practice of relevance. *MIS Quarterly, 23(1)*, 3-16.

Bennett, D. (2011), I'll have my robots talk to your robots, Bloomberg BusinessWeek, February 21-27, 52-61.

Bloom, B.S. (Ed.), Engelhart, M.D., Furst, E.J., Hill, W.H., & Krathwohl, D.R. (1956), *Taxonomy of educational objectives: The classification of educational goals. Handbook 1: Cognitive domain.* New York, NY: David McKay.

Buchanan, L. (2011), How great entrepreneurs think, *Inc. Magazine, 1 February*, Retrieved 2/25/2011 from http://www.inc.com/magazine/20110201/how-great-entrepreneurs-think.html

Burawoy, M. (1998), The extended case method, *Sociological Theory, 16(1)*, 4-33.

Carney, D.R., Cuddy, A.J. & Yap, A.J. (2010), Power posing: Brief nonverbal displays affect neuroendocrine levels and risk tolerance,

Psychological Science OnlineFirst, September 21,
doi:10.1177/0956797610383437

Christensen, C.M., (1997), *The innovator's dilemma*, Boston, MA: Harvard Business School Press.

Christensen, C.M., Horn, M.B. & Johnson, C.W. (2008), *Disrupting class*, New York, NY: McGraw Hill.

Christensen, C.R. (1991), The discussion teacher in action. In Christensen, C.R., Garvin, D.A. & Sweet, A. (Eds) *Education for judgment: The artistry of discussion leadership*, Boston, MA: Harvard Business School Press, 153-172.

Christensen, C.R., Garvin, D.A. & Sweet, A. (Eds) (1991), *Education for judgment: The artistry of discussion leadership*, Boston, MA: Harvard Business School Press.

Cohen, E. (1999), Reconceptualizing information systems as a field of the transdiscipline informing science: From ugly duckling to swan. *Journal of Computing and Information Technology*, 7(3), 213-219.

Colquitt, J. A., & Zapata-Phelan, C. P. (2007), Trends in theory building and theory testing: A five decade study of the Academy of Management Journal. *Academy of Management Journal*, 50(6), 1281-1303.

Cook, T.D. & Campbell, D.T. (1979), *Quasi-experimentation: Design & analysis issues for field settings*, Boston, MA: Houghton Mifflin.

Copeland, M.T. (1958) *And mark an era: The story of the Harvard Business School*, Boston, MA: Little, Brown and Company.

Cuddy, A.J., Fiske, S.T. & Glick, P. (2008), Chapter two: Warmth and competence as universal dimensions of social perception: The stereotype content model and the BIAS map, In *Advances in Experimental Social Psychology, 40, Elsevier*, 61-149.

Datar, S.M., Garvin, D.A. & Cullen, P.G. (2010), *Rethinking the MBA: Business education at a crossroads*, Boston, MA: Harvard Business Press.

Datar, S.M., Garvin, D.A. & Knoop, C. (2008), Harvard Business School, *Harvard Business School Publishing, 9-308-012*.

Davis, M. (1971), That's interesting!: Towards a phenomenology of sociology and a sociology of phenomenology. *Philosophy of the Social Sciences, 1*, 309-344.

Eccles, R.G. & Gladstone, J. (1991), KPMG Peat Marwick: The shadow partner, *Harvard Business School Publishing, 9-492-002*.

Elam, J. (Ed.)(1997), *Prentice hall case studies for management information systems*, Englewood Cliffs, NJ: Prentice Hall.

Elias, J. (2011), The "raw" vs. the "cooked", *Yale School of Management*, Retrieved on 2/22/2011 from http://mba.yale.edu/news_events/CMS/articles/pdf/RawvsCooked.pdf

Ellet, W. (2007), The case study handbook: how to read, discuss, and write persuasively about cases, Bonst, MA: Harvard Business School Press.

Fiske, S.T., Cuddy, A.J. Glick, P. & Xu, J. (2002), A model of (often mixed) stereotype content: Competence and warmth respectively follow from perceived status and competition, *Journal of Personality and Social Psychology, 82(6)*, 878-902.

Garvin, D.A. (2003), Making the case: Professional education for the world of practice. *Harvard Magazine, 106(1)*, 56-65, 107.

Gill, T.G. (1995a), High tech hidebound: Case studies of information technologies that inhibited organizational learning. *Accounting, Management. & Information Technologies, 5(1)*, 41-60.

Gill, T.G. (1995b), Early expert systems: Where are they now?, *MIS Quarterly*, 19(1), 51-81.

Gill, T.G. (1996), Expert systems usage: Task change and intrinsic motivation, *MIS Quarterly*, 20(3), 301-329.

Gill, T. G. (2005a), Learning C++ 'submarine style': a case study. *IEEE Transactions on Education.* 48(1), 150-156.

Gill, T. G. (2005b), *Introduction to programming using Visual C++.NET.* Hoboken, NJ: Wiley.

Gill, T. G. (2005c), The peer reviews and the programming course. *Issues in Informing Science and Information Technology, 2*, 205-217. Retrieved from http://2005papers.iisit.org/I17f83Gill.pdf

Gill, T.G. (2005d), A protocol for online case discussions, *Decision Sciences Journal of Innovative Education, 3(1)*, 141-148.

Gill, T. G. (2006a), The mystery of the self paced course (A), *Informing Faculty.* 1(3), 1-26.

Gill, T. G. (2006b), A learner-centered capstone course for a MIS master's degree program. *Decision Line.* 37(2), 4-6.

Gill, T.G. (2007), Using the Tablet PC for instruction, *Decision Sciences Journal of Innovative Education, 5(1)*, 183-190.

Gill, T. G. (2008), Reflections on researching the rugged fitness landscape. *Informing Science: the International Journal of an Emerging Transdiscipline*, 11, 165-196. Retrieved from http://inform.nu/Articles/Vol11/ISJv11p165-196Gill219.pdf

Gill, T.G. (2010), *Informing business: Research and education on a rugged landscape*, Santa Rosa, CA: Informing Science Press.

Gill, T.G. (2011), When what is useful is not necessarily true: The underappreciated conceptual scheme, *Informing Science, 14*, 1-32.

Gill, T. G., & Bhattacherjee, A. (2007), The informing sciences at a crossroads: The role of the client. *Informing Science: the International Journal of an Emerging Transdiscipline, 10*, 17-39. Retrieved from http://inform.nu/Articles/Vol10/ISJv10p017-039Gill317.pdf

Gill, T.G. & Bhattacherjee, A. (2009), Whom are we informing? Issues and recommendations for MIS research from an informing sciences perspective. *MIS Quarterly, 3(2)*, 217-235.

Gill, T.G., El-Rady, J. & Myerson, M. (2006), Classroom response units in human sexual behavior, *Informing Faculty, 1(4)*, 1-26.

Gill, T.G. & Jones, J. (2010). A tale of three classes: Case studies in course complexity, *Journal of IT Education, 9*, 1-29.

Gill, T.G. & Holton, C. (2006), A self-paced introductory programming course. *Journal of Information Technology Education. 5.* 95-105.

Gill, T.G. & Hoppe, U. (2009), The business professional doctorate as an informing channel: A survey and analysis, *International Journal of Doctoral Studies, 4*, 27-57, Retrieved from http://ijds.org/Volume4/IJDSv4p027-057Gill267.pdf

Gill, T.G. & Shaunessy, E. (2006), Counseling gifted students: A web-based course. *Informing Faculty*, 1(2), 1-18.

Gill, T. G., & Sincich, A. (2008), Illusions of significance in a rugged landscape. *Informing Science*, 11, 197-226. Retrieved from http://inform.nu/Articles/Vol11/ISJv11p197-226GillIllusions.pdf

Goldberg, R.A. (1968), *Agribusiness coordination: A systems approach to the wheat, soybean and Florida orange economies*, Boston, MA: Harvard Business School, Division of Research.

Goold, A. & Rimmer, R. (2000), Factors affecting performance in first-year computing. *ACM SIGCSE Bulletin*, June, 32(2), 39-43.

Gordon, R.A. & Howell, J.E. (1959), *Higher education for business*. New York, NY: Columbia University Press.

Hagan, D. & Markam, S. (2000), Does it help to have some programming experience before beginning a computing degree program? *ITiCSE Helsinki, Finland*, July, 25-28.

Hambrick, D. C. (2007), The field of management's devotion to theory: Too much of a good thing? *Academy of Management Journal, 50(6)*, 1346-1352.

Harmon, P., Maus, R. and Morrissey, W. (1988). *Expert systems: Tools and applications.* New York, NY: Wiley.

Heath, C. & Heath, D. (2007), *Made to stick*, New York, NY: Random House.

Kirchheimer, S. (2004), Coffee: The new health food? *WebMD.* Accessed on 9/8/2008 from http://men.webmd.com/features/coffee-new-health-food.

Kuhn, T. S. (1970). *The structure of scientific revolutions* (2nd ed., enlarged). Chicago, IL: University of Chicago Press.

Halpin, Gl., Halpin, Ge., Raju, P.K., Sankar, C.S. & Belliston, L. (2004), Real-World: Vital in engineering education, *34th ASEE/IEEE Frontiers in Education Conference, October 20 – 23, Savannah, GA*, T2F-13-18.

Harmon, P., Maus, R. and Morrissey, W. (1988). *Expert systems: Tools and applications.* New York, NY: Wiley.

Herried, C.F. (Ed.)(2007) *Start with a story: The case study method of teaching college science*, Arlington, VA: NSTA Press.

Holden, E. & Weeden, E. (2003), Software development: The impact of prior experience in an information technology programming course sequence. *Proceeding of the 4th Conference on Information Technology Education. Lafayette, Indiana*, October 16-18, 41-46.

Hubbard, R. & Armstrong, J.S. (1994). Replications and extensions in marketing: Rarely published but quite contrary, *International Journal of Research in Marketing, 11(3)*, 233-248.

Hubbard, R. & Vetter, D.E. (1991). Replication in the finance literature: An empirical study. *Quarterly Journal of Business and Economics, 30*, 70-81.

Hubbard, R. & Vetter, D.E. (1996). An Empirical Comparison of Published Replication Research in Accounting, Economics, Finance, Management, and Marketing, *Journal of Business Research, 35*, 153-164.

Kauffman, S.A. (1993), *The origins of order*, Oxford, UK: Oxford University Press.

Kerlinger, F.N. (1986), *Foundations of behavioural research*, New York, NY: Holt, Rinehart & Winston

Khurana, R. (2007), *From higher aims to hired hands*, Princeton, NJ: Princeton University Press.

Konsynski, B., Warbelow, A. & Kokuryo, J. (1996), AUCNET: TV auction network system, *HBS Publishing.*

Krathwohl, D.R. (2002). A revision of Bloom's taxonomy: An overview, *Theory Into Practice*, 41(4), 212-218.

Krumme, G. (1995), Major categories in the taxonomy of educational objectives, Retrieved from http://www.krummefamily.org/guides/bloom.html

Lambert, C. (2010), The psyche on automatic, *Harvard Magazine*, November/December, *113(2)*, 48-52.

Majaran, V., Muller, E., & Bass, F. M. (1991). New product diffusion models in marketing: A review and directions for research. In N. Nakicenovic & A. Grubler (Eds.), *Diffusion of technologies and social behavior* (pp. 125-177). New York, NY: Springer.

McKeachie, W.J. (1990), Research on college teaching: the historical background. *Journal of Educational Psychology*. 82(2), 189-200.

McFarlan, F.W. (Ed.) (1985). *The information systems research challenge: proceedings*. Boston: HBS Press.

Miller, G. A. (1967), *The psychology of communication*. New York, NY: Basic Books.

Mintzberg, H. (2004), *Managers not MBAs*. San Francisco, CA: Berrett-Koehler.

Mitnik, B. (2009), The case against the case method, *Harvard Business Review Blogs*, Retrieved from http://blogs.hbr.org/how-to-fix-business-schools/2009/04/the-case-against-the-case-meth-1.html

Morison, E. (1966). *Man, machines and modern times*. Cambridge, MA: MIT Press.

Newell, A., & Simon, H. A. (1972), *Human problem solving*. Englewood Cliffs, NJ: Prentice-Hall.

Patton, M.Q. (2002), *Qualitative research and evaluation methods, third edition*, Thousand Oaks, CA: Sage.

Pfeffer, J. (2007), A modest proposal: How we might change the process and product of managerial research. *Academy of Management Journal*, 50*(6)*, 1334-1345.

Pfeffer, J. & Fong, C. (2002), The end of business schools? Less success than meets the eye, *Academy of Management Learning & Education*, 1(1), 78–95.

Pierson, F.C. (1959), *The education of American businessmen: A study of university-college programs in business administration*, New York, NY: McGraw-Hill.

Porter, M. E. (1980), *Competitive strategy*. New York, NY: Free Press.

Rangan, K. (1995), Choreographing a case class, *HBS Case Note 9-595-074*.

Rhine, J. (2009), What is grounded theory. *Grounded Theory Institute*, 16 March, Retrieved from: http://www.groundedtheory.com/what-is-gt.aspx

Roberts, E. (2000), Strategies for encouraging individual achievement in introductory computer science courses. *SIGCSE '00. Austin, TX*, March, 295-299.

Rogers, E. M. (2003), *Diffusion of innovations* (5th ed.), New York, NY: Free Press.

Roethlisberger, F. (1977), *The elusive phenomena*. Boston, MA: HBS Press.

Rynes, S., Giluk, T. and Brown, K. (2007), The very separate worlds of academic and practitioner periodicals in human resource management: implications for evidence-based management. *Academy of Management Journal*. 50(5), 987-1008.

Sarasvathy, S.D. (2001), Causation and effectuation: Toward a theoretical shift from economic inevitability to entrepreneurial contingency, *Academy of Management Review, 26(2)*, 243-263.

Shanteau, J. (1992), Competence in experts: The role of task characteristics. *Organizational Behavior and Human Decision Processes, 53*, 252-266.

Shugan, S.M. (2006).Editorial: Save research—abandon the case method of teaching, *Marketing Science*, 25(2), 109–115.

Simon, H. (1981), *The Sciences of the Artificial, Second Edition*. Cambridge, MA: MIT Press.

SSRN (2010), Social science research network (SSRN) home page, Retrieved from http://www.ssrn.com/

Taleb, N. N. (2007), *The Black Swan*. New York, NY: Random House.

Tetlock, P. E. (1999), Theory driven reasoning about plausible pasts and probable futures in world politics: Are we prisoners of our preconceptions? *American Journal of Political Science, 43*(2), 335-366.

Thompson, R. (2008), Harvard Business School discusses future of the MBA, *HBS Bulletin, 24 November*, Retrieved from http://hbswk.hbs.edu/item/6053.html

Webb, H., Gill, T.G. & Poe, G. (2005). Teaching with the case method online: Pure vs. hybrid approaches, *Decision Sciences Journal of Innovative Education, 3(2)*, 223-250.

Willingham, D.T. (2009), *Why don't students like school?* San Francisco, CA: Jossey Bass.

Winter, S. & Gill, T.G. (2001), OfficeTech, *Journal of Information Technology*, 16(1), 14-33.

Wood, R. (1986), Task complexity: definition of the construct. *Organizational Behavior and Human Decision Processes*, 37, 60-82.

Yin, R.K. (2009), *Case research: Design and methods, fourth edition*, Thousand Oaks, CA: Sage.

Ziliak, S.T. & McCloskey, D.N. (2008), *The cult of statistical significance*. Ann Arbor, MI: University of Michigan Press.

Index

EMBA 2002, 60, 73, 121, 184,
185, 192, 218, 250, 463, 464,
474, 487, 489, 490, 494, 495
entrepreneurs, 275, 276
Environmental MBA, 296, 298,
474
ERP, 61, 62, 454, 481
Essence of Decision, 5, 129, 135,
200
eugenics and statistics, 51
European Case Clearing House.
See ECCH
Exercise Case, 71
exhibits, 191
expanders, 55
expert system, 146
expert systems, 87
extended case method, 15
external validity, 154
Fables, 69
facilitator persona, 280
fair use, 96, 205
FAU, 82, 346, 347, 470, 471,
472, 474, 475, 477
fill in the blanks, 99
First Meeting, 89
Fisher, R., 140
Fiske, S., 280, 281
fitness, 36, 37, 38, 39, 40, 41,
42, 43, 44, 46, 47, 51, 52, 87,
92, 107, 110, 111, 119, 120,
121, 122, 123, 124, 126, 127,
128, 130, 131, 133, 137, 141,
149, 151, 157, 158, 159, 244,
407, 408, 410, 411, 412, 413,
414, 415, 417, 418, 419, 420,
421, 422, 423, 424,及425,
426, 427, 428, 429, 430, 431,
432, 433, 437, 438, 439, 441,
442, 443

fitness peak, 44
Florida Atlantic University. See
FAU, *See* FAU
Florida Virtual School, 318
FLVS. *See* Florida Virtual
School
Fong, C., 195
Ford Foundation, 4
Freud, S., 111
Frontier Airlines, 181
Galacticomm, 82
Garvin, D., vii, 2, 3, 4, 50, 53,
317, 321
Gill, Clare, 210
Gill, Tommy, 319, 321
Giluk, T.L., 161
Gladstone, J., 71
Gladwell, M., 341
Glick, P., 280, 281
goal-driven planning, 272, 275,
278, 285, 289
Goldberg, R.A., 331, 333, 334,
357
Google, vii, 86, 218, 383
Goold, A., 423, 440
Gordon, R.A., 4
Gosset, W.S., 118, 140, 333
Griffith, M., 87
grounded theory, 161, 170
guest protagonist, 292
Guinness Brewery, 333
Guinness, Alec, 78
Guinness, Sir Alec, 78
Hagan, D., 423, 440
Halpin, G., 225
Hambrick, D., 56, 153, 415
Hansen, A., vii
Harmon, P., 87, 88
Harvard Business Review, 32, 63,
161

Made in the USA
Charleston, SC
07 February 2014